635
RIC

copy 1

Rice, Eddy

How to grow,
preserve & store
all the food you
need

DATE			

How to Grow, Preserve & Store All the Food You Need

How to Grow, Preserve & Store All the Food You Need

Eddy Rice

RESTON PUBLISHING COMPANY, INC.
A Prentice-Hall Company
Reston, Virginia

Library of Congress Cataloging in Publication Data

Rice, Eddy,
    How to grow, preserve, and store all the food
you need.

    Includes index.
    1. Vegetable gardening. 2. Fruit-culture.
3. Vegetable—Preservation. 4. Fruit—Preservation.
I. Title.
SB321.R533   635   76-47669
ISBN 0-87909-350-1

© 1977 by Reston Publishing Company, Inc.
A Prentice-Hall Company
Reston, Virginia 22090

1 3 5 7 9 10 8 6 4 2

PRINTED IN THE UNITED STATES OF AMERICA

7931

To my wife, Dolores, who edited the manuscript,
to our son, Jack, and his wife, Linda,
and to our son, Eddy Paul and his wife, Ann,
whose constant encouragement and boundless enthusiasm
made my task much easier.

Acknowledgments

The following companies and individuals graciously permitted reproduction of their material: W. F. Allen Company, W. Atlee Burpee Company, Stark Bro's., Paul Stark, Jr., and Sudbury Laboratory, Inc. The United States Department of Agriculture provided the information on home canning as well as the frost charts and the various pictures of vegetables.

Contents

Preface xi

1: **Preparing the Garden Plot 1**
Economic Aspects 1, Soil Testing 2, Chemical Fertilizers 3,
Mulches 6, Top Dressing 9, Improving Soil with Leaves 9, Improving
Soil with Grass 11, Compost 12, Earthworms for Compost 14,
Lime 14, Green Manuring 15, Cover Crop 16, Organic Gardening 17,
Protecting the Garden Plot 18

2: **Planting And Care 20**
What to Grow 20, When to Plant 21, Cultivation 35, Watering 35,
Insecticides 38, Beneficial Insects 40, Fungicides 40, Legume
Inoculation 41, Canning and Preserving 42

3: **Basic Vegetables for Your Garden 44**
Beans 44, Beet 53, Broccoli 55, Cabbage 57, Carrots 58,
Chard 59, Cowpeas 61, Cucumber 61, Eggplant 64, Kale 69,
Kohlrabi 70, Lettuce 72, Okra 75, The Onion Family 77,
Parsley 83, Parsnip 85, Peas 87, Peppers 91, Potato 94, Radish 96,
Spinach 98, Squash 100, Sweet Corn 104, Sweet Potato 106,
Tomato 109, Turnip 124

4: **Additional Vegetables For Your Garden 126**
Asparagus 126, Brussels Sprouts 129, Cantaloupe 130,
Cauliflower 131, Celeriac 133, Celery 133, Celtuce 136, Witloof
Chicory 137, Chinese Cabbage 138, Collards 139, Comfrey 140,
Dill 143, Edible-Podded Sugar Peas 143, Endive 144, Horse-
radish 145, Jerusalem Artichoke 147, Mustard 149, Peanut 151,
Popcorn 152, Pumpkin 155, Rutabaga 156, Salsify 157,
Sunflower 158, Watermelon 159

5: **Herbs 162**

6: **Gardening Hints 166**

7: **Strawberries 171**
Bearing 171, Planting 171, Soil and Location 172, Irrigation 173,
Land Preparation 173, Putting Plants in Ground 174, Chemical
Fertilizer 174, Lime 174, Care of Plants 175, Cultivating, Hoeing,
and Training 175, Mulches 175, Types of Plant 176

8: **Fertilizers 178**
Mixing Liquid Fertilizers 182

9: **Save Your Own Garden Seed 184**

10: **Drying Food 189**
Advantages 189, Disadvantages 190, Selection 191, Tests for
Dryness in Fruits 192, Storage 192, Drying Fruits and Vege-
tables 194, How to Dry Beans 195, Drying Herbs 196, Sun
Drying 197, Air Drying 198, Oven Drying 198, Steam Drying 198,
String Drying 198, Electric Dehydrators 199, Bulb-in-box Dryer 199,
Cabinet Type Dryer 200, Solar Dryer 201

11: **Fruits, Berries, Grapes, and Nuts 203**
What You Should Know About Pollination 203, Mini-Trees 205,
Apples 206, Peaches 214, Nectarines 219, Apricots 220,
Prunes 222, Plums 223, Pears 224, Cherries 228, Blackberries 230,
Raspberries 231, Grapes 232, Nuts 235

12: **Soil Testing 238**
Soil Should be Analyzed 239, General Information 239, Testing pH
(Acidity or Alkalinity) 240, Tests for Plant Food Deficiency 241,
What to Do After You Test Your Soil 247

Appendix A 249
Appendix B 271
Index 299

Preface

It has been a matter of only a very few years since there were vast surpluses of food in America. A little over a decade ago there was a worldwide reserve of a four-months supply of grain. We have on hand today a reserve supply of grain sufficient for only three weeks.

This move to *no reserves* of grain has frightening implications. Are we heading into an era of famine in our country? Our primary concern about the real possibility of critical shortages of food stems directly from the alarming yearly growth in world population. This growth continues unabated in many parts of the world and appears to be prevalent in most of South America, Africa, and India. Best estimates place annual growth of world population at approximately 75 million people.

The so-called "green revolution" that has occurred during the past 20 years has been responsible for vastly increased yields in bushels per acre of corn, rice, sorghum, wheat, and other major foodstuffs. However, at no time during the past 20 years has the annual increase in food supplies offset the annual increase in worldwide population. Now the gap is widening daily owing to a shortage of fertilizer coupled with an increase in the annual birthrate.

A prime factor in this greatly improved agricultural productivity has been the use of more and better fertilizers. These fertilizers require large amounts of petroleum for their manufacture. The recent quadrupling of the price of petroleum has had a most adverse effect on the supply of fertilizer throughout the world. The countries most in need of increased supplies of fertilizers to ensure an increase in annual yields of food supplies are unable to afford the prohibitive costs of fertilizers directly attributable to the unreasonable costs of petroleum and rampant inflation.

You are probably aware of the fact that 600 to 800 million people on the earth are existing in a perpetual state of chronic hunger and are suffering from the effects of being malnourished, and that an estimated 15 to 20 million die each year as a direct result of famine. Furthermore, you are probably wondering what all this has to do with you and your well-being.

The United States Department of Agriculture is committed to a policy of exporting the maximum amount of food supplies in order to try to balance our import-export trade. Many of our people in all walks of life believe that we are morally obligated to share our food with the needy throughout the world. These two significant factors will cause our foodstuffs to remain in short supply as far as we can see into the future.

Short supplies inevitably lead to critical shortages, which become severe when people begin panic buying and hoarding. Needless to say, this action has a snowballing effect that increases prices and demand, leading to further shortages. The only way to be a winner in such a situation is not to be a participant.

It is recommended that you pause and reflect on the changes in your life style caused by inflation and the energy crisis. Project your thoughts along these lines for the next five to ten years and make your own decision about the source of an adequate supply of high-quality, nutritious food for your family. Will these foodstuffs always be available in the varieties and quantities that you require, and at prices that you can afford? If you have any doubts about this last question, I would urge you to become as self-sufficient as possible in this area.

A plot of soil encompassing an area of 2500 square feet is large enough to produce all of the basic vegetables a family of four or more can use profitably. I am referring to fresh seasonal use on the table, as well as canning, freezing, preserving, and storing for later use. Naturally, on a small plot one must take every advantage accruing from good tilth and the use of hybrid seeds and plants when available in the types and varieties desired, as well as proper and adequate fertilization, watering when required, and cultivation to control weeds and conserve soil moisture. Strict attention to early and late planting in conjunction with well-planned succession planting will enable you *actually to double* and to come very close to tripling the yield of vegetables on a small garden plot.

It has only been a matter of 75 to 100 years ago since most of our ancestors were producing about 95 per cent of their annual supply of food. Their food was used directly from the vegetable patch and adjacent fields—fresh, tasty, and nutritious. Reserve supplies were canned, dried, and then stored in pantries, cellars, and in both above- and below-ground mounds and pits.

There is nothing mysterious or complicated about the idea of being self-reliant and producing most of your food supply. Our ancestors did it without benefit of our hybrid seeds and plants and without unlimited access to well-stocked libraries and free assistance from county agricultural extension agents.

I would suggest that most of us have grown fat and lazy and become entirely too dependent on supermarkets and convenience foods. There is an old expression which goes like this: "Close examination proves that work is less boring than trying to amuse oneself." It is just possible that gardening, canning, freezing, preserving, and storing your annual supply of food will serve to eliminate many of the ideas you now have with regard to what to do with your spare time.

To embark on an independent food supply project does not require a large outlay of cash. It is not necessary for you to buy a Rototiller, a pressure canner, or a good dehydrator. The only tools essential to your gardening success are a spade, a hoe, and a gardening rake. The most essential ingredient is a positive can-do attitude! If you have an earnest desire to provide your own security in this most important aspect of your life, success is right within your grasp. You are sincerely encouraged to start now and not to procrastinate until the issue is forced upon you.

This is a real challenge—a return to our true American heritage—the pioneer spirit—the idea of each man's being able to provide for his family, come what may.

Nothing, absolutely nothing, provides better physical exercise or mental relaxation than vegetable gardening. There is no substitute for the sense of well-being that comes from achieving a large measure of independence by planning, planting, harvesting, canning, freezing, preserving, and storing your own supply of food. What are you waiting for? These are violent times, filled with change, and the best way to avoid being drowned in the social tidal wave is to maximize your independence.

1

Preparing The Garden Plot

Borrow a garden plot from someone who is not gardening on his property. Most property owners would rather "share" their land than see it lie fallow and idle. The only compensation expected for use of borrowed garden space is a small sharing of what is grown.

Do not restrict your gardening activities to the next-door neighbors' backyard or a vacant lot in your block. If unable to borrow a garden plot in your immediate area, look for one elsewhere. As long as it is fence, your garden will be relatively safe from roaming animals and other scavengers.

If you have a lawn but have never had a garden, it is well worth your time to consider "digging up" at least half of it to plant vegetables. Even a plot 10 by 20 feet is big enough to provide a family of four with all the tomatoes, squash, and bell peppers that they need. Naturally, this is but one example; a plot of this size could provide you with snap beans, lettuce, kale, onions, beets, and carrots. You will never fully appreciate the glowing terms that others use to describe the abundance of food that can be produced on a small plot of land until you give it a try. Actually, there is literally no limit to what a creative person can do with a small piece of land. All you have to do to receive benefits that will exceed your wildest dreams is to plan in advance, choose varieties carefully, follow best gardening techniques, and har-

1

vest on schedule. It is a relatively simple matter to double and even triple the yield from a given plot by careful attention to initial planning, variety, and seed selection, coupled with timely succession planting.

"Happiness belongs to the self-sufficient."

ARISTOTLE

SOIL TESTING

Much has been written about the acidity (sourness), and the alkalinity (sweetness), of soil. Fortunately, chemists have shown how to use the hydrogen ion concentration in soils to measure the relative degree of acidity or alkalinity. This measurement is based on the proportion of positive hydrogen ions and negative hydroxyl ions in the soil solution being tested. The positive ions indicate acidity, whereas the negative ions indicate alkalinity. When the number of hydrogen and hydroxyl ions are in balance, the soil solution will be neither acid nor alkaline, but neutral—the same as distilled water. The amount of divergence from neutral is known as the hydrogen ion concentration, and the symbol in universal use is pH.

The pH scale for measuring the acidity or alkalinity of soil is numbered from 4 to 9 and includes the entire range of soil in which plants can grow. A soil with a pH above 7 is alkaline, or "sweet," whereas one with a pH below 7 is acid, or "sour." Chemical indicators are used to establish the known color reaction of certain pH values.

For practical purposes, most common garden soils lie in the range of 6 to 7 on the pH scale. Most garden plants thrive in this pH range and are very tolerant of slight variations below 6 and above 7.

The various intervals (measurements) on the pH scale are classified in this manner:

pH value	4.0	5.0
	Very acid (strong)	Acid
pH value	6.0	7.0
	Slightly acid	Neutral
		(not acid; not alkaline)
pH value	8.0	9.0
	Alkaline	Strongly alkaline

There are several soil testing kits on the market that are easy to use and quite accurate. One of the better known is the Sudbury Soil Testing Outfit®, which comes in half a dozen different-sized kits and models.

State agricultural colleges provide soil-testing service either free or for a small handling fee—they will test the soil and let you know the fertilizer and lime requirements for a group of plants or a particular field crop. Your country extension agent has the necessary forms and pint cartons for taking the soil sample.

To obtain the sample of soil: In a garden plot, lightly scrape off the surface debris on the immediate site where a soil sample is to be taken. Then take a shovel and push it vertically into the soil about six inches deep. Push the handle forward, with the shovel still in the soil, to expose a hole big enough to take a soil sample. With a tablespoon, scrape the side of the hole about three inches below the surface. Take one tablespoon of soil from this part of the hole and put it into the pint carton or whatever container you are using. Now withdraw the shovel and push the soil back in place with your foot. Take samples of soil in this same manner from at least fifteen random spots all over the area, putting it all into the pint carton. This pint of soil constitutes one soil sample.

Fill out the soil-testing forms, being sure that each area's sample is properly designated to avoid any confusion about area recommendations when more than one sample is submitted for testing.

When taking tablespoons of soil for sampling, avoid spots that are wet and areas where trash has been burned, where manure or compost has been piled, or where excessive amounts of fertilizer have been used. Remember that your soil sample of a pint, taken from one-twentieth of an acre—an area 33 by 66 feet—represents a tremendous amount of soil. The top eight inches or so of this small section of land weighs approximately 100,000 pounds. When you consider that your sample of a pint of soil weighs about one pound, you begin to appreciate the necessity for careful, precise, representative sampling of the exact garden area in which you are interested. However, if the garden area produces healthy plants with good yields when it is properly tilled, adequately fertilized, and generally well-tended, forget about soil testing—it is a superfluous luxury.

CHEMICAL FERTILIZERS

Basically, the complete, balanced fertilizers are used to feed the soil so the soil can feed the plants. Cultivated soils are usually deficient in one or more of three primary elements—nitrogen, phosphoric acid, or potash.

Nitrogen

Nitrogen is responsible for producing vegetative growth—the development of stems and leaves. An oversupply of nitrogen will greatly increase the amount of foliage at the expense of fruits and flowers. On the other hand, nitrogen deficiency causes stunted growth, yellowing of leaves, and a decidedly lower yield of fruits and flowers.

A complete, balanced fertilizer with a high percentage of nitrogen (10-10-10) supplies the two other major elements as well as nitrogen.

One of the quickest available sources of nitrogen is found in 34.5-0-0. This fertilizer can be mixed with 5-10-5 in any desired ratio to increase the percentage of nitrogen. 34.5-0-0 is especially good around spinach, kale, lettuce, mustard, and early cabbage. However, one has to use this fertilizer very sparingly around most plants unless it is first mixed with a balanced fertilizer.

Phosphoric Acid

Phosphoric acid is necessary for a strong root system, increases the vitamin content of plants, aids in early maturity, and increases the yield of fruits, flowers, and seeds.

The least expensive and most readily available source of phosphoric acid is in a balanced or complete fertilizer, such as 10-20-10, or 15-30-15.

If you are looking for phosphoric acid in a concentrated form, superphosphate is a common source. Superphosphate comes in various concentrations, ranging from 16 to 45 percent. When applied as a top dressing it should be thoroughly raked and cultivated into the soil.

Potash

Potash, the third member of the big three, exerts a balancing influence on other plant nutrients. Potash promotes vigorous root systems and is essential for best yields and top quality root crops. Potash increases disease resistance and improves color and keeping qualities of fruits and vegetables.

A readily available, inexpensive, and highly concentrated source of potash is found in a complete fertilizer, 5-10-10 or 3-18-18. Muriate of potash contains potash in a readily available form with concentrations ranging from 45 to 60 percent. Recommended rate of application is one pound per hundred square feet of soil.

Iron Chelate

Iron is one of the elements necessary for the formation of chlorophyll. Most soils have enough iron in very minute qualitities to provide for adequate plant growth. However, when these traces of iron are not available, leaves turn yellow and eventually go to a pale ivory hue. Of course, this same condition may be caused by other factors. However, unless the condition is corrected, the plant will eventually die.

Iron chelates (pronounced *key-lates*) are used extensively by home gardeners for protection of valuable ornamental plants and shrubs that are suffering from iron starvation. The iron chelates may be applied to the soil in dry or liquid form and are available under several trade names. Directions for use should be carefully observed.

Usage

You should shy away from all high-priced, small-packaged brands of chemical fertilizers. The fertilizer one uses in a garden should come in a bag with a weight of between 50 and 100 pounds. It should have a guaranteed analysis of nitrogen, phosphoric acid, and potash: 5-10-5, 5-10-10, and 10-10-10 are all good mixtures. The first figure is the percentage of nitrogen; the second figure, the percentage of available phosphoric acid; the third figure, the percentage of available potash in the mixture. Most of these fertilizers also contain small quantities of calcium, magnesium, and sulphur.

Since most gardeners of small plots will be using chemical fertilizers, it is necessary to offer a caution with regard to the amounts to be used. A pound of fertilizer for every fifty square feet of soil is enough to provide nutrients for most vegetables; one pint of 5-10-5 is about a pound. Weighing is never required, and good judgment coupled with rough measuring is all you need to do. Please be reminded that it is better to err toward the lean side. You can always apply some more in the form of top dressing, whereas too heavy an application may actually burn and kill your seeds and plants. Small applications in the form of top dressing at two- or three-week intervals is a highly desirable method for ensuring an adequate and continuous supply of plant nutrients.

Apply fertilizer when the crop is planted or a few days before, taking care to mix it with the soil and to prevent direct contact with the seed. A bit of experimentation, coupled with close observation of your growing plants, will soon enable you to determine if you are using too much or too little fertilizer. Too little will result in spindly plants and low yields. Too much will cause the plants to shed their leaves and become barren. Placing the fertilizer so that it will be two or three inches to one side of the seed and about the same level, or an inch lower, will eliminate the danger of having seed damaged by direct contact.

Good, sustained yields of quality vegetables will not be attained unless there is an abundance of available plant food in the soil. That is the primary reason for using fertilizer. However, you must be exceedingly careful in applying fertilizer around individual plants in order not to use too much and also not to get it too close to the roots—stay about eight inches away from stalk or stem, and mix a small quantity with the soil in a small circle around the plant.

MULCHES

Mulches are used to good advantage in conserving moisture, reducing the temperature of the soil, and controlling weeds in the vegetable garden. Anything that can be used to cover the soil without injuring plants or damaging the soil may be considered a mulch. Mulching materials should be inexpensive, readily available, and easy to use.

Plastic

Black polyethylene film is widely used in truck gardening and has most of the features that are desirable in a mulch. It is relatively inexpensive and will last for at least five years if properly handled. It is placed between rows or around stems of tomatoes, peppers, and eggplants, and is weighted down on the edges with soil, bricks, or rocks. The black color absorbs the rays of the sun and elevates the soil temperature—a highly desirable asset for heat-loving plants such as tomato, pepper, and eggplant. This feature also helps such plants to attain vigorous growth when they are first set out in the garden in the early spring. However, unless the film comes with perforations, it is necessary to slit many holes, evenly spaced, through it with a pen or paring knife, so that even a light rainfall will drain through to the soil underneath.

This mulch is good in strawberry beds; it keeps the berries free of grit and assists them in reaching earlier maturity. Because of its heat-absorbing and retaining qualities, soil temperatures under this black film may be too high for some plants. Close observation of the plants, especially on days with high temperatures, will enable you to resolve this question.

Hay

Hay is a good mulch for the vegetable garden and may be used long or chopped for convenience. It breaks down into good humus, and if it is from a legume crop, it will supply additional nitrogen to the soil while decomposing. A layer of hay three to four inches thick is sufficient for a good mulch. This type of mulch frequently harbors mice. However, with or without hay for a mulch, mice are usually present in the garden. The mice can be eliminated by use of D-Con®.

Black plastic film conserves moisture, warms the soil, controls weeds, and hastens maturity of vegetable crops

Leaves

Leaves are nature's natural mulch; these add humus to the soil, but they tend to blow away or drift with the wind into piles against the tallest plants. This difficulty is eliminated by lightly working them under the soil. Shredded leaves tend to stay put, and the depth of the mulch can be made more uniform. In this way, they decompose and add humus to the soil much more quickly.

Mulching Paper

Black mulching paper is made in rolls of various widths as well as squares for individual plants and is more weather-resistant than ordinary paper. It has many of the characteristics of black polyethylene film and is used in the same manner. Ordinary newspapers can be used to good advantage for conserving moisture and controlling weeds in small areas. Use five or six thicknesses and weight the edges down evenly and firmly in order to exclude all light. However, you must remove them to take full advantage of a rainfall.

Pine Needles

Pine needles are plentiful in most areas of the country and may be had for the gathering. They are weed-free and easily handled. They make an attractive mulch that may be removed at the end of the gardening season and stored for use in the following years. A layer of needles three to five inches deep is enough for a good mulch. Pine needles do not readily decompose and may be used for at least three years if properly handled and stored in a dry place. Although they are acid in reaction, they tend to shed water and resist decomposition. Since they are around your vegetables for only a short period of time, you will not notice any reaction in your soil or in your plants. However, hard and fast rules cannot be applied for all types of mulches and all kinds of soil in all localities. One must experiment a bit, occasionally, and pay close attention to the results. If an acid condition of the soil should result from the use of pine needles over a period of years, it is easily corrected by the application of a small amount of lime.

Grass Clippings

Grass clippings provide a good mulch if they are allowed to dry out for two or three days before use. When applied green, they tend to form a dense mat that air and water cannot penetrate. Apply the clippings loosely, after they are comparatively dry. A better mulch is composed of about a 50-50 mixture of shredded leaves and dry grass clippings.

Other Mulches

There are many more organic mulches that are very effective, such as ground corncobs; sawdust; wood chips and wood shavings; straws, such as wheat, rye, oat, and barley; salt or marsh hay; sugar cane; and peat moss. However, all, except the last three named, extract nitrogen from the soil during the process of decomposition. This could deprive your plants of much-needed nitrogen, unless you increase the supply of nitrogen available in the soil at the time the mulches are applied. Application of a pound of a complete fertilizer (10-10-10) per 100 square feet, or one-half pound of nitrate of soda, or one-third pound of ammonium nitrate is recommended to offset the nitrogen loss due to these mulches.

Manure

Barnyard manures, when well-rotted, make excellent mulches for the vegetable garden and add both humus and plant food to the soil. Their non-availability in most areas precludes their use by gardeners. They are invaluable for adding humus to the soil.

TOP DRESSING

Top dressing is the application of fertilizer, manure, or compost to crops without benefit of plowing. The beginner may get the idea that mulching and top dressing serve the same purpose; this is not so. Mulching, during the growing season, conserves moisture and keeps down the weeds. Top dressing is strictly used to feed the plant. The amount and type of top dressing used depends on the crop. Top dressing is the most advantageous method to use on rich-feeding crops, on sandy soil, and where quick growth is desirable. When top dressing your vegetables, take care not to get fertilizer or manure on the plants. Scatter it lightly between the rows and in a wide circle around individual pepper, cabbage, and tomato plants.

Whatever material is used for top dressing should be lightly raked into the soil. Top dressing is the easiest and surest method to use for providing adequate nutrients for your plants. Heavy, continuous yields of top-quality vegetables cannot be attained without an adequate supply of plant nutrients in the soil.

IMPROVING SOIL WITH LEAVES

Leaves are nature's tools for constantly putting back into the soil all the elements that plant life extracts. In addition to the big three—nitrogen, phosphorus, and potassium—leaves contain many of the essential "trace" elements, such as magnesium, boron, and cobalt. These mineral elements are required for sturdy, vigorous plant growth—although in rather minute amounts when compared with the big three.*

Ever wonder why the topsoil in a deciduous forest is so rich in plant nutrients? This is due to the continuous and never-ending decomposition of leaves and other vegetable and animal matter. The top layer is known as humus and is the one ingredient most sought by knowledgeable gardeners. Humus acts as a storehouse for plant foods by slow release of nutrients and by prevention of leaching in extremely porous soils. Humus aids in soil aeration and in water absorption and retention, provides chemical plant foods while decomposing, and greatly improves the texture of the soil. Woodland topsoil with a large percentage of pure humus will absorb up to 500 percent of its dry weight in water.

Appreciation of the readily available minerals stored in leaves should cause us to stop and ponder the senselessness of burning or disposing of them as trash. Many people now use leaf-shredding machines to greatly reduce the volume and aid in leaf disposal. If you have access to the spoils from such an autumn leaf disposal operation, you are indeed fortunate. Turn the shredded leaves under the soil in the fall and they will be a part of it the following spring. Needless to say, leaves do not have to be shredded to be turned under the soil for decomposition. Shredding, however, eases the task for the small gardener without power tools and hastens decomposition and consequent soil improvement.

Leaf mold added to ordinary garden soil—about 50 percent by volume— will add greatly to its enrichment and moisture retention. It provides an excellent mixture for potted plants without the expense of purchasing potting soil.**

Leaves are used in making compost, and as a winter mulch in strawberry beds and around shrubs. People in rural areas have always used leaves to line and cover the pits they use for winter storage of root crops, as well as cabbage and apples. The insulating properties of leaves have been used to good advantage down through the centuries.

---

*When one refers to "trace" elements it is with regard to the infinitesimal amounts needed by the plants, not to the amount of the element in the soil.

**Flaky leaf mold will provide the necessary organic matter for most potted plants. This consists of leaves that have decayed to the point where the integral parts crumble easily. This material is gathered from the forest floor and is readily recognized by its texture. Where there is a thick layer of leaves, you may have to remove some of the top portion to reach those that are sufficiently decomposed.

IMPROVING SOIL WITH GRASS

Grass clippings obtained from lawn mowing and turned under the soil will add humus and nitrogen to it. These clippings are of such small dimensions and are so succulent that they literally disappear into the soil in about two weeks. Given warm earth and adequate moisture, biochemical processes in the soil are accelerated, which further hastens decomposition of the grass.

Plan to work the green clippings into the soil as soon as they become available. They have their maximum nitrogen content when first cut. Use plenty of clippings in a small area and systematically enrich the soil of the entire garden as more and more clippings become available for this purpose. It is well to bear in mind that most good garden soil is enriched and properly conditioned by man's efforts. The best garden soils are not often found in nature. Stop and consider: most natural plants bear only one crop per season. Nature provides for that one crop, and, where mankind has not upset her balance, she does a fine job. However, we must examine the other side of the coin. We expect our green beans, squash, tomatoes, eggplant, and cucumbers to continue pumping out their fruits over a two- or three-month season. In order for vegetable plants to give us continuing yields of top-quality produce, we must do our part in putting extra humus and nutrients into the soil. And we must go one step further to control the inevitable weeds, to keep them from stealing plant food needed by our crop of vegetables.

When grass clippings are being used for a mulch, let the clippings remain spread out to dry for a day or two so they will not mat or pack down. Then place the mulch around unstaked tomatoes, eggplants, and any or all of your vegetables to conserve moisture and keep down weeds. You will not usually have enough grass mulch for the entire garden, so mulch the earliest bearing vegetables first and the remainder as clippings become available. Put the mulch around plants and between rows to a depth of three to five inches. This mulch will stay where you put it and actually improves the appearance of your garden. It breaks down completely in one gardening season and should be incorporated into the soil for its humus content.

Green grass clippings are a decided bonus on the compost pile. A three-to-six-inch layer under a similar layer of topsoil or barnyard manure will generate the heat so necessary for proper decomposition. Up to about two-thirds of the entire compost pile can be green clippings.

Green grass clippings constitute an excellent way to physically condition an unused plot of heavy clay for gardening. The green clippings are turned under the soil in large quantities; this is the process of green manuring —the plowing under of quick-growing succulent crops to add humus and fertility to the soil. When enough green clippings have been incorporated into the heavy clay, its physical texture will be much lighter, it will absorb and retain more moisture, and soil aeration will be greatly improved. When it has these qualities, you can grow vegetables very successfully on this piece of land.

Our vast and productive country has always been blessed with an abundance of good agricultural land. However, urban and suburban sprawl, coupled with our national obsession for more and still more highways, has gobbled up approximately one million acres of good farmland each year during the past two decades. This land is gone forever, with regard to food production. Looming big on the horizon is a constantly growing world shortage of food. Many complex factors will make this shortage much more critical as time goes on. We mention this here to stimulate your thinking about wastefulness and to encourage you to use grass clippings and leaves for soil improvement.

Nature, with her never-ending bounty for mankind, provides us with a seemingly inexhaustible supply of grass clippings and leaves. Their potential for physical conditioning and enrichment of the soil staggers the imagination, because it is almost beyond belief. We have the organic materials at hand to build good soil from any plot of land we choose to work over. The question is, will we, as responsible individuals, make the necessary effort?

COMPOST

Compost is the man-made substitute for manure. It consists of fermented and decomposed organic matter, such as leaves, grass clippings, straws, vegetable refuse, weeds (either green or dry), peat moss, all types of animal manures, muck, and sand. Chemicals are added to aid in the decomposition and to add fertility to the compost. Composting is the easiest way to dispose of garden trash, lawn clippings, and leaves. It is also the simplest and least expensive way to add humus to the garden soil and improve its texture and fertility. Properly composted fresh organic matter yields a decidedly superior soil that is rich in plant nutrients and very high in humus content.

Making a Compost Pile

The decomposition of organic matter is due to the activity of microorganisms that are present in all healthy soils. To ensure bacterial action and a rapid rate of decomposition, alternate thin layers of topsoil with the organic matter.

Building a compost pile is a simple matter, and its location will be largely dictated by one's surroundings. However, a partially shaded area is preferable to one in the full sun, simply because a more even moisture content is easier to maintain. As you build the compost pile, keep it from four to six feet in width so that you can occasionally rebuild the pile by forking or turning the outer portion of the old pile into the center of the new pile. On the bottom of the pile place a six- to twelve-inch layer of leaves, grass clippings, weeds, or garden trash. Tramp this layer down well to compress it and then sprinkle either ammonium sulfate or ammonium nitrate on top of it. Use about one-half cup of either of these activators to a square yard of area, and water it well. Then add a six-inch layer of manure and a two-inch layer of topsoil. Water these first three layers. Continue until the pile is about four feet high—with a covering of topsoil. Be sure to add the chemical activator to each layer of organic material.*

If manure cannot be obtained, construct your compost pile with alternate layers of fresh organic matter and topsoil. The yield from such a pile will be just as good an additive as barnyard manure to your garden soil.

A mixed fertilizer (5-10-10, or similar) applied at a rate of 3 cups per square yard is an excellent activator for the organic matter.

Do not put twigs or woody materials into the compost pile. Keep the pile moist at all times. Decomposition is accelerated by heat and moisture. The chemical activators hasten bacterial action and greatly assist in fermentation and decomposition of organic matter. The time from the start of the pile until everything is decomposed and ready to use will vary from three to six months. This variance in time is due to materials used, temperature, moisture, and turning the pile over at four- to six-week intervals.

The compost pile may be enclosed for aesthetic reasons. It also may be covered (to advantage) with black plastic to increase the temperature inside the pile. You do not have to build a compost pile six feet wide and four feet high in a single day—or ever, for that matter. Start with whatever is available and use the proper procedure for layering, a chemical activator, moisture, and a top layer of soil. Then continue to build the pile as additional materials become available.

The addition of barnyard manure to garden soils tends to lighten heavy, clayey soils and vastly improves the texture and the moisture-retention qualities of light, sandy soils; it also improves soil aeration and assists bacterial activity. Controlled experiments by several state agricultural extension services have proven that mineral fertilizers are much more effective when applied after an application of humus or well-rotted manure. Yields have been increased by as much as 30 percent when humus (or manure) and chemical fertilizers were both used. When either is used alone, doubling the amount does not have the same effect on crop yields.

----

*The compost pile should be shaped like a pyramid so that it will shed rain.

EARTHWORMS FOR COMPOST

The small gardener can enjoy the benefits of a superior compost by profiting from the activities of earthworms confined to boxes. Earthworm manure is known as castings. Earthworm castings are finely granulated and far superior to other manures.

Either construct or obtain wooden boxes that are two to three feet square and 2½ feet deep. Fill the boxes to a depth of two feet with a mixture of about 75 percent of shredded leaves and grass clippings. Add about 15 percent of barnyard or chicken manure. Then add about 10 percent of good topsoil. If you cannot obtain manure, substitute table garbage. Mix the materials thoroughly and moisten until the mixture is damp.

Purchase breeding worms or go out and dig your own. You must feed the worms. Dry cornmeal mixed with coffee grounds in a one-to-three ratio makes good food for earthworms. Dry oatmeal mixed with coffee grounds and any grain can also be ground and used.

The castings in the bottom of the box will get blacker and blacker. This material is finely granulated and bears no resemblance to the mixture you put into the box. About every two months you can remove these castings and replace their volume with your favorite earthworm box-filling mixture.

Earthworms thrive under many different types and combinations of soils and moisture. The combinations of materials and foods for successful earthworm composting are seemingly endless. Experiment and closely observe your results. The main points to bear in mind are food and moisture. (Do not keep them wet, just a little damp.)

LIME

The many types of lime on the market tend to confuse the gardener. Horticultural hydrated lime, ground limestone, or ground dolomitic limestone are best for the garden.

Lime is used primarily by the gardener to sweeten the soil by lowering the acidity. But lime has several beneficial side effects, such as loosening the granular structure of clay soils, accelerating bacterial action, aiding in decomposition of organic matter, and supplying some calcium.

Indiscriminate use of lime is to be avoided. It is not required as an additive to all soils. It is not a fertilizer, even though it does add calcium as a nutrient. The intended use is to correct soil acidity, and for this purpose it is superbly effective. Lime tends to release some of the phosphorus and potash from their insoluble compounds, making them available for plant food. Thus, in fact, it does enhance the fertility of the soil.

The usual prescription for general liming of cropland that has become too acid is a ton of lime per acre. Some authorities maintain that this ton-per-acre formula applies only to ground limestone and dolomitic limestone and that when hydrated lime is used 80 percent of a ton per acre is enough.

The ton-per-acre formula, translated for the gardener, means applying about a half-pound per square yard of soil. Measuring is not necessary if you use care in spreading the lime thinly and evenly, applying just enough to completely whiten the ground.

Either fall or early spring applications of lime are satisfactory. Spread it thinly and evenly on a windless day, preferably on freshly cultivated soil. If the soil is not freshly cultivated, either rake, harrow, or disk the lime into the soil. Spread it evenly and thoroughly, because there is no noticeable lateral action. The effects will last for about five years.

GREEN MANURING

Green manuring is the term used to describe the turning under of quick-growing succulent crops. The green plants decay quite rapidly, thereby incorporating humus and plant nutrients into the soil. Green manuring is preferable and more effective than composting, because the green crops are turned under when they are at their peak of plant nutrient content. Green manure crops should be turned under the soil when they are two-thirds to three-quarters grown and still succulent. Young, tender plants decompose much more quickly than full-grown, tougher plants. When the weather is warm and the soil has an adequate supply of moisture, almost complete decomposition occurs within 6 to 8 weeks.

Nothing is superior to green manure crops for conditioning soil, adding humus, and maintaining fertility. They also provide the quickest, easiest, and least expensive way to accomplish these objectives.

It is an almost impossible task to compost enough materials to provide for the requirements of a larger garden. The answer here is to use part of the garden area to grow a green manure crop and to rotate this green manuring each year so that it eventually covers the entire garden plot.

Some of the best green manure crops are the nitrogen gatherers, such as the legumes, which absorb nitrogen from the air and then add it to the soil. These legumes include alfalfa, clover, cowpeas, field peas, soybeans, and the different varieties of vetch.

Green manuring does things for the soil that are impossible to accomplish by composting, fertilizing, or plowing under barnyard manure. The roots of green manure plants penetrate the soil quite deeply and provide a good source of organic matter. The cowpea has a root system powerful enough to crack hardpans. (Hardpans are hard layers of earth beneath the soil composed mainly of clay and impervious to water.) Alfalfa regularly sends roots down to a depth of three feet in two years' time. As the roots decay, they add humus and provide channels for aeration of the soil. This minute channeling of the subsoil also increases the amount of water it receives and retains. The action of bacteria and fungi, the microorganisms that make fertile soil a living, breathing medium for earthworms and other soil-building entities, is greatly increased or even initiated by the green manuring.

Long before the relationship between leguminous cover crops and their ability to add nitrogen to the soil was understood, the plowing under of these crops was known to have a tremendous impact on the fertility of the soil. It is now known that such a crop—plowed under while still succulent and before it reaches maturity—can add as much nitrogen to an acre as would the application of 12 to 15 tons of barnyard manure.

COVER CROP

A cover crop, as the name implies, is planted primarily to cover the ground and to prevent erosion by holding the soil in place. The subsequent addition of humus to the soil is also a matter for prime consideration.

Good winter cover crops are wheat, rye, the various vetches, and rye grass. These cover crops have large fibrous root systems that also add humus to the soil when they are plowed or tilled under. Good summer cover crops are buckwheat, soybeans, millet, and sudan grass.

Cover crops are used both winter and summer to prevent soil erosion, to maintain soil fertility by encouraging constant bacterial and fungial action, which is concomitant with all plant growth, and finally, to incorporate humus and plant nutrients into the soil, when turned under.

As with green manuring, you have a choice of nonleguminous or leguminous cover crops. The choice should depend on whether you want to add extra nitrogen to the soil along with the organic matter. For both winter and summer cover crops, one has to choose a variety adapted to the temperature range of these seasons.

There is one cover crop that can be grown successfully on poor subsoil or even on landfill, although several crops will add enough humus to the soil to make it fertile enough to support a vegetable garden. This crop is ordinary buckwheat. Successive crops of buckwheat turned under will incorporate humus into the soil and greatly increase its water retention. Sandy and light soils deficient in humus will not hold much moisture. Heavy, clayey soil devoid of humus will not support vegetable plants.

The procedure for building poor or acid soil into a suitable garden plot is quite simple. First plow the weed crop under and let the furrows stand as they are for two weeks. Then disk or rake the area smooth and sow a very thick crop of buckwheat. When the buckwheat is about 8 to 10 inches high, turn it under. Wait 10 to 14 days and sow another crop of buckwheat. Plow this second crop under when it is 8 to 10 inches high. In 10 to 14 days sow another crop of buckwheat. Keep this rotation of buckwheat going until enough humus has been added to the soil or until you want to increase the fertility with one of the leguminous green manure crops. You will be pleasantly surprised to note that each succeeding crop of buckwheat grows much better than the last. This increase in rate of growth is due to the humus you have been adding to the soil with each crop turned under.

ORGANIC GARDENING

Organic gardening is a system of maintaining soil fertility by the constant addition of humus. Organic materials are used for composting and mulching in an effort to duplicate nature's own way of maintaining and increasing the texture and the fertility of the soil.

Various compositions of rocks are sources of fertilizer for the organic gardener. The rocks must be finely ground or pulverized in order to become soluble and release their plant nutrients. Raw ground phosphates become soluble and release their plant nutrients. Raw ground phosphate rock, pulverized limestone, and granite dust are all sources of plant food.

The proponents of organically grown foods are merely expressing a desire for garden produce that is free of chemicals. They do not approve of the use of chemical fertilizers and poisonous insecticides on garden crops. Furthermore, these same people do not think much of the food processing chemicals that are used for coloring and preservation in so much of our canned and dry foods.

There can be no quarrel with their tenets of what is good for the maintenance of soil texture and fertility. Humus is nature's own method of building topsoil. Nor can we question the quality of organically grown produce. The real problem occurs when one tries to envision enough compost and barnyard manure to fertilize the entire agricultural production of the United States.

Knowledgeable people in the Department of Agriculture have recently estimated that we could not feed more than three-quarters of our population if the use of chemical fertilizers and insecticides were suddenly banned from further use—a sobering thought.

Unless one has access to an almost unlimited source of organic materials or maintains an exceptionally large compost pile, the cost of organic material can be prohibitive. For example, 50-lb bags of composted sheep and cow manure cost about $3.50 a piece. The guaranteed analysis of available nitrogen, phosphoric acid, and potash is one percent each. By way of comparison, an 80-lb bag of 10-10-10, a balanced chemical fertilizer, sells for about $4.60 and has a guaranteed analysis of 10 percent each of available nitrogen, phosphoric acid, and potash.

It is our understanding that the Department of Agriculture is doing extensive experimental work in trying to develop plants that will act as "attractors" for insects that damage vegetable plants. The idea is to develop a plant that provides better food and protection for the insect than it is accustomed to having on its favorite vegetable plant. When this occurs, it is expected that the insect will abandon its favorite vegetable plant and take up residence on the new plant. These "host" plants would be grown alongside the vegetable plants they are protecting.

PROTECTING THE GARDEN PLOT

A fence sufficiently high and close-woven to keep out rabbits, chickens, dogs, and other animals is necessary to protect one's vegetables. The sides may be used as a trellis (support) for peas, pole beans, and cucumbers. However, although this is a good preventative device, you must know what to do when animals manage to get into your garden.

Mole Damage

Many people contend that moles are harmless, even beneficial to the gardener, because they help aerate the soil in their ceaseless quest for insects and worms. Perhaps it is true that moles do not eat the roots and bulbs of your plants, but in their frenzied tunneling for food just beneath the surface, they do a lot of damage to plants by burrowing under and around the plants and causing the soil to dry out around the roots. The primary damage is caused by plant roots being dislodged and exposed to air, causing loss of moisture. Furthermore, it is a well-known fact that field and pine mice use the mole runs to sally forth and do their bit of damage by destroying newly planted seeds and young plants. In order to get rid of the moles, it becomes necessary to either eliminate or drastically reduce their supply of food. In other words, you must treat the soil with a pesticide that will kill the insects and worms on which the moles depend for their supply of fresh food. As soon as their supply of insects and worms is drastically reduced, the moles will abandon the area and seek out better living quarters in which to satisfy their voracious appetites.

Chlordane 10-G is a pesticide that is used to control Japanese beetles, grubs, wireworms, white fringe beetles, chinch bugs, chiggers, ticks, ants, sowbugs, millipedes, sod webworm, armyworm, box elder bugs, cutworms, white grubs, mole crickets, and earwigs. Some of these soil pests may be controlled for as long as four to five years by a single application of Chlordane 10-G. However, you must follow the directions on the label exactly, because this product is toxic to fish and wildlife.

Small areas that have recently become infested with moles can usually be effectively cleared out by the liberal use of Mole-Nots. Mole-Nots are acorn-sized packages of tiny pellets that contain an active ingredient of one percent of thallium sulphate. They are effective when used according to the directions on the package.

If you have a very small garden area or seedbed in an area adjacent to mole territory over which you have no control, it may become necessary for you physically to block the moles from entering your domain. Simply enclose your garden area with hardware cloth, sheet metal, or discarded plywood. This barrier should extend downward from the surface for at least twelve inches and then extend outward at an angle of 90 degrees for another twelve inches. For the barrier to be effective, all connections must be secure and present no holes for entry.

Control of Mice

Areas of the garden or lawn that are interlaced with mole runs and frequented by field or pine mice will need to be treated for control of the mice as well as the moles. Fortunately, this can be accomplished quite easily by waging war on the mice with D-con.® The manufacturers of D-con® provide explicit directions for your successful campaign against the mice.

Rodent Damage

Various kinds of rodents damage garden crops throughout the country. The extent of damage depends on the size of the garden, the type of control being used, and the numbers and kinds of rodents in the immediate vicinity. If you find yourself faced with a seemingly insurmountable rodent or mole infestation, your best bet is immediately to contact the county extension agent for assistance. These people are experts on local rodent control problems.

2

Planting And Care

WHAT TO GROW

Most beginners plant too many different kinds of vegetables without considering what they really expect to harvest. It is far better to begin with the most widely used and more easily grown things, such as string beans, tomatoes, beets, lettuce, cucumbers, cabbage, squash, chard, peas, onions, and turnips. Naturally, one can expand, contract, or change these items as desired; we are merely trying to get you to be a practical gardener and plan on lots of string beans and perhaps no cabbage—if you like the beans and do not like cabbage. Plant the things you enjoy eating and plant in sufficient quantities to lower your food bill and last throughout the season.

Where space limitations compel a choice, it is well to consider the value of the yield of a vegetable plant in deciding what to plant. So, in planning the size of your garden, you must decide what you want to grow as well as consider the relative yields and values. In order to get maximum use of your garden plot, you may grow both a crop of early vegetables and a crop of late vegetables on the same plot of land. After the peas, early potatoes, and green onions are harvested, one can plant late cabbage, turnips, and kale. These are but a few of the successive plantings that are easy to accomplish. Where a medium-to-long growing season makes such successive plantings possible, a small garden plot can actually be doubled in size with regard to actual yield of vegetables. There are seemingly endless combinations of early, mid-season, and late vegetable crops that may be used for a succession planting or intercropping.

Plan your garden with care. Plant pole beans and corn where they will not shade lower plants. It is best to group the tall-growing plants at one end and in rows running east to west to best use the orbit of the sun. Rotation of crops will help keep the soil fertility in balance, inasmuch as different plants take different amounts of nutrients from the soil. Also, bear in mind the grouping of early vegetables so that, when they are harvested, one can till the area and prepare the soil for successive planting of later crops. For example, peas, potatoes, and early cabbage may be followed by turnips, kale, and beets. One can have a continuous supply of lettuce, beets, and carrots by successive sowings of ten-foot rows of each type at intervals of two to three weeks, depending on rate of growth and use. Furthermore, a 30-foot row need not be reserved for one vegetable—three kinds will grow as readily as one in a row. Radishes may be used to mark the rows of any vegetable—they germinate rapidly, thus marking the row. Planted thinly, at intervals of twelve inches, they also provide a bonus wherever used.

On a small plot, it is feasible to grow many vegetables in rows only a foot apart. This includes beets, carrots, leaf lettuce, onions, dwarf peas, radishes, and spinach. Others require more room. Plan on a circle 5 feet in diameter for a hill of squash. A well-planted hill of zucchini will keep pumping out fruits for the table over a period of two to three months. They are vigorous, highly productive, and easily grown. After the vines attain full growth, they require no further attention other than keeping the fruits picked.

WHEN TO PLANT

The time for planting or transplanting is very important—both from the standpoint of vigorous, productive plants and that of their mere survival. For example, eggplants that are set outdoors before the ground is warm and daily temperatures are high simply will not grow and thrive. Conversely, peas that are planted too late in the spring to mature before summer heat and high temperatures prevail will not be productive. We must time our planting to coincide with the temperature requirements of the various vegetables. Knowing this, we can group them according to their relative hardiness or resistance to cold.

The extremely cold-hardy plants include turnips, potatoes, lettuce, onions, peas, and cabbage. All of these may be planted as early in the spring as the ground can be worked and a month to six weeks before the frost-free date.

Table 2-1

EARLIEST DATES, AND RANGE OF DATES, FOR SAFE SPRING PLANTING OF VEGETABLES IN THE OPEN

Planting dates for localities in which average date of last freeze is

Crop	Jan. 30	Feb. 8	Feb. 18	Feb. 28	Mar. 10	Mar. 20	Mar. 30
Asparagus*	Feb. 1-Apr. 15	Feb. 10-May 1	Mar. 1-May 1	Mar. 15-June 1	Jan. 1-Mar. 1	Feb. 1-Mar. 10	Feb. 15-Mar. 20
Beans, lima	Feb. 1-Apr. 1	Feb. 1-May 1	Mar. 1-May 1	Mar. 15-June 1	Mar. 20-June 1	Apr. 1-June 15	Apr. 15-June 20
Beans, snap	Jan. 1-Mar. 15	Jan. 10-Mar. 15	Jan. 20-Apr. 1	Mar. 10-May 1	Mar. 15-May 15	Mar. 15-May 25	Apr. 1-June 1
Beet	Jan. 1-30	Jan. 1-30	Jan. 20-Apr. 1	Feb. 1-Apr. 15	Feb. 15-June 1	Feb. 15-May 15	Mar. 1-June 1
Broccoli, sprouting*	Jan. 1-30	Jan. 1-30	Jan. 15-Feb. 15	Feb. 1-Mar. 1	Feb. 15-Mar. 15	Feb. 15-Mar. 15	Mar. 1-20
Brussels sprouts*	Jan. 1-30	Jan. 1-30	Jan. 15-Feb. 15	Feb. 1-Mar. 1	Feb. 15-Mar. 15	Feb. 15-Mar. 15	Mar. 1-20
Cabbage*	Jan. 1-15	Jan. 1-Feb. 10	Jan. 1-Feb. 25	Jan. 15-Feb. 25	Jan. 25-Mar. 1	Feb. 1-Mar. 1	Feb. 15-Mar. 10
	**	**	**	**	**	**	**
Cabbage, Chinese							
Carrot	Jan. 1-Mar. 1	Jan. 1-Mar. 1	Jan. 15-Mar. 1	Feb. 1-Mar. 1	Feb. 10-Mar. 1	Feb. 15-Mar. 1	Mar. 1-Apr. 10
Cauliflower*	Jan. 1-Feb. 1	Jan. 1-Feb. 1	Jan. 10-Feb. 10	Jan. 20-Feb. 20	Feb. 1-Mar. 1	Feb. 10-Mar. 10	Feb. 20-Mar. 20
Celery and celeriac	Jan. 1-Feb. 1	Jan. 10-Feb. 10	Jan. 20-Feb. 20	Feb. 1-Mar. 1	Feb. 20-Mar. 20	Mar. 1-Apr. 1	Mar. 15-Apr. 15
Chard	Jan. 1-Apr. 1	Jan. 1-Apr. 1	Jan. 10-Apr. 1	Feb. 1-May 1	Feb. 15-May 15	Feb. 20-May 15	Mar. 1-May 25
Chervil and Chives	Jan. 1-Feb. 1	Jan. 1-Feb. 1	Jan. 20-Apr. 15	Jan. 15-Feb. 15	Feb. 1-Mar. 1	Feb. 10-Mar. 10	Feb. 15-Mar. 15
Chicory, witloof					June 1-July 1	June 1-July 1	June 1-July 1
Collards*	Jan. 1-Feb. 15	Jan. 1-Feb. 15	Jan. 1-Mar. 15	Jan. 15-Mar. 15	Feb. 1-Apr. 1	Feb. 15-May 1	Mar. 1-June 1
Cornsalad	Jan. 1-Feb. 15	Jan. 1-Feb. 15	Jan. 1-Mar. 15	Jan. 1-Mar. 1	Jan. 1-Apr. 1	Jan. 1-Mar. 1	Jan. 15-Mar. 15
Corn, sweet	Feb. 1-Mar. 15	Feb. 10-Apr. 1	Feb. 20-Apr. 15	Mar. 1-Apr. 1	Mar. 10-Apr. 15	Mar. 15-May 1	Mar. 25-May 15
Cress, upland	Jan. 1-Feb. 1	Jan. 1-Feb. 15	Jan. 15-Apr. 1	Feb. 1-Mar. 1	Feb. 10-Mar. 15	Feb. 20-Apr. 15	Mar. 1-Apr. 1
Cucumber	Feb. 15-Apr. 1	Feb. 15-Apr. 1	Feb. 15-Apr. 15	Mar. 1-Apr. 15	Mar. 15-Apr. 15	Apr. 1-May 1	Apr. 10-May 15
Eggplant*	Feb. 1-Mar. 1	Feb. 10-Mar. 15	Feb. 20-Apr. 1	Mar. 10-Apr. 15	Mar. 15-Apr. 15	Apr. 1-May 1	Apr. 15-May 15
Endive	Jan. 1-Mar. 1	Jan. 1-Mar. 1	Jan. 1-Mar. 15	Feb. 1-Mar. 1	Feb. 15-Apr. 15	Mar. 1-Apr. 1	Mar. 10-Apr. 10
Fennel, Florence	Jan. 1-Mar. 1	Jan. 1-Mar. 1	Jan. 15-Mar. 1	Feb. 1-Mar. 1	Feb. 15-Mar. 15	Mar. 1-Apr. 1	Mar. 10-Apr. 10
Garlic							
	**	**	**	**	**	Feb. 1-Mar. 1	Feb. 10-Mar. 10
Horseradish*							
Kale	Jan. 1-Feb. 1	Jan. 10-Feb. 1	Jan. 20-Feb. 10	Feb. 1-20	Feb. 10-Mar. 1	Feb. 20-Mar. 10	Mar. 1-20
Kohlrabi	Jan. 1-Feb. 1	Jan. 10-Feb. 1	Jan. 20-Feb. 10	Feb. 1-20	Feb. 10-Mar. 1	Feb. 20-Mar. 10	Mar. 1-Apr. 1

Leek	Jan. 1-Feb. 1	Jan. 1-Feb.	Jan. 1-Feb. 15	Jan. 15-Feb. 15	Jan. 25-Mar. 1	Feb. 1-Mar. 1	Feb. 15-Mar. 15
Lettuce, head*	Jan. 1-Feb. 1	Jan. 1-Feb.	Jan. 1-Feb. 15	Jan. 15-Feb. 15	Feb. 1-20	Feb. 15-Mar. 10	Mar. 1-20
Lettuce, leaf	Jan. 1-Feb. 1	Jan. 1-Feb.	Jan. 1-Mar. 15	Jan. 1-Mar. 15	Jan. 15-Apr. 1	Feb. 1-Apr. 1	Feb. 15-Apr. 15
Muskmelon	Feb. 15-Mar. 15	Feb. 15-Apr.	Feb. 15-Apr. 15	Mar. 1-Apr. 15	Mar. 15-Apr. 15	Apr. 1-May 1	Apr. 10-May 15
Mustard	Jan. 1-Mar. 1	Jan. 1-Mar.	Feb. 15-Apr. 15	Feb. 1-Mar. 1	Feb. 10-Mar. 15	Feb. 20-Apr. 1	Mar. 1-Apr. 15
Okra	Feb. 15-Apr. 1	Feb. 15-Apr. 15	Mar. 1-June 1	Mar. 10-June 1	Mar. 20-June 1	Apr. 1-June 15	Apr. 10-June 15
Onion*	Jan. 1-15	Jan. 1-15	Jan. 1-15	Jan. 1-Feb. 1	Jan. 15-Feb. 15	Feb. 10-Mar. 10	Feb. 15-Mar. 15
Onion, seed	Jan. 1-15	Jan. 1-15	Jan. 1-15	Jan. 1-Feb. 15	Jan. 1-Mar. 1	Feb. 1-Mar. 1	Feb. 20-Mar. 15
Onion, sets	Jan. 1-15	Jan. 1-15	Jan. 1-15	Jan. 15-Mar.	Jan. 15-Mar. 10	Feb. 1-Mar. 20	Feb. 15-Mar. 20
Parsley	Jan. 1-30	Jan. 1-30	Jan. 1-30	Feb. 15-Mar.	Feb. 1-Mar. 15	Feb. 15-Mar. 15	Mar. 1-Apr. 1
Parsnip			Jan. 1-Feb.	Jan. 15-Feb. 15	Jan. 15-Mar.	Feb. 15-Mar. 15	Mar. 1-Apr. 1
Peas, garden	Jan. 1-Feb. 15	Jan. 1-Feb. 15	Jan. 1-Mar.	Jan. 15-Mar. 15	Jan. 15-Mar. 15	Feb. 1-Mar. 15	Feb. 10-Mar. 20
Peas, blackeye	Feb. 15-May 1	Feb. 15-May 15	Mar. 1-June 15	Mar. 10-June 20	Mar. 15-July	Apr. 1-July	Apr. 15-July 1
Pepper*	Feb. 1-Apr. 1	Feb. 1-Apr. 1	Mar. 1-May	Mar. 15-May	Apr. 1-June	Apr. 10-June	Apr. 15-June 1
Potato	Jan. 1-Feb. 15	Jan. 1-Feb. 15	Jan. 15-Mar.	Jan. 15-Mar.	Feb. 1-Mar.	Feb. 10-Mar. 15	Feb. 20-Mar. 20
Radish	Jan. 1-Apr. 1	Jan. 1-Apr. 1	Jan. 1-Apr.	Jan. 1-Apr.	Jan. 1-Apr.	Jan. 20-May	Feb. 15-May 1
Rhubard*				Jan. 1-Feb.	Jan. 1-Feb.	Jan. 15-Mar.	Feb. 1-Mar. 1
Rutabaga	Jan. 1-Feb. 1	Jan. 1-Feb. 10	Jan. 1-Mar.	Jan. 15-Mar.	Jan. 15-Mar.	Feb. 15-Mar.	Mar. 1-15
Salsify	Jan. 1-Feb. 1	Jan. 1-Feb. 10	Jan. 15-Feb. 20	Jan. 1-Mar.	Jan. 15-Mar.	Feb. 10-Mar. 20	Feb. 15-Mar. 15
Shallot	Jan. 1-Feb. 1	Jan. 1-Feb. 10	Jan. 1-Feb. 20	Jan. 1-Mar.	Jan. 1-Mar.	Feb. 1-Mar. 10	Feb. 20-Apr. 1
Sorrel	Jan. 1-Mar. 1	Jan. 1-Mar. 1	Jan. 1-Mar. 15	Feb. 1-Mar.	Feb. 1-Mar. 10	Feb. 10-Mar. 20	Mar. 1-Apr. 1
Soybean	Mar. 1-June 30	Mar. 1-June 30	Mar. 10-June 30	Mar. 20-June 30	Apr. 10-June 30	Apr. 10-June 30	Apr. 20-June 30
Spinach	Jan. 1-Feb. 15	Jan. 1-Feb. 15	Jan. 1-Mar.	Jan. 15-Mar.	Jan. 15-Mar. 10	Jan. 15-Mar. 15	Apr. 1-Mar. 20
Spinach, N.Z.	Feb. 1-Apr. 15	Feb. 15-Apr. 15	Mar. 1-Apr. 15	Mar. 15-May 15	Mar. 15-May	Apr. 1-May 15	Apr. 10-June 1
Squash, summer	Feb. 1-Apr. 15	Feb. 15-Apr. 15	Mar. 1-Apr. 15	Mar. 15-May	Mar. 15-May	Apr. 1-May 15	Apr. 10-June 1
Sweet potato	Feb. 15-May 15	Mar. 1-May 15	Mar. 20-June 1	Mar. 20-June	Apr. 1-June	Apr. 10-June	Apr. 20-June
Tomato	Feb. 1-Apr. 1	Feb. 20-Apr. 10	Mar. 1-Apr. 20	Mar. 20-May 10	Mar. 20-May 20	Apr. 1-May	Apr. 10-June
Turnip	Jan. 1-Mar. 1	Jan. 1-Mar. 1	Jan. 10-Mar.	Jan. 20-Mar.	Feb. 1-Mar.	Feb. 10-Mar. 10	Feb. 20-Mar. 20
Watermelon	Feb. 15-Mar. 15	Feb. 15-Apr. 15	Feb. 15-Apr. 15	Mar. 1-Apr. 15	Mar. 15-Apr. 15	Apr. 1-May	Apr. 10-May 15

*Plants.
**Generally fall-planted (Table 5).

Table 2-1 (continued)

EARLIEST DATES, AND RANGE OF DATES, FOR SAFE SPRING PLANTING OF VEGETABLES IN THE OPEN

Planting dates for localities in which average date of last freeze is

Crop	Apr. 10	Apr. 20	Apr. 30	May 10	May 20	May 30	June 10
Asparagus*	Mar. 10–Apr. 10	Mar. 15–Apr. 15	Mar. 20–Apr. 15	Mar. 10–Apr. 30	Apr. 20–May 15	May 1–June 1	May 15–June 1
Beans, lima	Apr. 1–June 30	May 1–June 20	May 15–June 15	May 25–June 15			
Beans, snap	Apr. 10–June 30	Apr. 25–June 30	May 10–June 30	May 10–June 30	May 15–June 30	May 25–June 15	
Beet	Mar. 10–June 1	Mar. 20–June 1	Apr. 1–June 15	Apr. 15–June 15	Apr. 25–June 15	May 1–June 15	May 15–June 15
Broccoli, sprouting*	Mar. 15–Apr. 15	Mar. 25–Apr. 20	Apr. 1–May 1	Apr. 15–June 15	May 1–June 15	May 10–June 10	May 20–June 10
Brussels sprouts*	Mar. 15–Apr. 15	Mar. 25–Apr. 20	Apr. 1–May 1	Apr. 15–June 1	May 1–June 15	May 10–June 10	May 20–June 10
Cabbage*	Mar. 1–Apr. 1	**	Mar. 15–Apr. 10	Apr. 1–May 15	May 1–June 15	May 10–June 15	May 20–June 1
Cabbage, Chinese		**		Apr. 1–May 15	May 1–June 15	May 10–June 15	May 20–June 1
Carrot	Mar. 10–Apr. 20	Apr. 1–May 15	Apr. 10–June 1	Apr. 20–June 15	May 1–June 1	May 10–June 1	May 20–June 1
Cauliflower*	Mar. 1–Mar. 20	Mar. 15–Apr. 20	Apr. 10–May 10	Apr. 15–May 15	May 10–June 15	May 20–June 1	June 1–June 15
Celery and celeriac	Apr. 1–Apr. 20	Apr. 10–May 1	Apr. 15–May 1	Apr. 20–June 15	May 10–June 15	May 20–June 1	June 1–June 15
Chard	Mar. 15–June 15	Apr. 1–June 15	Apr. 15–June 15	Apr. 20–June 15	May 10–June 15	May 20–June 1	June 1–June 15
Chervil and chives	Mar. 1–Apr. 1	Mar. 10–Apr. 10	Mar. 20–Apr. 20	Apr. 1–May 1	Apr. 15–May 15	May 1–June 1	May 15–June 1
Chicory, witloof	June 10–July 1	June 15–July 1	June 15–July 1	June 1–20	June 1–15	June 1–15	June 1–15
Collards*	Mar. 1–June 1	Mar. 10–June 1	Apr. 1–June 1	Apr. 15–June 1	May 1–June 1	May 10–June 1	May 20–June 1
Cornsalad	Feb. 1–Apr. 1	Feb. 15–Apr. 15	Mar. 1–May 1	Apr. 1–June 1	Apr. 15–June 1	May 1–June 15	May 15–June 15
Corn, sweet	Apr. 10–June 1	Apr. 25–June 15	May 10–June 15	May 10–June 10	May 15–June 1	May 20–June 1	
Cress, upland	Mar. 10–Apr. 15	Mar. 20–May 1	Apr. 10–May 10	Apr. 20–May 20	May 1–June 1	May 15–June 1	May 15–June 15
Cucumber	Apr. 20–June 1	May 1–June 15	May 15–June 15	May 20–June 15	June 1–15		
Eggplant*	May 1–June 1	May 10–June 1	May 15–June 10	May 20–June 15	June 1–15		
Endive	Mar. 15–Apr. 15	Mar. 25–Apr. 15	Apr. 1–May 1	Apr. 15–May 15	May 1–30	May 1–30	May 15–June 1
Fennel, Florence	Mar. 15–Apr. 15	Mar. 25–Apr. 15	Apr. 1–May 1	Apr. 15–May 15	May 1–30	May 1–30	May 15–June 1
Garlic	Feb. 20–Mar. 20	Mar. 10–Apr. 1	Mar. 15–Apr. 15	Apr. 1–May 1	Apr. 15–May 15	May 1–30	May 15–June 1
Horseradish*	Mar. 10–Apr. 10	Mar. 20–Apr. 20	Apr. 1–May 1	Apr. 15–May 15	Apr. 20–May 20	May 1–30	May 15–June 1
Kale	Mar. 10–Apr. 10	Mar. 20–Apr. 20	Apr. 1–20	Apr. 10–May 1	Apr. 20–May 20	May 1–30	May 15–June 1
Kohlrabi	Mar. 10–Apr. 10	Mar. 20–May 1	Apr. 1–May 10	Apr. 10–May 15	Apr. 20–May 20	May 1–30	May 15–June 1

Leek	Mar. 1-Apr. 1	Mar. 15-Apr. 15	Apr. 1-May 1	May 1-May 20	May 1-15	May 1-15
Lettuce, head*	Mar. 10-Apr. 1	Mar. 20-Apr. 15	Apr. 15-May 15	May 1-June 30	May 10-June 30	May 20-June 30
Lettuce, leaf	Mar. 15-May 15	Mar. 20-May 15	Apr. 1-June 15	May 1-June 30	May 10-June 30	May 20-June 30
Muskmelon	Apr. 20-June	May 1-June 15	June 1-June 15	—	—	—
Mustard	Mar. 10-Apr. 20	Mar. 20-May 1	Apr. 1-May 10	May 1-June 30	May 10-June 30	May 20-June 30
Okra	Apr. 20-June 15	May 1-June 1	May 10-June 10	June 1-20	—	—
Onion*	Mar. 1-Apr. 1	Mar. 15-Apr. 10	Apr. 10-May 1	Apr. 20-May 15	May 1-30	May 10-June 10
Onion, seed	Mar. 1-Apr. 1	Mar. 15-Apr. 1	Apr. 1-May 1	Apr. 20-May 15	May 1-30	May 10-June 10
Onion, sets	Mar. 1-Apr. 1	Mar. 10-Apr. 1	Apr. 10-May 1	Apr. 20-May 15	May 1-30	May 10-June 10
Parsley	Mar. 10-Apr. 10	Mar. 20-Apr. 20	Apr. 15-May 15	May 1-20	May 10-June	May 20-June 10
Parsnip	Mar. 10-Apr. 10	Mar. 20-Apr. 20	Apr. 1-May 1	May 1-20	May 10-June	May 20-June 10
Peas, garden	Feb. 20-Mar. 20	Mar. 10-Apr. 10	Mar. 15-June	Apr. 15-June 1	May 1-June 15	May 10-June 15
Peas, blackeye	May 1-July 1	May 1-June 1	May 15-June 10	—	June 1-15	—
Pepper*	May 1-June 1	May 10-June	May 20-June	May 25-June 15	May 1-June 15	—
Potato	Mar. 10-Apr. 1	Mar. 15-Apr. 10	Mar. 20-May 1	Apr. 15-June 15	May 1-June 15	May 15-June 1
Radish	Mar. 1-May 1	Mar. 10-May 10	Mar. 20-May 20	Apr. 15-June 15	May 1-June 15	May 15-June 1
Rhubarb*	Mar. 1-Apr. 1	Mar. 10-Apr. 10	Mar. 20-Apr. 15	Apr. 1-May 10	May 1-20	May 15-June 1
Rutabaga	—	May 1-June	May 1-June 1	May 1-20	May 10-20	May 20-June
Salsify	Mar. 10-Apr. 15	Mar. 20-May 1	Apr. 1-May 1	May 1-June 1	May 10-June	May 20-June 1
Shallot	Mar. 1-Apr. 1	Mar. 15-Apr. 15	Apr. 1-May 1	Apr. 20-May 10	May 1-June	May 10-June
Sorrel	Mar. 1-Apr. 15	Mar. 15-May 1	Apr. 1-May 1	May 1-June	May 10-June 10	May 20-June 10
Soybean	May 1-June 30	May 10-June 20	May 15-June 15	—	Apr. 20-June 15	—
Spinach	Feb. 15-Apr. 1	Mar. 1-Apr. 15	Mar. 20-Apr. 20	Apr. 10-June 15	Apr. 20-June 15	May 1-June 15
Spinach, N.Z.	Apr. 20-June 1	May 1-June 15	May 1-30	May 20-June 15	June 1-15	—
Squash, summer	Apr. 20-June 1	May 1-June 15	May 1-30	May 20-June 15	June 1-20	June 10-20
Sweet potato	May 1-June 1	May 10-June 10	May 10-June 10	—	June 10-20	—
Tomato	Apr. 20-June 1	May 5-June 10	May 10-June 10	May 25-June 15	June 5-20	June 15-30
Turnip	Mar. 1-Apr. 1	Mar. 10-Apr.	Mar. 20-May 20	Apr. 15-June	May 1-June 15	May 15-June 15
Watermelon	Apr. 20-June 1	May 1-June 15	May 15-June 15	June 15-July	June 1-15	—

*Plants.
**Generally fall-planted (Table 5)

The cold-hardy plants include beets, radishes, chard, carrots, and parsnips. All of these should be planted from two to four weeks before the frost-free date.

Those vegetables to be planted after the last killing frost and when temperatures begin to rise, both day and night, include snap beans, squash, New Zealand spinach, tomatoes, and sweet corn.

Table 2-2

SOME COMMON VEGETABLES GROUPED ACCORDING TO THE APPROXIMATE TIMES THEY CAN BE PLANTED AND THEIR RELATIVE REQUIREMENTS FOR COOL AND WARM WEATHER

COLD-HARDY PLANTS FOR EARLY-SPRING PLANTING		COLD-TENDER OR HEAT-HARDY PLANTS FOR LATER-SPRING OR EARLY-SUMMER PLANTING			Hardy plants for late-summer or fall planting except in the North
Very hardy (plant 4 to 6 weeks before frost-free date)	Hardy (plant 2 to 4 weeks before frost-free date)	Not cold-hardy (plant on frost-free date)	Requiring hot weather (plant 1 week or more after frost-free date)	Medium heat tolerant (good for summer planting)	(plant 6 to 8 weeks before first fall freeze)
Broccoli	Beets	Beans, snap	Beans, lima	Beans, all	Beets
Cabbage	Carrot	Okra	Eggplant	Chard	Collard
Lettuce	Chard	New Zealand	Peppers	Soybean	Kale
Onions	Mustard	spinach	Sweet potato	New Zealand	Lettuce
Peas	Parsnip	Soybean	Cucumber	spinach	Mustard
Potato	Radish	Squash	Melons	Squash	Spinach
Spinach		Sweet corn		Sweet corn	Turnip
Turnip		Tomato			

The truly heat-hardy plants that thrive only on hot weather include lima beans, eggplant, peppers, sweet potatoes, and cucumbers. These are all best planted about two weeks or more after the frost-free date.

The cold-hardy plants that thrive in the fall include kale, beets, mustard, turnips, late cabbage, and lettuce. Planting must be made in late summer in time to allow for maturity before the first freeze, except for turnips and kale. Both of these thrive on repeated frosts.

Table 2-3

LATEST DATES, AND RANGE OF DATES, FOR SAFE FALL PLANTING OF VEGETABLES IN THE OPEN

Planting dates for localities in which average date of first freeze is

Crop	Aug. 30	Sept. 10	Sept. 20	Sept. 30	Oct. 10	Oct. 20
Asparagus*					Oct. 20-Nov. 15	Nov. 1-Dec. 15
Beans, lima					Jun. 1-15	Jun. 15-30
Beans, snap		May 15-Jun. 15		Jun. 1-Jul. 1	Jun. 15-Jul. 20	Jul. 1-Aug. 1
Beet	May 20-Jun. 15	May 1-Jun. 1	May 1-Jun. 15	Jun. 1-30	Jun. 15-Jul. 25	Jul. 1-Aug. 5
Broccoli, sprouting	May 1-Jun. 1	May 1-Jun. 1	May 1-Jun. 15	Jun. 1-30	Jun. 15-Jul. 15	Jul. 1-Aug. 1
Brussels sprouts	May 1-Jun. 1	May 1-Jun. 1	May 1-Jun. 15	Jun. 1-30	Jun. 15-Jul. 15	Jul. 1-Aug. 1
Cabbage*	May 1-Jun. 1	May 1-Jun. 1	May 1-Jun. 15	Jun. 1-Jul. 1	Jun. 1-Jul. 15	Jul. 1-20
Cabbage, Chinese	May 15-Jun. 15	May 15-Jun. 15	May 15-Jun. 15	Jun. 1-Jul. 1	Jun. 15-Aug. 1	Jul. 15-Aug. 15
Carrot	May 15-Jun. 15	May 15-Jun. 15	Jun. 1-Jul. 1	Jun. 1-Jul. 1	Jun. 1-Jul. 20	Jun. 15-Aug. 1
Cauliflower*	May 1-Jun. 1	May 15-Jul. 1	May 1-Jul. 1	Jun. 1-Jul. 1	Jun. 1-Jul. 25	Jul. 1-Aug. 5
Celery* and celeriac	May 1-Jun. 1	May 1-Jul. 1	May 15-Jul. 1	May 10-Jul. 1	May 10-Jul. 15	Jun. 1-Aug. 1
Chard	May 15-Jun. 15	May 15-Jul. 1	May 15-Jul. 1	Jun. 1-Jul. 1	Jun. 1-Jul. 20	Jun. 1-Aug. 1
Chervil and chives	May 10-Jun. 10	May 1-Jun. 15	May 15-Jun. 15	**	**	**
Chicory, witloof	May 15-Jun. 15	May 15-Jun. 15	May 15-Jun. 15	Jun. 1-Jul. 1	Jun. 1-Jul. 1	Jun. 15-Jul. 15
Collards*	May 15-Jun. 15	May 15-Jun. 15	May 15-Jun. 15	Jun. 15-Jul. 15	Jul. 1-Aug. 1	Jul. 15-Aug. 15
Cornsalad	May 15-Jun. 15	May 15-Jul. 1	May 15-Aug. 15	Jul. 15-Sept. 1	Aug. 15-Sept. 15	Sept. 1-Oct. 15
Corn, sweet		May 15-Jul. 1	Jun. 1-Jul. 1	Jun. 1-Jul. 1	Jun. 1-Jul. 10	Jun. 1-Jul. 20
Cress, upland	May 15-Jun. 15	May 15-Jul. 15	Jun. 15-Aug. 15	Jul. 15-Sept. 1	Aug. 15-Sept. 15	Sept. 1-Oct. 15
Cucumber			Jun. 1-15	Jun. 1-Jul. 1	Jun. 1-Jul. 1	Jun. 1-Jul. 15
Eggplant*		May 15-Jun. 15	Jun. 1-15	May 20-Jun. 10	May 15-Jun. 15	Jun. 1-Jul. 15
Endive	Jun. 1-Jul. 1	Jun. 1-Jul. 1	Jun. 15-Jul. 15	Jun. 15-Aug. 1	Jul. 1-Aug. 15	Jul. 15-Sept. 1
Fennel, Florence	May 15-Jun. 15	May 15-Jul. 15	Jun. 1-Jul. 1	Jun. 1-Aug. 1	Jun. 15-Jul. 15	Jun. 15-Aug. 1
Garlic	**	**	**	**	**	**
Horseradish*	**	**	**	**	**	**

Table 2-3 (continued)

LATEST DATES, AND RANGE OF DATES, FOR SAFE FALL PLANTING OF VEGETABLES IN THE OPEN

Crop	Planting dates for localities in which average date of first freeze is					
	Aug. 30	Sept. 10	Sept. 20	Sept. 30	Oct. 10	Oct. 20
Kale	May 15-Jun. 15	May 15-Jun. 15	Jun. 1-Jul. 1	Jun. 15-Jul. 15	Jul. 1-Aug. 1	Jul. 15-Aug. 15
Kohlrabi	May 15-Jun. 15	Jun. 1-Jul. 1	Jun. 1-Jul. 15	Jun. 15-Jul. 15	Jul. 1-Aug. 1	Jul. 15-Aug. 15
Leek	May 1-Jun. 1	May 1-Jun. 1	[2]	[2]	[2]	[2]
Lettuce, head*	May 15-Jul. 1	May 15-Jul. 1	Jun. 1-Jul. 15	Jun. 15-Aug. 1	Jul. 15-Aug. 15	Aug. 1-30
Lettuce, leaf	May 15-Jul. 15	May 15-Jul. 15	Jun. 1-Aug. 1	Jun. 1-Aug. 1	Jul. 15-Sept. 1	Jul. 15-Sept. 1
Muskmelon			May 1-Jun. 15	May 15-Jun. 1	Jun. 1-Jul. 15	Jun. 15-Jul. 20
Mustard	May 15-Jul. 15	May 15-Jul. 15	Jun. 1-Aug. 1	Jun. 15-Aug. 1	Jul. 15-Aug. 15	Aug. 1-Sept. 1
Okra			Jun. 1-20	Jun. 1-Jul. 1	Jun. 1-Jul. 15	Jun. 1-Aug. 1
Onion*	May 1-Jun. 10	May 1-Jun. 10	**	**	**	**
Onion, seed	May 1-Jun. 1	May 1-Jun. 10	**	**	**	**
Onion, sets	May 1-Jun. 1	May 1-Jun. 10	**	**	**	**
Parsley	May 15-Jun. 15	May 1-Jun. 15	Jun. 1-Jul. 1	Jun. 1-Jul. 15	Jun. 15-Aug. 1	Jul. 15-Aug. 15
Parsnip	May 15-Jun. 1	May 1-Jun. 15	May 15-Jun. 15	Jun. 1-Jul. 1	Jun. 1-Jul. 10	[2]
Peas, garden	May 10-Jun. 15	May 1-Jul. 1	May 15-Jun. 15	Jun. 1-Jul. 1	**	**
Peas, blackeye			Jun. 1-Jul. 15	Jun. 1-Aug. 1	Jun. 1-Jul. 1	Jun. 1-Jul. 1

Pepper*	May 15-Jun. 1		Jun. 1-Jul. 1	Jun. 1-Jul. 1	Jun. 1-Jul. 10
Potato	May 1-Jul. 15	May 1-Aug. 15	May 1-Jun. 15	May 1-Jun. 15	May 15-Jul. 15
Radish	Sept. 1-Oct. 1	Sept. 15-Oct. 15	Sept. 15-Nov. 1	Jul. 1-Sept. 1	Aug. 1-Oct. 1
Rhubard*	May 15-Jun. 15		Oct. 1-Nov. 1	Oct. 15-Nov. 15	Oct. 15-Dec. 1
Rutabaga	May 15-Jun. 15	May 10-Jun. 10	Jun. 1-Jul. 15	Jun. 1-Jul. 15	Jul. 10-20
Salsify			May 20-Jun. 20	Jun. 1-Jul. 1	
Shallot	**	**	**	**	**
Sorrel	May 15-Jun. 15		Jun. 1-Jul. 15	Jul. 1-Aug. 1	Jul. 15-Aug. 15
Soybean			May 25-Jun. 10	Jun. 1-25	Jun. 1-Jul. 1
Spinach	May 15-Jul. 15	1-20	Jul. 1-Aug. 15	Aug. 1-Sept. 1	Aug. 20-Sept. 10
Spinach, New Zealand			May 15-Jul. 1	Jun. 1-Aug. 1	Jun. 1-Aug. 1
Squash, summer	Jun. 10-20	May 15-Jul. 1	Jun. 1-Jul. 1	Jun. 1-Jul. 15	Jun. 1-Jul. 20
Squash, winter		May 20-Jun. 10	Jun. 1-15	Jun. 1-Jul. 1	Jun. 1-Jul. 1
Sweet potato				May 20-Jun. 10	Jun. 1-15
Tomato	Jun. 20-30	Jun. 10-20	Jun. 1-20	Jun. 1-20	Jun. 1-Jul. 1
Turnip	May 15-Jun. 15	Jun. 1-Jul. 1	Jun. 1-Aug. 1	Jul. 1-Aug. 1	Jul. 15-Aug. 15
Watermelon			May 15-Jun. 15	May 15-Jul. 15	Jun. 15-Jul. 20

*Plants.
**Generally spring-planted (Table 4).

Table 2-3 (continued)

LATEST DATES, AND RANGE OF DATES, FOR SAFE FALL PLANTING OF VEGETABLES IN THE OPEN

Planting dates for localities in which average date of first freeze is

Crop	Oct. 30	Nov. 10	Nov. 20	Nov. 30	Dec. 10	Dec. 20
Asparagus*	Nov. 22–Jan. 1	Dec. 1–Jan. 1				
Beans, lima	Jul. 1–Aug. 1	Jul. 1–Aug. 15	Jul. 15–Sept. 1	Aug. 1–Sept. 15	Sept. 1–30	Sept. 1–Oct. 1
Beans, snap	Jul. 1–Aug. 15	Jul. 1–Sept. 1	1–Sept. 10	Aug. 15–Sept. 20	Sept. 1–30	Sept. 1–Nov. 1
Beet	Aug. 1–Sept. 1	Aug. 1–Oct. 1	Sept. 1–Dec. 1	Sept. 1–Dec. 15	Sept. 1–Dec. 31	Sept. 1–Dec. 31
Broccoli, sprouting	Jul. 1–Aug. 15	Aug. 1–Sept. 1	Aug. 1–Sept. 15	Aug. 1–Oct. 1	Aug. 1–Nov. 1	Sept. 1–Dec. 31
Brussels sprouts	Jul. 1–Aug. 15	Aug. 1–Sept. 1	Aug. 1–Sept. 15	Aug. 1–Oct. 1	Aug. 1–Nov. 1	Sept. 1–Dec. 31
Cabbage*	Aug. 1–Sept. 1	Sept. 1–15	Sept. 1–Dec. 1	Sept. 1–Dec. 31	Sept. 1–Dec. 31	Sept. 1–Dec. 31
Cabbage, Chinese	Aug. 1–Sept. 15	Aug. 15–Oct. 1	Sept. 1–Oct. 15	Sept. 1–Nov. 1	Sept. 1–Nov. 15	Sept. 1–Dec. 1
Carrot	Jul. 1–Aug. 15	Aug. 1–Sept. 1	Sept. 1–Nov. 1	Sept. 15–Dec. 1	Sept. 15–Dec. 1	Sept. 15–Dec. 1
Cauliflower*	Jul. 15–Aug. 15	Aug. 1–Sept. 1	Aug. 1–Sept. 15	Aug. 15–Oct. 10	Sept. 1–Oct. 20	Sept. 15–Nov. 1
Celery* and celeriac	Jun. 15–Aug. 15	Jul. 1–Aug. 15	Jul. 15–Sept. 1	Aug. 1–Dec. 1	Sept. 1–Dec. 31	Oct. 1–Dec. 31
Chard	Jun. 1–Sept. 10	Jun. 1–Sept. 15	Jun. 1–Oct. 1	Jun. 1–Nov. 1	Jun. 1–Dec. 1	Jun. 1–Dec. 31
Chervil and chives	**	**	Nov. 1–Dec. 31	Nov. 1–Dec. 31	Nov. 1–Dec. 31	Nov. 1–Dec. 31
Chicory, witloof	Jul. 1–Aug. 10	Jul. 10–Aug. 20	Jul. 20–Sept. 1	Aug. 15–Sept. 30	Aug. 15–Oct. 15	Aug. 15–Oct. 15
Collards*	Aug. 1–Sept. 15	Aug. 15–Oct. 1	Aug. 25–Nov. 1	Sept. 1–Dec. 1	Sept. 1–Dec. 31	Sept. 1–Dec. 31
Cornsalad	Sept. 15–Nov. 1	Oct. 1–Dec. 1	Oct. 1–Dec. 1	Oct. 1–Dec. 31	Oct. 1–Dec. 31	Oct. 1–Dec. 31
Corn, sweet	Jun. 1–Aug. 1	Jun. 1–Aug. 15	Jun. 1–Sept. 1			
Cress, upland	Sept. 15–Nov. 1	Oct. 1–Dec. 1	Oct. 1–Dec. 1	Oct. 1–Dec. 31	Oct. 1–Dec. 31	Oct. 1–Dec. 31
Cucumber	Jun. 1–Aug. 1	Jun. 1–Aug. 15	Jun. 1–Aug. 15	Jul. 15–Sept. 15	Aug. 15–Oct. 1	Aug. 15–Oct. 1
Eggplant*	Jun. 1–Jul. 1	Jun. 1–Jul. 15	Jun. 1–Aug. 1	Jul. 1–Sept. 1	Aug. 1–Sept. 30	Aug. 1–Sept. 30
Endive	Jul. 15–Aug. 15	Aug. 1–Sept. 1	Sept. 1–Oct. 1	Sept. 1–Nov. 15	Sept. 1–Dec. 31	Sept. 1–Dec. 31
Fennel, Florence	Jul. 1–Aug. 1	Jul. 15–Aug. 15	Aug. 15–Sept. 15	Sept. 1–Nov. 15	Sept. 1–Dec. 1	Sept. 1–Dec. 1
Garlic	**	Aug. 1–Oct. 1	Aug. 15–Oct. 1	Sept. 1–Nov. 15	Sept. 15–Nov. 15	Sept. 15–Nov. 15
Horseradish*	**	**	**	**	**	**
Kale	Jul. 15–Sept. 1	Aug. 1–Sept. 15	Aug. 15–Oct. 15	Sept. 1–Dec. 1	Sept. 1–Dec. 31	Sept. 1–Dec. 31

Kohlrabi	Aug. 1–Sept. 1	Aug. 15–Sept. 15	Sept. 1–Oct. 15	Sept. 1–Dec. 1	Sept. 1–Dec. 31	Sept. 15–Dec. 31	Sept. 15–Dec. 31
Leek	**	**	Sept.	Sept.	Sept.	Sept. 1–Nov. 1	Sept. 15–Nov. 1
Lettuce, head*	Aug. 1–Sept. 15	Aug. 15–Oct. 15	Sept. 1–Nov. 1	Sept. 1–Dec. 1	Sept. 1–Dec. 1	Sept. 15–Dec. 31	Sept. 15–Dec. 31
Lettuce, leaf	Aug. 15–Oct. 1	Aug. 25–Oct. 1	Sept. 1–Nov. 1	Sept. 1–Nov. 1	Sept. 1–Nov. 1	Sept. 15–Dec. 31	Sept. 15–Dec. 31
Muskmelon	Jul. 1–Jul. 15	Jul. 15–Jul. 30					
Mustard	Aug. 15–Oct. 15	Aug. 15–Nov. 1	Sept. 1–Dec. 1	Sept. 1–Dec. 1	Sept. 1–Dec. 1	Sept. 15–Dec. 1	Sept. 15–Dec. 1
Okra	Jun. 1–Aug. 10	Jun. 1–Aug. 20	Jun. 1–Sept. 10	Jun. 1–Sept. 20	Jun. 1–Sept. 20	Aug. 1–Oct. 1	Aug. 1–Oct. 1
Onion*		Sept. 1–Oct. 15	Oct. 1–Dec. 31	Oct. 1–Dec. 31	Oct. 1–Dec. 31	Oct. 1–Dec. 31	Oct. 1–Dec. 31
Onion, seed		Sept. 1–Oct. 15	Sept. 1–Nov. 1	Oct. 1–Nov. 1	Oct. 1–Nov. 1	Oct. 1–Nov. 1	Sept. 15–Nov. 1
Onion, sets			Nov. 1–Dec. 31	Nov. 1–Dec. 31	Nov. 1–Dec. 31	Nov. 1–Dec. 31	Nov. 1–Dec. 31
Parsley	Aug. 1–Sept. 15	Oct. 1–Dec. 1	Sept. 1–Dec. 31	Sept. 1–Dec. 31	Sept. 1–Dec. 31	Sept. 1–Dec. 31	Sept. 1–Dec. 31
Parsnip	**	Sept. 1–Nov. 15	Aug. 1–Sept. 1	Sept. 1–Nov. 15	Sept. 1–Dec. 31	Sept. 1–Dec. 31	Sept. 1–Dec. 31
Peas, garden	Aug. 1–Sept. 15	Sept. 1–Nov. 1	Oct. 1–Dec. 1	Oct. 1–Dec. 1	Oct. 1–Dec. 31	Oct. 1–Dec. 31	Oct. 1–Dec. 31
Peas, blackeye	Jun. 1–Aug. 1	Jun. 15–Aug. 15	Jul. 1–Sept. 1	Jul. 1–Sept. 10	Jul. 1–Sept. 20	Jul. 1–Sept. 20	Jul. 1–Sept. 20
Pepper*	Jun. 1–Jul. 20	Jun. 1–Aug. 1	Jun. 1–Aug. 15	Jun. 1–Aug. 15	Jul. 15–Sept. 1	Aug. 15–Oct. 1	Aug. 15–Oct. 1
Potato	Jul. 20–Aug. 10	Jul. 25–Aug. 20	Aug. 10–Sept. 15	Aug. 10–Sept. 15	Aug. 1–Sept. 15	Aug. 1–Sept. 15	Aug. 1–Sept. 15
Radish	Aug. 15–Oct. 15	Sept. 1–Nov. 15	Sept. 1–Dec. 1	Sept. 1–Dec. 1	Sept. 1–Dec. 31	Oct. 1–Dec. 31	Oct. 1–Dec. 31
Rhubarb*	Nov. 1–Dec. 1						
Rutabaga	Jul. 15–Aug. 1	Jul. 15–Aug. 15	Aug. 1–Sept. 1	Aug. 1–Sept. 1	Sept. 1–Nov. 15	Oct. 15–Nov. 15	Oct. 15–Nov. 15
Salsify	Jun. 1–Jul. 10	Jun. 15–Jul. 20	Jul. 15–Aug. 15	Jul. 15–Aug. 15	Aug. 15–Sept. 30	Sept. 1–Oct. 31	Sept. 1–Oct. 31
Shallot	**	Aug. 1–Oct. 1	Aug. 15–Oct. 1	Aug. 1–Oct. 1	Aug. 15–Oct. 15	Sept. 15–Nov. 1	Sept. 15–Nov. 1
Sorrel	Aug. 1–Sept. 15	Aug. 15–Oct. 1	Aug. 15–Oct. 15	Aug. 15–Oct. 15	Aug. 15–Oct. 15	Sept. 1–Dec. 1	Sept. 1–Dec. 1
Soybean	Jun. 1–Jul. 15	Jun. 1–Jul. 25	Jun. 1–Jul. 1	Jun. 1–Jul. 1	Jun. 1–Jul. 30	Jun. 1–Jul. 30	Jun. 1–Jul. 30
Spinach	Sept. 1–Oct. 1	Sept. 15–Nov. 1	Oct. 1–Dec. 1	Oct. 1–Dec. 1	Oct. 1–Dec. 31	Oct. 1–Dec. 31	Oct. 1–Dec. 31
Spinach, New Zealand	Jun. 1–Aug. 1	Jun. 1–Aug. 15	Jun. 1–Aug. 15	Jun. 1–Aug. 15	Jun. 1–Sept. 1	Jun. 1–Sept. 1	
Squash, summer	Jun. 1–Aug. 1	Jun. 1–Aug. 10	Jun. 1–Aug. 20	Jun. 1–Aug. 20	Aug. 15–Sept. 15	Aug. 15–Sept. 15	Jun. 1–Oct. 1
Squash, winter	Jun. 10–Jul. 10	Jun. 20–Jul. 20	Jul. 1–Aug. 1	Jul. 1–Aug. 1	Aug. 15–Aug. 15	Aug. 1–Sept. 1	Aug. 1–Sept. 1
Sweet potato	Jun. 1–15	Jun. 1–Jul. 1	Jun. 1–Jul. 1	Jun. 1–Jul. 1	Jun. 1–Jul. 1	Jun. 1–Jul. 1	Jun. 1–Jul. 1
Tomato	Jun. 1–Jul. 1	Jun. 1–Jul. 15	Jun. 1–Aug. 1	Jun. 1–Aug. 1	Aug. 1–Sept. 1	Aug. 15–Oct. 1	Aug. 15–Oct. 1
Turnip	Aug. 1–Sept. 15	Sept. 1–Oct. 15	Sept. 1–Nov. 15	Sept. 1–Nov. 15	Sept. 1–Nov. 15	Oct. 1–Dec. 31	Oct. 1–Dec. 31
Watermelon	Jul. 1–Jul. 15	Jul. 15–Jul. 30					

*Plants.
**Generally fall-planted (Table 4).

Table 2-4

QUANTITY OF SEED AND NUMBER OF PLANTS REQUIRED FOR 100 FEET OF ROW, DEPTHS OF PLANTING, AND DISTANCES APART FOR ROWS AND PLANTS

| Crop | Requirement for 100 feet of row | | Depth for planting seed (Inches) | Distance apart | | |
| | Seed | Plants | | Rows | | Plants in the row |
				Horse- or tractor-cultivated (Feet)	Hand-cultivated	
Asparagus	1 ounce	75	1–1-1/2	4–5	1-1/2 to 2 feet	18 inches
Beans, lima, bush	1/2 pound		1–1-1/2	2-1/2–3	2 feet	3 to 4 inches
Beans, lima, pole	1/2 pound		1–1-1/2	3–4	3 feet	3 to 4 feet
Beans, snap, bush	1/2 pound		1–1-1/2	2-1/2–3	2 feet	3 to 4 inches
Beans, snap, pole	4 ounces		1–1-1/2	3–4	2 feet	3 feet
Beet	2 ounces		1	2–2-1/2	14 to 16 inches	2 to 3 inches
Broccoli: heading	1 packet	50–75	1/2	2-1/2–3	2 to 2-1/2 feet	14 to 24 inches
Broccoli: sprouting	1 packet	50–75	1/2	2-1/2–3	2 to 2-1/2 feet	14 to 24 inches
Brussels sprouts	1 packet	50–75	1/2	2-1/2–3	2 to 2-1/2 feet	14 to 24 inches
Cabbage	1 packet	50–75	1/2	2-1/2–3	2 to 2-1/2 feet	14 to 24 inches
Cabbage, Chinese	1 packet		1/2	2–2-1/2	18 to 24 inches	8 to 12 inches
Carrot	1 packet		1/2	2–2-1/2	14 to 16 inches	2 to 3 inches
Cauliflower	1 packet	50–75	1/2	2-1/2–3	2 to 2-1/2 feet	14 to 24 inches
Celeriac	1 packet	200–250	1/8	2-1/2–3	18 to 24 inches	4 to 6 inches
Celery	1 packet	200–250	1/8	2-1/2–3	18 to 24 inches	4 to 6 inches
Chard	2 ounces		1	2–2-1/2	18 to 24 inches	6 inches
Chervil	1 packet		1/2	2–2-1/2	14 to 16 inches	2 to 3 inches
Chicory, witloof	1 packet		1/2	2–2-1/2	18 to 24 inches	6 to 8 inches
Chives	1 packet		1/2	2-1/2–3	14 to 16 inches	In clusters
Collards	1 packet		1/2	3–3-1/2	18 to 24 inches	18 to 24 inches

Cornsalad	1 packet		1/2	2-1/2–3	14 to 16 inches	1 foot
Corn, sweet	2 ounces		2	3–3-1/2	2 to 3 feet	14"-16" drills; 2½-3 ft. hills
Cress, upland	1 packet		1/8–1/4	2–2-1/2	14 to 16 inches	2 to 3 inches
Cucumber	1 packet		1/2	6–7	6 to 7 feet	3 ft. drills; 6 ft. hills
Dasheen	5 to 6 pounds	50	2–3	3-1/2–4	3-1/2 to 4 feet	2 feet
Eggplant	1 packet	50	1/2	3	2 to 2-1/2 feet	3 feet
Endive	1 packet		1/2	2-1/2–3	18 to 24 inches	12 inches
Fennel, Florence	1 packet		1/2	2-1/2–3	18 to 24 inches	4 to 6 inches
Garlic	1 pound		1–2	2-1/2–3	14 to 16 inches	2 to 3 inches
Horseradish	Cuttings	50–75	2	3–4	2 to 2-1/2 feet	18 to 24 inches
Kale	1 packet		1/2	2-1/2–3	18 to 24 inches	12 to 15 inches
Kohlrabi	1 packet		1/2	1/2	14 to 16 inches	5 to 6 inches
Leek	1 packet		1/2–1	2-1/2–3	18 to 24 inches	2 to 3 inches
Lettuce, head	1 packet	100	1/2	2-1/2–3	14 to 16 inches	12 to 15 inches
Lettuce, leaf	1 packet		1/2	2-1/2–3	14 to 16 inches	6 inches
Muskmelon	1 packet		1	6–7	6 to 7 feet	Hills, 6 feet
Mustard	1 packet		1/2	2-1/2–3	14 to 16 inches	12 inches
Okra	2 ounces	400	1–1-1/2	3–3-1/2	3 to 3-1/2 feet	2 feet
Onion, plants	1 packet		1–2	2–2-1/2	14 to 16 inches	2 to 3 inches
Onion, seed	1 pound		1/2–1	2–2-1/2	14 to 16 inches	2 to 3 inches
Onion, sets	1 packet		1–2	2–2-1/2	14 to 16 inches	2 to 3 inches
Parsley	1 packet		1/8	2–2-1/2	14 to 16 inches	4 to 6 inches
Parsley, turnip-rooted	1 packet		1/8–1/4	2–2-1/2	14 to 16 inches	2 to 3 inches
Parsnip	1/2 pound		1/2	2–2-1/2	18 to 24 inches	2 to 3 inches
Peas	1 packet		2–3	2–4	1-1/2 to 3 feet	1 inch
Pepper	1 packet	50–70	1/2	3–4	2 to 3 feet	18 to 24 inches
Physalis	1 packet		1/2	2–2-1/2	1-1/2 to 2 feet	12 to 18 inches
Potato	5 to 6 pounds, tubers		4	2-1/2–3	2 to 2-1/2 feet	10 to 18 inches
Pumpkin	1 ounce		1–2	5–8	5 to 8 feet	3 to 4 feet
Radish	1 ounce		1/2	2–2-1/2	14 to 18 inches	1 inch
Rhubarb		25–35		3–4	3 to 4 feet	3 to 4 feet

Table 2-4 (continued)

QUANTITY OF SEED AND NUMBER OF PLANTS REQUIRED FOR 100 FEET OF ROW, DEPTHS OF PLANTING, AND DISTANCES APART FOR ROWS AND PLANTS

	Requirement for 100 feet of row		Depth for planting seed (Inches)	Distance apart			
				Rows			Plants in the row
Crop	Seed	Plants		Horse- or tractor-cultivated (Feet)	Hand-cultivated		
Salsify	1 ounce		1/2	2–2-1/2	18 to 26 inches		2 to 3 inches
Shallots	1 pound (cloves)		1–2	2–2-1/2	12 to 18 inches		2 to 3 inches
Sorrel	1 packet		1/2	2–2-1/2	18 to 24 inches		5 to 8 inches
Soybean	1/2 to 1 pound		1–1-1/2	2-1/2–3	24 to 30 inches		3 inches
Spinach	1 ounce		1/2	2–2-1/2	14 to 18 inches		3 to 4 inches
Spinach, New Zealand	1 ounce		1–1-1/2	3–3-1/2	3 feet		18 inches
Squash, bush	1/2 ounce		1–2	4–5	4 to 5 feet		15″-18″ drills; 4 ft. hills
Squash, vine	1 ounce		1–2	8–12	8 to 12 feet		2-3 ft. drills; 4 ft. hills
Sweet potato	5 pounds, bedroots	75	2–3	3–3-1/2	3 to 3-1/2 feet		12 to 14 inches
Tomato	1 packet	35–50	1/2	3–4	2 to 3 feet		1-1/2 to 3 feet
Turnip greens	1 packet		1/4–1/2	2–2-1/2	14 to 16 inches		2 to 3 inches
Turnips and rutabagas	1/2 ounce		1/4–1/2	2–2-1/2	14 to 16 inches		2 to 3 inches
Watermelon	1 ounce		1–2	8–10	8 to 10 feet		2-3 ft. drills, 8 ft. hills

34

CULTIVATION

Some people cannot bear the thought of pulling up healthy plants and casting them aside. Consequently, their plants are always too crowded and never bear heavy crops nor yield top-quality vegetables. Adequate spacing between plants is necessary for the leaves to draw nutrients from the air and receive the beneficial rays of the sun as well as to give the roots adequate room to draw nutrients from the soil. For a plant to enjoy its best environment, other plants or weeds must not be allowed to encroach on its ground or air space. Thus, cultivation and weeding insure that the plant can take full advantage of the nutrients around it. When a plant can take full advantage of the fertility of the soil and does not have to share the nutrients with weeds, a healthier, more productive plant results.

The practice of cultivating one's plants as soon after a rain as the ground can be worked is the best means of controlling weeds. This kills sprouted weeds and loosens the soil so that it readily absorbs the next rainfall. Care should be exercised in hoeing in order not to injure plants. Hand weeding is very effective on small plots, and can be used close to plants on any size plot. It is best done after a rain when the soil is soft and weeds can easily be pulled out by the roots.

WATERING

Plants require about an inch of rainfall a week for best growth in most areas. If the rainfall is inadequate and moisture in the soil is depleted, you must provide water to ensure good production. A good soaking once a week is far better than daily sprinkling. In fact, light sprinkling is actually harmful, inasmuch as it causes roots to seek the surface for the bit of water supplied. The best way to water your garden is to run the water in furrows between rows until the ground is well soaked. For small plots use a sprinkler or a bucket and a cup. Watering your plants in a haphazard fashion and inadequately may do more harm than good. Late evening is the best time for watering, inasmuch as the sun will not evaporate the water before it sinks into the soil.

You can easily make provisions for deep irrigation around a few tomato plants, pepper plants, or eggplants by cutting the tops and bottoms out of some tin cans, digging holes adjacent to the plants, and putting the cans in the holes. Make the tops level with the surface and then fill with gravel or small stones. Water poured into the can will provide moisture down at the roots where it is most effective. Keep filling the can until the water is no longer being quickly absorbed by the soil. This method of watering plants will en-

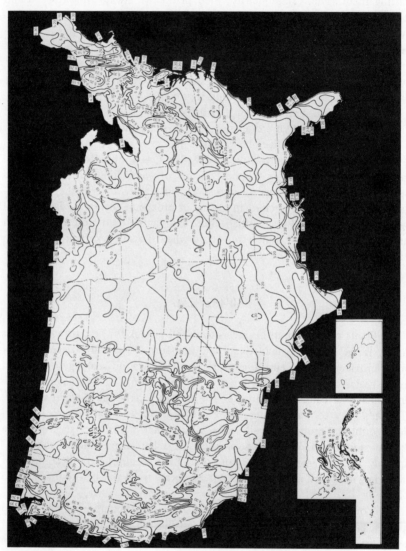

Average dates of the last killing frost in spring (USDA photo)

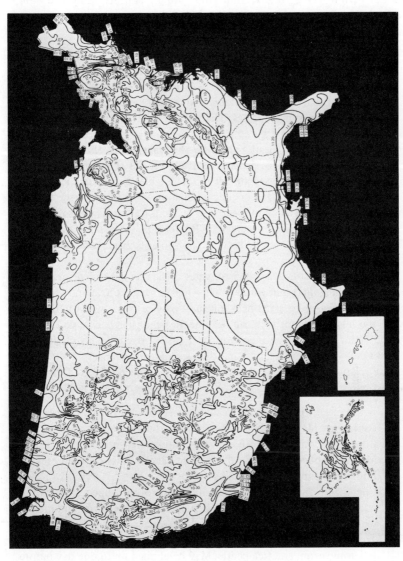

Average dates of the first killing frost in fall (USDA photo)

courage deep root structure, thereby enabling plants to better withstand heat and drought. Naturally, this method of watering is not limited to a few individual plants and may be employed as extensively as desired. The moral here is: Do not permit lack of rain to ruin your garden. You may also feed your plants with liquid fertilizer by this method of watering.

INSECTICIDES

Most insects that damage vegetable plants may be effectively controlled with chemicals known as insecticides. There is a bewildering variety of insecticides on the market. However, one need not become a chemist nor study the habits of the various insect pests that chew the leaves, suck the sap, and occasionally cut off the stalk of a plant. Fortunately for the gardener, an all-purpose insecticide can be used on all the vegetables grown in the average garden, and it will be effective on approximately 90 percent of the garden pests encountered. Such an all-purpose insecticide is Carbaryl (it is sold under several brand names). It is a 50 percent WP (wettable powder). Carbaryl is a synthetic carbonate that acts as a stomach poison as well as a contact insecticide.

Two tablespoonsful per gallon of water is the recommended spray mixture for everything in your garden. This means that you do not have to change from a weaker to a stronger mixture, or vice versa, when you finish spraying the bush beans for Mexican bean beetles and then decide you should spray the summer squash because you have just noticed some squash bugs. This insecticide can be a real labor- and time-saving convenience.

The many uses of Carbaryl have to be seen to be appreciated; here is a partial listing:

1. Beans. For control of Mexican bean beetle, leafhopper, lygus, and stink bugs. May be applied up to one day before harvest.
2. Corn. For control of corn earworm, sap beetle, and Japanese beetle. May be applied up to one day before harvest on sweet corn ears for human consumption.
3. Cucumbers and summer squash. For control of striped and spotted cucumber beetles, squash bugs, flea beetles, pickleworm, and melonworm. May be applied up to day of harvest.
4. Tomato, eggplant, and pepper. For control of tomato fruitworm, fall armyworm, and flea beetle. May be applied up to one day before harvest.
5. Strawberries. For control of meadow spittlebug and strawberry leaf roller. May be applied up to one day before harvest.

Carbaryl is equally effective on lettuce, cabbage, and most all fruits.

For small gardens, insecticides can be applied with a minimum amount of equipment, either by dusting or spraying. Some of the dusts can be applied by shaking the powder onto the plants, although this is effective only for small areas. You can also use a plunger-type duster with a capacity of from one to three pounds. They are usually constructed so you can easily spray the undersides of leaves. Carbaryl and Malathion with four percent of active ingredients are good all-purpose dusts for the vegetable garden. Apply an even, light coating of dust, in still air, and force it through the foliage in order to reach both sides of the leaves.

Dusting can be done only when there is relatively low wind. Dust is more easily washed off by rain; it is also more expensive to dust than it is to spray. The most effective method of applying insecticides for the average gardener is by use of the small plunger-type sprayer. However, spraying cannot be done effectively when the foilage of the plant is wet with dew, whereas this is an ideal time for dusting. For the person with a small outdoor garden or with plants growing in containers, there are hand atomizers that come in many sizes, from approximately a pint to three quarts.

The small-scale gardener should not become too concerned with insecticides and spraying. The large-scale gardener, however, who is interested in spraying, should look into the advantages of a three- or four-gallon sling-type hand sprayer.

Fill your new sprayer (or old sprayer at the beginning of the season) with clean water and try it out before using an insecticide in it. Occasionally oil the pump plunger leather.

Empty your sprayer as soon as the job is finished and rinse it out thoroughly with clean water. You can prolong the life of your equipment by spraying some clean water through the hose and nozzle after you clean the tank. This, of course, rids the small channels and orifices of any particles of spray mixture that may have settled out. Hang the sprayer upside down, with pump removed, so that it can drain and thoroughly dry out. Replace the pump in the tank as soon as the tank is dry. Mud daubers and other insects will inhabit the tank if it is left open. Rust inside the tank and tiny foreign objects in the spray mixture are your only hazards.

For your insect spray to be effective, it is necessary that you mix it in exactly the recommended proportions, keeping the solution agitated to prevent settling while it is being used. Spray the undersides of leaves where insects deposit their eggs and do most of their sucking and chewing damage.

The primary idea is to apply the spray where the trouble is; spray only to the point of runoff, using a fine cone-shaped mist. Drenching with its attendant runoff is wasteful and not as good for your plants as a fine covering of mist-like droplets.

Remember these points when spraying and dusting; In spraying, try to coat the foliage with a fine mist, without drenching, which results in "runoff"; when dusting, try to cover the foliage with a light cloud of the dust, as it is more effective and less damaging than a heavy application of powder.

If you are vigilant and spot insects when they first appear and start feasting on your plants, the battle is already half won. Wipe out these first few, and you will have fewer insects to contend with all summer long.

Remember that improper use of insecticides can be injurious to plants, man, and animals. Heed all precautions and follow directions very carefully. The labels list both the vegetables on which the products are to be used and the varieties of insects that they will control. If you are purchasing the product for the first time, read the labels of the various brands. If you are still in doubt, get the opinion of your seedsman or nurseryman. Avoid inhalation of the insecticide and wash immediately after handling.

BENEFICIAL INSECTS

Certain insects do not damage garden plants; instead, they destroy other insects that are injurious to vegetables. One of the best-known is the praying mantis, which devours beetles, aphids, cutworms, and other insects. Praying mantis egg cases (approximately 300 eggs) may be purchased from some mail order seed outlets for a very nominal amount. Ladybugs also devour larvae and worms of many harmful insects. A half-pint of ladybugs, about 5000, can be purchased for less than five dollars. These insects can be used for natural control of garden pests. Among the many other beneficial insects are lady beetles, ground beetles, spiders and mites, and the ant lion (doodlebug).

The mere presence of these beneficial insects is reason enough to deter one from preventative or indiscriminate spraying or dusting. In fact, when close observation of plants reveals very few pests, simply pick them off by hand and check again on succeeding days to determine if spraying or dusting is necessary.

FUNGICIDES

Fungicides are used to control or prevent plant diseases such as early blight, leaf spot, seed decay, damping-off, late blight, and black rot. However, fungicides will not eradicate all plant diseases, and one of the best measures is to pull up and burn all diseased plants. Treatment of seeds with Captan (Captan 50-W), Thiram (Arasan 75, Thiram-50), or Dichlone (Phygon Seed

Protectant) is effective in preventing seed decay and damping-off. This treatment is a standard procedure for certified seed.

The best-known fungicides are Captan, Maneb, Thiram, and Zineb. Do not let the many varieties lead you astray. Read the labels and if you are still undecided, get the advice of the closest nurseryman or your county agricultural agent.

Just as is the case with insecticides, you do not need to study plant pathology to become a successful gardener. Many of our ancestors living in rural surroundings often produced more than 95 percent of their annual supply of food. Yet they were totally unacquainted with insecticides and fungicides as we know them today. Furthermore, their seeds were quite inferior to those available today, both in percentage of germination and resistance to disease. Furthermore, most hybrids in the vegetable world did not exist at that time. Why not garden for the sheer joy of it and not become burdened with the negative side of the project? A positive "can-do" attitude, coupled with close observation of what is happening to your plants, can be your biggest asset in your gardening endeavor. It is worth remembering that seeds do not know if they are being handled by an amateur or an old pro; consequently, many beginners have splendid results simply because they follow directions carefully and observe their plants closely.

LEGUME INOCULATION

Some plants of the pea family will not grow satisfactorily unless large numbers of certain nitrogen-fixing bacteria are present in the soil. Bacteria are obtained from a healthy legume root nodule, and cultures are grown in a laboratory. These bacteria are prepared for particular legumes, and the seeds are inoculated just before planting. The bacteria make atmospheric nitrogen available to the plant. The plant, in turn, supplies food to the bacteria on its roots; rapid multiplication of the bacteria results. This interaction is known as *symbiosis.*

Some of the legumes are very dependent on these nitrogen-fixing bacteria and simply will not produce a good crop if these bacteria are not present in large numbers in the soil. Alfalfa is a typical example of a leguminous crop requiring large numbers of the proper strain of bacteria for the very best yields. Consequently, seed inoculation is most desirable.

Inoculation of seed is particularly important when a crop of something new is planted in a field for the first time—soybeans, for example. If soybeans have never been grown in that soil, the nitrogen-fixing bacteria will not be present in large enough numbers to ensure best plant growth and maximum production of beans. Yields have been increased 10 to 25 percent by seed inoculation with proper strains of bacteria.

Legume bacteria are easily applied to seeds moistened with water. Plant seeds immediately after treating to reduce chances of bacterial loss due to exposure to air and heat.

CANNING AND PRESERVING

The recent "back to nature" trend came at a time when the ancient arts of preserving and storing vegetables seemed destined to be lost amongst supermarket shelves crammed with convenience foods. People are beginning to realize that the ability to be self-sufficient brings not only satisfaction, but a sense of security. Furthermore, you cannot "buy" the flavor and nutrition that you can get from freezing, canning, or drying your own vegetables.

The methods used to preserve vegetables and fruits are the very epitome of simplicity and convenience. Here are a few examples for your consideration.

Leather Breeches Beans

Use only select, tender green beans. Take a three- or four-foot length of strong thread and tie a kitchen match stem (or similar-sized piece of wood) onto one end and put the other end through a long needle. Push the needle through the center of the bean, pushing the beans together down against the other end of the thread, filling from end to end. The beans will dry better if they alternate in layers at right angles to each other. Hang the string on a nail or rafter in a warm, airy space, but never in direct sunlight. The direct rays of the sun rob them of some of their flavor. Keep them hanging until the beans are thoroughly dry. They are now dehydrated and will keep almost indefinitely if stored in a dry area. Store them in a paper bag or box until you are ready to use them.

When you get ready for a meal of leather breeches, remove the string and drop your dried green beans into a pot of boiling water. Add one or two pieces of salt pork and cook for two or three hours. Add just enough hot water to keep them covered while cooking, and take care not to cook them too long. An occasional sampling will let you know when they are at their best—tender, but not mushy, not overcooked.

Apples

Apples may be thinly sliced and strung on thread in exactly the same manner as green beans. Or the apples may be cored, then sliced and put on thin poles. The apples to be dried are hung in the sun or around a source of heat. If they are outdoors, they should be brought inside at sundown. The drying process takes from three to five days, depending on the temperature and relative humidity. The sliced apples become brown and rubbery while becoming dehydrated. When dry, they may be stored in sacks or boxes, in a dry area, for winter use.

Use the dried apples for frying, desserts, and pies. You may be pleasantly surprised to find that they have retained all of their delicious flavor.

Pickled Beans

Break string beans, remove any strings, wash, and then cook for a few minutes until barely tender. Soak in cold water until they are thoroughly chilled and pack them tightly in a clean crock jar. Add enough salty water to cover the beans. Use one-half cup of salt (do not use iodized salt for pickling) per gallon of water. Weight the beans inside the crock with a dinner plate or a piece of heavy aluminum foil; they will be ready for table use in about two weeks. They may be used directly from the crock and will remain good for several months. Exclude light from top of crock and store in a cool place.

3

Basic Vegetables For Your Garden

BEANS
Phaseolus vulgaris

Experienced home gardeners often grow only two types of beans, snap beans and lima beans. However, there are beans and beans and beans—more kinds, strains, and varieties than you would ever imagine. Beans originated in Central America, and several varieties used in the United States today were developed from beans grown by the American Indians.

Snap beans are easily grown but not foolproof. Snap, or green beans, grow in two main types, the low-growing bush beans and the tall-growing pole beans. Both types are highly productive, but the pole bean will produce more in a given ground space, and the beans are more easily harvested. The pole variety will climb a trellis or fence or a hill of sweet corn and does not necessarily require a pole if planted near these supports. Three inches is about the correct distance to plant beans away from their intended support.

Pole beans will climb corn stalks that are in rows six inches or more apart as well as stalks grouped three or so to a hill. However, it is important to allow the corn to get a head start on the beans in order for the stalks to be strong enough to support the bean vines once they start climbing. This is accomplished by planting the corn first and waiting until the stalks are about six inches tall before planting the beans. Naturally, you must exercise due

44

care when planting beans close to small stalks of corn and not injure or expose their root system. Tall varieties of sunflowers and the Jerusalem artichoke also provide good support for pole beans if allowed to obtain a bit of growth *before* the beans are planted. If a pole is used for support, it must be firmly planted in the ground. A small sapling seven or eight feet long and about two inches in diameter is satisfactory. Leave the bark on it and do not trim too smoothly, as any projections aid the beans in climbing and clinging to the support.

Green beans are grown well on land that has received a generous application of compost, fertilizer, or manure. However, a top dressing of compost, fertilizer, or manure when the plants are about a foot high is very conducive to heavy yields if the plants have not been grown in excessively fertile soil. (See page 9 for a discussion of top dressing.) Also, when the plants have reached about a foot or more in height, is is of inestimable value to bank soil around the stalks of the plants to a depth of three or four inches. Use your bare hands or a hoe, but be careful not to injure the roots. Do not firm the soil—merely move it into place. This banking or mounding of soil around the plants assists in moisture retention, retards weeds, and is good cultivation.

Beans should not be planted until the ground is warm. This is usually about two weeks after the last killing frost in your area. However, it is good gardening practice to take a chance on one row or even a half row of snap beans and plant them two weeks *earlier* than local gardening sages recommend. Ours have germinated nicely under these conditions, and we have enjoyed fresh snap beans long before those who insist on playing it safe. If you plant too early and they do fail to germinate, you only lose a few seeds while enjoying early gardening and the personal satisfaction of doing your own experimentation. There are lots of old wives tales connected with gardening, most of which are pure myth. You are urged to have fun with your gardening by being innovative and experimenting on a continuing basis. Of course, you must observe good basic gardening techniques of proper tilth, good seed, and correct fertilization to ensure that plant nutrients are always available, and when nature does not provide enough water, you must make up the shortage. Once your first beans are under way, you can enjoy a continuous supply for fresh table use, canning, drying, and freezing by making one or two successive plantings at one-month intervals. There is not much profit to be realized from planting the last time within 60 days of the first expected killing frost, so we recommend that you make the last planting at least 90 days before this date. This will allow you a minimum of 30 days of bean picking, and if the first killing frost is late, you may have 45 to 60 days of picking from this last planting. Incidentally, it is a fact of gardening that the first vegetables are usually the choicest, and you will soon learn to do your canning, freezing and drying from these early and mid-season harvests. Also, over most of the

United States we experience more dryness and more bugs as we get into the later part of our respective gardening seasons. A lack of moisture, coupled with bugs on an increasing scale, is not conducive to quick growth and top-quality produce.

Cultivation

If hand cultivation is used, make the rows 18 inches apart. Trace the furrows two inches deep and space the beans two to three inches apart in the row. Cover with fine soil about one inch deep in heavy soil and about one and one-half inches deep in light soil. Firm the soil gently to assist in germination. On very heavy soil it is a good idea to cover the beans in the furrow with a mixture of sand, light humus, and peat or other suitable material that will not bake or form a hard crust. A thin layer of well-rotted cow manure, old sawdust, or shredded leaves on top of the furrow will retain moisture in the soil and greatly assist germination under dry, difficult conditions. An occasional light sprinkling of this covering late in the day is very beneficial and under extreme conditions can spell the difference between success and failure. It is well to remember that a sprouting bean must pull its folded leaves through the soil in order to spread them above the surface. Close observation of crusted or heavy soil will show you some struggling and broken shoots that have tried and failed.

When the seeds have germinated and the plants are two to four inches high, thin them to stand with about four inches between plants. However, it is best not to handle or cultivate bean plants when they are wet from a rainfall or a heavy dew; all evidence indicates that this is likely to spread disease.

Bush Beans

Recommended Varieties Burpee's Tenderpod (50 days to maturity). Burpee's most popular bean and an *All-America* winner with real adaptability and vigor. Early and productive over a long period.
Commodore (Bush Kentucky Wonder, 58 days). Delicious 6½-inch, tender, stringless pods.
Old Dutch or White Half Runners (55-60 days). White seeds. Tender pods, 4-4½ inches long, have good, sweet, beany flavor; 3-foot runners need no staking. Produces bountifully; excellent when used fresh, canned, or frozen.
Purple Pod Royalty (51 days). A purple-pod snap bean that is good in colder soils. When boiled two minutes, pods turn green, providing a blanching indicator for home freezing.

Bountiful, Tendercrop, Topcrop, Provider, Blue Lake, Gardengreen, Brittle Wax, Golden Wax, Roma (bush form of Italian Pole Romano), Tenderette, Lika Lake and Improved Tendergreen are all excellent choices for the home gardener and mature in 49 to 60 days. Study their descriptions in various seed catalogs and make your choice according to intended uses and personal whims.

Tendercrop is a mosaic-resistant, heavy yielding snap bean with tender, round, green pods and a wide range of adaptability (USDA photo).

You will never really appreciate the bountiful yield and exquisite flavors of freshly harvested green beans until you pick them from your own bean patch.

Pole Beans

Pole beans are planted and cultivated in a manner similar to the low or bush type. Plant five or six beans in a circle around the pole and when they are well started—about five to six inches tall—thin to two or three plants per pole. Poles should be about three feet apart each way. Pole beans alongside a trellis or fence should be spaced at least six inches apart. When corn stalks are used for support, wait until the corn is three to six inches tall before planting the beans. It is a good idea to assist the bean tendrils in getting started around and up the support, remembering that they tend to twine in a counterclockwise direction. Use your hands to gently start them around and up the support. In windy weather or in windy locations, it may become necessary to use a few loose ties of one-inch-wide strips of soft cloth to hold them in place long enough for nature to take over.

> *Recommended Varieties* Kentucky Wonder (65 days to maturity). Noted for the distinctive tasty flavor of both fresh pods and dried light brown seeds, desirable as shell beans.
> Purple Pod (68 days). Burpee Golden (60 days).
> Blue Lake stringless or Oregon Blue Lake (60 days).
> Romano (Italian Pole, 60 days). Heavy yielder with a distinctive flavor; often referred to as "the gourmet bean."
> Oregon Giant Paul Bunyon (68 days). Giant pods that are 12 inches long, free of fiber, thick-meated, with a delicious flavor. An old Oregon favorite; four or five pods make a meal.

Lima Beans

Limas need a longer growing season than snaps. Whereas bush snaps mature in 47 to 60 days, bush limas take 65 to 75 days. While pole green beans mature in 60 to 70 days, it takes pole limas about 78 to 92 days to reach maturity, depending, of course, on the variety planted and on local weather conditions. Both the large- and small-seeded lima beans are available in bush and pole varieties. Planting and culvitation are the same as for green or snap beans—but it must be kept in mind that higher temperatures and longer growing seasons are required.

Limas will stand more dryness, as a general rule, than snaps. Bean beetles and other bugs seem to show a minimum interest in them. If the

weather is extremely dry, you can encourage them to bloom and fill pods two
or three times by soaking the soil thoroughly between the rows.

Recommended Varieties—Bush Dixie Butterpeas (Geo. W. Park Seed
   Co.). Our favorite bush limas. The finest, meatiest, most delicious
   bush lima, without a question. (75 days to maturity).
Burpee's Improved Bush Lima (75 days).
Henderson's Bush (65 days). Popular "baby" lima with a buttery flavor
   that is an old standby—fine fresh, canned, frozen, or dried.
Clark's Green Seeded (68 days).
Fordhook No. 242 (75 days). Heavy yielder and most certain of all to
   produce an abundant crop under adverse circumstances due to its
   vigor, heat resistance, and ability to withstand dry weather.
   Other fine varieties are Baby Bush (70 days), Speckled Dixie Butterpea
(75 days), Jackson Wonder (65 days), Burpee's Fordhook (75 days), and
Baby Fordhook Bush Lima (70 days).

*Fordhook 242 bush lima beans are vigorous, productive, and heat-resistant
(USDA photo)*

Recommended Varieties—Pole King of the Garden (88 days to maturity). An old favorite home-garden pole lima for fresh use, freezing, or drying. Pods are 5 to 6 inches long and 1-1/8 to 1-1/2 inches wide with three to five large, flat beans.

Carolina or Sieva (78 days). The dried beans are small and white; grown extensively for winter use.

Christmas Limas (85 days). Big yielder of high-quality, buttery-flavored beans. Delicious fresh, maintaining flavor and quality canned or frozen. (Nichols Garden Nursery, Albany, Oregon.)

Prizetaker (90 days). Unique, extra-large beans. Quality and flavor excellent fresh or frozen.

Burpee's Best (92 days). Best features of Fordhook Bush—thick seed, rich tenderness, large pods—with three or four times as many pods per plant.

Green-Shell Beans

The Long Pod Fava (English Broad Bean) is a hardy bush bean that can be used as a substitute for pole limas in the northern parts of the country with short growing seasons. Fava beans are much hardier than other beans and may be planted early, at the same time as peas, as soon in the spring as the ground can be worked. The plants are true bush form, heavy yielders, large, and erect. Pods are glossy green, about seven inches long, and contain from five to seven large, oblong-shaped, flat, light green beans with a flavor a bit like that of the pea. The beans resemble limas and should be used in the same way.

Even if you are not planting the Fava as a substitute for the pole lima, you should still consider this bean, because you can be eating it in the middle of June—long before your other beans mature. (The date of first harvesting is naturally dependent on local climatic conditions and the date of plantings.)

Cultivation Plant in rows, placing the seed about five inches apart in the row and covering with three inches of soil. Rows should be 1-1/2 to 2-1/2 feet apart, depending on the space available and the method of cultivation. When they are up and growing, thin to stand ten inches apart. These thinnings are hardy and, if removed with a dibble or garden trowel, can be very successfully transplanted to another row that has already been prepared. It is not unusual to have close to one hundred percent germination with most varieties of beans, and experience will soon enable you to dispense with most thinning by planting only what you want in the final stand. The Fava takes 85 days to mature. Dwarf Horticultural (65 days) is another green-shell bean with outstanding qualities; it is delicious, either green or dried.

Bush Shell Beans (for use as dry beans)

Bush shell beans are grown for use as dry beans. Culture is similar to that used for green or snap bush beans, but shell beans should be left on the plants until the pods are mature. When beans have matured, pull the plants and hang them in the shade to dry. Any ventilated area is suitable—garage rafters, breezeways, woodsheds and attics are fine for this purpose. However, the mature beans may be left on the plants in the garden until ready to be shelled. Your only problem in leaving them in the garden to dry is when an unusually damp or rainy spell occurs and the pods tend to collect moisture. If the soil stays wet and high winds topple some plants, some pods will burst, and others will become soiled. You cannot leave limas and soybeans on the plants to dry, as the shells will split and drop your crop on the ground. Some people contend that beans dried in the shade are tastier and retain more of their natural flavor. We are inclined to agree with this theory.

Dampness will mold organic substances at ordinary temperatures; accordingly, your beans *must* be dry before you store them. If there is any doubt, heat them on a tray in an oven with a temperature of 125 to 135 degrees for about an hour. This procedure also eliminates any residual or potential weevil troubles. Dry beans store nicely in any glass jar or container that can be capped or sealed to make it bug-proof.

Recommended Varieties Red Kidney (95 days to maturity). Large, kidney-shaped, pinkish red- to mahogany-colored beans. Good baked, boiled, in soups and Spanish or Mexican dishes.

Chestnut Bean—Garbanzo or Chick Pea (100 days). These beans have a chestnut-like flavor and are superb for soups, stuffings, and in salads (Burgess Seed and Plant Co. and Nichols Garden Nursery).

Great Northern. A large white bean excellent for baking and cooking. Great for Boston baked beans.

White Kidney Bean. Large, white kidney-shaped beans are fine for baking and are delicious in minestrone soup. (This and Great Northern are from Gurney Seed and Nursery Co.)

Other fine varieties are Michilite, Black Valentine, Pinto, Navy, White Marrowfat, and Santa Marie Pinquito.

Soybeans

Soybeans are planted, cultivated, and grown as easily as snap beans. Make the furrows 1-1/2 to 2 inches deep and space the beans 2 to 3 inches apart in rows that are 24 to 36 inches apart. As is true with all members of the bean family, avoid cultivation or other work around the soybeans when they are wet from dew or rain, as the plants are easily bruised and broken.

In order to realize maximum yields, it is necessary for you to inoculate the seed with nitrogen-fixing bacteria. However, soybean bacteria live in the soil for a number of years, and inoculation is not absolutely mandatory if soybeans have been grown in that particular soil within the past three to four years. The inoculant *must* be one specifically prepared for soybeans, as the inoculant containing bacteria from other legumes is not effective on soybeans.

The difficulty of shelling soybeans seems to deter some gardeners from growing them. Pour boiling water over the fresh picked pods and let them stand in this hot water for about four minutes. Then drain the pods, break them crosswise, and easily squeeze out the beans.

The Orientals, who consume more soybeans than any other people, have a novel way of getting around the hard-shelling process. They merely cook them in the pods in salted boiling water and let the diner squeeze out the beans as they are eaten.

By now it is common knowledge that soybeans are very rich in food value, having twice as much protein as meat or fish, ten times as much as milk, and three times as much as whole wheat flour. The beans are also rich in calcium and lecithin.

Recommended Varieties Soybeans are versatile, and there are many varieties to suit the taste, growing conditions, and climate of almost anyone living in a region having a growing season of 100 to 130 days. Kuromane, the famous Oriental Black soybean, is probably the first choice of experienced users. However, there are many fine varieties, among them being Kanrich, Disoy, Giant Green, Okuhara Early, Verde, and Sodefuri.

More Beans

It would not be fair to the reader to close this section on beans without mentioning the Scarlet Runner (Nichols Garden Nursery) and the Yard Long Bean (Burgess Seed and Plant Co.). The Scarlet Runner is native to the tropics, where it grows as a perennial. Its fast-growing vines are ideal for screening purposes. It produces beautiful, brilliant, red flowers that can be cut and brought indoors. The flowers are followed by pods, which contain three or four large beans that are delicious when used "green-shelled." Use young pods for snap beans, or let the mature pods dry and have shell beans for winter use. The Scarlet Runner matures in 60 days. The Yard Long Bean matures in 70 days. This bean produces long, slender pods, the thickness of a pencil and as much as 3 feet long. Vines are vigorous and produce an enormous crop. Young beans are of good quality and excellent flavor when used as snap beans.

BEET
Beta vulgaris

Beets can be grown anywhere in the United States, but they prefer the northern sections. They are grown in the cooler months of fall, winter, and early spring in the South. Beets are one of the most popular and most important vegetables in the home garden. They are easy to grow and make a valuable contribution to your diet. Beet roots provide good amounts of vitamins B, C, and G, and the tops or greens are rich in vitamins A and C, and in iron with many trace elements. Not only is the entire plant edible, but it adds fiber to your food intake and thereby contributes to overall health.

Beets are tolerant of both heat and cold and may be planted as much as four weeks before the last frost-free date. They are rich feeders, and good quality depends on quick growth. Quick growth results from friable land with plenty of plant nutrients and adequate moisture in the soil. Top dressing when plants are about six inches high tends to speed their growth. If you are growing beets during really hot weather, you *must* see that they get plenty of water, and a thick layer of organic mulch will ensure a good crop. Their roots seem to resent really warm soil and will become tough and stringy unless you provide protection from dryness and heat. Adequate water and a thick, organic mulch will take care of these incipient problems.

What appears to be a beet seed is actually a little crinkled seedball containing several seeds—unless, of course, you are planting the "mono" King Explorer variety, which is a monogerm type with a single seed to each seedball.

Culture

Make shallow furrows one inch deep and space the seedballs three inches apart. Cover with one-half inch of fine soil and firm lightly to assist germination. If you are planting the monogerm variety, space seeds one inch apart. When the plants are three to four inches tall, thin to stand about three inches apart in the row. Rows can be 15 to 18 inches apart. Beets do not require a lot of cultivation, and you must not scratch or nick the bulb, because it will bleed and not develop properly. Hand-pick weeds before they become big enough to interfere with root development. Quick, uninterrupted growth is essential for top quality, and during periods of inadequate rainfall you must supply the needed water. It is best not to plant more beets than you can readily use at the table, or can, freeze, pickle, or store. Accordingly, for a continuous supply, make additional sowings when the preceding planting is up and growing; allow time for the last sowing to mature before frost.

Harvesting and Storage

Early beets are pulled from the ground when they are one to one-and-one-half inches in diameter, and the beets are prepared for table use, for freezing, canning, or pickling. Leave about two inches of stem and the taproot so that the vegetable will not bleed while cooking. The tops can be washed, sorted, blanched, and then frozen.

The main crop of beets to be stored for winter use can be reasonably mature when harvested. Their many uses are the same as for the early crop, except for storage. Late beets for storage may be left in the ground until you expect heavy frosts. It is best to harvest them when the soil is not too wet. Let them lie on the ground for two or three hours to dry out. Now cut off the tops about one inch above the crown. Do not wash and do not disturb the tap root. Cull out any defective roots. Store in layers of moist sand, peat, or sphagnum moss in boxes where the temperature ranges between 32° and 42°F. Properly harvested and stored, beets will remain in good condition for a period of four to five months. Their big enemies are high temperatures and low humidity, which cause them to sprout new tops, shrivel up, and become woody.

Recommended Varieties

Your choice is not critical, except for the fact that some varieties are better for greens and storage. All varieties can serve for both greens and roots. Study their descriptions in seed catalogs to determine the varieties you think will be best for your intended uses. Some recommended varieties are:

Detroit Dark Red (60 days)
Burpee Golden (55 days)
Cylindra (60 days)
Lutz Green Leaf, Winter Keeper (80 days)
"Mono" King Explorer (59 days)
Hybrid Pacemaker (55 days)
Ruby Queen (52 days)
Early Wonder (52 days)
Green Top Bunching (58 days)

BROCCOLI
Brassica Oleracea Italica

Broccoli is a hardy member of the cabbage family that will do well in almost any type of garden soil that is moderately rich and fairly easy to work. However, it takes more than average moisture to keep producing the abundance of stems and buds that will give you four to six cuttings from every stalk. This nutritious vegetable is rich in vitamins and is delicious fresh, canned, or frozen. Nutritionists insist that this vegetable should be a regular part of every diet. It is an excellent source of vitamins A, B, and C, in addition to providing calcium and iron.

Sprouting broccoli with center head and side shoots (USDA photo).

We are talking about the kind of broccoli that is known as Italian Green Sprouting, which continues to produce smaller heads on side branches after the large center head is cut.

Culture

Sprouting broccoli is grown in the same way as cabbage. For the early spring crop, sow seeds in flats in the house and transplant the young seedlings into the garden after the last frost. Of course, you can buy started plants from a nursery; six to twelve will give you an excellent crop. Space the young plants 18 inches apart in rows that are 30 inches apart. The plants respond generously to top dressings of 10-10-10, well-rotted cow manure, or mature compost applied at three-week intervals until heads begin to form. Unless natural rainfall keeps an adequate supply of moisture in the soil, you must water regularly. Do not let weeds steal plant food and moisture from the soil surrounding your broccoli.

Inasmuch as broccoli is a cool-season grower, you can plan on a second crop for early fall. Sow the seeds directly into rows or a seedbed in your garden and then thin or transplant as required.

Harvesting

This must be done at just the right time if broccoli is to be at peak flavor and edible best. Cut the heads when they are hard and green. If you wait until the clustered buds begin to open, their freshness will be dispersed. Include about 6 inches of stem and leaves when cutting; these are also edible.

Recommended Varieties

Calabrese or Green Sprouting (85 days)
DeCicco—Burpee's Greenbud Brand (60 days)
Green Comet Hybrid (40 days)
Spartan Early (55 days)
White Broccoli (75 days)
Green Mountain (60 days)
Premium Crop Hybrid (58 days)

CABBAGE
Brassica oleracea capitata

Cabbage is a common vegetable that thrives in almost any kind of soil and is one of our most important garden crops. It is a heavy feeder and requires plenty of moisture and fertile soil to produce quick growth and top quality. Well-rotted manure and balanced fertilizers should be used liberally. It is a good idea to cover the entire area to be used for cabbage with three to four inches of well-rotted manure. Then plow or rototill it well under the soil. Do this two or three weeks before setting out the cabbage plants. In addition to the initial preparation of the soil before setting out the plants, a top dressing of 10-10-10-, 34.5-0-0, or compost is beneficial during the growing season.

Early varieties may be set out as soon as danger from frost is past in your area. Early varieties are usually set 14 inches apart with the rows twice that far apart. Late-season cabbage should be set two feet apart in the row, with rows three feet apart.

If you prefer to grow your own cabbage plants, they must be started four to six weeks before you plan to set them out in the garden. Sow the seeds very thinly in fine soil in any container, pot, or flat that you consider to be suitable. They will thrive in any cool room or other cool space. When the seedlings are two or three inches tall, they should be carefully transplanted to individual paper cups or other suitable cups or pots to get good, stocky plants.

If you are in doubt about the best varieties to plant in your locality, see what the local nurseries and seed stores handle. If you do not want to start with seed, you can obtain excellent varieties of plants from local sources. However, be sure to have the soil ready before you purchase plants in order to get them into the ground in a minimum of time.

Late cabbage plants are easily grown in open seed beds in your garden. Seeds should be sown about four weeks before you plan on transplanting into rows. Late cabbage is especially prized for storage, kraut, and table use.

Mounding of the soil around the stems will encourage growth of additional roots and will provide better support for the cabbage heads.

There are many varieties of cabbage, and you have a choice of early or late, green or red—or a combination of both.

Recommended Varieties

Early, small heads. Earliana, Copenhagen Market, Savoy King Hybrid, Red Head, Stonehead, Early Jersey Wakefield, Red Acre, Emerald Cross.

Late, very large heads. All Seasons, Burpee's Surehead, Danish Ball-head, Premium Flat Dutch, and Perfection Drumhead.

CARROTS
Daucus carota sativa

Carrots have aptly been called king among the root crops. They are becoming increasingly important because of their high vitamin A content and the ease with which they may be kept or stored for long periods of time. They may be left in the ground and harvested as needed all winter long. Merely cover the row with a thick layer of spoiled hay to protect the carrots from freezing temperatures and to prevent heaving of the soil, which occurs when it alternately freezes and thaws. This heaving action produces cracks in the soil, thereby admitting cold air, which will dry out, freeze, and ruin your carrots.

The seeds are tiny and slow to germinate. Place the seeds in shallow furrows at a rate of two or more per linear inch and cover with a half-inch of fine soil. Sow a radish seed every foot or so to mark the row to allow weed pulling if that becomes necessary before the carrots come up. A half-inch mulch of well-rotted cow manure, well-rotted sawdust, or flaky leaf mold applied over the row after sowing will eliminate crusting of the soil and help retain moisture. Light sprinkling of the row at regular intervals greatly assists and improves germination. Do the thinning while plants are still small so as to disturb the roots of remaining seedlings as little as possible, and be sure to firm the soil back around the plants left in the row. Thin plants to stand two to three inches apart. Leave at least 12 inches between rows.

Carrots come in various lengths, and the varieties to be planted should be chosen according to individual preference for shape and size although the type of soil in which they will be planted must be a consideration. The Royal Chantenay, Goldinhart, Short 'n Sweet, Gueranade, Oxheart, Sucram, and Sweetheart are short-to-medium length and good choices for heavy soils. Most of them are very tolerant to wet spring and fall weather. In fact, carrots do best when sown in the spring and fall, yet they will succeed in the summer unless the weather is extremely hot and dry. The long, slender varieties thrive best in light, loamy, and sandy soils that have been cultivated rather deeply. These longer varieties include Nantes Coreless, Imperator, Gold Pak, Touchon, Tendersweet, and Danvers Half Long. All of these varieties mature in 65 to 80 days.

Carrots can be grown successfully in extremely heavy soil by making a vee-shaped trench six to eight inches deep and two to three inches wide at the surface. Fill the vee-shaped trench with light topsoil or a 50-50 mixture of compost and sand. If you do not have any compost, use a 50-50 mixture of topsoil and sand. If no topsoil is available, simply fill the trench with sand. When using the trench method in heavy soil, it is essential that you give the trench a thorough soaking before sowing the seeds, and that a mulch be used to retain the moisture. If you use black plastic, several thicknesses of newspaper, or burlap to retain moisture, be sure to check daily and to remove it as soon as the seedlings begin to emerge. One or two top dressings with a balanced fertilizer coupled with adequate moisture will assure the fast growth that is necessary for tender, juicy carrots.

CHARD
Beta vulgaris cicla

Chard, or Swiss chard, is developed from the beet, but is used for its top instead of its root. Chard is a hardy plant that can be grown throughout the United States. It will thrive during cool weather and go right on producing during the hot summer months. It is a healthful and nutritious, easily grown vegetable that is valued as a leaf crop. The large, green crinkly leaves are cooked and served like spinach, and the mid-ribs may be prepared like asparagus, or both may be cooked together. Leaves are good in raw salads and may be substituted for lettuce in sandwiches. Chard is an ideal source for a continuous abundant source of summer greens. It is generally free of disease and rarely bothered by pests. Harvesting is done by removing the outer leaves of various plants and thus allowing the center and remaining leaves to grow, or entire plants may be cut off about two inches above the crown; new leaves will be produced very quickly.

Culture

The culture of chard is identical to that of beets, except that the plants grow larger and should be thinned to six inches or more apart in the row. Since leaves can be cut on a continuing basis from various plants, there is no requirement for successive sowings. Chard is suitable for freezing, and just one 20-foot row will provide for a family of four for several months. Sometimes the plants may become exhausted and begin producing smaller and fewer leaves over a longer period of time. This condition may be due to prolonged periods of excessive heat and dryness or to a decided lowering of available plant nutrients in the soil. Whatever the reason, when this occurs, it is the signal for you to plant another row of chard. Chard will continue to produce all winter long in milder areas, and the season can be prolonged in more

Swiss chard is especially suitable for hot-weather culture (USDA photo)

severe areas by covering with a straw mulch or by providing other protective covering.

Recommended Varieties

Lucullus. The best general variety; has a fine flavor. The broad white
 stalks are splendid for creaming.

Burpee's Fordhook Giant. Leaves are rich dark green, much crumpled
 and savoyed, thick, and fleshy, and make the most tender "greens."
 Very heavy yielding plants. The pearly white stalks, 2-1/2 inches
 across, make an excellent dish prepared like asparagus, as do the
 broad midribs of the leaves.

Rhubard Chard. The stalks look like rhubarb, being bright, but delicate,
 translucent crimson. The rich color extends out through the veins into the dark green heavily crumpled leaves. Leaf stalks, considered by
 many to be the most delicious part of chard, and leaves have a sweet,
 tasty flavor. This variety is so handsome that it is frequently grown
 as a border plant in flower beds.

All varieties mature in 60 days from seed. Naturally, some variation is
to be expected, depending on the season, locality, and time of sowing.

COWPEAS
Vigna sinensis

Also known as Southern table peas, black-eyed peas or table field peas. They are highly nutritious and, in the light of the effort necessary to grow them, few, if any, other vegetables will yield higher dividends. They have a delicate, but delicious flavor and may be used either green or dried. Their storage life in sealed containers with favorable temperatures is almost indefinite. After the seeds are fully developed, they may be picked and used while in the green stage, or they may be allowed to ripen fully and become hard while still remaining on the plant. Then they are harvested, shelled, and stored as dried peas. They develop long pods that grow seven to nine inches in length and mature in 60 to 90 days. The time from planting to maturity will depend on the variety, the time of sowing, the soil, and the local weather.

Culture

Cowpeas are very susceptible to cold and should not be planted until the soil is warm and both daytime and nighttime temperatures remain fairly high. However, they will thrive on most any type of well-drained soil when their temperature requirements are met. Sow the seeds in shallow furrows that are about 1-1/2 inches deep and cover them with 1 to 1-1/2 inches of soil. In heavier soils it is best to plant quite shallowly. With lighter soils you may want to plant a bit deeper. Space seeds about four inches apart in the row. You can expect 80 percent or more germination, and it is not necessary to plant more closely and then resort to thinning. Firm the soil very lightly to ensure good contact of seed with soil. As a general rule, this practice of very lightly firming the soil over seeds assists in quicker and better germination. Space the rows 18 to 30 inches apart, depending on whether you use hand or machine cultivation.

Recommended Varieties

Recommended varieties are California Blackeye, Brown Crowder, Mississippi Silver, Dixilee, Monarch, Purple Hull, and White Acre.

CUCUMBER
Cucumis sativus

Because of its short growing season, the cucumber can be grown almost anywhere in the United States. The vines tend to sprawl for distances of eight to ten feet across the ground. However, if your gardening space is limited, do not be discouraged. Many varieties produce strong, vigorous vines that are natural climbers, which are ideal for growing on fences and for trellising. In the Orient, where all fertile soil is much more intensively cultivated than throughout most of the world, cucumbers are habitually trained to climb a tripod or teepee arrangement of three to six poles tied together at the tops and secured over the hills or groups. Fasten the vines to the poles loosely by means of inch or so widths of soft cloth or old nylons. These ties can be made from old sheets or from any soft, discarded clothing. Remember that the vines are tender; be careful lest you injure them while handling.

Cucumbers are a warm-weather crop requiring lots of moisture, plenty of heat, and a rich soil. No other way of assuring plenty of available plant nutrients is as satisfactory as removing two buckets of soil from an area 15 to 18 inches in diameter and then replacing one bucket of soil with a bucketful of well-rotted cow or horse manure. Then sprinkle a generous handful of 10-10-10 (or similar fertilizer) on top of the manure. If manure is not available, use topsoil mixed with peat moss, or well-rotted sawdust, compost, or some other organic material. Tramp on the manure to firm it for good capillary action. Cover with soil and, again, firm the soil to ensure capillarity. Seed should be four inches from the manure or other filler. Just in case you have *no* organic material on hand, thoroughly mix about a pint of 10-10-10 with a bucketful of soil; replace this mixture in the excavation and tramp down to firm it well. Replace the remaining soil, being sure to have three or four inches of soil between the seed and the fertilizer. Plant six seeds in each group; plan to thin to half that number when the plants are growing vigorously. Plant seeds two or three inches apart with the pointed ends of the seeds down and cover with 1/2 to 1 inch of fine soil.

Cucumbers come in assorted lengths and sizes, ranging from the West India Gherkin with small, burr-like fruits, two to three inches long and 1 to 1-1/2 inches thick, to the China Long, which attains a length of up to two feet. Cucumbers are divided into two families: "white spine" and "black spine." The spines are the miniature stickers that protrude from the warts when fruits are young. White-spine cucumbers turn creamy white when old; black-spine varieties turn yellowish orange.

Failure to set fruit with the first flowers occurs because these flowers are male, and female flowers must have pollen supplied by air or insects from the male before any fruit is set. Male flowers bloom first. There are all-female (gynoecious) hybrids on the market that set fruit with the first flowers.

Harvesting and Yields

Cucumbers may be harvested at any size, depending on their intended use. However, it is absolutely necessary for you to pick all fruits from the vines as they reach a usable size. Failure to keep almost mature fruits picked will cause the plants to stop setting new fruit. If you want to keep them coming, pick *all* of them before they mature. Give any surplus to neighbors or bury them for soil enrichment, but get them off the vines at the proper time to encourage the setting of more fruits.

Many ingenious methods of overcoming soil and watering difficulties with cucumbers and other members of the cucurbitaceae family have been devised by home gardeners. One method is to cut the bottoms out of some tin cans, to dig holes adjacent to the plants, and to put the cans in the holes. Make the tops level with the surface and then fill with gravel or small stones. Water poured into the can will provide moisture down at the roots where it is most effective. Keep filling the can until the water is no longer being quickly absorbed by the soil. This method of watering plants will encourage deep root structure, thereby enabling plants to better withstand heat and drought. Another method is to sink a large coffee can or similar container with the bottom removed into the center of the planting area and then to plant around it. Water applied at regular intervals will ensure quick, vigorous growth. These two methods are especially valuable on slopes and in hot, dry regions with scanty rainfall. In addition, they provide excellent means of getting liquid fertilizer down to the root zone, where it is most effective.

Diseases and Insect Pests

Healthy, vigorous vines are usually free of disease and are not likely to be damaged by insects, but it is helpful to be able to recognize Mosaic, which is a viral disease that causes a yellowing on either side of the veins of a leaf. This chlorosis is a failure to produce the normal green coloring matter in leaves, causing them to become yellowish, pale, and resulting in an unhealthy plant. It may be spread from diseased plants to healthy plants by aphids or by touching the plants with hands or tools. Downy mildew is spread by wind-blown spores and can usually be controlled with either Maneb or Zineb. It is identified by the appearance of black spots on the leaves, frequently accompanied by a gray or brown fungus on the opposite side of the leaf and directly beneath the black spot.

Cucumber Beetle. The striped cucumber beetle in the adult stage is colored from yellow to black and has three black stripes down the back. This is the Eastern variety; the Western variety has 12 black spots on the wing. Adults feed on leaves, stems, and fruit, and spread bacterial wilt. The symptoms and damage of bacterial wilt are readily apparent, inasmuch as large vines gradually wilt and die with no yellowing of the leaves. Young plants die rapidly when they become infected. Older, stronger plants may first have only one shoot affected. Bacteria, spread by cucumber beetles, enter and plug the water vessels of stems and leaves. The best remedy is to remove and destroy wilted or damaged plants as soon as they are observed. The larva of the cucumber beetle is white, slender, and brownish at the ends. These larvae attack the plants below the soil line, boring into roots and stems. Damaged plants first wilt and then sometimes die. If you suspect that you have cucumber beetles, dust with Sevin at weekly intervals until you have them under control. **Caution**: Do not apply insecticides within one day before a harvest. **Note**: Dusting is preferable to spraying, since moisture can cause mildew on cucumber vines.

Pickleworm. The pickleworm is another adversary of the cucumber, especially in the South and along the east coast as far north as Connecticut as as far west as Iowa, Illinois, and Kansas. It winters in southern Florida and Texas, spreading northward late in the season. It is a yellowish-white worm with a brownish head, attaining a length of up to three-quarters of an inch. Its appetite is unbelievable as it feeds on all parts of the plant—the flowers, leaf buds, terminal buds, vines, and fruits. Begin treating plants at first sign of worms in blossoms and buds; worms must be killed before they enter the fruits. Dust with Sevin or other insecticide containing carbaryl. Do not dust within one day of harvest. This dusting will also control any aphids that may be on the vines.

Your best means of combatting Mosaic, Downy Mildew, and insects is to plant hybrids with built-in resistance in fertile, light, well-drained soil.

Recommended Varieties

Cucumbers are grown for two purposes: for slicing and eating fresh or cooked and for pickling. The larger varieties are used for slicing as well as for large dills and other types of pickles. Some of the best are Burpee Hybrid, Green Ice, Burpless Hybrid, Gemini 7 Hybrid, Surecrop Hybrid, Spartan Valor Hybrid, Twilly's Early Hybrid, Victory Hybrid, Park's Comanche, Fertila Hybrid, Marketmore 70, China Hybrid, Early Fortune, Burpee's M&M Hybrid, Damascus Hybrid, China Long, and Poinsett. For most pickling the recommended smaller-fruited varieties are Spartan Dawn, Earliest of All, Burpee Pickler, Pioneer, Everbearing, Wisconsin SMR 18, Salty Hybrid, Picadilly, Ohio MR 17, Patio Pik Hybrid, Armenian Yard Long, Lemon, and Early Hycrop Hybrid.

EGGPLANT
Solanum melongena esculentum

The eggplant is essentially a tropical plant that requires heat for its development. It is related botanically to the pepper and tomato, and the culture of all three is similar. However, it is a heavier feeder than either of the other two crops and much more exacting in soil moisture requirements, inasmuch as it must continue to grow steadily in order to yield a good amount of quality fruits. Keep the soil uniformly moist with a thorough soaking every seven to ten days. Then cultivate very lightly to a depth of about one inch to create a dust mulch for soil moisture retention. An organic mulch of hay or straw two to four inches thick will greatly assist in holding water in the soil while eliminating weeds and stabilizing the temperature of the soil. Do not apply the layer of mulch until the young plants have put out considerable new growth and both day and night temperatures remain high.

The fruits are handsome and add beauty and variety to your garden. The flavor of eggplant is reminiscent of fried oysters, and it is very easily cooked in several different ways. It is an excellent substitute for meat. Please do not make up your mind about liking or not liking eggplant until you have tried it in at least half a dozen different ways. There are many different methods of serving eggplant, and most of the recipes are delectable. It is an excellent pickler. We have to label the jars to identify them from cucumber pickles.

The eggplant is a popular vegetable that requires little space (USDA photo).

Culture

If you are interested in growing your own plants, start the seed indoors in flats or pots about eight or nine weeks before you anticipate setting them out in the garden. However, be sure to transplant the young seedlings into peat pots, when they are about three inches tall, for later setting out in the garden. It is important that you do not lose or disturb the soil around the root system while handling or transplanting. Most gardeners prefer to buy the few plants they grow each year. Whatever your method, do not set the plants into the garden until the soil temperature is quite high—65 degrees or more. This *real* warming of the soil occurs only after both day and night temperatures hit and hold in the higher ranges. Eggplants will grow in a variety of soils but prefer rich, sandy loams. The young plants are quite sensitive to weather conditions, and you may have to provide some kind of protection when they are first transplanted into the garden. A top dressing of well-rotted cow manure, compost, or a balanced fertilizer will be quite beneficial when the plants are first set out—with a repeat at three- to five-week intervals thereafter. Naturally, you are expected to use a starter solution to settle the soil, eliminate air pockets, and lessen the shock of transplanting. Set the plants three feet apart each way. However, if you are cramped for space, do not hesitate to space them only two feet apart. These handsome plants thrive in five-gallon containers when properly fed and watered. On cool days place the container where it will get the reflected heat from a south wall. Varieties that bear small- to medium-sized fruits carried high on the plant are better adapted to container growing. The Golden Yellow (and other varieties bearing small fruits) is especially decorative when grown and used for a house plant.

The fruits of eggplant come in a large variety of sizes, shapes, and colors. They range from small to medium to large and are round, cylindrical, and pear-shaped. The fruits are very ornamental with colors that range through whites, yellows, purples, and on to purplish black.

Better yields of quality fruits can be attained by pinching off some of the blossoms and then pinching back some of the terminal growths on the stems. Do not overdo this disbudding, however, lest you seriously decrease the yield.

Harvesting

For best eating quality, pick the young fruits when they are one-half to three-fourths of their normal, fully mature size with a high skin gloss. One test for maturity is to indent the side of the fruit with the ball of your thumb. If the indentation does not spring back, the fruit has already become mature or is rapidly approaching that stage. The fruits are so heavy and so well attached to a tough, woody stem that it is best to harvest them with pruning shears. When you cut open an eggplant and find that it has brown seeds, this is an indication that it is no longer edible.

Recommended Varieties

Burpee Hybrid, Mission Bell Hybrid, Peerless Hybrid, Black Beauty, White Italian, Florida Market, Golden Yellow, Jersey King, Japanese Fl Hybrid, White Beauty, and Early Beauty Hybrid. All of these varieties reach maturity in 62 to 85 days from the time that plants are set outdoors.

KALE
Brassica oleracea acephala

Kale, also known as borecole, is a kind of cabbage that does not produce a head. It is closely related to wild cabbage and has been cultivated for as long as man has grown vegetables. Kale is cold-hardy and lives through winter as far north as the Pennsylvania border and in other northern areas where similar climatic conditions exist. It can be grown easily anywhere in the United States. It furnishes greens to home gardeners during fall and winter months at a time when other leafy vegetables are both scarce and expensive. In areas where winters are not extreme, and throughout the South, it is grown all winter. Kale is very rich in vitamins A and C and is one of the most wholesome of all vegetables. Young, tender leaves can be chopped or torn up for use in salads or sandwiches to take full advantage of the vitamins. However, it is generally agreed that the best-testing way to eat kale is as a pot herb. Boil the leaves with a slice or two of smoked bacon or smoked ham along with seasoning to taste of salt and bacon grease. As with all leafy vegetables, do not overcook and do not use too much water. Vinegar and finely chopped onions scattered over the greens complement their flavor and add to their enjoyment.

Culture

For late summer or early fall, work the soil lightly and very sparsely broadcast the seed by hand. Then lightly rake the seed into the soil. Germination is improved and speeded up by firming the soil. This can be done by pressing the soil lightly with a piece of wide board or thin plywood. Kale and all members of the cabbage family thrive in soil that is neutral or on the verge of being on the sweet or alkaline side of the pH scale. Consequently, a liberal application of crushed calcium limestone or an average liming of the soil with horticultural lime during the working and cultivating, prior to planting, will prove beneficial. Rapid growth is essential for top-quality kale. This, of course, means that adequate nutrients and moisture must be available. When the plants are up and growing vigorously, thin to stand about a foot apart each way. If you encounter slow growth, apply liquid manure in a shallow furrow about four inches from the base of each plant. Mix a quart of dry cow manure with two gallons of water and stir it well two or three times during a 36- to 48-hour period. It is then ready to use. Do not use more often than every three weeks. An alternative liquid fertilizer is made by mixing two tablespoonfuls of 10-10-10 to each gallon of water. Stir vigorously several times to thoroughly dissolve the granular chemicals. There will always be a residue of undissolved inert filler material left in the bottom of the container.

Kale, a hardy green, is mulched here with spoiled hay (USDA photo)

For midsummer plantings, finely worked soil retains more moisture. Germination is improved by planting the seeds about one-half to three-fourths inch deep in shallow furrows that are spaced about one foot apart. This planting succeeds best if done immediately after a rain. If the soil is fairly dry when you plant, give it a good soaking to get germination off to a good start.

During hot weather, mulches are especially valuable in conserving soil moisture and controlling weeds. The root system is developed close to the surface and extends almost horizontally just beneath the top of the soil. This explains the need for extremely shallow cultivation or a layer of mulch. Mulch also gives you a clean surface on which to walk when harvesting kale in an otherwise muddy garden.

Harvesting

Kale is harvested by taking the larger leaves while they are still young and tender and continuing to take the lower ones that are in good condition, while leaving the uppermost to attain more growth. You may, of course, cut the entire plant and enjoy the tender, succulent leaves at the top near the rosette, but this is needless waste, because the removal of a few prime leaves as needed for the table does not harm the plant, and it will continue to produce until its life cycle is ended. Your plants will be healthier and more productive if you cut the kale close to the main stalk with a pair of 10-inch scissors. Invariably, you will have more kale than needed. In order to keep the plants vigorous and productive, it is a good idea to cut all mature leaves and use them for small animal forage or to bury them in your garden for enrichment of the soil.

Kale is exceedingly easy to grow and productive for many months with a minimum of attention from the gardener. It can be used fresh from the garden; it is easily canned and still more easily put in the freezer, either blanched or merely washed and stored in plastic bags. It will withstand a fair amount of summer heat but loves cool weather. In fact, the flavor and crispness is improved by a light touch of frost. A light snowfall does no harm, and a scattering of pine boughs throughout the patch will provide protection from fairly heavy snows. Any kind of temporary cover to hold off heavy snows will prolong its productive cycle. Kale is ideal for succession planting to follow some early-season vegetable such as peas, potatoes, or beets. Kale has few bug enemies; in some areas the only insect problem occurs in late spring or late fall, when aphids cluster on one or two leaves of a plant. Most of the leaves remain uninfested. The aphids can be removed from picked leaves by a vigorous shake or by washing them off under the faucet.

Recommended varieties are Blue Curled Scotch, Dwarf Siberian, and Vates, also known as Dwarf Blue Curled and Dwarf Blue Scotch. All these varieties attain maturity in 55 to 70 days. The plants are so attractive that some leaves may be used in flower arrangements. They enhance a bed of flowers when used as a border plant. The leaves of the several varieties have colors ranging from dark green, to blue, to even a purplish cast. Some leaves are plume-like, some beautifully fringed, while some are densely curled. It is certainly one of the most useful and prettiest members of the vegetable world.

KOHLRABI
Brassica caulorapa

Kohlrabi is a minor member of the cabbage family. It was developed from wild cabbage in northern Europe, and records indicate its introduction into the United States at the start of the eighteenth century. This vegetable is unusual in appearance, inasmuch as it grows on a stem above the ground and sprouts leaves on long stems all over. It has been aptly described as a turnip growing on cabbage roots. The flavor is unique in that it is reminiscent of both turnip and cabbage. However, it is milder and sweeter than either of these vegetables. Although many gardeners are not familiar with this vege- table, it certainly is well worth adding to your "must" list of vegetable crops. The edible portion, a bulb produced by the enlarged stem base, is tender and juicy when about the size of a golf ball or a bit larger—about 2 to 2-1/2 inches in diameter. It may be prepared in the same way as turnips, eaten raw, or sliced and used in salads. It is excellent when dipped raw into the "hot bath" of an Italian Bagna Cauda sauce. Raw sliced vegetables are dipped into the bubbling hot bath to coat them and to enhance their flavor—not to cook them. It is versatile when added to stews and a taste treat when mashed and served with butter and cream. Always cook kohlrabi in its skin to preserve its flavor. It may be served as a relish with sour cream dips.

Culture

The culture of kohlrabi is similar to that of cabbage; the principal re- quirements are fertile soil and adequate moisture to ensure rapid growth. Generous use of well-rotted manure, compost, and old organic mulches turned into the soil will ensure plenty of humus, which adds so much to the quick growth of this crop. Kohlrabi does best in soil that is very slightly on the acid side. However, when the pH reading falls below 6.0, it is time to lime the planting area with an application of horticultural lime two or three weeks prior to planting. Sow the seed in well-prepared and enriched ground as early in the spring as possible. Make a shallow furrow and drop a seed every inch and cover with about three-fourths inch of soil. Firm the soil with your hand or foot, but gently; do not tamp it down. When the plants are about four inches tall, thin them to stand about four inches apart. The culls that have been removed for thinning can be transplanted into another row, previously prepared for this use, and the harvest season can thereby be extended. For hand cultivation, rows may be 15 to 18 inches apart. The transplanting shock will slow down the growth of the thinned-out plants, and they will mature quite a bit later than the original stand of kohlrabi. A top dressing of 5-10-5 or a similar organic fertilizer is beneficial right after thinning, both for the transplanted row and the original stand. The young roots spread out just under the surface of the soil and are very shallow. Consequently, until the plants are big enough to mulch, cultivate very lightly, about one-half inch deep, and weed around plants by hand-pulling. Cultivate thoroughly, but very shallowly, before putting on a thick mulch. If natural rainfall is not adequate, you must be sure that enough watering is done to keep the soil moderately moist at all times. Rapid growth is a must for tender, succulent bulbs. The soil must be rich in plant food and always have an adequate supply of moisture in order to ensure rapid growth.

Harvesting

Harvest the plants when they are quite small; pull up the entire plant to avoid disease from rotting roots and leaves. If they are growing and maturing faster than you can use them, pick them anyway. Harvest them at the right time before they get too large and store them in a cool basement. Kohlrabi may also be stored deep in the soil in straw-lined pits, where they will stay crisp and fresh well into the winter. Some gardeners give up on kohlrabi simply because they do not harvest when the plants are at their best—young, tender, and small. When the bulbs get as big as a baseball, they are too old and too tough.

Varieties

Only two varieties are grown:

Early White Vienna (55 days). The flesh is creamy white, tender, and of mild flavor. The bulb is light green with very smooth skin. It freezes well.

Early Purple Vienna (60 days). Matures five days later than White Vienna and has bulbs of a purplish color that grow a trifle larger. Same creamy white flesh of fine quality. Early Purple is very hardy and is the choice for late sowing for maturing in late fall and early winter.

LETTUCE
Lactuca sativa

This is undoubtedly the most popular salad vegetable in the home garden and the largest seller in food stores and supermarkets thoughout the United States. It can be grown anywhere in our country and is widely adaptable to a variety of soils and gardening situations. The three types grown in home gardens are head lettuce (crisphead and butterhead), leaf or bunching (loosehead, nonheading), and cos or romaine.

Crisphead lettuce forms well-folded heads of crisp, brittle texture that will stand more heat than the butterhead varieties. When the plants are grown under favorable conditions and properly spaced, they make large, round firm heads that are blanched silvery white or creamy yellow in the center. Popular and widely adapted varieties maturing in 70 to 90 days are Great Lakes, Iceberg, Mesa, Early Great Lakes, Hot Weather, Fulton, Premier Great Lakes, and Imperial.

Butterhead lettuce develops loose to well-folded heads of good form with outer leaves of dark green that are sometimes tinged with brown or red. The heart is tightly folded and blanches to a light golden or buttery yellow. Some varieties are slow to bolt (go to seed) and react to hot weather by producing tender, tasty leaves while not heading the way they do in cooler weather. Trying to choose the best varieties for you and your locality would be utterly impossible, inasmuch as there are hundreds of strains and varieties. However, the culture is the same for all of them. If you provide adequate plant food and moisture in the soil, and then thin them enough to allow full plant development, you cannot go wrong. Popular varieties maturing in 70 to 80 days are Buttercrunch, Burpee Bibb, Dark Green Boston, Butter King, White Boston, Fordhook, and Deer Tongue or Matchless.

Leaf or bunching lettuce is considered by many to be the easiest of all to grow. It does well in window boxes and patio containers for those people without other gardening areas. Maturing in 40 to 45 days, it naturally requires less nutrients than varieties that take twice this long to reach maturity. The shorter growing season means that the plants will be subjected to smaller extremes of temperature and natural rainfall which, of course, is conducive to better growing conditions.

Culture

All types of lettuce grow best during cool weather, despite the fact that some varieties have been specifically developed for their resistance to heat. Plant as early in the spring as the ground can be worked. To enrich the soil, thoroughly mix about three wheelbarrow loads of well-rotted manure or compost humus to 50 feet of row. In addition, use about three pounds of a balanced fertilizer on the same 50-foot row. If only one of these is available, try to use the manure or compost humus simply because they add humus to the soil, thereby increasing its moisture-holding capacity in addition to enriching it. Sow the seeds thinly in shallow furrows 18 inches apart and cover with 1/4 to 1/2 inch of fine soil. Light, daily sprinkling to keep topsoil moist will greatly assist germination.

Head lettuce or romaine should be thinned or transplanted to stand 12 inches apart. Leaf lettuce should be thinned to about six inches to allow for development and removal of outer leaves over a long period of harvesting. Butterhead does quite well when spaced about ten inches apart. A bit of trial and error will soon teach you the merit of proper spacing in order to give plants room to spread or head, to prolong the harvesting season, and to help keep plants from bolting.

For the spring crop you may want to start seeds indoors in flats, boxes, or pots in a cool, sunny location where the temperature ranges between 50 and 60 degrees. Plants from seeds started four to six weeks before the last heavy frost can be hardened off and set out in the garden very early in the spring. Lettuce is extremely cold-hardy, and properly hardened-off transplants will readily cope with any late, unexpected frosts. Many gardeners prepare a good seedbed outdoors and sow their seeds in the fall, early enough to permit the seedlings to attain good growth before the first heavy, killing frost. As colder weather approaches, the seedlings are gradually covered with an ever-increasing layer of loose straw, hay, pine boughs, or similar material. The small plants will survive winter temperatures under this protective cover, and you will have an ample supply of sturdy, vigorous seedlings available for transplanting just as soon as the ground can be worked in the spring.

Popular varieties of leaf lettuce are Green Ice, Black Seeded Simpson, Saladbowl, Prizehead, Slobolt, Curled Simpson, Grand Rapids, Oak Leaf, and Ruby.

The dark green leaves of lettuce are a good source of many minerals as well as being a rich source of vitamins A, B_2, and K. The lettuce picked in your own garden is far superior in food value and flavor to that which has been shipped hundreds of miles and stored endlessly in food markets.

Cos or romaine lettuce is much esteemed for its fresh crispness and sweet flavor. The elongated oval heads have light green outer leaves; and inner leaves are blanched greenish white and have a piquant, endive-like flavor. It is distinctive from other lettuce; the head is upright, the leaves are tightly folded, and at maturity it is about ten inches tall. The Paris White variety reaches maturity in 80 to 85 days and is widely grown in northern states to provide tightly folded, elongated heads in the home garden. Another excellent variety is Dark Green Cos.

Saladbowl lettuce is an outstanding leaf lettuce with considerable heat-resistance (USDA photo)

Here are some ideas to enhance your success with lettuce:

1. The small seeds are sometimes reluctant to germinate in dry, hot weather. Refrigerating the seeds for at least 24 hours before planting appears to speed up the germination process. Unless the soil moisture content is very high, wet the furrow thoroughly, press seeds lightly into soil, and then cover them very lightly with fine, dry soil. Keep the topsoil moist with a daily, fine sprinkling. If weather is very hot and dry, either cover the rows with wet burlap or rig a temporary shade to conserve soil moisture.

2. Considerable evidence points to the fact that lettuce grows best in soil that is neutral or a bit on the "sweet" or alkaline side of the pH scale. Consequently, to provide the best conditions possible for lettuce growth, lime the soil lightly before sowing seeds or transplanting seedlings. Do this unless you are sure that your soil is not acid.

3. Quick growth and top quality depend on a continuous, adequate supply of moisture in the soil, and during excessively hot weather a full or partial shade.

4. Study the descriptions in various seed catalogs in order to select the types of varieties you think are best adapted to your locality and your needs.

5. It costs only a few cents to buy a packet of seeds to try out a new or different variety. Why not experiment with two or three each season until you are happy and fully satisfied with your lettuce crop?

6. If you want to try a few plants without starting from seed, why not

purchase a few from a nursery or seed and plant center? Fresh lettuce can be enjoyed by the home gardener throughout most of the year in possibly two-thirds of the United States.

7. Excessive crowding in the row and high moisture content in the soil often combine to cause a form of rot to appear on the lower leaves. This condition can be corrected by spreading a layer of clean sand around the base of the plants or by mulching lightly with straw, leaves, or similar material to prevent contact of lower leaves with the soil.

8. Leaf lettuce will continue to thrive and produce for a much longer time if you cut the outer, larger leaves from the plants as they begin to attain maximum size. If you and your friends cannot use all that you harvest, use it for mulch or bury it in the garden for soil enrichment.

OKRA
Hibiscus esculentus

Okra is grown for its immature edible pods, which have a distinctive, mucilaginous taste. The tender small pods are eaten as a vegetable, and they also are used as an herb to flavor soups and stews. Some Southern dishes utilizing okra cannot be compared with anything you have ever tasted. Their flavor and aroma are peculiar and delightful. Fresh okra is a source of vitamins A and E as well as calcium, iron, niacin, and phosphorus. It is also one of the fiber foods so necessary for buoyant health. It is a valuable addition to the diet because of the nutritionally important minerals it provides.

The common name of okra is *gumbo*. It is widely thought of as being strictly a tropical crop; however, it can be grown successfully wherever cucumber and eggplant thrive. It is a tall, rank grower and thrives on heat and any fertile, well-drained soil.

Okra is quite versatile in both its uses and its climatic adaptation. It is a rich feeder and will produce tremendous yields, pods growing to an edible size almost overnight, when plenty of plant food and adequate moisture are available. The ground-up mature seeds are used as a coffee substitute in some countries and as a basic ingredient in the manufacture of perfume in others. The leaves and immature fruit possess demulcent and emollient properties, which result in their being used in fomentations and poultices in many eastern countries.

Regular varieties grow four to six feet tall, attaining eight feet or more in the deep South. Dwarf varieties reach heights of two to four feet. Their vigorous growth and space requirements scare some home gardeners into giv-

ing up on okra. However, they are only cheating themselves. You can successfully grow a wide variety of vegetables between rows of okra. Try lima beans,
tomatoes, and cucumbers beneath the canopy of okra leaves. Try pole beans
alongside the sturdy plants—and reinforce both beans and tomatoes with a
pole where needed. Lettuce, cauliflower, and late cabbage will thrive amidst
your okra. However, remember that all these vegetables will require plenty of
nutrients and moisture.

Culture

Generous applications of mature compost, well-rotted cow manure, or
other organic matter should be worked into the soil long before you plan to
plant okra. Make a shallow furrow and sow the seeds about eight inches apart,
covering with 1/2 inch of fine soil. Firm the soil lightly over the seed. Space
the rows three feet apart. When the plants are well established, thin to stand
16 inches apart in the row. Top dressings of mature compost or well-rotted
manure are very beneficial when the plants are about half-grown and again
when they just begin to bloom. If your okra is producing vigorous growth and
you have interplanted, some pruning of branches may be necessary. Simply
cut or snap off some branches and leaves immediately below each pod as it is
harvested. In fact, in midseason, you can cut back the main trunk to about
three feet and induce a fall crop. The stump will immediately start producing
new sprouts, which will grow vigorously and produce pods within a month or
so. You are encouraged to experiment with pruning back to a few branches
and cutting some main trunks back to three feet. Do this with half or less
than half of your plants, initially, to learn how to grow the most pods over
the longest season and how to interplant successfully. You can condense
years of gardening experience into one year by intelligent planning, taking
proper action at the correct time, and then recording the results for future
reference.

Harvesting

Pick the small immature pods when they are one to four inches long,
depending on variety, and at their flavor peak. They must be picked daily for
continuous production. Freeze or pickle any excess not to be used while still
green and fresh. Pods to be kept longer than 24 hours should be slightly
moistened and spread out in an area where there is good circulation of air.
They seem to generate or release heat when stored in containers. As is true of
all vegetables, any pods left on the plant after it reaches full growth will stop
or greatly reduce all further production.

Recommended Varieties

Clemson Spineless, Dwarf Green Long Pod, Emerald Green, Early Dwarf Green, and Louisiana Green Velvet. All these varieties produce edible pods in 50 to 60 days. The okra plant is so vigorous that it is not subject to attack from many insects. Consequently, you can usually hand-pick those insects that are causing injury to your plants.

THE ONION FAMILY
Allium cepa

Onion The underground bulb of this hardy, pungent, strong-smelling plant has been highly prized since the days of antiquity. Onions are a large family, which includes chives, garlic, leeks, and shallots. A well-known gourmet of the nineteenth century expressed it well for onion lovers everywhere: "Without onions there would be no gastronomic art. Its absence reduces the rarest dainty to insipidity and the diner to despair." The *allium* genus of onion-scented, perennial herbs also includes at least fifteen varieties grown for their ornamental flowers. Surprisingly, their colors range from white, to yellow, to pinkish-rose, to lilac, to rose-purple, to a purple that is almost black. These showy ornamentals of the onion family nearly all grow bulbs and are easily grown from seeds or bulbs. They make fine border plants that are of easy culture in any ordinary garden soil. Some attain a height of 30 inches, and some have leaves as long as 24 inches. This is a very interesting family of the plant world and well worth your further consideration.

Green onions are the most popular variety for the home gardener. They are easily grown from sets (small bulbs) and young plants. One of the best varieties of sets and young plants for green bunching and pickling when small is the White Sweet Spanish. The Evergreen Long White Bunching is widely grown for its long, slender, silvery white stalks, which are produced in clusters and used for green bunching onions or scallions. Seeds sown in the spring or summer will provide mild, green scallions late in the fall or, if wintered over, very early the following spring. Young plants will require some protection in sections where winters are severe. Any standard variety can be used for "green onions." It is merely a matter of harvesting at the proper growth stage.

Planting Instructions

Onions do best in a well-drained, rich soil. They thrive under varied conditions of climate and soil because of their tolerance of cold and heat and their vigor. The soil should be friable and free of stones, clods, and foreign matter. If the soil is light and sandy or exceptionally heavy (clayey), this condition should be corrected months in advance of planting by the generous addition of well-rotted animal manure, grass clippings, leaves, or other organic material that has been deeply dug in and thoroughly mixed with the soil. To enrich the soil about two weeks prior to planting, apply both well-rotted manure and a balanced fertilizer. About a pound of manure to each square foot of ground plus about five pounds of 10-10-10 to each 100 square feet is about right.

Onions are most easily grown by using "sets." The set is a small, dried bulblet raised from seed the previous year and picked when young. The best sets to plant are those from 1/2 to 3/4 inch in diameter. Smaller sets are usually lacking in vigor and growing potential. Each bulblet will produce a mature onion during the growing season. The sets are relatively inexpensive in the amounts needed by the average gardener. However, you are urged to get a packet of seed and sow them in the garden. You may be quite pleasantly surprised at the ease with which you can grow scallions, and you may want to propagate sets of a favorite variety. You can get a much larger variety by growing from seeds. Seed should be sown as early as you can work the ground. Give it a try.

Sets should be planted in a two-inch deep furrow. Set them in their natural position, upright, roots down, about 1-1/2 to two inches apart and about two inches deep. Firm the soil around each set. Keep the rows about 15 inches apart—although in small plots (well fertilized) they may be grown successfully in rows as close as six inches. When you start harvesting and eating young, green onions, thin them to stand about four inches apart for those you want to grow to maturity.

Chicken manure between the rows, gently worked into the soil, provides a valuable fertilizer for the onions because of its high nitrogen content. It is necessary to cultivate them enough to keep down weeds and conserve soil moisture. Keep in mind that onions are a shallow-rooted crop; one must be careful not to injure the roots or bulbs. The ordinary dry onion is a weather-wise plant, tending to concentrate on growing green tops in cool weather while preferring to form bulbs when the weather is warmer.

Most varieties reach maturity in 80 to 115 days. As onions reach maturity, the tops turn yellow, begin to wilt, and gradually fall to the ground. Some, not mature, but perfectly satisfactory for immediate use, can be harvested as needed. It is best to allow those that you intend to store to reach full maturity. The tops should be cut from pulled onions about an inch above the bulb. The onions should then be spread out in an airy space or placed on racks to dry off the surface moisture. This curing process usually takes from one to two weeks, depending on soil moisture at time of harvest, relative humidity, average temperature, and movement of air over and around the drying onions. A good indicator of curing is when the cut-off stem is no longer green but dry and shriveled. At this stage the onions may be safely stored in net sacks or airy crates in a well-ventilated, dry, cool, storage area.

Varieties

Burpee Yellow Globe Hybrid (102 days). Outstanding hybrid for earliness, uniformity, high yield, and exceptional keeping quality.

Early Yellow Globe (100 days). Globe-shaped, deep yellow-skinned onions with clear, white flesh and mild flavor. Early, uniform, solid, and large; an enormous cropper and a good one for storage.

Sweet Spanish Yellow Utah (110 days). Large, globe-shaped, mild, fine-grained and sweet—excellent cooked or raw. Will store for short periods better than Bermuda varieties.

Indian Queen Yellow Globe (115 days). Uniform in size, shape, and color. Very high yields and a very good keeper.

Grainex Hybrid (80 days). Excellent eating quality, mild flavor, good keeper.

Southport Red Globe (115 days). White flesh, tinged pink, with deep purplish red skin; perfectly round. Excellent for long storage.

Southport White Globe (110 days). Medium-sized, round onion with thin delicate skin and mild flavor. Good keeper.

Patti King Hybrid (100 days). Golden brown-skinned onions are of the Sweet Spanish class. This large bun-sized onion with its firm and mild flesh is tops in raw eating qualities. Hybrid vigor is your assurance of big, uniform yields. Good keeper.

Ebenezer (105 days). Bulbs are flattened globes, 2-1/2 to 3-1/2 inches across with yellowish-brown skin and firm yellowish-white flesh of exceptionally mild flavor. Excellent for winter long storage.

Downing Yellow Globe (110 days). Bright golden-yellow skin with creamy yellow flesh. Tremendous yielder. Has excellent keeping qualities for long-term storage.

Ringmaster (110 days). An improved white sweet Spanish onion with very mild, sweet flavor and pearl-white flesh. Absolutely ideal for onion rings, as it has only one center point, so rings come off perfectly round, slice after slice. Delicious fried in batter and excellent in salads and all cooking.

You can enjoy tastier and better onions than you ever knew existed, if you will carefully select two or more varieties and grow them from seed. Repeat this little experiment with selection of best and tastiest varieties each year until you are satisfied that you are growing the very best. Of course, this is the method to use for *final* selection of all your vegetables. Grow only the best. Commercial growers are not concerned about flavor and cooking qualities. They select varieties on the basis of adaptability, uniformity, and good shipping and keeping qualities.

   Chives *Allium schoenoprasum* An onion-scented, hardy, perennial herb that produces neat clumps of hollow, cylindrical leaves. These leaves are cut and then snipped with scissors into tiny pieces that are used for seasoning in fresh vegetable salads, omelets, cheeses, butters, soups, and stews, as well as various chicken, fish, and meat dishes. Chive butter adds a delightful flavor and succulence to broiled seafood and steaks. Their tasty, zestful, mild flavor is sought by many. Frozen chopped chives are almost as good as the fresh.

A pot of chives grown indoors (USDA photo)

   Chives are frequently planted as a border in flower beds or alongside walkways. They may be started from clumps of bulbs or seed. If using seed, sow them in rich, pebbly soil. Sow them rather thickly and cover about 1/4 inch, firming soil gently to ensure good contact of seeds with soil. Germination of seeds is slow, and the easiest method of propagation is to use bulbs. Chives prefer a rich, coarse soil with full sun. Whether planting outdoors or in pots, plant three of four of the tiny bulbs in one spot. Cover with about one inch of soil, gently firmed down. Keep the soil moist—not wet, not dry. This is one extraordinarily useful herb that thrives in pots and window boxes, providing an excellent source of seasoning all year long.

The plant is hardy and readily withstands repeated clippings. If not clipped and allowed to flower, it produces tiny, lavender-colored pompoms. The bulbs multiply rapidly, and it will be necessary for you to dig them every two or three years, divide, and then replant or repot them.

Garlic Allium sativum The dried bulblets or cloves of an onion-like vegetable plant. Two types are available to the home gardener: the type you buy at the market—a bulb containing eight to 12 sections called *cloves*—and "elephant garlic," which is milder and six times larger, often weighing over a pound. Elephant garlic gives vegetables and meats the wonderful, delicious seasoning flavor of garlic, with none of the strongness. It is so mild in flavor that it can be served, thinly sliced or minced, in fresh salads.

Garlic is a bit more exacting in its cultural requirements than are onions, but it may be successfully grown in any home garden where good results are obtained with onions. The compound bulbs are composed of eight to 12 cloves. The cloves should be planted root end down about four to six inches apart and covered with about 1-1/2 inches of soil firmed around them for good contact. Rows can be short and need not be spaced more than 12 inches apart. Garlic is usually planted in early spring. However, the cloves may be planted in the fall. The jumbo strain of elephant garlic withstands subzero weather. The culture of garlic is the same as that for onions.

The crop reaches maturity any time from June to September, depending on locality, weather, and time of planting. When the tops begin to turn yellow and show signs of wilting, it is time to pull them from the ground. (First loosen the soil with a trowel or dibble.) Dry the bulbs in a cool, airy place by spreading on papers or hang them in bunches from rafters in a breezeway, garage, or attic. After drying, remove any loose dirt and any loose pieces of the outer sheath. Trim roots fairly close to the base. They may be stored in net sacks or well-ventilated boxes, like onions, or tied in bunches and hung in a convenient place.

By selecting the largest bulbs for seed, you will be assured of having large, well-formed cloves for planting the following season. This selection of the largest and best bulbs for seed will result in a decidedly superior harvest of large, top-quality garlic cloves. It usually takes two years for the giant-size elephant garlic bulbs to develop from the cloves that you buy. They are relatively expensive; however, it is a one-time investment, inasmuch as you will grow your own cloves for all future crops of garlic.

Leek *Allium porrum* A hardy, onion-like plant, used much like the onion, but of a milder flavor. Both the leaves and edible stems are used for seasoning and in cooking. It is highly esteemed as a fall and winter substitute for green onions. It is superb when creamed and delicious for soups and stews.

Leeks are used for almost any purpose that onions are used for (USDA photo)

Culture

Leeks prefer a rich, deep loam but will tolerate a rather wide range of soil so long as it is rich in nitrogen and well supplied with moisture-holding compost, well-rotted manure, or other organic matter. Seed are sown rather thickly in an outdoor seedbed, covering them with 1/2 inch of fine soil. When the seedlings are about eight inches tall, carefully remove them from the seedbed, cut off about half the tops and transplant six inches apart in trenches about six inches deep and four inches wide. As the plants begin to thrive in their new location, cultivate often, drawing the soil up around the stems to blanch them. A good supply of sifted, mature compost or well-rotted manure should be mixed with the soil in the bottom of the trench before the leeks are set in it. During their early growth they require an abundance of plant food, and consequently they also require a plentiful supply of moisture. They can be dug before hard frosts appear and stored in a frost-free garage or cellar. They keep for long periods when heeled-in, in a box of moistened sand. Broad London (Large American Flag) takes 130 days from seed and is probably the most popular variety.

Shallot *Allium ascalonicum* An onion-like plant of the Multiplier type, often called *eschallot.* It is far superior to ordinary scallions for all seasoning. The young leaves are sometimes harvested, as are those of bunching onions. The cloves are separable from the bulb (like garlic) and are considerably milder than onions. They add a "gourmet" touch to most vegetable and meat dishes.

It is a hardy perennial and may be left in the ground from year to year. However, larger and better bulbs are realized from annual plantings. The culture is exactly the same as that for onions grown from sets. Propagation is by means of the small cloves or divisions into which the plant splits during its growth. Harvest, dry, and store as you would mature, dry onions.

PARSLEY
Petroselinum crispum

Parsley is the most popular and best-known member of the herb family. It is a biennial that tries to become a perennial. We now have a ten-foot row that is producing well in its third year. While thought of as being purely to season food and please the eye when used as garnish, parsley is a good source of vitamins A, B, and C. It dries or freezes well.

Parsley is cold-hardy and at the same time is able to withstand heat to the extent that it will continue to thrive throughout the summer. It can be carried through the winter in most of the north with a bit of protection in the form of a straw mulch. At the onset of winter, entire plants can be removed from the garden and potted, then moved indoors to provide fresh parsley all winter long. Put them back in the garden in late spring if you care to.

Culture

Parsley is widely adaptable and will thrive on any friable, fertile soil. The seeds are exceedingly slow to germinate. You can assist and speed up germination by soaking the seeds in tepid water for 24 to 48 hours immediately prior to planting. Parsley requires lots of nitrogen, which can be supplied by filling a four-inch-deep trench—beneath the row—with a 50-50 mixture of sifted compost and well-rotted cow manure. Alternatively, you can top dress with this same mixture of compost and manure or use a tiny bit of 34.5-0-0 or nitrate of soda. Regardless of your fertilization method, make a very shallow drill about 1/4 inch deep and sow the seeds very thinly, covering with 1/4 inch or less of fine soil. In most parts of the United States, parsley may be planted in March, April, or May. Early spring plantings are preferable. Firm it gently to give good contact of soil with seed, thereby assisting germination. Water often enough to keep the soil moist but not wet. Sprinkle very lightly so as not to disturb the soil and tiny seeds. Avoid any puddling or runoff. Covering the row with a board until the first seedlings emerge is beneficial. When young plants are two to four inches tall, thin so that mature plants will be six inches apart. Parsley will thrive either in full sun or partial shade. You can also get a start of parsley for either your garden or a window box from a fresh bunch purchased at the market. Select the freshest bunch with the best roots. Cut off the stems about an inch above the roots, then carefully plant the roots. Water, and tend the same as you would any other transplant.

Harvesting

You may start cutting the first outer sprigs as soon as the leaves are fully formed. Cut the outer leaves and sprigs as you need them, and leave the inner sprigs and hearts to continue to grow and produce more leaves. The chopped leaves freeze well.

You can prevent parsley from going to seed by cutting off the blossoms as soon as they begin to appear.

The dried leaves are very good when used for flavoring. Cut young sprigs from the plants and dry on a screen in a dry, out-of-the-sun, well-ventilated area. When leaves are thoroughly dry, crush and store in small, airtight containers.

Recommended Varieties

Extra Curled Dwarf (85 days). Compact plants with finely cut and curled, beautiful, dark green, moss-like leaves. Plain or single.

Italian (72 days). Plain, dark green, deeply cut, flat leaves with a fine rich flavor.

Parsnip-rooted or Hamburg (90 days). Principally grown for the parsnip-like roots of white flesh. Used for flavoring soups, stews, etc. Slender roots six inches or longer and about two inches thick at the neck.

Giant Italian Parsley (85 days). This variety grows to three feet tall and produces thick-stalked plants and leafstems that can be eaten like celery. Excellent for use in salads, soups, and stews.

PARSNIP
Pastinaca sativa

Parsnips are a good source of vitamins B, C, and G, potassium, and the micronutrient or trace elements. The stalks also are edible and both look and taste like celery. The dark green leaves are rich in vitamins and minerals and are delicious when used in late fall or winter salads or as "boiling greens" mixed with kale, mustard, or turnip tops. You can eat the whole thing and be relatively well nourished, in many respects, from one single root crop. Inasmuch as nothing about the parsnip has to be discarded or wasted, you certainly should give serious consideration to growing them regularly. However, it may take two or three seasons for you to fully appreciate their many virtues.

Parsnips can be grown almost anywhere in the United States. However, it is generally conceded that parsnips are improved by cold, or even by freezing, more than any other vegetable. They are among the most nutritious of the root crops. If planted in nonfreezing areas, they should be grown in late fall and winter and used as soon as they mature. In freezing areas of the country they can be left in the ground and harvested when you want some for cooking. In areas where the ground freezes hard, protect your crop from alternate freezes and thaws with a thick layer of mulch. There is no doubt that freezing improves them by giving them a more delicate flavor.

Culture

Parsnips mature in 80 to 120 days, depending on the variety planted. The seeds have a short vitality and germinate very slowly. Consequently, you should get fresh seeds each season and soak them overnight before planting to improve and speed up their germination. Seeds should be sown in the spring as early as the ground can be worked. Timing is most important for your main crop of fall and winter parsnips. They prefer a long, cool growing season, and for best results your main crop should be planted just in time to reach maturity shortly before the first freeze. Soil should be spaded, dug, or rototilled to a depth of 12 to 15 inches. Parsnips will easily grow 12 to 15 inches long, and the deeper down you loosen the soil, the easier it will be for the roots to lengthen and thicken. Any small stones, pieces of wood, or other objects in the soil will cause the roots to fork and become distorted. At the soil surface an eight-inch and a 15-inch parsnip require about the same amount of space. However, beneath the surface, in terms of food value, vitamins, and trace elements, the 15-inch root is far more efficient and just as easy to grow. Make a very shallow furrow and sow the seeds thickly, covering to a depth of 1/2 inch. Firm the soil lightly to ensure good contact of soil with seed. You should sow some early radish seeds in the row with the parsnip seeds, to mark the row to allow for one or two cultivations to control weeds before the young parsnip seedlings emerge. It is imperative that adequate soil moisture be present during the long period of germination. Germination is assisted by covering the seeds with something that will not bake and harden, such as a mixture of leafmold and sand or peat and topsoil. Another method is to use a 1/4-inch mulch of well-rotted sawdust or vermiculite over the furrow. Clear plastic will also hold soil moisture and prevent surface crusting, but must be removed as soon as seedlings begin to break through the surface. You can be assured of good germination by watering liberally and keeping the furrow moist, but not wet. Sprinkle gently with a light touch or use a fine, gentle, mist spray from a hose. You must be careful enough not to cause puddling of water, which causes crusting, and not disturb the surface over the seeds. Rows can be 14 to 30 inches apart, depending on whether you use hand or machine cultivation. Cultivate often enough to control weeds and conserve moisture. When the young parsnips are well started, thin to stand four to five inches apart. (Of course, all radishes used to mark the row should have been pulled and eaten long before now.) Parsnips are remarkably free from harmful pests and plant diseases.

The slow germination and painstaking care required to get the young seedlings started on their way may sound like too much fuss and bother for you. However, the resultant crop of nutritious and delicious parsnips with their unsurpassed keeping qualities, when left in the ground until needed for the table, will more than repay your efforts in their behalf.

Recommended Varieties

Hollow Crown (105 days). Long and smooth roots broad at shoulder, well tapered. Does best in deeply prepared soil. The fully developed roots are 12 inches long and 2-3/4 inches thick at the shoulder. Flesh is fine-grained, white, and of good quality.

All American (95 days). A vigorous grower and very dependable. Hollow crown, white flesh. Exceptional quality.

Harris Model (120 days). The whitest in color and the smoothest-skinned. Does not discolor as quickly as some varieties after harvesting and is probably the most attractive variety for roadside marketing and general sales.

Premium (80 days). Has shorter roots and matures more quickly. These two features could be advantageous in shallow soils and areas with short growing seasons.

PEAS
Pisum sativum = tall varieties
Pisum sativum humile = dwarf varieties

The garden pea is one of our most delicious and nourishing vegetables, combining all the attributes of green garden freshness with a rich supply of vitamins A, B, and C. Peas are called "English peas" in the South to differentiate them from Southern or cowpeas.

Peas have so much full-bodied flavor and are so nourishing that many Europeans make a meal out of them. The French cooks add a pinch of sugar to the water when cooking peas to further emphasize their sweet, mellow flavor. Napoleon's armies depended on dried peas because of their high nutritional value for most of their sustenance when on the march in hostile territory.

Peas are cool-season plants and should be sown just as early as the ground can be worked. In fact, the sowing of pea seed should be almost your first spring activity in the vegetable garden. They are easy to start and still easier to grow. The only cultivation required is enough to control weeds.

Most dwarf or low varieties have shorter pods and smooth seeds as compared to the tall varieties with their longer pods and usually wrinkled seeds. The low varieties mature in 52 to 65 days and appeal to most home gardeners because of this feature, coupled with the fact that they do not require support. However, you will encounter some experienced gardeners who rely on tall varieties for their main crop, which they dry, can, freeze, and use for the table. These same people contend that tall varieties are more flavorful because of a larger sugar content. Tall varieties mature in 62 to 80 days and require some type of support. Any variety up to about 3-1/2 feet tall can be propped up on either side with spoiled hay. Varieties that get no more than three feet tall can be well supported on 24-inch poultry netting that is either stapled, or tied to, one-by-four stakes or round posts. Have the bottom of wire eight inches above the surface. Always "double row"—plant on both sides of the support. While requiring a bit more care in the way of supports and a longer growing season, tall varieties bear for a longer time and can be counted on to produce bigger and better crops—all other considerations being equal.

Culture

Plant as early in the spring as the ground can be worked. Peas are cold-hardy and can be planted four to six weeks before the frost-free date. Peas under the soil surface are not harmed by heavy frosts and those above ground recover quickly, since only the bloom can be seriously damaged by frost. For first planting of the low varieties, make a furrow two inches deep in light soil and only one inch deep in heavy soil. Scatter the seeds rather thickly in the furrow—an inch apart, although some experienced gardeners sow them twice this thick. Cover with two inches of fine soil (one inch for heavy soil) and firm lightly to assist germination. An alternate method is to make a shallow furrow as wide as the blade of your garden hoe and scatter seeds quite thickly— at least an inch apart—and cover and firm the same as for a regular furrow. Rows should be 18 to 30 inches apart.

Tall varieties are planted in a different manner. The seeds are planted in double rows that are only six inches apart. Make two parallel furrows (or one trench six inches wide) about four inches deep and drop seeds every two inches. Cover the seeds with 1-1/2 to two inches of soil or enough to half fill the furrow. Finish filling the furrow after plants are up. This extra covering of soil keeps the roots cooler and moister. However, you can accomplish the same objectives by planting tall varieties in the same way as low varieties and then using a thick layer of organic mulch.

The reason for the double row six inches apart is to take full advantage of the support that you must provide for tall varieties. Poultry netting makes an ideal support for peas and can be rolled up and stored for future use in the pea patch for many seasons. It should be put up before the peas are planted. You must consider the tremendous load that tall peas will put on supports if strong winds and heavy rains occur at a time when the vines are fully grown and laden with pods. Use strong supports and put extra props in place to take care of any serious sags. Of course, there are extra compensations for all the effort going into the making of a support for the tall varieties, among them being:

1. Some tall varieties hold their flavor and sweetness a long time after the pods are ready to pick.
2. They produce bigger yields over a longer period—thus giving you more time for table use and for processing.
3. Some of the crop can be left to dry in the pods on the vines, providing you with one of the finest and richest foods for use in soups and other winter dishes.
4. Some gastronomic experts insist that the flavor of tall variety, wrinkle-seeded peas is superior to that of the other varieties, and they just may be right.

Harvesting

Your peas will be tender and sweet, full of flavor, and loaded with vitamins A, B, and C if you pick them as soon as the pods become swollen and filled. The longer they are exposed to air after being picked from the vine, the more tenderness and sweetness they lose. Consequently, either freeze or can them as quickly as possible after picking. For those for fresh use at the table, the best place for freshly shelled peas is in a tightly covered container in the refrigerator.

The following ideas may help you make better utilization of your crop of garden peas and save you some hard-earned cash in the process.

(1) Dried Peas You can grow the tall varieties on a fence or other type of support and harvest the first crop as they mature and leave the second crop to dry on the vine. When the peas are through blooming and the pods begin to bulge with full-grown peas, the vines will begin to wither and die. As the vines wither away and turn brown, the pods lose their moisture and turn to a yellow-brown with a stiff, papery texture. By the time that some of them begin to split open and drop their contents to the ground, the peas will have dried to a golden color. Now is the time to harvest and store them for future use. Some of the pods will contain fat worms, so they must be culled. Once your dried peas are ready to store, you want to ensure that no bugs are present and also add an extra bit of drying. Put them in shallow trays and expose them to oven heat of about 125°F for two or three hours. As soon as they cool and reach room temperature, store them in clear glass jars and cover them to exclude air. Naturally, any clean airtight container will be suitable for storage of this valuable food.

(2) Frozen Peas You can forget about conventional plastic bags and rigid freezer containers. We have found that peas keep perfectly for 12 months or longer when frozen in a cotton bag. They retain their flavor and keep better than when frozen in plastic containers. You can make these bags out of old cotton pillow cases or sheets. Try a size of 10 by 15 inches to start with and then go to larger or smaller sizes as desired. The 10-by-15-inch bag will hold about a gallon of peas with room to fold the top back on itself and pin shut or, if you leave enough room, to twist and tie. Heavy cotton is the best material to use and the bags can be laundered and used for many years. You are cautioned not to use anything but 100 percent cotton cloth.

To freeze your peas in cotton bags, shell and immediately put them into the bags and then into the freezer. Forget about blanching. Keep your fresh peas dry and ready to be quick-frozen in the coldest section of your freezer. The peas remain separated and freeze individually. To remove enough for a meal, open the bag and pour out the required amount. Immediately close the bag and return it to your freezer.

(3) Legume Inoculation Some plants of the pea family will not grow satisfactorily unless large numbers of certain nitrogen-fixing bacteria are present in the soil. This inoculant is also known as Legume Aid and Nitragin. A packet large enough to inoculate 10 pounds of seed costs less than a dollar. It is applied to beans and peas for sturdier growth and increased yields. These nitrogen-fixing bacteria greatly increase the pea plant's ability to take nitrogen out of the air and put it into the soil where it can be used by growing plants. The soil is enriched with nodules of nitrogen that grow on the plants' roots.

Legume bacteria are easily applied to seeds moistened with water. Either shake moistened seeds in a jar to get some inoculant on each seed, or stir them around in a container to accomplish the same purpose. Plant seeds immediately after treating to reduce the chances of bacterial loss due to exposure to air and heat.

Recommended Varieties

Dwarf or Low: Burpeeana Early (63 days).
Blue Bantam (64 days).
Little Marvel (63 days).
Early Alaska (52 days).
Frosty (63 days).
Laxton's Progress (60 days).
Sweet Green (62 days).
American Wonder (61 days).

Semi-dwarf and tall varieties: Wando (67 days). Heat resistant; sure cropper.
Freezonian (62 days). Wilt resistant, good quality. All-American winner.
Drought-Proof (70 days).
Green Arrow (70 days). Combines high yield with exceptionally sweet tender peas that are wonderful fresh or frozen.
Alderman (74 days). Very productive over a long season.
Fordhook Wonder (79 days). Peas are of the finest flavor and retain their sweetness for a long time after the pods are ready to pick.
Lincoln (68 days).
Tall Telephone (74 days). The standard large-podded main crop peas. Yields a heavy crop and is excellent for the home garden.

PEPPERS
Capsicum frutescens

The mild-flavored peppers are sweet and are used for salads, slicing, and stuffing. Most gardeners pick them when they attain a good size and are still green in color. However, their vitamin C content is higher and their flavor is improved by allowing them to remain on the plant until they ripen and turn red or yellow. Allowing the large, blocky sweet peppers to grow for a longer time and get sweeter and more mellow is a privilege of the home gardener that is unique and without duplication. Peppers that are fully ripened on the plant provide a rare culinary treat that is overlooked by the majority of home gardeners. The sweet, succulent, satisfying flavor of a fully ripened bell pepper is beyond comparison when eaten fresh from the garden like an apple, sliced and served in a salad, or sautéed in butter and served to complement meat or fish. Your own homemade pepper relish will add special savor to meat and vegetable dishes.

California Wonder variety of sweet pepper (USDA photo)

The hot peppers come in several varieties of *capsicum frutescens.* Originally used as a preservative and to mask the taste of not-so-fresh meat before the days of refrigeration, chili peppers (all hot peppers are chilis) are a very rich source of vitamin A. The New Mexico State University reports that the red chili is a natural preservative, acting as an antioxidant to retard the oxidation of meat and fats. Beef, chicken, and pork casseroles containing chili can be kept in frozen storage for longer periods, and still retain their original flavor.

There is some evidence to indicate a lowering of blood fat by people who eat chili-rich foods. These same chili-eaters (in New Mexico and other parts of the Southwest) enjoy robust health and a low incidence of heart disease and cancer. Be that as it may, there is no doubt that hot peppers lend flavor and special appeal to many favorite international dishes: African stews, Indian curries, Mexican salads, and Portugese and Spanish dishes. Hot peppers are universally used in sauces, for flavoring, and for pickling, either fresh or dried.

The Mexicans grind dried peppers daily for a hot, fresh supply of chili, which is used in most of their meat and vegetable dishes. Just a little of this "dynamite" enhances the flavor of almost any dish, and it is easy to completely change the flavor by varying the amount of chili that is used.

Container Growing

Many of the hot peppers are especially attractive when grown in containers. They add beauty to your surroundings while contributing to your health and dining pleasures. Container-grown hot peppers respond generously to regular feedings of a soluble fish fertilizer and regular watering. Container-grown peppers can be treated as perennials by keeping them in a frost-free area after their annual fruiting cycle ends. When kept in an area of low light, the plant will shed its leaves. At this time you decrease watering by at least 50 percent and feed the plant once per month. However, observe its "state of health," and do not let it die at this time. Prune the plant to proper shape and dimensions while it is without leaves, taking into account the growth that it will produce during the coming season and fruiting cycle. After a sufficient dormant period, or after the winter season is past, gradually expose the plant to sunlight again and slowly increase the frequency of watering and feeding. However, do not "shock" the plant by going to the full schedule of all its growing and fruiting requirements overnight.

These pretty plants bear shiny green leaves with dainty white flowers. The fruits come in greens, reds, and yellows; they are two to five inches long. Their nutrient requirements are fully satisfied by regular feeding with a soluble fish fertilizer. However, you are cautioned not to use too much fertilizer too often. Just like people, lean plants are healthier than overfed ones. These plants are pest-free and have their own inherent pest-repellent features.

Prime candidates for container growing are long red Cayenne, Fresno Chili, Jalapeno, and Red Chili. They utilize plant nutrients very thriftily, while responding generously to regular watering and all-day-long exposure to sunshine.

Culture

Buy your transplants locally or grow your favorite varieties from seed. Set them in your garden after all danger of frost has passed and the soil has definitely warmed up. You will gain nothing by putting pepper plants into cold soil. They will not take root and start new growth unless the soil is warm. Pepper plants like heat, and you must consider this requirement when setting them into your garden. You can grow them around your tomatoes and treat them much alike, bearing in mind that your pepper plants require less nutrients than your tomatoes. They thrive when spaced 1-1/2 to 2 feet apart in rows; however, circular planting permits more crowding.

Harvesting

Here is where you can experiment selectively and let your taste buds make the decision. Pick some of your sweet peppers as soon as they attain a good size for use in salads or for stuffing. Carefully evaluate their flavor. Let some of the others stay on the plants until they turn about half red or yellow and then critically sample them. Let some of the peppers remain on the plants until they ripen fully and turn all red or all yellow. Now, compare their flavor and their texture with those you harvested at their two earlier stages of growth. You should be selectively critical and make your own decision as to what stage of growth or maturity you prefer to harvest sweet peppers. Your pepper plants will be healthier if you cut off the peppers with about 1/2 inch of stem attached instead of pulling them free at the pepper.

Hot varieties can be picked when they attain maturity and used for pickling or in sauces, or the peppers can be left to dry on the plants for future use. The plants can be cut off at ground level and hung in a ventilated area to allow full drying of the pods. Alternatively, the pods can be pierced with a finishing nail or long needle—preferably at the thickest end—and strung up like beads to dry on a string. After thorough drying they store almost indefinitely in airtight containers.

Recommended Varieties

There is a great difference between varieties, and you will profit by studying their descriptions in seed catalogs. The most popular sweet peppers include: California Wonder, Bell Boy Hybrid, Golden Bell Hybrid, Sunny-brook, Aconcaqua, Sweet Banana, Cubanelle, Florida Giant, Merrimack Wonder, King of the North, Hybrid Peter Piper, Wisconsin Lakes, Italian Sweet, Yolo Wonder, Hercules Sweet Red, California Mammoth Green, Italian Pepperoncini, Canape Hybrid, New Ace Hybrid, and Hercules Golden Yellow.

The most popular hot varieties include: Long Red Ceyenne, Hungarian Wax, Mexican Chili, Tabasco, Large Cherry, Red Chili, Jalapeno, Fresno Chili, Anaheim, and Golden Spike Hybrid.

POTATO
Solanum tuberosum

Potatoes are native to South America; the first cultivated varieties were grown by the Incas high up in the Andes. Its high starch content, as well as vitamin C, give it a high food value and make it a most important garden plant. Potatoes store well for long periods of time when the home gardener provides adequate storage conditions. When treated to control sprouting, potatoes are stored for months and shipped to points all over the world. Both Germany and the Soviet Union produce enormous crops annually. In dollar value and volume of production, the potato equals or exceeds all other crops in the world.

Culture

Any fertile, well-drained soil is suitable if properly fertilized. Potatoes need plenty of moisture and an acid soil with a pH factor of 5.0 to 6.0. Commercial fertilizers, 5-10-10 or 3-18-18, should be applied at a rate of eight to 15 pounds per 100-foot row. The lower rate of application is sufficient for very fertile soils; the higher rate for less fertile ones. If manure, either animal or a green manure crop, is used, it should be plowed or raked well under the topsoil in the autumn before the spring planting. The commercial fertilizer must be mixed with the soil in such a manner that the seed pieces will not come in direct contact with it. This is easily accomplished by making the furrows an inch deeper than required for planting, scattering the fertilizer in bottom of furrow, and then raking or pulling about an inch of soil down onto the fertilizer.

Potatoes are grown by cutting up seed potatoes, allowing one or two "eyes" (buds of the underground stem) to each piece. Cut the potato into blocky, square-shaped pieces, trying to avoid thin or wedge-shaped pieces. Cut seed pieces should be allowed to dry for 24 hours before planting. This allows a protective tissue to form over the cut surface. A light sprinkling of fine, powdery soil over the cut surfaces greatly hastens the formation of callus. It is essential for the seed piece to weigh more than an ounce, inasmuch as the plant will live on this stored, fleshy food while sprouting. Potatoes can be grown from pieces of thick peelings with eyes. However, your chances of a heavy yield are decreased by this practice. The best seed potatoes are small ones that do not need cutting but are planted whole.

Potatoes are susceptible to a number of disastrous diseases, and you would not want to handicap a new crop with them. Consequently, you should buy certified, disease-free seed potatoes from a reliable dealer. Federal regulations require them to be tagged as such. Of course, you could use your own seed potatoes from last year's crop, if you think they are free of disease. If you had healthy, vigorous plants that produced good yields, you would need five to eight pounds of seed potatoes to plant a 100-foot row. The amount needed depends on their size and the number of eyes. Your own potatoes will surely be quite satisfactory to use for seed.

Make furrows about five inches deep and put a piece of seed potato every 12 to 15 inches. Cover the seed pieces thoroughly to the full depth of the furrow. The rows should be two to three feet apart, depending on whether you use hand or machine cultivation.

Potatoes are a cool-weather crop and should be planted early in the spring—not later than two weeks before the last killing frost. In areas where it gets too hot for good yields, a thick mulch of hay or straw should be applied as soon as planting is finished. A ten-inch layer of mulch will conserve moisture, stabilize soil temperature, and foster healthier plants with better yields.

Potatoes require two to three weeks to come up, depending on the depth of planting and the temperature of the soil. If an early planting results in frost damage to sprouts, the plants will usually keep right on growing from parts of the underground stem unharmed by the frost.

Clean cultivation, often enough to control weeds and conserve moisture, is essential. In six to eight weeks the plants will become too bushy and sprawling for further cultivation. Before this happens, at the last cultivation, mound the soil to a depth of six to eight inches around the plants. This mounding or ridging of the soil is necessary to keep the tubers beneath the surface of the soil. When potatoes surface, they turn green and are not fit for human consumption.

Harvesting

Potatoes are ready to be dug when most of the tops have withered. However, it is common practice for home gardeners to start digging "new" potatoes when the plants bloom and the little tubers reach an inch or so in diameter. At this stage of their growth they are unbelievably good. Mature early potatoes can be left in the ground for two to four weeks if the weather is not too hot and wet. The late varieties can be left in the ground four to eight weeks. However, after the tops have withered, it is a good idea to dig a hill every three to four days just be sure that the entire crop is not deteriorating. At the very first sign of deterioration, get them out of the ground and into proper storage.

You will find a garden spade the best tool for digging potatoes. After digging, let them remain in the sun for two or three hours to dry out to remove soil moisture and loose soil. They must then be stored in a cool, dark place. Careful handling to avoid bruising and skinning is desirable, and protection from long exposure to light is necessary to prevent their becoming green and unfit for table use. Store in a well ventilated place where the temperature is low—35 to 50°F is best, if possible—but where there is no danger of freezing. When stored where temperatures are too high, they sprout.

Recommended Varieties

In the North, plant two types of potatoes—one to provide early potatoes for summer use, the other for storage and winter use. Early varieties include Anoka, Irish Cobbler, Early Gem, Norland, Norgold Russet, and Superior. Best late varieties are Katahdin, Kennebec, Chippewa, Russet Burbank, Sebago, and the golden nematode resistant Wanseon. Irish Cobbler is the most widely adapted of the early varieties and Katahdin of the late. In the Great Plains States, Pontiac and Red La Soda are preferred for summer use; the Katahdin and Russet Burbank for winter. In the Pacific Northwest, the Russet Burbank, White Rose, Early Gem, and Kinnebec are used. In the Southern states, the Irish Cobbler, Pungo, Red La Soda, and Red Pontiac are widely used.

RADISH
Raphanus sativus

Radishes are the easiest and quickest of all vegetables to grow in your garden, in a window box, or in almost any container. While traditionally considered a salad vegetable or relish, radishes have been cooked by the Chinese for thousands of years and are excellent when butter-steamed or fried in oil. They are a good source of vitamin C and will grow anywhere in the United States at some time of the year.

Culture

Radishes are divided into three types: the early or spring, the midseason or summer, and the winter. All of the early radishes will also grow well in the fall. Early types mature from seed in 21 to 28 days. Midseason radishes are ready to eat in 45 to 60 days; the winter types usually mature in 60 to 70 days. Culture of all three types is identical. They do best in fertile, loose, deeply prepared soil. Sow seed of the earliest and midseason varieties as early in the spring as the ground can be worked. There is a big variation in size of the seeds, and quick growth of select roots is enhanced by sifting out the largest seeds and rejecting the smaller ones. Make a shallow furrow and space the seeds about one inch apart and cover with 1/4 to 1/3 inch of fine soil, lightly firmed to assist germination.

It is best to curb your inclination to plant a packet of seeds all at one time. Instead, plant a 10- or 15-foot row and make second and third plantings when the first planting is up and well started. Thin to stand far enough apart in the row to attain full size without touching.

Early radishes grow so quickly that they are ideal for interplanting—anywhere and everywhere. Early radishes mature so quickly that those sown with slowly germinating seed like carrots and parsnips will be pulled and eaten before any crowding occurs. This practice is called *companion cropping* or *intercropping*. Try planting them in between cabbages, broccoli, eggplant, peppers, and tomatoes. If you are cramped for space, plant them in odd nooks and crannies. However, you must meet their requirements for fertility and moisture in order to realize quick growth of top-quality roots. By all means, use radishes to mark the rows of more slowly germinating crops such as parsnips and carrots. A radish seed planted at six- to 12-inch intervals will enable you to cultivate and weed between the rows before the carrots and parsnips are up.

Harvesting

Radishes should be pulled from the soil as soon as they are big enough to eat. As is true with almost all vegetables, early, young radishes are crisper and have a milder flavor. Midseason varieties should be harvested as they get big enough to eat—with the exception of the All Seasons White Radish, which will hold up to six weeks after attaining edible size, without becoming pithy or strong. Winter varieties can be pulled when size is attained or left in the ground until heavy frosts. Even then, a covering of mulch to prevent alternate freezing and thawing will protect them.

Recommended Varieties

Cherry Bell, Burgess Special, Champion, French Breakfast, Red Devil, Stop Lite, White Icicle, All Seasons White, French Golden, Hailstone, Takinashi, Miyashige, Black Spanish, China Rose, White Chinese, and California White Mammoth.

SPINACH
Spinacia oleracea

Spinach is rich in minerals and vitamins, and is one of our most important potherbs. Potherbs or "greens" are leafy plants that are cultivated and grown exclusively for their foliage. The darker green winter varieties are very high in calcium, protein, iron and vitamins A, B_1, B_2, and C.

Spinach is tasty and nutritious, either raw or cooked. It is choosy with regard to temperature, and good growth is made only during the cool weather of early spring and again during the colder weather of fall. However, the long-standing varieties of Bloomsdale and America are slow to bolt to seed and produce heavy yields in about 50 days. Virginia Blight Resistant Savoy is hardy to frost and matures in 39 days. It is extremely tolerant of adverse conditions and is the fastest growing Savoy. Spinach varieties also differ in the physical structure and appearance of their leaves or foliage; some are savoyed and some are smooth. The Savoy types tend to be a bit darker green and more attractive to the eye; they are a trifle harder to clean but are usually preferred. Cleanleaf is the name of a variety that bears its leaves well away from the soil, thus avoiding splashes of soil in heavy rain. Other good varieties include Northland, Hybrid No. 7, Nobel, and Longstanding Winter.

Culture

Spinach is a quick-growing, leafy plant that requires an abundant supply of plant food, especially nitrogen, coupled with adequate moisture. It will thrive in any fertile, well-drained garden soil that is not too acid. Spinach appears to do best in soil with a pH rating just below to just above neutral. Soils with a pH factor below 6.0 should be limed sufficiently to bring the pH factor up to the range of 6.5 to 7.5. Compost and manure worked into the soil will increase its moisture-holding qualities and assure a steady supply of plant food. It is a cool-season crop that should be planted as early in the spring as the ground can be worked. It can also be planted in late summer, about the first of August, and then cut until the ground freezes. Sow the seed rather thinly in shallow drills, covering with 1/2 inch of fine soil, firmed gently. Rows can be 18 to 24 inches apart. When seedlings are well established, thin to stand four to six inches apart. Sow again when the preceding planting is up, but omit sowings of regular spinach that would mature in hot weather. For early spring use, where winters are mild, sow in early fall and mulch with a few inches of hay or straw. Remove any of the mulch that hinders emergence of plants in early spring. One or two applications of a nitrogenous top dressing will ensure rapid growth and top-quality spinach. 34.5-0-0 and nitrate of soda are good sources of nitrogen. They can be used either dry or dissolved in water to make a liquid fertilizer.

Harvesting

Spinach matures in 40 to 50 days; individual plants are cut off at the roots and either washed and prepared for immediate fresh table use, freezing, or canning, or stored in plastic bags in the refrigerator. All varieties can and freeze well.

Similar Greens

Tampala is a valuable green that stands hot weather. This tropical plant is a cultivated variety of *Amaranthus gangeticus*. Those who grow it prefer it to spinach. They claim that it is tastier and sweeter. The young tender leaves can be cooked like asparagus and are much like artichoke in flavor.

Malabar Spinach (*Basella alba*—70 days). Thrives on hot weather and can be grown on a trellis or fence. This potherb is an excellent substitute for spinach. The young leaves are large and a bright glossy green. They can be harvested repeatedly, because they are produced in succession on long viney stems. It is not only a good vegetable but also an attractive, ornamental plant.

New Zealand Spinach (*Tetragonia expansa*—70 days). This native of New Zealand so greatly resembles spinach in appearance and flavor that most persons will not be aware of the difference. It is much more tolerant of heat than regular spinach and much easier to grow. The big, sturdy plants produce an abundance of fleshy, brittle, green leaves and young stem tips that can be picked repeatedly, as new leaves and stem tips are successively produced all during summer and fall, until the plants are killed by frost.

Culture

New Zealand spinach seeds are large, very hard, and slow to germinate, taking from three to five weeks to come up (this is a good one to mark with radishes). Germination can be speeded up by soaking the seeds in warm water for 24 to 36 hours to soften the hard outer covering. Seeds may be sown as soon as danger of frost is past. Space the seed about six inches apart in a shallow furrow and cover with 1/2 inch of fine soil, gently firmed. When plants are well established, thin to stand three feet apart in the row. Rows should be four feet apart, because these big plants sprawl and cover a lot of ground when full grown, and you must have enough room to get around between the plants to harvest the leaves and tips.

These plants are so vigorous and so productive that four to six of them will provide an ample supply of greens for a family of four, including freezing and canning requirements. New Zealand spinach is highly recommended for a continuous supply of fresh, nutritious, flavorful greens. The plants respond generously to repeated, scant top dressings of 34.5-0-0 and 10-5-5, and top dressings of chicken manure give excellent results due to its nitrogen content.

Many home gardeners are thoroughly familiar with regular spinach and grow a crop in the spring and another one in the fall. This provides them with garden-fresh table greens for, at most, a four-month period. By growing the substitutes that thrive in hot weather and produce over a period of several months, you can easily enjoy fresh greens for 8 to 12 months, depending on your geographic location. All types can or freeze well. They are easily grown and make a significant contribution to your family's nutrition requirements.

SQUASH
Cucurbita

The squash is native to the Americas and will thrive in any section of the country with enough moisture. Squash need enough water to keep the root zone continually moist. You can either plant in a feeding and watering circle, as described under tomatoes on page 121, or build a small dike around the hill to hold water so that it will soak down to the roots. Summer squash mature in 48 to 57 days and are very easy to grow. Winter squash take about twice as long to ripen—80 to 115 days. However, culture of summer and winter types is identical. Both summer and winter types can make a significant contribution to your annual food supply and provide good, nutritious, tasty food that can be prepared in many delightful ways.

The home gardener with an average-sized plot may be tempted to forego the winter types, because most of the better-known varieties are of the vining kind and require lots of space. Vining types can be grown, by careful handling, in hills six feet apart, with eight feet between rows. However, they really do need lots of room for best production and will respond generously when spaced ten feet apart each way. However, you can grow either the bush or semi-bush varieties in much, much less space and have squash to enjoy at the table throughout the winter. Gold Nugget, Golden Nugget, Table King, and Table Queen are good examples of this type. Kindred, an All-American Selection, bears a great quantity of eight-inch tuber-shaped fruit on bush-type plants that start vines in midseason, needing only a small space. The golden fruit keep their delicious flavor even after long storage.

A mulched plant of Yellow Straightneck summer squash (USDA photo)

Culture

Squash prefer a rich, warm, sandy loam but will thrive in any light soil where the fertilizer, compost, or manure is concentrated under the hills. Any spot in the garden where more than one plant is to grow in a group is called a *hill*. It is essential that your squash plants have an adequate supply of nutrients and moisture to enable them to "pump out" a continuous supply of top-quality fruits.

A good plan is to remove a bucketful of soil and replace half of the volume with well-rotted cow manure, packing and tramping it down firmly to provide good capillary action. Now sprinkle a handful of 10-10-10 or similar fertilizer on top of the manure and cover it with four inches of fine topsoil; firm it well. Do not hill or mound the soil above general ground level.

A second method for fertilizing is to remove a bucketful of soil and mix a pound (a pint) of 10-10-10, or similar fertilizer, with half of the removed soil. Finish preparing the hill for planting as you do when using manure.

Still a third method of soil enrichment *beneath* the hill is to replace a bucketful of excavated soil with a bucketful of compost. Then finish preparation for planting by adding a firm, two-inch layer of topsoil. By now, it should be readily apparent that almost any method of enriching the soil in the hill will be satisfactory.

When all danger of frost has passed and the soil really begins to get warm (the seeds will not germinate in cold soil), place five or six seeds in a hill. Either space the seeds around the perimeter of a ten-inch circle, or at the center and ends of a ten-inch X. You want the seeds to be spaced about five inches apart. Cover the seeds with one inch of fine topsoil and firm it gently to ensure good contact of soil with seed to assist germination.

When plants are up and beginning to make vigorous growth, thin to two or three of the most vigorous ones. Keep weeds under control and cultivate lightly around the hill to conserve moisture. If rainfall is not adequate, water thoroughly every three or four days.

Setting of Fruit

Some gardeners get quite concerned when the first blossoms fail to set fruit. This is natural for the squash and not a disease. Some female flowers bloom before there are male flowers for pollination. The first few female blossoms either dry up or produce small fruits that abort and then rot. This natural aborting of imperfect young fruits is a self-pruning process for the plant, which also occurs when a good load of fruit is set and all the plant's resources for fruit development are being stretched to the limit.

Harvesting

Summer squash should be picked while it is young, tender, and comparatively small. Zucchini types are at their peak for flavor and tenderness when not more than seven inches long and about 1-1/2 inches in diameter. The time-honored test of rind's being tender enough to pierce readily with slight thumbnail pressure is not valid. Flavor, small size, and tenderness are the only proper and valid criteria. For example, ten-inch-long zucchinis with diameters of three inches will readily pass the thumbnail test. Yet any experienced gardener or any competent cook knows that squash this big have lost their flavor and are pithy.

White Bush (White Patty Pan) is delicious when cooked whole—about an inch across—and so is the St. Pat Scallop. Crookneck and straightneck types are at their flavor peak when about four inches long. Under favorable conditions, summer squash grow so fast that it is advisable for you to selectively harvest them on a daily basis.

Winter squash should be left on the vines until they are fully ripened. Their flavor is improved by the onset of cold weather, which increases their sugar content. Immature fruits have poor flavor, are watery, and do not store well. Observe the colors of different varieties as they reach full maturity in order to avoid premature harvesting. All of them change color as they ripen, and "Butternut" loses all its green and turns to a distinct, even tan. Light frosts do not harm mature fruits and may actually improve their flavor. However, all winter squash should be taken in before hard frosts. When harvesting, leave about an inch of the stem attached to the fruit.

Storing

Select only hard-shelled, sound squashes for long-term storage. Wash them carefully, dry thoroughly, and examine for injury, especially that part which rested on the ground. They keep best when placed in single layers of rows on shelves in an area that is dry, with a temperature of 40 to 55°F. They will keep quite well at temperatures up to 65°F. However, higher temperatures cause them to dry out more rapidly, and they do not remain edible for quite as long.

Stored squash should be examined at two- or three-week intervals for evidence of superficial molds caused by moisture condensation. Carefully wipe any surface that appears to be damp or moldy. Neglected moldy spots can ruin large parts of the inside of the squash with little or no damage to the outer surface. Proper storage and occasional checking will enable you to enjoy squash throughout the winter.

Recommended Varieties

There are dozens of varieties to choose from, and a brief study of their descriptions in seed catalogs will enable you to make a better choice. Since properly stored seeds remain viable for four years or longer, you can plant a different variety or two each year—at slight expense—until you decide on what varieties you like best. Most popular summer varieties include Burpee Golden Zucchini, Hybrid Zucchini, Astrocrat Hybrid, Greyzini, Cocozelle Bush, Clarita, Chefini, Diplomat, President, Blackini, Early Straightneck, Golden Crookneck, Early White Bush, St. Pat Scallop, Seneca Butterbar, and Seneca Prolific.

The best-flavored and best-keeping winter varieties include True Hubbard, Blue Hubbard, Improved Green Hubbard, Golden Hubbard, Warted

Hubbard, Faribo Hybrid "R," Sweet Meat, Big Red, Umatilla Marblehead, Kikuza, Sakata F$_j$ Hybrid, Banana, Jumbo Pink Banana, Gold Nugget, Ebony, Golden Delicious, Buttercup, Emerald, Butternut, Hercules Butternut, Waltham Butternut, Table Queen, and Table King.

New Hampshire's Experimental Station has developed an Eat-All Sweet Potato Squash with tasty hulless seeds of high nutritional value. Compact five-foot vines produce green-and-white-striped fruits. The seeds, when baked, make a wholesome confection. Their sweetnut squash has a rich, nutlike flavor with edible seeds that are nutritionally equal to peanuts. It is a compact, bush-type squash.

SWEET CORN
Zea mays rugosa

Historians generally agree that corn supported the early civilizations of North and South America. It is the most valuable food plant contributed to the Old World by the New. Many gardeners have been led to believe that they should not attempt to grow their own sweet corn because it takes up entirely too much room in proportion to the returns. Like many other facets of gardening, this is pure myth and can be readily proven as such. Corn will thrive when the plants are spaced six inches apart in rows that are 30 inches apart. The only requirements are a fertile, well-drained, light soil that is provided with a good supply of plant food and adequate moisture during the time from tasseling to picking. You can produce still more corn in a given area by growing it in a permanent mulch. Many, many gardeners have shown this to be a practical way to get maximum yields of sweet corn from a small area. Periodic hoeing and cultivating is not a requirement for a good crop of sweet corn. However, plenty of plant food must be available, and you can ensure this by an adequate application of fertilizer before the mulch is applied. Adequate moisture is essential, but the mulch vastly improves the moisture-holding capability of the soil. You are urged to try growing sweet corn with a permanent mulch. Space the rows one foot apart with the plants spaced six, nine, or twelve inches apart in the rows. Experiment by alternately spacing plants at intervals of six inches in one row, nine inches in another row, and twelve inches in a third row, etc. Observe the growth and yields to determine the most satisfactory spacing and arrangement for you and your garden. This experimenting for maximum yields will require consistency with varieties planted and fertilization methods used. Locality, rainfall, and temperature also influence results. Nevertheless, planning on a continuing basis can be very rewarding. Corn is pollinated by the wind. Consequently, plant it in blocks of at least four rows. It is definitely a warm-weather plant, and will not thrive until all danger of frost is past and the ground has begun to warm up.

Culture

It is good practice to scatter about five pounds of 10-10-10 along a 50-foot row and lightly cultivate and thoroughly mix it with the soil prior to planting. Then make a shallow furrow about 1-1/2 inches deep and space the seeds six inches apart. Cover to a depth of one to 1-1/2 inches and firm the soil lightly over seed. By spacing the seeds six inches apart, you are not planning on doing any thinning, and you are expecting 100 percent germination. This kind of germination is assured by going through the seeds and *selecting* the large kernels for planting this distance apart. The smaller kernels will not give this percentage of germination, and it takes from three to six days longer for them to come through the surface of the soil. Germination is assisted and speeded up by soaking the seeds in water for about 12 hours immediately prior to planting. Soaking fills the kernel with moisture and causes it nearly to double in size.

When the corn is about 10 to 12 inches high, top dress it with about the same amount of the same fertilizer. As the corn continues to grow, it develops a ring of secondary or prop roots just above the surface. When the corn is 16 to 18 inches high, give it a second top dressing and then mound soil around the prop roots to a depth of six to eight inches. This procedure stiffens the plant in strong winds or at times of excessive rainfall.

One of the most mouth-watering experiences in the world of fresh vegetables is *fresh* corn on the cob. It is an outstanding taste treat. However, this superb treat can only be enjoyed by those who pick their corn and cook it immediately. The flavor deteriorates quite rapidly, and speed in handling the corn from stalk to table is essential. Harvesting at the proper time is just as important. Test for harvesting by opening the tip of the husk and puncturing the kernels with your thumbnail. If the kernel is easily pierced and squirts milky juice, pick immediately. *Twist* the ear off the stalk; do not try to do a straight pull. Really good, fresh, sweet corn, picked at its peak, is simply delicious when eaten right off the cob uncooked and unbuttered. Just like tomatoes and sweet peppers, the flavor is best when it is picked and eaten right in the garden.

Corn is easily cut from the cob for freezing or for drying, and with either method retains its exquisite flavor. When corn is exactly at its peak, harvest the ears and husk them at once. Then remove the silk, cut the corn off the cob, place in plastic bags, seal, and freeze. Blanching is not necessary, and we believe the flavor to be better when it is not blanched.

Recommended Varieties

Silver and Golden Queen are rated by experts as being the highest-quality corn ever developed. However, there are taste treats in store for those who try Illini Xtra Sweet, Early Xtra Sweet, and Honey and Cream. Most varieties mature in 65 to 90 days. Good varieties of hybrid yellows are Barbecue, Iochief, Earliking, Bantam Evergreen, Golden Cross Bantam, Carmelcross, Illini Chief, Early Sunglow, and Corneli's Gold Rush Hybrid. Good varieties of hybrid whites are Silver Sweet, Hi-Sugar, Snowcross, Country Gentlemen, and Stowell's Evergreen.

SWEET POTATO
Ipomoea batatas

This is one of the important fiber foods and an excellent source of vitamins A and C. One ordinary sweet potato of the *Allgold* variety contains a third of the daily vitamin C and 150 percent of the vitamin A requirements for adults. It is worthwhile to compare *Allgold* with Porto Rico, which is grown by many home gardeners. In addition to its remarkable vitamin qualities, *Allgold* has produced almost double the yield of Porto Rico in extensive field trials.

The sweet potato is a member of the morning glory family and a native of Central and South America. It is distinctly a warm weather crop, requiring 100 to 120 days of warm weather with a soil temperature of 65 to 80°F. Sweet potatoes can thrive on less moisture than any other crop that you will grow and still produce enormous yields under ordinary conditions of rainfall. They are grown along the east coast as far north as southern New York and southern Michigan, in the middle of the United States as far north as Illinois, and along the west coast all the way up to the Pacific Northwest. Needless to say, they thrive in almost all southern parts of the country.

Sweet potatoes do their best on sandy, warm soils, of medium fertility. However, they can be grown on heavier soils, especially when they are worked deeply and the soil is lightened by addition of leaves and grass cuttings, compost, or well-rotted manure. Well-rotted sawdust is also a good soil lightener. If the nitrogen content of the soil is too high, you may get lots of vines and leaves and not many tubers. Consequently, some gardeners do not fertilize for sweet potatoes when they follow a crop that was fertilized the year before.

Sweet potatoes are grown from "slips" or "draws" that are thrown off from their swollen roots. These sprouts are called sweet potato plants. They are grown commercially by specialists who capitalize on the habit of the sweet potato to throw off from its swollen root a "sprout" that develops from adventitious buds. These sprouts or slips are carefully detached from the tuber by removing the soil and grasping the stem at its base or point of attachment to the tuber. They are now ready to be planted in the field or in the garden. If you are not ready to plant them in a permanent location, they can be "heeled in" and kept for weeks. The best time to remove the plants from the tuber is when they are three to four inches high above the soil. If you have grown plants from tubers kept in a pan of water, wait until the potato has produced two to three dozen sprouts about six to nine inches tall, each bearing four to five leaves. Detach the plants carefully, either by pulling at the base or by cutting. You can grow sweet potatoes from larger plants, but the smaller ones are easier to set out and have a better rate of survival. As soon as you remove one crop of sprouts or plants from the tuber, it immediately starts producing a second crop, which will reach plantable size in about eight to 14 days. The tubers sometimes produce a third crop. Under favorable conditions, they are a veritable gold mine of reproduction.

Culture

Prepare the planting site well in advance of actual planting. You cannot obtain top quality and high yields unless you ridge the soil. The height of the ridge should be at least ten inches to provide a well-worked, friable soil for good root development and for easy harvesting. Work the soil to a depth of eight to 10 inches and then do one of the following: Spread a two-inch layer of compost or well-rotted manure in a six-inch-wide band where the ridge will center. Or spread about five pounds of 3-18-18 (or similar low nitrogen and high potash fertilizer) to a 100-foot ridge. Rake the compost, manure, or fertilizer into the surface of the soil and mix it to reduce the concentration. Then, using a hoe or rake, draw up the soil from either side of the fertilized bank to form a ridge 10 to 12 inches high and about the same width. Subsequent rains will settle and firm the soil until its height is reduced by two to four inches. When the time arrives for sweet potato planting—about a month after the last frost—or when the soil temperature reaches 65°F or more, set the plants 12 to 15 inches apart in the middle of the ridge. Use a 12- to 15-inch length of broom handle to make the hole to set the plant and to space distance between plants. Set the plants about 1/2 inch deeper than the bleached part, cover halfway, and then pour a cup of water around the plant to settle the soil and to eliminate any air pockets. When the water is absorbed by the soil, finish filling the hole and packing the soil around the plants. After the plants become established in the ridge, hoe lightly and cultivate the sides and tops of the ridge to keep down weeds and grass. Gradually build up the size of the ridge by pulling soil up from the sides and around the plants. Sweet potatoes, like beets, always want to expose the tops of their roots. For best growth and top quality, it is necessary to remove soil from between the ridges or from the sides of the ridges up and around the base of the plants. Try to work them at least two or three times during the first six to eight weeks. The vines grow to lengths of eight to 10 feet, four to five feet on each side of the ridge, so culti-vate frequently in the early stages, lifting the vines to prevent rooting at the joints, and hand weeding as required. When plants begin to reach maturity, the entire area will be shaded and covered with leaves and vines, and no further cultivating can be done. Do not be concerned about the vines intermingling with other plants and vines. They are compatible and do not handicap cucumber, squash, peppers, eggplant, tomatoes, and many others.

Harvesting and Storage

There is no surface indication as to when the tubers reach maturity. When you think they are big enough to dig, 90 days or so from the setting of plants, investigate by digging a hill. A spade or shovel is excellent for this purpose. If you are satisfied with the size of the tubers, proceed with your digging; if not, investigate each week thereafter. It is generally conceded that frost-blackened vines pass undesirable juices back to the tubers. If an early or an unexpected frost blackens your sweet potato vines, either harvest the potatoes immediately or else cut all vines at their base. If possible, dig your sweet potatoes on a clear, dry day when the soil is not wet enough to cling to the roots. Do not expose the roots to the direct rays of the sun for more than one or two hours. As you dig, place them in ventilated wooden or plastic containers about the size of a bushel. Then move them to an area where the temperature is 75 to 90°F and spread them out on the floor, or on tables or benches where air can circulate freely around them. This drying or *curing* process enables them to lose a lot of moisture and gets them into condition for subsequent long-term storage, preferably at temperatures ranging between 50 to 65°F. You should allow 10 to 18 days for curing. After curing, store the sweet potatoes in cardboard boxes in the coolest area of your home or in another area with a suitable temperature range—never below 45° and never above 70°F. They should not be stored in a damp place. Outside ventilation is desirable when weather conditions permit.

When harvesting, do not toss the tubers into the containers. They bruise very easily and rot soon thereafter. Place them into the containers as if you were handling fresh eggs. On all subsequent handling use the same care. Discard or use immediately all tubers that are cut or bruised during the harvesting. No other crop is so easily damaged by careless harvesting and rough handling. Do not handle and do not move them until you are ready to eat them or place them on the market. You may get the impression from the foregoing that you are dealing with the prima donna of the vegetable world. Not so. When properly harvested, handled, cured, and stored, they are easily kept in prime condition for periods of nine to 12 months. The most important point about growing sweet potatoes is that they may be enjoyed all winter long and make a significant contribution to your year-round supply of food.

TOMATO
Lycopersicum esculentum commune

The tomato is easily grown and is a good source of vitamins A, B and C. It is probably the most popular and most widely grown member of the home vegetable garden. Tomatoes grow under a wide variety of conditions and require only a relatively small space for a large production. Of tropical American origin, the tomato does not thrive in very cool weather and will not yield good fruits of top quality in areas having cool nights or long periods of foggy weather. Tomato plants will bear and ripen fruit in 45 to 90 days after they are planted in the garden. Tomato plants are probably more tender than any other garden plants in general cultivation and are blackened and set back by the least touch of frost. They grow well only where there is plenty of heat. Despite their tenderness and their love of heat, tomatoes will grow in almost any kind of soil, so long as they receive direct sunlight for most of the day. Talk to a dozen gardeners about tomatoes and you will likely get a dozen different ideas on planting, feeding, pruning, spraying, etc. All of the ideas are workable and will produce good crops. This is good evidence of the versatility of the different varieties and their ability to adapt to various types of soil, fertilization, and the whims of individual gardeners.

Culture

Plants purchased locally are adapted to your locality and are desirable if you do not want to start from seed. When buying, select strong, sturdy plants. Short, thick-stemmed plants are much more desirable than long, spindly plants.

In setting a plant into the ground, use a trowel to make a generous-sized hole and set the plant deeply (about two-thirds of it in the ground), filling soil around the stem carefully so as not to injure the roots. There are several advantages in planting tomatoes deeply. Roots form rapidly all along the buried stem and make for quicker and more vigorous growth. Long or taller plants are better supported when planted deeply. However, carefully "pinch off" all side branches and leaves from the part of the stem to be buried in the soil. When the hole is half full of soil, pour a cup of water around the plant to settle the soil and to eliminate air pockets. A cup of starter solution poured around the plant at this time is very beneficial in giving the plant a boost in its new location and offsetting the shock of transplanting. If frost or freezing weather is expected or forecast *after* you have set out tomato plants, protect them overnight with cardboard boxes, buckets, baskets, paper bags, or "hot-kaps" placed over the plants. This temporary covering will prevent the plants from being injured or retarded by frostbite. Remove the covers during the day.

You can get exceptional results by using a shovelful of well-rotted cow manure in the hole where the plant is set. Make the hole about six inches deeper than required for regular planting. Place the manure in the bottom of the hole and tamp it down firmly. Sprinkle a handful of 10-10-10 or steamed bone meal on top of the manure and mix it into the manure by pouring all the water into the hole that the manure will absorb. Now cover the manure with three or four inches of topsoil and firm it to ensure good capillary action. Try to have about two to three inches of soil between the roots of the plant and the manure. Then go ahead and set the plant just as you would if there were no manure beneath it. When the roots grow enough to reach the manure, the tomato plant will "suddenly" start growing vigorously, and it will continue to show exceptional vigor throughout its life cycle.

You can stake the plants and tie them to the supports at regular intervals to prevent undue sagging. You can surround the plant with a cylinder of wire about 20 inches across, made from a length of concrete reinforcing wire. Drive two short stakes into the ground on opposite sides of the wire cylinder and tie it to them. Alternatively, you can let the plants sprawl on the ground. If you let them sprawl, mulch with spoiled hay or other organic material to keep your tomatoes away from damp soil and its tendency to cause rotten spots. We urge you to try all three systems in order to choose what is best for you and least expensive. Six plants—two each way—would enable you to decide in one growing season. The only way to determine what you prefer is to give it a try. Gardening is just like engaging in any other productive activity—to get best results you must do a bit of experimenting and try some different approaches. Do not rely on someone's enthusiasm or "best" method; instead, find out for yourself and have the fun of making your own discovery.

Tomato fanciers like to divide the varieties into *early* (45 to 60 days), *midseason* (60 to 75 days), and *late* or main crop (75 to 90 days). However, there is a generous overlapping of these groups, and size of the fruit does not determine number of days from planting to maturity.

Distances between plants depend on the variety used and on whether the tomato plants are to be pruned and staked. Staked plants should be 18 inches apart in rows three feet apart. Plants growing unsupported and left to sprawl should be planted three feet apart in rows four to five feet apart. Do not hesitate to experiment with closer planting—sunlight, plant nutrients, and adequate moisture are more important than wide spacing between individual plants.

Tomato plants staked with a wire cylinder to hold them off the ground so the fruit does not rot. The grass mulch around the plants controls weeds and conserves moisture (USDA photo)

Harvesting

To get the best flavor and color, harvest tomatoes after they are fully ripe. If tomatoes are picked green, they can be ripened at temperatures between 55 and 75°F. Light will increase the color of tomatoes somewhat, but light is not essential to ripening. When tomatoes are placed in direct sunlight, the added heat often deteriorates their quality.

Just before the first frost you may harvest the remaining green fruits and let them ripen on a bench or other area where temperatures range between 55 and 75°F. Green tomatoes are also used to good advantage in making green tomato marmalade, green tomato mincemeat, and piccalilli. You can wrap them individually in pieces of newspaper and store them in cardboard boxes, being careful not to bruise them and not to store defective fruits. They will usually ripen in one to six weeks, depending on their degree of maturity when harvested and the temperature of the area where they are stored.

Disease Control

Two of the most common tomato diseases occurring in home gardens are fusarium and verticillium wilts. They are caused by fungi that live in the soil. Before the development of resistant varieties, gardeners were urged to plant in a different plot each year; this is still a good idea. The best control, however, is to grow one of the resistant varieties. Spraying or dusting is ineffective in controlling either of the wilt diseases. As soon as you spot a diseased plant, pull it up, getting all the roots, and either burn it or seal it in a plastic bag for later disposal.

Blossom-end rot is the most troublesome fruit rot for the home gardener. It is caused by a calcium deficiency and is aggravated by any kind of drought stress on the plants. Calcium, in the form of finely ground dolomitic limestone, will help prevent blossom-end rot. It must be applied before tomatoes are planted.

Do not become worried about fusarium and verticillium wilts and blossom-end rot. Chances are that your tomato plants will be healthy, strong, and vigorous, and will produce lots of fruits. However, it is best to know that such things do exist and can occur. This knowledge should encourage you to exercise due care in selecting superior varieties of disease-resistant plants and seeds.

Determinate and Indeterminate

When reading the descriptions of different varieties of tomatoes, you will encounter the two terms above. *Determinate* means that the terminal growth is stopped by the production of a terminal flower (and fruit) cluster. Such plants bear nearly all their crop at one time, a distinct advantage in short-season regions. This distinguishing trait is most desirable for all crops grown commercially for canning, catsup, and juice.

Indeterminate is a term used to describe tomato plants in which terminal growth is not prevented by flower (and fruit) clusters at the apex. Such plants grow and bear until frost, a distinct advantage to the home gardener.

Some varieties have plants that are semi-determinate, which continue to yield fruits long after determinate varieties have stopped bearing.

Hybrid

Each seed of a hybrid tomato is a controlled cross by hand of two distinct parent lines. This produces a hybrid of extreme vigor, more uniform in growth, with bigger yields and better quality.

Hybrid tomatoes are such strong, vigorous growers and have such ability to outyield regular varieties that they must be fed more. To produce a maximum crop of large fruit, maintain good fertility and moisture in your soil.

Recommended Varieties

There are hundreds of varieties and strains that have been developed for flavor, yield, shipping qualities, canning, catsup, juice, and slicing. If this is your first season of growing your own, select the most promising of local varieties and get advice from an experienced gardener, local nurseryman, or your county extension agent. The following varieties are grown throughout most of the United States and are considered best for their intended use: Ace VF, Atkinson, Beefmaster, Bellarina, Big Boy, Bonanza, Burpee's Big Early Hybrid, Burpee Hybrid, Burpee VF Hybrid, Cal-Ace VF, Campbell's 1327, Caro-Red, Climbing Triple Crop, Colossal Hybrid, Cura, Delicious, Double-rich, Droplet, Earliana, Everbearing, Fantastic Hybrid, Fireball VF, Firesteel, Floradel, Gardener's Delight, Giant Beefsteak, Glamour, Gurney's Crimson Giant, Gurney's Golden Giant, Gurney's Vigor Boy Hybrid, H-1350, Homestead 24, Jetstar, Jubilee, Manalucie, Manapal, Marglobe, Marion, Monte Carlo, Morden, Morton Hybrid, Moscow VR, Nemared, New Yorker, Nichol's French Primabel, Nichol's Kurihara, Oxheart, Paul Bunyan, Pinkdeal, Pixie, Ponderosa, Porter, Ramapo, Red Glow, Red Pear, Rex-Chico, Rockingham, Roma VF, Rushmore Hybrid, Rutgers, San Marzano, Saturn, Small Fry, Spring Giant, Springset, Starfire, Sub-Artic, Sugar Lump, Sunray, Sunset, Supercross, Supermarket, Supersonic, Tiny Tim, Tropic, Twilley's Market King, Twilley's Red Glow, Twilley's Red King, Twilley's Selected Rutgers, Venus, VFN-8, Walter, White Beauty, Wonder Body VF, and Yellow Plum.

Growing Tomatoes

The following ideas will afford you many happy hours of productive effort with your plants. Your tomato crop and your gardening know-how can be vastly improved by intelligent experimentation.

Insect Control

Flea Beetles: These are many species, varicolored, brown, black, or striped; also called jumping beetles. They are small, about 1/16 inch long, and they attack beet, eggplant, potato, pepper, tomato, spinach, turnip, radish, and cabbage and related crops. Young plants, especially transplants, are severely damaged; the leaves look as if they had been shot full of holes. You can eliminate them with a dust or a spray containing carbaryl.

Hornworms: Green, two species, diagonal lines on sides, prominent horn on rear end; up to four inches long. They eat the foliage and fruit of eggplant, pepper, and tomato. On light infestations you can hand-pick the worms. If damage is heavy, apply a dust or spray containing carbaryl.

Tomato Fruitworm: When this insect occurs on corn, it is called corn earworm. It can be green, brown, or pink with light stripes along the sides and on the back; up to 1-3/4 inches long. Fruitworms eat holes in fruits and buds. Control is same as that for hornworms.

Other hazards are stalk borers, aphids, leafminers, spider mites, and stink bugs. However, just as we said about disease, you should not be too concerned about insects. Healthy, disease-resistant plants are more than a match for inroads made by insects on a normal scale.

Seeding Outdoors: In areas with a long growing season, tomatoes may be started in a seedbed in the garden. Work the soil into a fine, friable condition and sow the seeds about two inches apart, covering with about 1/4 to 1/2 inch of fine soil, gently firmed. Keep the soil moist until the seeds germinate. When seedlings are about 2 or 2-1/2 inches tall, with a second set of leaves, either thin them to stand at least three inches apart each way or transplant them to their new location in the garden. Thinned plants may be left in the seedbed until they reach heights of one foot before transplanting.

Seeding Indoors: Throughout the northern half of the United States, the growing season is likely to be too short for heavy tomato yields; it is desirable to increase the length of the growing season by starting tomato plants indoors.

Sow the tomato seeds six to eight weeks before the plants are to be transplanted into the garden. This should be no earlier than the frost-free date in your area. You can sow seeds in a flat (5 X 10 inches with a three-inch depth—with seeds one inch apart) or in any improvised container that you can provide with drainage holes. Half-gallon milk cartons make good flats. Wash them out thoroughly. Lay the carton on its side with spout up and cut out the top panel with a sharp knife. Close the spout, and either staple or punch a nail hole through the flap and tie together for a more firmly holding flat. Cut small drainage holes in all four bottom corners, and puncture the sides and bottom with a small nail to provide additional drainage. You have many options for starting mixtures to use in the flats. Loam or sandy top soil, sand, shredded sphagnum peat moss, vermiculite, compost, and perlite may be used in various combinations to start seedlings.

Some of these combinations are one part compost–one part sand–two parts topsoil; one part vermiculite–one part topsoil; one part peat moss–two parts sand; one part peat moss–one part vermiculite–one part perlite. Alternatively, you may sow the seeds in small, individual peat pots, which are made of 85 percent peat and 15 percent wood fiber to which soluble fertilizer has been added. You can plant the pot and ensure less root disturbance and a fast start in your garden.

Various prepared mixtures for starting seeds are available commercially. However, the only item that you need in order to mix a thoroughly dependable starting "medium" mixture is vermiculite. It is a sterile, seed-growing medium obtained from a mica-like ore. It is light in weight, retains moisture, and permits good plant aeration. It eliminates damping off. It keeps soil from compacting and allows roots to spread and form a strong root system. Seedlings are easier to remove, without injury, from a mixture containing vermiculite. It is relatively inexpensive, does not wear out, and may be purchased in garden centers and many other places.

When seeding into flats, place seeds about one inch apart and cover with 1/4 to 1/2 inch of the mixture. This is best done by pressing each seed 1/4 inch deep until you have planted the flat. Now cover the top with 1/4 inch of vermiculite. Now take a glass or other object with a flat bottom and press down on the vermiculite, firming it into the mixture and bringing the seeds into good contact with it.

Watering: Set the newly seeded pot or flat into a pan of tepid water. Do not put too much water into the pan, because you want the flat to absorb from the bottom without water pouring into the flat from the top. Let it sit in the water until you see the vermiculite or planting medium become wet. Adequate watering for germination has now been attained. Again, with a flat object, gently firm the vermiculite into the soil. As soon as the flat stops dripping, cover it with a plastic wrap or slip the container into a plastic bag and close it. This covering is to reduce evaporation and provide miniature greenhouse conditions of high humidity for rapid germination. As soon as the seeds germinate, in five to ten days, you must remove the cover, because the young seedlings require air and light. The flat should be kept in an area with a temperature of 70 to 80°F and out of direct sunlight until the seeds germinate. Hybrid varieties especially need plenty of warmth. After the cover is removed, gradually expose the seedlings to direct sunlight for the first few days. Seedlings grow strongest at 60 to 70°F. Then let them have the sun all day long. Sun will dry out the flat, so water when necessary from the bottom, and do it thoroughly. The plants will lean towards the sun, so turn the flat daily to keep the seedlings growing straight. When the seedlings are about two inches tall and have a second set of leaves, it is time to transplant them into other flats to give them adequate growing space.

Transplanting the Seedlings: Space the seedlings three inches apart each way. Tobacco mosaic virus is transmitted by direct contact, and smokers should wash their hands and tools before touching or handling plants. Do not smoke while handling tomato plants. Water the seedlings to be transplanted in order to have some of the soil adhere to the roots when they are removed from the flat. Use a sharpened wood pencil to dig down near the seedling and gently lift it out. Make a hole in the new flat big enough to accommodate the root structure without forcing the plant into the hole. Grasp the plant gently by the leaves when transplanting. Even slight pressure on the stem can cause permanent injury at this stage of growth. Lower the plant in the hole to the same depth as it grew before and firm the soil gently around each plant. When the flat is filled, gently water the plants from the top to settle the soil and eliminate any air pockets. Transplanting of young seedlings should be done as carefully and as gently as possible in order to minimize the shock of root disturbance to the plant.

Hardening Off: Plants can be hardened off in one week, but a period of two weeks is less of a shock and will give them a better start when they are set out in your garden. This "toughening up" process is done to acquaint an indoor plant with the outdoor environment. Start by moving the flats to a cooler section of your home. Then gradually reduce the amount of watering. Start the outdoor conditioning by exposing the plants outside for about two hours, avoiding direct rays of hot sun and windy spots. Double the outdoor exposure time each day and continue to cut down the watering. Check the appearance of your plants closely while conditioning them to the outdoors. If they appear to be suffering from shock or exposure, slow down the process and take whatever action is indicated to harden them off successfully.

Special Varieties: In choosing varieties to grow in the home garden, you should study their descriptions in various seed catalogs and be very discriminating. The fruits may be orange, pink, red, white, or yellow and the shape may be round, rectangular, plum-shaped or pear-like. Disease resistance is indicated by the initals "F"—fusarium; "N"—nematode; "V"—verticillium. The initial "H" means a hybrid variety. Most hybrids have been developed for increased yields and disease resistance. By all means, grow and compare both hybrid and standard varieties.

Doublerich: The experimental station at the University of New Hampshire developed the Doublerich Tomato. It has much, much more vitamin C content than other tomatoes and is aptly named nutritionwise; it is a bonus to the home gardener.

Caro-Red: Another "special" is Caro-Red, which was developed at Purdue University by research personnel of the agriculture experimental station. The meat of this tomato has a distinctive orange-red color. Caro-Red is ten times richer in vitamin A than ordinary varieties.

Sunray: Compares well with best standard red varieties, but its flavor is preferred by many. Fruits are a bright golden orange.

Oxheart and Ponderosa: These are large pink tomatoes, having small seed cavities, and a delightful mild flavor.

Roma VF: A superior paste-type tomato with resistance to verticillium and fusarium wilts. Produces large crops of bright red plum-shaped fruits with very meaty interiors and few seeds. Excellent for paste or canning whole; also used to give more body to tomato juice.

Tiny Tim: Truly a midget in the world of tomatoes. Plants grow only 15 inches tall and are covered with 3/4-inch, brilliant scarlet tomatoes. The plant can be grown anywhere—in the garden, in a pot on the porch, or in a window box.

Gurney's White Beauty: When ripe, turns from green to ivory white. If you like tomatoes, but are troubled by their acidity, this is the tomato for you. It is so low in acid that it could almost be called subacid. Large-sized, fine flavor, and used for slicing, canning, and juice.

Yellow Plus: A productive, small, fleshy tomato, the size and shape of a plum with lemon-yellow skin.

Mulching: There is no question that you can grow fine tomatoes *without* mulching. However, during periods of infrequent or spotty rainfall, a good layer of spoiled hay or other organic material will conserve ground moisture, stabilize soil temperature, and completely eliminate weeds. These three functions will considerably lessen your work load in the garden and will usually result in more uniform fruits and better yields when the weather is both dry and hot. A two- to four-inch layer of organic mulch, applied *after* the soil is warm and both day and night temperatures are high, will invariably prove beneficial to your tomato plants. Snug the layer of mulch up close to the base of the stem; you are preparing a layer of insulation, and the smaller the breaks in it, the more effective it will be. Mulch should extend for a distance of 12 to 24 inches from the stem, all around the plant. On sprawling, unstaked plants, a layer of mulch two to three feet wide around the plant will keep fruits clean and conserve maximum soil moisture.

Stone Mulch: Small rocks may be used to trap heat from the sun, and its subsequent release during the night may ward off the effects of a late frost on your young transplants while extending the life of your plants in the fall, when an unexpected early frost will kill them. The ability of stones to absorb and trap heat in the daytime and then slowly to release it during the night means that your plants enjoy the benefits of a local, miniature, heat-regulating system. To mulch with stones, start with those that are two to three inches wide and place them within about half an inch of the base of the stalk. Extend the stone mulch to a width of ten to 12 inches all around the plants. The closer the fit of the stones against each other, the better their insulation and consequent soil temperature and moisture stabilization. Fewer cracks mean fewer weeds. Needless to say, earthworms enjoy living under rocks, and their presence greatly enhances soil bacteria development and provides much better aeration of the soil.

Newspaper Mulch: Five or six layers of newspapers will last all season and effectively control weeds, conserve moisture, and stabilize soil temperature. Overlap the layers about six inches and hold them in place with stones, soil, or small pieces of lumber. Weeds may be placed on top of the papers and especially around the sides and ends of the layers to hold them in place.

These three ideas on mulching barely scratch the surface and should encourage you seriously to consider the use of mulch throughout your garden. Mulch can be defined as any material spread on the ground around plants to prevent loss of water from the soil, to control weeds, to stabilize soil temperature, and to prevent freezing of roots. In addition, organic mulch also adds humus and plant nutrients to the soil. However, because of its convenience and serviceability, plastic mulch is used almost exclusively by commercial tomato growers.

Trickle Irrigation: Leading growers of tomatoes in southern Florida reported dramatic gains of as much as four tons per acre, with significant gains in size and quality, at the end of their first season of commercial experience with trickle irrigation.

The systems were based on Dupont's new "Viaflo" porous plastic tubing for both fall and winter crops. The south Florida growers buried the tubing under the plastic mulch covering tomato beds. When pressurized at three to four psi, the half-inch polyethylene tubing begins to weep water through micron-sized pores. The tubing delivers a steady cone of moisture to the plant root zone, replacing overhead sprinklers, which have been used in some areas, or a flood-and-seep irrigation system common in other parts of the state.

One grower finds that the drip system cuts water consumption drastically. About 100,000 gallons per week is needed to irrigate a 50-acre block of tomatoes, compared with more than 900,000 gallons weekly with over-head irrigation in an adjacent block. Trickle irrigation also results in additional savings from more efficient use of fertilizer and better control of disease.

Trickle irrigation is the most exciting recent development for vegetable growers; early studies also show promise on peppers. Snap bean, sweet corn, potato, and other commercial growers are looking closely at trickle irrigation tomato plots. Trial plantings are already underway.

These facts concerning the enormous benefits derived from trickle irrigation vividly point up the need for you to provide a continuous supply of moisture to your tomato crop.

Cutworm Protection: An occasional cutworm will cut down one of your young tomato plants. They can easily be located within a six- or eight-inch circle around the plant stem, usually within the top 1/2 inch of soil. However, it is best to frustrate the cutworm with a bit of prevention. The cutworm wraps its saw-toothed body around the plant stem to cut it down. A slender stick or piece of coat hanger wire about five inches long pushed into the ground about two inches, parallel to and touching the plant stem, will extend up about three inches. The stick or wire is effective and prevents plant loss to this pest. They are not able to anchor themselves to the stem in order to accomplish their deadly cutting. Coat hangers are always available, and the wire rods can be used for several seasons.

Pruning: Staked tomatoes appear to bear larger fruits when they are pruned during early growth to not more than three main stems. Some growers advocate the removal of all sucker growth—small shoots that appear at the point where the leaf stem joins the main stem. The theory is that these excess growths take energy from the plant and yield nothing in return. However, if you prune too severely and remove too much growth, your fruits will get sun-scald and in drastic cases your plants will lose their vigor. It is well to bear in mind that the fruits do not need direct sunlight to ripen. It is recommended that you limit your experimentation with pruning to not more than three plants, initially, and determine for yourself whether or not to continue with this phase of your experience with advanced culture of the tomato. There is no doubt that a little bit of pruning at the proper time will do much to help produce fine yields of quality tomatoes on strong, vigorous plants. But take it easy.

Staking: Staking makes it easier to cultivate and harvest tomatoes, and helps prevent fruit rot from contact with wet soil. However, staked plants are more subject to losses from blossom-end rot than plants allowed to grow naturally. If you plan to stake your tomatoes, sink the stakes into the ground soon after transplanting to prevent root damage. Insert stakes four to six inches from the base of the plant and imbed them deeply enough that they will not topple over when the plants get tall and are loaded with fruit at all stages of growth.

There are many types of support: single or multiple wooden stakes, wire cages or cylinders, wooden cages or racks, and wire and wooden fences and trellises. However, the simplest and least expensive method of staking is the single wood stake or pole that is about eight feet long and about 1-1/2 inches wide. Stakes should be imbedded 12 to 18 inches deep, depending on whether the soil is heavy or light. There are many ways to tie the plants to the stakes when they get weighty and start to climb. Here is one good method. Tie strips of soft cloth (old sheets and old nylons are excellent) tightly around the stake two to three inches above a leaf stem, then loop the strip of cloth loosely around the main stem just below the base of the leaf stem, and tie with a square knot. As the plants grow taller and fuller, it will be necessary for you to add additional ties and maybe adjust or change the position of some of the lower ones. It will not take you very long to gain enough experience to see when ties need to be added or repositioned.

Fertilization: Compost, or well-rotted manure placed in the hole beneath the plant and laced with a handful of 10-10-10 (as described under "Culture") will carry the plant successfully through its complete cycle.

Scant top dressings of 10-10-10 at three-week intervals throughout the fruiting season are beneficial to plants that have not been fertilized *beneath* the root structure at time of setting out in the garden. Plants are just like people in that they require continuous nourishment for peak performance.

Top dressings of steamed bone meal at the time of setting plants in the garden last for long periods and result in a continuous supply of the phosphorus on which tomatoes thrive.

Fish emulsion provides good nutrients for tomato plants and should be mixed and applied according to instructions on the label. You will find that fish emulsion is very effective in boosting the growth of young transplants and in encouraging growth of top-quality fruits all season long.

Seaweed is a complete, natural fertilizer containing all the "trace elements." Dried out, it can be used as a mulch or readily dug into and mixed with the soil. If you can obtain it, by all means use it.

Any organic matter that will decompose can be used to feed the soil that will feed the plants. The simplest method is to bury it in the garden.

Cottonseed meal and liquid manure can be used at regular intervals to provide nutrients for your tomato plants.

We could go on "ad infinitum" with this discussion on various methods of fertilizing tomato plants. However, it should be obvious by now that tomato plants will respond generously to many different methods and types of feeding.

Your primary concern should be to fertilize as often as needed for strong, vigorous plant growth coupled with top yields of quality fruits. It is well to bear in mind that an overfeeding of nitrogen will give your plants excessive growth of foliage with a corresponding reduction in fruits.

Feeding and Watering Circles: If you want to be certain that you can grow a good supply of top-quality tomatoes with a minimum outlay of fertilizer, time, and water, then you should seriously consider the many advantages of this idea of planting tomatoes around the outer edges of a 30-inch diameter circle.

By setting from four to eight plants around the perimeter of a 30-inch circle you not only conserve planting space, but you also provide a common feeding and watering area for all plants in the circle.

First, establish dimensions on the ground of the outer 30-inch circle and then remove the soil from an inner circle to a depth of 10 to 15 inches. Leave a marginal band of soil eight to 10 inches wide between the excavated area and perimeter of the outer circle. Later, you will set your tomato plants just outside the center of this band of topsoil. Now, fill the excavated area about three-quarters full with a 50-50 mixture of cow manure and topsoil lightly laced with 10-10-10 or similar fertilizer. Or use compost that is lightly laced with a balanced fertilizer. The reason for not filling in the center to a level area is to provide a depression that will hold about six gallons of water. This depression in the center of the plants prevents any runoff and waste, while at the same time enabling you to gauge the amount of water that your plants are getting.

Whenever you wish to water all the plants in the circle, merely fill the depression (watering hole), and the resulting seepage to nearby areas will satisfy the moisture requirements of all plants in the circle. When you wish to feed the plants directly with liquid manure or liquid fertilizer, all that you have to do is pour it into the center of the circle. You will soon realize the efficiency of this unique plant feeding and watering arrangement; then you will probably curtail your inclination to overfeed your plants.

This circular planting lends itself to individual staking or to group support in large wire cylinders—or plants can be left to sprawl and grow naturally. Whatever method you choose, a good mulch, preferably organic, will control weeds, conserve moisture, and stabilize the temperature of the soil.

Circular planting works equally as well for eggplant, peppers, summer squash, cantaloupes, celery, and cucumbers. Of course, there is no reason why it would not be a good way to grow all of your vegetables in an area of scant rainfall where the gardener *must* irrigate regularly.

Growing Tomatoes in Containers: Tomatoes are very easy to grow in containers, and a number of varieties have been developed especially for this purpose. The containers are easily moved from sun deck or patio to breeze-way or garage—or even into any room of your home.

The same sensible ideas for growing tomatoes in your garden also work for those grown in containers. The main ingredients are a suitable container (small varieties can be grown successfully on a gallon of soil, whereas the larger varieties require twice this much) and a suitable growing medium, which can be topsoil, topsoil with 50 percent vermiculite or perlite or any of the synthetic soils. The sterile, synthetic mixes are almost foolproof for the container-growing of vegetables, because they cannot become waterlogged if your container has the requisite drain holes. You cannot expect to have strong, vigorous plants that produce good yields of quality fruits unless you start with a container of adequate size and then feed and water your plants on a regular schedule. Plant roots spread easily throughout the container and make maximum use of plant nutrients and available moisture.

The container can be a plastic pail, a metal bucket, a bushel basket, a small, deep box, or almost anything that will hold the "soil" and not absorb all the moisture and nutrients. Naturally, good drainage must be provided at the bottom.

Because of the restricted area in which container plants grow, it is nec-essary for you to water and feed them regularly. Watering is best accom-plished by use of a liquid fertilizer or plant nutrient. This feeding of the plant should be with a weak solution, but it must be done regularly to ensure strong, vigorous growth and good setting of the fruits. Furthermore, tomatoes require lots of sunshine, plus an even, warm surrounding temperature.

The following varieties are especially adapted for container growing:

Tiny Tim (55 days). Plants grow about 15 inches tall and are covered with 3/4-inch tomatoes; fruit is brilliant scarlet and fine-flavored.

Burpee's Pixie Hybrid (52 days). Pixie grows 14 to 18 inches tall and bears heavy loads of bright scarlet, smooth, attractive fruits about 1-3/4 inches in diameter.

Early Salad Hybrid (45 days). Produces hundreds of bright red 1-1/2 inch fruits on a compact plant six to eight inches tall with a spread of two feet.

Blossom Drop: Home gardeners often find that blossoms drop off pre-maturely and the fruit fails to develop. Blossom drop is caused by (1) cold temperatures, (2) hot temperatures, or (3) excessive nitrogen fertilization. Nothing can be done to remedy the situation, and you can only wait for later flowers to produce fruit. Rarely does a plant continue to drop its flowers.

FLAT FOR TOMATO SEEDLINGS 10 X 6 X 3 INCHES

	1	2	3	4	37
	5	6	7	8	38
	9	10	11	12	39
	13	14	15	16	40
	17	18	19	20	41
	21	22	23	24	42
	25	26	27	28	43
	29	30	31	32	44
	33	34	35	36	45

Leave a small space between the sides and the bottom for drainage and for watering from the bottom.

A single packet of tomato seed contains more than enough seeds to provide plants for at least two home gardens. Hybrid varieties will have 30 to 50 seeds per packet, and standard varieties will contain about a hundred. You can count on at least 75 percent germination, and extra plants are a bonus when you lose some when transplanting or from other causes.

TURNIP
Brassica rapa

Turnips have been cultivated for over two thousand years and are still one of our least appreciated vegetables. There are three major reasons why turnips should be grown in *every* home garden: (1) *Its food value.* The turnip root is outstanding as a source of vitamin C and supplies carbohydrates, B vitamins, and minerals. It also supplies fiber, which is so vitally necessary for proper functioning of the lower intestinal tract. Turnip greens (the cooked leafy turnip tops) are an excellent source of vitamins A and C, as well as calcium. (2) *Its storage qualities.* Turnips can be kept for months in an above-ground earthen mound, in moistened sand, or in cans, bins, or boxes surrounded by straw. They keep best at a temperature just above freezing with a high relative humidity. All you have to do to get them ready for storage is to pull them (preferably, when they are about two-thirds full size) and cut off the tops (leaving about one inch of the stems). Do not wash or bruise, and store only perfect turnips. Of course, they can be left in the ground and will survive light snows and short periods below freezing. A thick mulch of spoiled hay or leaves, held in place with pine branches, chicken wire, or rocks will enable you to remove turnips from the soil in which they grew all winter long. Pine branches alone provide enough mulch for light snows and mild winters. (3) *Its ease of cultivation.* Turnips are one of our hardiest vegetable plants and have only two real enemies, root maggots and flea beetles. Furthermore, you may grow turnips for several years before root maggots and flea beetles appear on the scene. You can evade the root maggot by growing your turnips in a different place each year or each growing season—this is crop rotation. The flea beetle is easily controlled by frequent cultivation and the virtual elimination of weeds in and around the garden.

Culture

Turnips do well in almost all parts of the United States, and when planted in succession after another crop, they require no additional fertilizer. Cold-hardy, they may be grown in the spring and fall. In the spring, sow the seed as soon as the ground can be worked. Grow them in a row: make a very shallow furrow, drop the seeds very thinly in it, and cover with 1/8 to 1/4 inch of soil. When the plants are up and growing, thin to stand two to three inches apart. The thinner the original sowing of seed, the less work required in thinning. Shallow cultivation and a slight mounding of soil over the roots coupled with weed control will give you better-quality turnips in quicker time.

Another popular way to grow turnips is to broadcast the seeds onto a smoothly prepared seedbed and then rake it lightly to cover the seeds. However, the percentage of germination is so high and the emerging seedlings so vigorous that you can get a good stand of turnips by thinly scattering the seeds along an eight-inch-wide band (row) of well-raked soil and then simply walking on them in order to trample them into the loose soil. This trampling will bury them in the loose soil and firm the soil around them to ensure good contact of soil with seed and assist germination. For successive harvest of top-quality young roots and a continuous supply of tender greens, make two or three sowings at two- or three-week intervals.

Recommended Varieties

Turnips are at their best when growth is made during cool weather. Plant early Purple-Top Milan (45 days) and Tokyo Cross (35 days) in the early spring for their roots, and Foliage or Shogoin (30 days for greens) for their tops, which are popular for "greens." Sow any variety in late summer for fall use or storage of roots for a winter vegetable. Frost improves the flavor of foliage turnips.

4

Additional Vegetables For Your Garden

ASPARAGUS

Asparagus is a perennial and one of the earliest spring vegetables. It is a prolific, tall grower—5 to 6 feet tall—with many reed-like stalks emanating in a tight cluster from a central crown. In late summer and fall these stalks are covered with dozens of thin, light, branching stems bearing fern-like leaves and literally loaded with pretty orange-red berries or seed pods. Once a "patch" is established, it requires very little maintenance to remain very productive for fifteen or twenty years—some gardeners contend, for a lifetime. It does best in areas where winter temperatures get down low enough to freeze the surface of the soil. However, asparagus is grown very successfully by home gardeners in Florida. Their success is due to initial care in preparing the bed. The light, sandy soil is fortified with more than liberal quantities of animal manures, compost, and leaves dug in to a depth of two feet or more and thoroughly mixed with the soil, with a follow-up program of constant mulching with organic residues, such as oak and pine leaves intermixed with grass clippings.

Asparagus does well on nearly any fertile, well-drained soil. It is a rich feeder and will not produce the quick-growing, tender shoots one is looking for unless properly planted.

In selecting a site to establish an asparagus bed, you should stay clear of trees and off to the side of the regular garden plot, so as not to interfere with its cultivation. As early as the ground can be worked in the spring, re-move the soil from an area as long as you intend to make the row. A fifty-foot row will provide for a family of four. Make the planting trench 15 inches deep and 18 inches wide. Fill the bottom of the trench to a depth of six inches with manure, compost, well-rotted leaves, or peat mixed with topsoil.

Asparagus shoots ready for cutting (USDA photo)

Now lightly cover this area with a balanced fertilizer (10-10-10), using five to ten pounds for a fifty-foot row. Now thoroughly soak the area to settle the filling and to start off with adequate moisture *beneath* the plants. Cover with about four inches of topsoil and trample down firmly for good capillary action. Now you are ready for planting. It is well to use one-year old plants, or crowns of a variety that is resistant to asparagus rust, such as Mary or Waltham Washington. Set the crowns 18 inches apart and spread the roots well apart. Cover the fleshy roots with two or three inches of fine topsoil and firm it well. If the soil is dry, sprinkle it down to remove any pockets of air around the roots. When shoots poke through the soil (in two to three weeks), cover them lightly again; repeat this covering process until the trench is filled. It is advisable not to rush this filling of the trench, or you may tend to stifle the growing plants. If you are planting more than one row, the second should be spaced four to five feet from the first.

The proper site selection and careful, deep preparation of the planting trench are of inestimable value, because the powerful, fleshy roots will thrust their way downward as much as five feet and spread laterally an equal distance in searching for nutrients needed for sustained yields.

Cut none of the stalks the first year. They are needed for growth and nourishment of the crown and roots. A modest cutting of shoots may be made during the first four weeks of the second season; then allow the foliage to develop. Starting with the third season, you can harvest the shoots or spears for about eight to ten weeks, or until they become thin. When the spears become thin, it is evident that the food stored in the roots is nearly exhausted, and harvesting should stop immediately.

Asparagus spears are ready for use when five to eight inches long. Bending the spear over sharply until it breaks is the way to avoid injury to other shoots under the ground. With a little practice you will "snap" them off easily and forget about the cutting. When spears first appear above ground, it may take as much as three days for them to reach the size for harvest. However, as the soil warms up and growth increases, it will be necessary to cut once or twice a day.

In the fall, when the foliage turns brown, cut the stalks at ground level and burn them. This procedure will practically eliminate damage that is done by the asparagus beetle. The beetle is thus deprived of a concealed location in which to overwinter. When they cannot survive during the winter in the asparagus stalks, none are around to attack the young emerging spears in the springtime.

As is the case with all vegetables, do not let weeds rob your asparagus of nourishment and moisture. Since the tall, wiry bush is rather brittle, cultivation should be frequent, and the area should be kept weed-free until about the middle of July. After this, the plants' foliage will fill the row. Naturally, a heavy mulching of spoiled hay (six to eight inches) or other organic mulch will eliminate the need for weeding and cultivation and will conserve moisture in the soil. This practice is highly recommended.

A twice-a-year feeding program must be followed in order to have a good yield of thick spears. Make the first application of a complete fertilizer early in the spring before the start of new growth. Apply it in the middle of the rows or about one foot on each side of a single row. Rake or rototill it into the top two inches of soil. If applying compost or manure instead of fertilizer, use same procedure. Then, as soon as the harvest is over, make a second application of fertilizer, compost, or manure in order to assure heavy top growth and accompanying storage of food in the roots.

Each year new storage roots are formed on the uppermost side of the crown. This new growth causes the crown to continually move upward toward the surface. As a result, the soil is too shallow over the crown, and the shoots tend to open before they are long enough to harvest. Even if you are satisfied with unbleached asparagus, you will find it necessary to ridge or mound soil to a depth of 3 or 4 inches over the crowns. This buildup of soil over the row of asparagus is easily accomplished by drawing up soil from both sides with a hoe or rake—but take care not to expose or damage roots. If you have enough compost available, merely build a ridge over the row and reap the benefits of bleached shoots while adding additional plant nutrients to the soil.

BRUSSELS SPROUTS
Brassica Oleracea gemmifera

This peculiar member of the cabbage family is referred to as "thousand-headed-cabbage" or simply "sprouts." It is usually a single-stalked, stout plant with most of the leaves clustered at the top. The sprouts or buds grow thickly around the stem and vary in size from one to two inches in diameter. A good healthy plant will produce 60 to 90 sprouts that are the equal of broccoli and cauliflower in flavor and tenderness.

Brussels sprouts are primarily a fall and winter vegetable, and the best flavor is not attained until after a few sharp frosts. The sprouts are delicious fresh or frozen and are a good source of vitamins A, B, and C.

Culture

The same as for late cabbage. Sow the seeds in an outdoor seedbed about the middle or latter part of May. The plants should be six to eight inches tall in about eight to ten weeks and ready to transplant to rows that should be about two feet apart. Space the plants about 18 inches apart in the rows. Pinch off a few of the lower leaves while setting the young plants in the row. This means less plant for the root system to feed and tends to lessen the shock of transplanting. Any good, fertile garden soil will grow good sprouts if the plants are top dressed with 34.5-0-0 or nitrate of soda about two weeks after transplanting. Use one-half pound of 34.5-0-0 and one pound of nitrate of soda per 100 foot of row. Of course, well-rotted cow manure, hen manure, or compost will do a good job for this top dressing and should be applied at two- or three-week intervals when it is available. Frequent, shallow cultivation, especially after rains, is necessary to conserve moisture and control weeds. Brussels sprouts require lots of moisture and will not thrive in dry hot weather. Although you cannot control the temperature, you can certainly supply the water during periods of inadequate rainfall.

Harvesting

Sprouts or buds should be picked when they attain the size of a walnut or golf ball and before they change color. Always pick the lowest sprouts first and remove the lower leaves to alleviate some of the crowding. The buds develop at the leaf base, and their growth is stimulated by breaking off most of the lower leaves when they begin to form. Leave an inch or so of stump for stalk protection. Never disturb the cluster of leaves at the topmost part of the plant, as they are vital to its nourishment.

Winter Storage

When near-zero weather, or snows, threaten your unharvested sprouts, use a spade to remove the plants with lots of soil clinging to their roots and put them in a cold frame or a box and see that the roots are covered with soil. Store the boxes in a garage or shed where they will keep cold but not freeze. Pick and use the sprouts before they deteriorate. Storing plants with sprouts attached will prolong your season for this crop.

Recommended Varieties

Jade Cross Hybrid (80 days). We urge you to try this easy-to-grow hybrid. The rich, blue-green, firm "sprouts" are packed in tight rows on plants almost two feet tall.

Long Island Improved (Catskill—90 days). Round, dark green, tight buds are produced along the central stalk of plants growing to 20 inches.

CANTALOUPE
Muskmelon

The canteloupe, like all members of the melon family, does best in soil that is light and somewhat sandy. Planting should not be attempted until the soil is warm and days are warm and sunny.

To prepare the hills for planting, remove four shovelsful of soil and dump two shovelsful of well-rotted manure into the hole. A handful of 10-10-

10 scattered on top of the manure adds to the available plant food. Trample it down and cover with five to six inches of well-firmed soil. Space the hills or groups four feet apart each way. Plant eight to ten seeds per hill and cover with one-half inch of fine soil, firmed gently for good seed contact. Seeds are best spaced in concentric circles two or three inches apart. When the young plants are about four inches tall, thin out and leave the three strongest plants in each group.

Cultivate soil lightly to keep down weeds and provide a dust mulch to retain moisture.

To determine if a melon is "vine ripe," lift it or slightly turn it and see if the stem breaks away. To harvest for roadside markets or shipment, the "full slip" method is commonly used. This means that you can break the stem away cleanly with slight pressure. Pay particular attention to the way you detach the first few melons from their vines, and you will soon become quite an expert at harvesting them. Needless to say, those fully vine-ripened possess mouth-watering flavor. Their delicious flavor is fully retained when quick frozen.

Recommended Varieties

Burpee's Ambrosia Hybrid, Bender's Surprise, Cantaloup Charantais, Honey Dew Green, Burpee's Hybrid, Iroquois, Super Market Hybrid, Honey Rock, Samson Hybrid, Sungold Casaba, Early Crenshaw, Far North, Edisto, Saticoy, Queen of Colorado, Big Gurney's Mammoth, Schoon's Hard Shell, Golden Champlain, Chaca Hybrid, Harvest Queen, Samson F_i Hybrid, Honey Mist, Golden Beauty Casaba, Minnesota Midget, Luscious, Delicious, Tam-Dew, and Hale's Best Jumbo.

CAULIFLOWER

Cauliflower is often thought of as being difficult to grow. This idea, no doubt, stems from the fact that it is insistent with its demand for good, fertile soil containing a high percentage of nitrogen. Quick, vigorous growth is necessary for full development of the cauliflowers. Soil fertility can be enhanced by the plowing under of a green manure crop and/or the generous use of compost. One or two scant top dressings of 34.5-0-0 will greatly assist in vigorous, rapid growth.

Most evidence points to fall as being the best time for the main crop. However, with adequate care, spring planting can be highly successful. For a main or fall crop, sow the seeds rather thinly in a specially prepared seedbed or cold frame about four months before your first expected frost. Thin out from time to time to allow ample room for development. It is important that cauliflower seedlings not be allowed to become crowded in the plant bed.

A good head of cauliflower on a plant mulched with hay (USDA photo)

When plants are ready to be set in the garden, space them 1-1/2 to 2 feet apart, in rows 2-1/2 to 3 feet apart. It is *imperative* that the plants be kept in a healthy growing condition until heads are formed. Any stunting of growth due to lack of moisture or low fertility will definitely result in a poor and disappointing crop. Deep watering during dry spells is easy to accomplish by making shallow furrows between the rows and providing enough water for deep irrigation of the soil adjacent to the plants.

Spring planting will necessitate the starting of plants in flats or a hotbed. If you have never worked with cauliflower, it may be worthwhile for you to buy a half dozen or more plants from your local seed outlet and get acquainted with its cultivation. There is nothing like a bit of experience to give you that all-important confidence factor.

Recommended Varieties

Snow Crown Hybrid, Snow King Hybrid, Danish Giant, Metropole, Purple Head, Burpeeana, White Princess, and Early Snowball. All of these varieties mature, from plants, in 58 to 85 days.

CELERIAC

Celeriac, or turnip-rooted celery, has been developed for the root instead of the top. It is sometimes called *knob celery*. It has a flavor similar to celery and is good boiled or in vegetable soup, stews, and other dishes. It may be grated and eaten raw or used in green salads. Its flesh is white, and the edible portion is the large, thick root, which may be used when it has grown about two inches across.

Celeriac matures in about 120 days. However, half-grown roots may be harvested at a much earlier time. The culture is *exactly* the same as that for celery. Transplant the plants outdoors when they are four to six inches tall. For the main or fall crop, sow in the open ground as early in the spring as the soil can be worked. Transplant the main crop into the permanent rows during July. Since celeriac does not develop leafstalks and requires no blanching, it is a bit easier to grow than celery. For hand cultivation, the plants can be grown six inches apart in rows that are 18 inches apart.

Fully grown roots should average four inches in diameter. Roots are easily stored and keep well. For winter use, gather the roots when they are two to four inches in diameter, and store them in a cool, frost-proof cellar or similar storage area.

CELERY
Apium

Many gardeners consider the growing of celery to be too difficult for them to undertake. However, this thought can be put aside if they will take a few simple precautions. Celery is a very heavy feeder, and in addition an abundant supply of moisture must always be present in the soil. To achieve rich soil, spread four to five wheelbarrow loads of well-rotted manure to a 100-foot row. This will add plant food and humus for more water retention in the soil. Since celery is such a gross feeder, it is advisable to add about six pounds of 5-10-10 to this same 100-foot row. This manure and fertilizer should be thoroughly mixed and dug into the soil; take care to work the soil quite deeply, to a depth of 12 to 15 inches. Celery will not thrive unless the soil is neutral in its pH range, or on the "sweet" or alkaline side. Consequently, if you suspect your soil to be acid, test it for the pH factor and use lime to bring it above the neutral line. A pH factor of 7.5 is considered ideal by many growers. Lime is the universally accepted material for sweetening soil (raising the pH). Five pounds of finely ground limestone will raise the pH of 100 square feet of soil three-quarters of a pH point. This is equal approximately to one ton of lime per acre.

In order to get the variety you prefer, it will be necessary for you to grow your own plants. Start the seed in a flat indoors about the first of March. The sowing of seeds should be about eight to ten weeks before you plan on setting the young plants into their permanent location in the garden. Fill the flat about three-quarters full with a finely sifted mixture, made up of two-thirds flaky leaf mold and rich topsoil, thoroughly mixed with one-third of clean washed sand. Good drainage must be provided in the bottom of the flat. Alternatively, you can use a sterile growing medium (synthetic soil) that is usually prepared from vermiculite and peat moss. Germination of celery seed is slow, and many fail to germinate at all. Soaking the seeds in a cotton cloth in water for 24 hours will greatly enhance germination. Space the seeds as evenly as possible one-half inch apart. Cover the seeds very evenly to a depth of 1/16 to 1/8 inch with a careful sprinkling of clean, washed sand. Firm gently with the bottom of a glass or a small flat board to ensure good contact of sand with seeds. Bottom-water the flat by placing it in a container holding enough water to reach halfway up its side. Let the flat remain in the water until the layer of surface sand becomes damp. Keep the flat in an airy, sunny place, and do not let the surface dry out. Keep it moist, not wet and soggy. Seedlings should appear within 10 to 14 days. You must have additional flats ready to transplant the young seedlings when they are about four weeks old. These young seedlings are very delicate, and you should exercise great care in transplanting. At least one more transplanting, with the plants spaced even farther apart, should be done to give you stockier, more vigorous plants. When the plants are four to six inches high, with well-developed roots, set them out in the garden. Make a trench three to four inches deep and soak it thoroughly. Do not set plants any deeper than they were in the flats. Gradually fill in the trench as the plants grow. Set the plants five to six inches apart in the rows, and make the rows three to four feet apart. Clean cultivation and frequent watering are essential for thrifty plants. Never let the soil dry out to the point where the plants start to wilt. You must, however, strike a happy balance and not keep the soil so full of moisture as to induce plant disease and encourage mildew. All this means, of course, is that your celery requires close observation to be sure that it always has an adequate supply of moisture coupled with plenty of plant food. Many growers top dress with nitrate of soda or 10-10-10 every three weeks, starting two weeks after the plants are set out. No doubt, these additional feedings benefit the celery. Heavy rains and constant irrigation tend to leach plant nutrients out of the soil. Top dressing puts them back in.

In dry and hot areas you will find it most advantageous to plant celery in a circle and provide essential plant food and moisture from a "common" fertilizing and watering hole. Start with a 30-inch-diameter outside circle and then make an inside, concentric circle of 18 inches diameter. Remove the soil from the inner circle to a depth of 12 inches and replace with well-rotted cow manure or compost. Sprinkle the top generously with 10-10-10 or a similar balanced fertilizer. Now soak this area thoroughly, and you are ready to set out celery plants. Set eleven or twelve plants about eight or nine inches apart around the outer circumference of the 30-inch circle. As soon as the plants begin to grow in their new location, mulch them with some organic material to conserve soil moisture and to protect them from heat. Water as often as you deem necessary, and add a bit of a balanced fertilizer every two or three weeks to replace that which has been used for plant food and to ensure a continuous supply. Watering and fertilizing in the center of the circle of plants will ensure that each plant receives an equal amount of moisture and nourishment. This idea of a central feeding and watering reservoir is a great time- and labor-saver, and, obviously, leads to much more efficient utilization of both fertilizer and water. As the plants develop longer leaf stalks and additional leaves, they begin to shade the inner circle and create a much cooler area.

Tomatoes, eggplant, and peppers also thrive when planted in groups of four around a two-foot circle with a central watering and fertilizing reservoir.

Blanching and Harvesting

As the plants reach about two-thirds maturity, you can blanch as many as you want by placing boards alongside the row, on edge, and securing them in place by driving stakes into the ground on either side. Boards should not extend so high as to enclose the tufts or leaves—which would suffocate the plant. If you do not care to use boards, wrap the plants loosely, below the leaves, with four or five layers of old newspapers secured with strings or pins. The classical way to blanch is by mounding soil up around the plant 10 to 14 days before intended harvest. Tie plants together if they are too spreading. No soil should be allowed to fall into the heart of the plant. Alternatively, soil can be mounded gradually, as plants grow. It is a very good idea to try two or three methods to find out which one you prefer. There is no need to wait until full maturity before harvesting and enjoying your celery. Start using it when it is a month or more away from full growth.

Storage

Celery keeps well when placed upright in a trench dug deep enough to just let two or three inches of the top extend above the surface. Prepare a trench about one foot wide, of suitable depth, before digging the plants. Then dig the plants and leave about two-thirds of their roots intact. Stand the plants close together and firm the soil alongside the unfilled portions of trench. Before snow arrives, cover the trench with boards inverted to form a V-shaped roof. Celery also may be left in the row and covered with straw drawn close alongside and over the top. As the weather gets colder, you may want to increase the covering of straw or simply mound a bit of soil around the first application of straw to increase insulation.

Recommended Varieties

Burpee Fordhook (130 days). The best and finest-flavored fall and winter green celery. Excellent for fall use and winter storage. Stocky, compact plants, 15 to 18 inches tall.

Summer Pascal (120 days). One of the most popular of the green varieties. Blight resistant.

Giant Pascal (135 days). Has a rich, nutty flavor when earth-blanched. Stores well during winter by covering with straw or salt hay.

Tendercrisp (90 days). A new strain of the Utah 52–70 type. Grows to 24 inches with rib length of ten to twelve inches. Excellent for the home gardener.

Golden Self Blanching (115 days). Widely grown, early, yellow celery. Has a lighter color than Summer Pascal. Plants make a compact growth and form thick, ribbed stalks that blanch easily to a beautiful clear waxen yellow.

CELTUCE

This is a coined term suggestive of a cross between celery and lettuce. However, horticulturists agree that it is a derivative of lettuce (*Lactuca sativa*), probably an improved strain of the variety *asparagina*. Celtuce seeds were brought from Western China to America just before the outbreak of World War Two.

Celtuce combines the uses of celery and lettuce. Young leaves have four times the vitamin C content of head lettuce leaves. When plants are young, leaves may be used as lettuce or as "boiling greens," but its primary value is the heart of the central stem or stalk, which is eaten raw or cooked in the same ways as you would prepare celery.

The flavor of the edible stem is subtle and has been aptly described as a pleasant cross between a mild summer squash and artichoke. The flowering stalks attain a length of six to eight inches and a diameter of 1-1/2 inches. Outer skin of the stalk is greenish white, tough and woody. This outer skin must be peeled off before the pale green, crisp, delicate, heart of the stem is exposed and ready to be eaten either raw or cooked.

Culture

Exactly the same as that detailed for lettuce.

WITLOOF CHICORY
Cichorium itybus

Witloof chicory, or French endive, is a choice salad delicacy for fall and winter use. The main aim of planting chicory seeds in the spring is to produce tall, leafy plants with healthy root systems by fall.

Sow seeds in the spring in very shallow furrows and cover with not more than 1/4 inch of fine soil. Sow the seeds very sparsely, and when the young seedlings are up and growing vigorously, thin to stand six to eight inches apart in the row. It is a hardy plant and not especially sensitive to heat or cold. Any deep, well-dug soil, properly drained, with good fertility, is suitable for witloof chicory.

In early fall, dig the roots and cut the top off two inches above the crown to avoid damaging the crown buds. Trim the tips of the roots to a uniform length of six to eight inches and place them, with crowns up, in a vertical position in a box. Fill the spaces between the roots with fine soil and then thoroughly moisten the soil and roots. Now cover the crowns with six to eight inches of clean sand or a mixture of peat and sand. Keep the sand or mixture moist and keep the box in a warm, dark cellar or other similar storage area. Since the root and crown are forcing new growth through the sand, it is compacted, and the leaves are blanched because of the exclusion of light. It will take three to four weeks to produce heads that are four to seven inches long. The moisture and warmth must be provided continuously.

The main use of witloof chicory is for salads during the winter months. When forced* indoors, they produce crisp, creamy-yellow, blanched "chicons." These succulent, blanched chicons make one of the most delectable

---

*Forcing is the process of inducing a plant to grow faster than normal or out of its normal season. It is accomplished by use of extra heat, light, fertilizer, or moisture.

salads imaginable. They are also delicious when lightly steamed and served with appropriate sauces or seasonings.

CHINESE CABBAGE
Brassica pekinensis

The Chinese cabbage, or celery cabbage, is not related to celery and is more closely related to mustard than to cabbage. This plant is of Chinese origin and has few equals as a salad green. It may be served like lettuce or shredded for a delicious cole claw. It is tastier than ordinary cabbage when boiled. A handsome vegetable, it matures in 45 to 75 days, depending on variety, and grows well in all sections of the United States.

Culture

Chinese cabbage does best as an autumn crop, because it will *bolt* and go to flowers and seeds during the warmer days of late spring and the hot days of summer. Bolting is the term used to describe unwanted or premature production of flowers and seeds, often caused by deficiency of plant nutrients or excessive heat. It occurs in Chinese cabbage, lettuce, and other plants. Sow the seeds in the soil where it is to grow, as it is checked in its growth by transplanting. Sowings should be made in early spring or about three months before first frost in the fall. Space seeds quite thinly in shallow furrows and cover with one-half to one inch of fine soil. When seedlings are growing vigorously, thin to stand eight to ten inches apart in rows 12 to 18 inches apart. Surplus seedlings from thinnings can be transplanted. If you do sow in the spring, do it as early as possible in order to harvest the crop before hot weather sends it bolting. Chinese cabbage needs the same rich, fertile soil as cabbage crops and must have lots of water to ensure rapid growth. It is a rich feeder, and top dressings of well-rotted cow manure or a balanced fertilizer will ensure quick growth. If your soil is on the acid side with a pH rating below 7, lime should be raked into the soil to correct this condition. Chinese cabbage thrives best in neutral soil or one leaning slightly toward alkalinity.

Recommended Varieties

Burpee Hybrid (75 days). Giant cylindrical heads, up to 13 inches high, and eight inches across. The outer leaves are medium green, heavily savoyed, thick, succulent, and nicely folded over the top. The inner leaves blanch almost white.

Chinese cabbage is a desirable autumn crop in the northern states (USDA photo)

Michihli (70 days). Crisp, tender, and of good flavor, sure header, keeps
well. Heads grow 18 inches tall and up to four inches thick. Dark
green exterior. Leaves blanch pure white inside.

Crispy Choy Loose-leaved Chinese Cabbage (45 days). Grows compact
bunches of eight to 12 greenish-white stalks that are shaped like
celery, seven to eight inches tall. and topped by spoon-shaped leaves.

COLLARDS
Brassica oleracea acephala

Collards are rich in minerals and vitamins and are of major importance
in the South. They are a nonheading member of the cabbage family that can
take both the summer heat and the winter chill of the southern climes of the
United States. Collards are one of the oldest members of the cabbage family,

having been described by European writers in the first century. They have been a favorite in the South for over 300 years and are gradually moving northward as more and more gardeners become acquainted with them.

Culture

Cultivation is the same as for cabbage; collards are a rich feeder requiring plenty of plant nutrients in the soil plus an adequate amount of moisture. In the South sowing is done in early spring and midsummer. Farther north, sowing of seed is usually limited to once a year for fall and winter use. Just like kale, its flavor is improved by light frosts. Collards are easy to grow by sowing seeds rather thinly in shallow furrows and covering with one-half inch of fine soil. Firm soil gently for good contact—to assist germination. Light sprinklings late in the afternoon will greatly assist germination. Thin plants to stand 10 to 16 inches apart in rows 18 to 24 inches apart. Leaves are harvested as needed, when they are young and have small midribs. Thinnings can be used if seedlings are allowed to grow several inches tall before they are pulled. As bottom leaves are harvested and plants become top-heavy with their rosette of young leaves, an occasional plant may need staking.

Recommended Varieties

Georgia (Southern or Creole). (80 days). Tolerant of adverse soil and weather conditions. It attains a height of 30 or more inches and bears a loose cluster of broad, juicy blue-green leaves.
Vates (75 days). Low growing, thick, broad-bladed, grassy green leaves.
Louisiana Sweet (85 days). Thick, tender, short-stemmed leaves.
Morris Heading (85 days). Forms moderately tight head.
Cabbage collard (85 days). Forms small, cabbage-like heads and is resistant to hot weather.

COMFREY
Symphytum officinale

This little-known perennial garden green is loaded with food values that readily outstrip most of the vegetables that we grow from seed each gardening season. Comfrey is rich in vitamins A and C, calcium, phosphorus, potassium, and trace elements. It is one of the hardiest vegetable plants you will ever encounter and appears to be virtually immune to garden pests.

Comfrey is a strong-growing perennial with hairy leaves 10 to 18 inches long, rising from a central crown, on short, thick stems. Mature plants are about two feet high and will spread to as much as three feet.

The attractive dark green leaves have a protein content ranging from 20 to more than 30 percent. The high-protein content coupled with the rich, nutritive values, should influence your decision to make this easily grown, power-packed vegetable a part of your regular food supply.

When you have an excess of large leaves, bury them alongside any row crop for use as green manuring or instant compost.

Comfrey is such a prolific plant with such high-protein value that it is fed, with excellent results, to chickens, cows, ducks, geese, goats, rabbits, sheep, and swine. A variety named *asperum* grows to heights of five feet. It is also known as prickly comfrey, Quaker comfrey, or Russian comfrey. This variety produces a perennial fodder crop that can be cut—to within two inches of the ground—half a dozen times or more each season. Good growth on poor soil is possible due to a deep, powerful root system that penetrates the subsoil in search of nutrients and water.

Comfrey is quite versatile and can be used for boiling greens, like kale, mustard, and spinach. It also increases the food value and complements the flavor of other greens when mixed with them. The small, young, tender leaves can be cut finely and used in raw salads. For a different nutritive taste treat, combine with kale, mustard, or spinach, add some finely diced onions and sweet peppers, and then lightly sauté in oil. Tea with a wallop is made by mixing equal parts of dried comfrey and mint. Steep for about five minutes in an enameled or porcelain pot. Drink with honey as a sweetener. Like most foods, comfrey can be used in various combinations and will add to the nutritive content of broths, casseroles, soups, and stews.

Medicinal Uses

By now you are probably wondering if comfrey is an all-purpose plant. Well, it is, almost! It has been used for the treatment of skin lesions such as those caused by heat rash and poison ivy. The foliage is crushed and immediately applied so that the moisture comes into direct contact with the damaged tissue. Comfrey is also used in poultices to alleviate pain, reduce swelling, and promote healing of cuts and sores. Some of its curative properties have recently been traced to a substance called *allantoin*, which aids in new cell formation, thus assisting the healing process.

Culture

Comfrey is propagated from root cuttings, crown cuttings containing eyes or buds, and established one-year-old plants. Root cuttings are the preferred way to start, and you may order them for either spring or fall planting. They come in pieces that range from two to six inches long. Plant them in a flat or horizontal position three feet apart each way and cover with two to six inches of soil. In other words, plant shallow in heavy clay and a bit deeper in sandy or light loams. Firm the soil with your hands and water thoroughly to further settle the soil and eliminate any pockets of air. Of course, any plant or root cutting will send out rootlets and make new growth faster when it is surrounded with moist soil.

The roots are benefited by generous applications of compost or well-rotted manure, which is mixed with the soil near the plants. Unless you have an unlimited supply of compost or manure, it is best to restrict the soil enrichment to areas close to the plants.

Shallow cultivation, either by hand or machine, will help control weeds and provide a dust mulch for conservation of the moisture in the soil. Hand-pick all weeds close to the plants to keep them from stealing nutrients and water from the soil.

Harvesting

Spring-planted root cuttings will produce leaves big enough to cut in eight to ten weeks. They are at their best for fresh table use when the leaf itself—not counting stem length—is six to ten inches long. Either pull a bunch of leaves together or cut them off singly about two inches above ground with scissors. A clean cut is much better for the plant. After harvesting, the plants will put out new leaves and grow enough to be ready for cutting again in two to four weeks. This successive cutting followed by production of new leaves goes on throughout the entire season.

Drying

The leaves can be easily and quickly dried for use either by people or animals during the lean months of winter. Best information points up the fact that food value in the leaf is at its peak at the end of a clear, sunny day. This is the time to cut the leaves and spread them out on a grassy spot to dry. The leaves have a high moisture and protein content, which necessitates spreading them out to dry. If stacked or piled in layers, the leaves will quickly heat and spoil. Drying time will take from two to three days, depending on the relative humidity and temperature. When they are dry, pack in large cardboard boxes and store in any convenient dry area. You can store an incredible amount of dried comfrey in a very small space. Make sure the leaves are dry enough to be crumbly before you store them. Any remaining moisture will cause mold.

You can dry comfrey better, quicker, and long after heavy dews hinder the process by having a rack of small-mesh poultry netting up off the ground on which to place the freshly cut leaves for drying. Small quantities for table use are easily dried on window screens in the attic or similar areas.

Dried comfrey is valuable as a protein booster for broths, soups, and stews. Superb teas result from blending with mint and other herbs. Chickens and rabbits thrive on supplemental additions of dry comfrey to their regular food.

DILL
Anethum graveolens

Dill is an easily grown annual that reaches heights of two to four feet. The dry or green branches, stems, and seed are used to flavor pickles and vinegar. It is one of the most popular herbs and is good in salads, soups, and stews. It adds a distinctive touch to most vegetables and finely cut leaves and seeds are used in appetizers, most meat dishes, fish sauces, and salads.

Culture

As soon as frost is past and the soil begins to warm, make shallow drills not more than one-fourth inch deep in an area that gets full sun. Sow the seed very thinly and cover with one-fourth inch or less of fine soil. Firm lightly to assist germination. When the young plants are about three inches high, thin to stand six to 12 inches apart. Hand-pick the weeds and cultivate lightly to provide a light dust mulch for conservation of soil moisture.

Harvesting

As you cut stems and leaves from mature plants to use for pickling (or other uses), it is a good idea to top dress very sparingly to help the plants retain their vigor and produce more leafy stems. Do your cutting in the morning when they are still wet with dew. They contain more volatile oil, and are most aromatic just as the buds are about to open.

EDIBLE-PODDED SUGAR PEAS

Also known as Chinese or snow peas, sugar peas have the tenderness and fleshy-podded qualities of a green bean combined with the flavor and sweetness of garden-fresh peas. When they are young, cook them like snap beans, pods and all. At this stage, the pods are free of fiber, succulent, brittle, and stringless. These delicately flavored pods are a rich source of vitamins A and C, and have almost as much protein as meat. They are truly delightful when served with all kinds of fowl and seafood. They are especially delicious when used as "snow peas" in Chinese dishes. If pods develop too fast to cook whole, shell and use peas before they get too large.

Just like other peas, they are a cool-weather plant and lose most of their vigor and much of their flavor during hot weather. Pick them during a cool part of the day and immediately get them ready for freezing or table. Keep cool until cooked. Harvest them when the peas are about half developed in size, but do not shell as you would regular peas. Instead, cut pods into two or three pieces and cook peas and pods together. They are a real gourmet treat when steamed until just tender, seasoned, and served with butter.

Culture

The culture is the same as that detailed for regular peas on pages 87-88.

Recommended Varieties

Dwarf Gray Sugar (65 days).
Oregon Sugar Pod (68 days).
Burpee's Sweetpod (68 days).

ENDIVE
Cichorium endivia

This popular salad green is prized for the rosette of lacy, frilled leaves, which have a slightly pungent taste in early stages of growth. However, as the plants fill out, the inner leaves blanch and become sweet and tender. When the heads begin to form and get about two-thirds full size, draw the long outer leaves up around the head and tie them with strips of soft cloth to exclude sunlight. In two or three weeks cut and examine a head to determine if it has blanched enough to suit your taste.

Culture

Endive is grown in exactly the same way as lettuce and will respond to early spring planting and fall planting. When the young plants are well started, thin them out or transplant them to stand 12 inches apart in the row. It is best to make successive sowings of short rows every three weeks or so, instead of sowing more than needed and then neglecting to prolong the season by not making successive sowings. Blanching can also be accomplished by excluding the sunlight with inverted flower pots or other containers. Just be sure to provide for ventilation and to avoid scalding. Here, again, a bit of experimentation is in order for you to decide your own best method for blanching.

You may want to use some of the green, unblanched outer leaves to *add* flavor either cooked with other greens or in a mixed raw salad. These green leaves are rich in vitamins A, B, and C and should not be wasted simply because their pungent flavor may not appeal to you when they are served alone and raw. Use the green outer leaves instead of lettuce on sandwiches. They add color and flavor to bland soups and stews, not to mention nutritive value.

Late maturing plants can be dug up in the fall, with a good ball of soil around the roots, and placed in a dark, cool, unheated cellar or a darkened cold frame and kept for quite a while. In these cool dark, storage areas blanching is a natural function.

Recommended Varieties

There are many fine varieties to choose from. For example:
Green Curled (Giant Fringed Oyster—90 days).
Salad King (98 days).
Broad-leaved Batavian (90 days).
Endive is also called *chicory* in many areas, and the broad-leaved variety is marketed under the name *escarole*.

HORSERADISH
Armoracia rusticana

Horseradish is a perennial that has been grown for centuries to tickle the appetites of those who enjoy hot, peppy, pungent flavors. The grated root is beloved for its hotness and plays a role in cuisines throughout the civilized world. Freshly grated horseradish adds zest and flavor to stews, root vegetables, seafood, and to beef and pork dishes when served as an accompanying side dish. When the freshly grated root is blended with a white sauce, its versatility is greatly enhanced, and it is hard to surpass as a condiment for use with fish, beef, and pork dishes. The hotness and unique flavor is easily varied and controlled by the amount of white sauce with which it is combined. Consequently, it may be blended to please the palate of the most fastidious diner.

Horseradish rarely produces seed; when it does, they are likely to be infertile. The usual method of propagation is by crowns or root cuttings, known as *sets*. In propagating by crowns, a portion of an old plant, consisting of a piece of root and crown buds, is separated and planted in a new spot. If you are using roots for propagation, they may consist of small roots of a size for spring planting to furnish large roots for use in late fall or winter. Alternatively, you may plant a piece of a larger root that has been cut lengthwise to provide sets. The lengthwise cuttings should be four to seven inches long and about three-eighths of an inch thick—or thicker. These sets may be obtained from seedsmen—Maliner Kren and New Bohemian are the best-known varieties. They are easily grown in any good garden soil that is moist, fertile, deep, and medium heavy. The white root is shaped like a parsnip and produces several branches. The heavy stems are coarse and attain lengths of 20 to 30 inches, with large leaves that resemble dock.

How to Grow

Plant the sets, either small roots or cuttings, in the spring as soon as the soil can be worked. They must be planted with the thick, or larger, end up, either in an upright or horizontal position, 12 to 15 inches apart. Place the sets in the soil so that the upper end is two to four inches below the surface. Firm the soil around the set to ensure good contact and prompt growth. If the root is planted in a horizontal position, you must place it at a slight angle. Dig a hole long enough to accommodate the set and about three inches deep at one end, slanting to four inches deep at the other end. Place the set so that the thick end will be at least an inch above the smaller end. Cover with soil about two inches deep and fill in as the plants grow.

The taproot system is fleshy and will produce several laterals when grown under proper conditions. The roots are inferior and worthless during the summer months; consequently, none of the roots should be dug before October. Horseradish grows best after summer heat diminishes and the days begin to shorten. This is when you should make sure that adequate moisture and nutrients are available for vigorous, sustained growth.

Roots may be dug just before the ground freezes and stored for long periods in a dark, cool root cellar. The root is hardy, and many gardeners let it stay where grown, digging a few roots as needed. The fresh roots may also be grated or ground to form relish, which is then stored in glass jars. The relish has a comparatively long shelf life when stored in a dark, cool area.

Horseradish roots (and crowns) are quite hardy and may be planted in the spring or fall. Plants in the home garden can be allowed to grow from year to year, and portions of the root system can be removed as needed. Pieces of roots and crowns remaining in the soil throughout the winter season are usually sufficient to reestablish the plants in the springtime.

JERUSALEM ARTICHOKE
Helianthus tuberosus

Jerusalem artichoke is a member of the sunflower family. The name Jerusalem is a misnomer resulting from a corruption of the Italian *girasole*, meaning "turning to the sun." It also is known as sunchoke, Canadian potato, or American artichoke. It is not related to the green or globe artichoke botanically; neither does it bear any similarity in taste or appearance.

Jerusalem artichokes are similar to potatoes but contain no starch. They are exceptionally easy to grow and may be considered as a bonus vegetable that is ideally suited to a modern weight-conscious society. This artichoke is 100 percent starchless. It stores its carbohydrades in the form of inulin rather than starch, and its sugar as levulose, the way most healthful fruits and honey do. It has practically no caloric value. Because of these facts, medical authorities strongly recommend it as a substitute for other carbohydrates on the diabetic's menu, and in the diet of all who should or must restrict their starch and caloric intake. In addition to its nonstarch feature, it is a good source of some minerals and vitamins, particularly potassium and thiamine. It has a delicate nut-like flavor when eaten raw.

These artichokes are an invaluable source of fresh produce through the fall and winter. Leave them in the ground for safe storage. Even in localities where the ground freezes, a thick mulch to protect them from alternate freezes and thaws will ensure a winter-long supply of crisp, fresh, sweet tubers. They lose their platability quite rapidly if removed from the ground and handled like potatoes. However, they retain their flavor and crispness for two weeks or longer if dug, washed, sealed in plastic bags, and immediately stored in the refrigerator.

There are two strains of artichokes available to the gardener—the American and the French. The American strain is quite knobby but does not have as many crevices or dirt-holding crannies as the French. The best method for table use is to dig them not more than three or four days before intended preparation and let them soak for about five minutes in a bucket of water to loosen the dirt. Then scrub with a vegetable brush or an old toothbrush. They are very easily cleaned. Rinse and store, while still moist and damp, in a plastic bag in the refrigerator. Never peel Jerusalem artichokes for either raw or cooked eating or recipes, inasmuch as their skin is paper-thin. It is worth repeating that Jerusalem artichokes are a delicately flavored, nutritious vegetable high in food value and rich in vitamins. They are easy to grow and will not fail in either a wet or dry season. They are relatively pest-free. They can be prepared in any way that you would potatoes—plus many more, including its use as a sweetmeat. They can be substituted for water chestnuts in all

Oriental and other recipes using this item. It can become one of your staples, comparable to beans, rice, potatoes, or bread, and an unfailing mainstay for your winter menu.

Culture

Jerusalem artichoke tubers can be planted as early in the spring as the ground can be worked. They can also be planted as late in the spring as you wish. The only criterion is to have about 120 days before the first frost—to allow them time to produce full-sized tubers. They can also be planted in the fall, up until the time of the last heavy frosts. They are perennial and will sprout early in the spring when left in the ground. Incidentally, they retain their crispness and delicate flavor until the sprouts are several inches long. They will grow in poor soil. However, they produce bigger and better tubers when planted in well-fertilized, deeply cultivated soil. Plant small tubers whole and cut the larger ones in two or three pieces before planting. Plant the tubers four inches deep and 12 to 15 inches apart, in rows that are 36 inches apart, or more. Firm the soil over the tuber. Mature compost and well-rotted manure dug into and well mixed with the soil at planting sites will ensure top production of tubers. You may use a scant amount of 10-10-10 or similar balanced fertilizer in a three- or four-inch deep pocket within about four inches of the planted tuber for all the additional plant food it will need. You will only get to cultivate once or twice before the foliage fills most of the space between the rows. A hilling or mounding of the soil around the base of the plants—similar to that done for potatoes—is beneficial. However, do this early in the season before the plants get so tall as to make it difficult or impossible. Weeding by hand will prevent the weeds from stealing the food your artichokes need.

The individual plantings will send up one to twelve stalks, which attain a height of 10 to 12 feet. About 75 days after planting the flowers begin to appear. Your plants will be loaded with yellow, daisy-like flowers that are fragrant and pretty. These flowers last for several weeks, and when they die, the tubers in the ground have reached maturity. After the first frosts we like to cut the stalks just above the ground and shovel a bit of soil on each hill for additional protection until dug. Strong winter winds, especially after a ground soaking rain, will occasionally topple a cluster of stalks and partially expose some tubers. When this happens, immediately shovel a six-inch layer of soil onto them. The stalks and leaves make a good contribution to the compost pile or to leaf-shredding operations.

Tubers for planting may be ordered from several leading suppliers to home gardeners. It is well to bear in mind that these artichokes are disarmingly easy to grow, pest-free, withstand drought as well as excessive rains, and rarely, if ever, fail as a main crop. They are rich in vitamins, high in food value, and contain inulin and levulans, which are easily hydrolyzed to levulose, a natural sugar. They can be left in the ground and harvested as needed, all winter long.

MUSTARD
Brassica juncea

This is the species most frequently grown in home gardens. Mustard greens are one of our very best leaf crops. The young leaves make a delicious and sharp addition to raw salads. Mixed with kale, young beet tops, or young turnip tops, they make the finest "boiling greens," and the food value is extra high.

Mustard is cold-hardy and can be grown anywhere in the United States. It is essentially a short-day, cool-weather crop that should not be planted to mature during the hottest part of the year. However, a variety known as Tendergreen is heat and drought resistant.

Culture

Mustard withstands light frosts and should be sown as early in the spring as the ground can be worked. You can plant again around the first of September for fall use. Make shallow furrows, 12 to 16 inches apart, and sow seeds rather thinly, covering with 1/4 inch of fine soil and firm lightly to assist germination. Thin to stand four to six inches apart. For quick growth and tender leaves the young plants need fertile soil and adequate moisture. A ten-foot row followed by successive plantings about four weeks apart will produce enough greens for a family of four. Experience may cause you to lengthen the row slightly or to decrease time between plantings.

The nutritional value of a cup of cooked greens borders on the unbelievable. It contains over 8000 international units of vitamin A, more ascorbic acid than that found in an average orange, some of the B vitamins, and significant amounts of calcium, iron, and phosphorus.

Most of the complaints about mustard being too hot, tough, or peppery are directly traceable to the way it is harvested and used. Never allow the leaves to grow to full size. Pick the leaves when they are four to six inches long; this is when they are the most tender and flavorful.

Use any surplus mustard to feed poultry or rabbits. If some of the leaves get much larger than you prefer, try steaming them until just tender and serve with melted butter. This method will eliminate most of the hot taste.

If the crop is so large that some of it bolts and goes to seed, you can still profit from it. Wait until the pods dry and then collect them before they shatter. Save an ample supply of seeds for next year's crop. If you select seeds from your best plants, you can develop an improved strain that is ideally adapted to local climatic conditions. Seeds are removed from pods by hand over a suitable container or a piece of old sheeting. Of course, you can flay and winnow if you have enough seeds to warrant it.

Surplus seeds can be put through a home flour grinder to make your own mustard condiment. After grinding they may be used either dry or wet. Experiment with small amounts blended with water and vinegar to suit your taste. The storage life dry, in tightly sealed containers not subjected to temperature extremes, is for several years. When mixed with water and vinegar, it will keep for months in tightly sealed jars under good storage conditions.

Harvesting

Again, we repeat that leaves should be harvested before they grow over six inches long. Use all the plants that you pull when thinning. If circumstances compel you to use much larger leaves, steam until just tender and serve with melted butter. Mustard greens are easily prepared for freezing and retain most of their nutritive value if small leaves no longer than six inches are picked and properly processed.

Recommended Varieties

Florida Broad Leaf (43 days). Desirable for "greens" because of the ease of preparing the leaves, which are broad and smooth. It is harder to remove dirt and grit from leaves of varieties that are curled and fringed.

Tendergreen (35 days). A rapid-growing mustard with large, broad, thick, dark green leaves, which have a flavor like that of spinach.

Southern Giant Curled (40 days). A curled mustard for spring or fall planting.

Fordhook Fancy (40 days). Deeply curled and fringed dark green leaves that curve backward like ostrich plumes.

PEANUT
Arachis hypogaea

The peanut is a native of Brazil and was carried by early explorers to the Philippines, whence they soon spread to China, Japan, and India. The

Portugese explorers took peanuts from South America to Africa. Plantation records of the eighteenth century discuss peanut cultivation in Virginia. Wherever they were introduced into new parts of the world, peanuts were instantly recognized for being pleasing to the palate and a ready means of satisfying one's hunger. Peanuts are one of the original "convenience foods," in that they require no preservatives or other additives to retain their flavor and highly nutritious food value over a long period of time. They have always been enjoyed in their raw state in addition to being cooked and roasted.

Peanuts are easy to grow, easy to roast, and easier to eat. Some people regard them as being strictly a southern crop. No doubt this idea stems from the fact that most of our commercial crops are harvested in Virginia and states farther south. However, peanuts are successfully grown as far north as New York and the Dakotas.

Roast peanuts in their pods, in an oven preheated to 300°F, for about 20 minutes. Residual heat will cause the nuts to continue cooking after removal from oven. Therefore, it is best to start out by underroasting them. Experiment with the timing until you get them exactly the way you prefer them.

Make your own peanut butter by running the roasted peanuts through the meat grinder until you get the consistency you want.

Culture

Peanuts like a warm sandy loam that is well prepared. If your soil does not have a good mixture of organic material, or if it is a bit on the heavy side, turn in a generous application of compost, leaf mold, or well-rotted manure. Make the furrows about two inches deep and plant the nuts, shell and all. Space them about 12 inches apart in rows two to three feet apart. Place two shells in each spot. If you want to experiment, plant four kernels, shelled nuts, in each group 12 to 18 inches apart. Cover to a depth of one to two inches and firm soil lightly to ensure good contact. Plant peanuts after the last frost and when the soil has begun to warm up—about the same time that sweet corn is planted.

When plants are about six inches tall, begin cultivating to control weeds, conserve moisture, and aerate the soil. When the plants have attained about 12 inches, mound or hill the soil high around the plants as you would hill potatoes. This hilling of the soil is extremely important for the production of peanuts. The lower leaves are discarded as the branches grow, and in their place long, pointed slender shoots (peduncles) appear and force their way into the mounded soil as they grow. Peanut pods are formed at the tips of each peduncle. After mounding, an 8-to-10-inch mulch of spoiled hay or leaves and grass clippings between plants will relieve you of any further cultivation for the season. Furthermore, each rain will leach nutrients from the mulch and carry them down to the plant roots for better feeding.

Harvesting

To allow for full growth, it is best to wait until heavy frosts destroy the leaves. Loosen the soil all around each plant with a spade or garden fork and then lift each bush carefully out of the ground and shake off the soil. Check the hole for any peanuts that may have broken off. You can hang the entire plant, with peanuts attached, in a dry, airy building to cure, or they may be placed on racks or poles to dry. Another method is to pluck the pods from the roots as soon as the plants come out of the ground. Place the pods in shallow trays or on the floor in any available dry area for their curing. This curing will take about seven to nine weeks. After curing, the peanuts should be bagged and stored in a cool, dry area—naturally, the storage area must be rodent-free. They keep well in this type of storage for at least a year.

Pick out some of the largest and best-colored pods for seed to plant next year. These nuts are better than any that you can buy for the simple reason that they are adapted to your soil and the local climate. This successive selection will enable you to develop a strain ideally suited to your particular conditions.

Recommended Varieties

Jumbo Virginia (120 days). A productive, extra-large peanut of rich flavor with one or two large kernels to a pod. Vines spread 3-1/2 feet across.

Spanish (110 days). Kernels are small and sweet, with two or three to the pod. The dwarf bushes grow close, so they are easily culitvated and harvested. A heavy bearer and widely grown.

NC-2 (112 days). Virginia type with dwarf plant habit. Bunches pods in clusters near tap root.

POPCORN
Zea mays everta

Popcorn can be ornamental in addition to providing a healthful, pleasant snack for both children and grownups. Popcorn has smaller ears than sweet corn and very hard pointed kernels that explode when heated. Corn, of course, is native to the Americas; it is thought that this variety was first popped because the kernels are so hard, even when fresh, that that was the only way to make it edible.

There are several varieties of popcorn with startling differences between them. For example, Black Beauty has jet-black kernels that pop open into bright white, tender popcorn. Hybrid South American Mushroom has orange-yellow kernels that pop to white kernels that are large, tasty, and tender. Strawberry Ornamental is a double-purpose popcorn that is highly decorative for floral and table displays and is also a good popping variety. It is called "strawberry" for its delightfully tiny mahogany red ears. Calico has brilliantly colored ears that make fine fall decorations in addition to popping well. The colors range from white to black through yellows to blues and dark reds. The Calico variety is a favorite with children around Halloween.

Culture

The culture is exactly the same as that detailed for sweet corn on page 105. Good pollination depends on a block of at least four rows. For example, you should *never* plant a single 60-foot row. Instead, plant four 15-foot rows, side by side. However, you may want to experiment a bit from season to season; the following planting variations will give you excellent stands: (1) Lay off rows three feet apart and dig up a hill and plant three seeds to a hill, spacing the hills three feet apart. (2) Plant in rows, spacing seeds eight to 10 inches apart, rows three feet apart. You will gain absolutely nothing by planting farther apart. In fact, popcorn has a tendency to produce "suckers" when planted too far apart on fertile soil. Suckers are abortive attempts to produce extra ears or spurs but do nothing except drain or sap the stalk's vitality.

Your stand of popcorn should be planted at least 50 yards from the nearest field corn or sweet corn in order to avoid cross-pollinization and the resultant mixture, which will not be true popcorn. If you cannot get the required distance between field, or sweet corn and popcorn, you can avoid cross-fertilization by planting your popcorn 10 to 15 days earlier than the other two varieties. Popcorn is not very subject to seed-rot and withstands cold much better than field corn. Needless to say, cross-pollinization will ruin both crops.

Control of weeds will let your popcorn get more nutrients and moisture. If, by chance, some large weeds become established near your cornstalks, do not pull them out of the soil and loosen the roots of the corn. Instead, cut the weeds off at the base with a sharp knife or pruning shears. During dry weather, corn will die when the soil and roots are loosened.

Do not hesitate to plant pole or climbing varieties of beans on either side of the hills or groups—in line with the row. Plant the beans any time after the corn is about one foot high. Popcorn matures in 85 to 120 days and is always left standing a few weeks after the ears mature for them to dry on the stalk. Consequently, the stalks provide excellent support for the beans.

It is only natural for you to plant the variety of your choice—whether for ornamental use or for eating—regardless of the size of the ears. However, the short-eared varieties will definitely give you less yield. The hybrids are excellent and produce larger yields with bigger ears.

Harvesting

After the stalks have turned brown, your popcorn has matured. Pull back the shuck and try to pierce the kernels with your finger nail. The corn has not cured enough to harvest until the kernels become too hard to pierce or penetrate with a finger nail. The next test is to try to "shell" an ear. When it is cured and dry enough to shell, it is ready to be harvested. The best-quality popcorn appears to be that which is harvested as soon as the ears become "shellable." However, frost will not hurt your popcorn at this stage, and any delay in harvesting will have a neglegible effect on quality.

It is a good idea to go through your patch a second or even a third time to pick the ears that you missed on the other trips through.

Never, never cut the stalks and shock your popcorn; it needs unimpeded air circulation for curing.

Store the ears in well ventilated baskets, bins, or boxes in order to avoid natural heating, which damages popping qualities and the food value. Your popcorn can be shelled at any convenient time after harvesting.

The experts say that the corn pops best when it has 12 to 13 percent moisture content. In lieu of scientific testing, we recommend that you test it in a frying pan or a corn popper. If it pops well, it is ready to be stored in airtight containers. In the event that some of your popcorn becomes too dry to "explode" to the expected volume, add a small amount of water to the kernels in a fruit jar and tightly seal for about 48 hours to allow absorption of water.

You can store and hold popcorn for three years or longer by placing it in gunnysacks and hanging it from the overhead in a ventilated attic, breezeway, garage, or barn. There will not be a perceptible loss in quality when it is properly stored, on the ear, in this manner. Of course, you should make periodic checks to determine that it is not deteriorating.

Recommended Varieties

Hybrid South American Mushroom (105 days).
Hybrid Gold (120 days).
South American Hybrid Yellow (100 days).
Giant White Hybrid (100 days).
Minhybrid 250 White Hulless (95 days).

PUMPKIN
Cucurbita

Pumpkins and squash have been crossed and hybridized to the extent that their exact identity is often in doubt. However, all technicalities aside, it is easy for us to think of colorful autumn days, delicious pies, and laughing jack-O'-lanterns when we see those big, beautiful orange pumpkins in the fall. We seem to associate them with our American heritage of bumper crops of good food and the happy, carefree, youthful days of life spent in company with our parents and grandparents.

Pumpkins are an excellent source of good nourishing food often over-looked and most certainly underutilized here in America. Pumpkin pies can be one of the tastiest in the world, and they can be served year-round from fresh, stored, or canned pumpkin. The United States Department of Agriculture has developed a pumpkin for its seeds rather than its flesh. The "naked" or hulless seeds are delicious raw or roasted and are high in protein. The Greeks bake pumpkin between fila layers and then pour honey over it for a delicious dessert. Down in South America pumpkin is used in soups. It would not take much effort to make this wholesome, nourishing food a staple part of your long-range food plan.

To prepare "naked" pumpkin seed: Open the pumpkin, scoop the seeds out, and wash lightly to remove the fiber—or you can pick the fiber out by hand. Spread thinly on paper towels or cookie sheets and dry for a few days in a warm, airy place.

Quick Preparation: Heat a frying pan with one tablespoon of cooking oil, add the seeds and shake the pan or stir gently. Some seeds will "pop," so have a mesh cover handy. The seeds will swell in only a few seconds, and you should remove them from the heat at once. Dry them on absorbent paper, salt to taste, and eat.

Culture

The culture is identical with that of squash as detailed on page 101. Pumpkins thrive under partial shade, and can be grown very successfully with corn. If you want to grow a huge prizewinner, select Big Max, which often weighs 100 pounds or more. Pinch off all competition and grow only one per vine. Despite its huge size, Big Max is good for pumpkin pies.

Recommended Varieties

Big Max (120 days). For big pumpkin competition. Huge pumpkins often weighing one hundred pounds or more.

Small Sugar (100 days). Very sweet and a good keeper. Best for general use.

Connecticut Field (100 days). Largest Halloween type pumpkin. Good for carving and good for pies.

Winter Luxury (85 days). One of the sweetest and best flavored of all pumpkins.

Cinderella (85 days). Good choice for the home gardener because it is a new bush type requiring only six square feet of area per plant.

Lady Godiva (100 days). Naked edible seed. The "naked" or hull-less seeds are delicious raw or roasted and high in protein.

Big Tom (120 days). Thick, dry, sweet, orange-yellow flesh, desirable for canning and pies.

RUTABAGA
Brassica napobrassica

Rutabagas are a late crop that stores well to give you plenty of tasty, nutritious eating all through the winter. Properly prepared, they are really delicious. They are tops in food value, a good source of carbohydrates, calcium and vitamin C. They also contain traces of vitamin A, iron, niacin, riboflavin, and thiamine.

The rutabaga is a most attractive plant with powdery, blue-green leaves. If you have little space for fall gardening, you might want to grow some along the edge of a flower bed or walk. This is one vegetable that is referred to by several names, among them being Macomber and winter turnips, "big yellow turnips," or Canadian turnips.

Culture

Soil should be well prepared to a depth of eight inches or more. Rake it well to eliminate clods and form a good seedbed. Make a shallow furrow and space the seeds at least three inches apart in the row. Cover the seeds with 1/3 to 1/2 inch of fine soil. Rows should be 18 to 30 inches apart, depending on whether you use hand or machine cultivation. When plants are well started, thin to stand six to eight inches apart. Control the weeds to conserve moisture and nutrients for your plants.

Rutabagas mature in about 90 days and are best used as a fall crop. Planting dates range from July 15 through August 15, depending on your first expected freeze. They should be harvested after a frost, which seems to improve their flavor. However, they should not be allowed to freeze, as this impairs both their flavor and their keeping qualities.

Storage

Rutabagas can be stored in above-ground mounds, buried in sand, or stored in a root cellar. They can also be left in the ground and protected from freezing with suitable coverings of mulch. The primary concern is to keep them cool, to protect them from freezing, and not to let them dry out or lose too much moisture. A bit of experimentation will convince you that they store easily and keep well. You can depend on them as a major contribution to your staple supply of good, nutritious fall and winter food.

Recommended Varieties

Laurentian Neckless (90 days). Purple-topped globe having rich, yellow flesh; fine-grained, tender, and sweet. Splendid keeper.

Burpee's Purple-Top Yellow (90 days). The leading rutabaga for table use during fall and winter. Sweet, fine-grained, yellow flesh that cooks to bright orange. A good keeper for winter storing.

SALSIFY
Tragopogon porrifolius

Because this vegetable root crop tastes so much like oysters when cooked, it is commonly called the oyster plant. It is also known as the vegetable oyster.

Black salsify (*Scorzonera*) is a close relative of salsify. Although the skin of the root is black, its flesh is white.

While little known in America and still classified as a newcomer, salsify has been cultivated and used as one of the staple foods in southern Europe for almost two thousand years.

Stews made with salsify can taste almost unbelievably like fresh oyster stew. It is very tasty when served raw with dips. Almost any meat dish is improved with its delicate flavor.

This secondary root crop can make a substantial contribution to your annual supply of food. It is easy to grow, extremely hardy, and possesses a unique flavor that can add something entirely different to your table fare.

Culture

Salsify can be grown in exactly the same manner as that which is detailed for parsnips. Furthermore, harvesting and leaving in the ground until needed are identical to the method used for parsnips.

The recommended variety is Sandwich Island Mammoth, which takes 120 days to mature. The flavor is not unlike that of oysters; the flesh is creamy white. The roots grow eight inches and more in length and are 1 to 1-1/2 inches in diameter at the shoulder, slightly tapering, clean-cut and uniform.

SUNFLOWER
Helianthus annuus

This is the common, native annual grown throughout the United States. The Lewis and Clark expedition noted in 1805 that Indians along the Missouri and Mississippi Rivers were using sunflower seeds for food. Most varieties of sunflowers cultivated in the United States are derived from the Mammoth Russian strain. Some of these giants tower up to 15 feet or more.

Sunflowers are cultivated for their protein-rich seeds, which are eaten raw and also used as a valuable ingredient in many of the best poultry mixes. A valuable oil is extracted from dried and crushed seed. The seeds are high in protein (about 25 percent—on the same protein level as meat), calcium, niacin, phosphorus, thiamin, and riboflavin. The seeds are prized for winter feeding of songbirds.

Sunflowers are also grown for ornamental purposes. These stately plants range in size all the way from two to 16 feet, depending on variety. They can be used with excellent results for backgrounds or screens. Gardeners, farmers, and homesteaders can interplant them with corn and along the borders of gardens, fields, forage areas, and poultry runs. They thrive in almost any soil exposed to the sun. When they are grown primarily for ornamental effect, the seeds are a welcome bonus.

Culture

Although it has been noted that sunflowers will grow in almost any soil exposed to the sun, they prefer a deeply spaded, rich, moist soil. Like the vast majority of cultivated plants, they do their best when adequate nutrients and moisture are available in the soil. They prefer soil with a pH rating of 6.0 to 7.5. Sow the seeds when frost danger has passed in the spring. Cover the seeds to a depth of 1/2 inch and firm the soil lightly. Space the seeds six to 12 inches, depending on the variety and the intended purpose. Rows should be two to 3-1/2 feet apart. The tall-growing varieties require strong support from a trellis, fence, or stakes. Heavy rainfall followed by strong winds will cause them to topple over. When the seedpod heads start to get heavy, the plants become especially vulnerable to wind and rain.

Harvesting

Cut the heads with about 12 inches of stalk attached when the outer row of seeds matures. The next rows will be ripe but not dry and the center seeds may still be a bit green. Tie two or three stalks together and hang the heads in an airy breezeway, garage, or shed to dry. The seeds may be removed by rubbing them lightly, when they are thoroughly dry. Store them in airtight containers so that they will retain their food and vitamin content for a long time.

Recommended Varieties

Recommended varieties for seed production, background, and screening include Mammoth Russian, Gray Stripe and Manchurian. All three mature in 80 to 90 days, have husky stalks and produce huge seedpods loaded with big, thin-shelled seeds.

WATERMELON
Citrullus vulgaris

You may have your choice of cylindrical, oval, or round watermelons, ranging in weight from three to 100 pounds.

The time from planting to maturity is from 57 to 95 days, depending on the variety. Many home gardeners shy away from watermelon growing because they think of them either as being too difficult to grow or as too space-consuming. You are encouraged to experiment with a trial season if you have a garden plot as big as 2000 square feet, more or less.

These are four basics to pay strict attention to if you are to be eminently successful on your very first attempt: (1) Choose a variety that will have ample time to mature during hot weather or one that is adapted to relatively cool summers, depending on your local climatic conditions. (2) Plant only in soil that has been well prepared and enriched directly beneath the seed with compost or well-rotted cow manure, and a light sprinkling of 10-10-10. You can vary this soil enrichment procedure by using a 50-50 layer of green manure (any green organic material—leaves, green grass, clover, pea vines, etc.) and a top layer of compost or stable manure placed in the "planting spots" at least three months prior to planting of the seeds. Regardless of method employed, have a minimum of two inches of good topsoil between the seeds and the fertilizing materials. (3) Plant the seeds after the soil is warm, which can occur only after relatively high nighttime as well as high daytime temperatures. (4) Provide the growing plants with adequate moisture. When summer showers do not dump at least an inch of rain on your melon patch each week, water deeply at least once each week around the root zone.

Culture

Remove the soil from a circular area 18 inches wide and 12 inches deep. Fill to within three inches of the top with well-rotted cow manure or aged compost and sprinkle liberally with a handful or two of 10-10-10. Now trample the filler down firmly to ensure good capillarity. Finish filling the hole with fine topsoil and firm it well. Now plant eight to 10 seeds spaced four to six inches apart. Use any pattern you like in spacing the seeds, remembering that vigorously growing vines should not be close together. Cover the seed with one inch of topsoil and firm lightly to ensure good contact of soil with seed. This assists germination. When seedlings begin producing runners, thin them to three to a group. Space the groups or hills six to eight feet apart each way.

When rainfall is excessive, you may find runners developing at an excessive rate. When this happens, cut some of them from the plant to lessen demands on the root structure. Remove any fruits that appear to be aborted or misshaped. Rapidly growing vines mean rapidly growing melons. You will get larger melons by leaving only two, three, or four per vine. Prove this to yourself by leaving two per vine, three per vine, and four per vine on selected control groups.

Side or top dressings of aged compost or well-rotted cow manure worked carefully into the soil near the root zone will provide the rich supply of nutrients that the roots require for rapid growth and top quality. Do this at three-week intervals, being careful not to disturb the roots.

A trowel and hand-weeding will enable you to keep the patch weed-free until the vines begin setting fruit. Of course, a thick mulch of spoiled hay or pine needles will end your weed problem and conserve moisture. Many home gardeners in the South plant peanuts in the rows between the melons to get better soil utilization. This practice also conserves moisture and lessens weed growth.

Harvesting

It is a bit difficult for an inexperienced person to tell just when to pick a vine-ripened watermelon. The surest sign of ripeness of most varieties is the color of the bottom surface. As the melon begins to ripen, the "ground spot" turns from a white or light straw color to a richer yellow. As the fruits ripen, they gradually lose their surface sheen or slick appearance and acquire a dull look. The tendril attaching the fruit to the vine will die as soon as the fruit is ripe. Finally, just about everyone knows that the best way of telling if a watermelon is ripe is to thump it. However, it is sometimes hard to determine by thumping (a firm rapping with a knuckle) whether you are getting a "ping"—not quite ripe—or a "muffled plunk"—ready to pick. Have fun and enjoy the thumping. The Golden Midget has a built-in ripeness indicator. It turns a golden color when ripe. Sugar Baby loses its stripes and turns a very dark green when ripe.

Recommended Varieties

There are dozens to choose from, and your decision should be based on local adaptation, disease resistance, and size.

Burpee's Fordhook Hybrid (74 days)
Yellow Baby Hybrid (70 days)
New Hampshire Midget (70 days)
Jumbo-State Fair (90 days)
Super Sweet (90 days)
Jubilee (95 days)
Sugar Baby (75 days)
Family Fun Hybrid (75 days)
Charleston Gray (85 days)
Klondike (78 days)
Golden Midget (65 days)
Kleckley's Sweet (85 days)
Louisiana Queen (80 days)
Hybrid Dixie Queen (75 days)
Winter Queen (85 days)
Hybrid Summer Festival (75 days)
Early Canada (75 days)
Winter Melon (85 days)
Black Diamond (90 days)
Faribo Hybrid (57 days)
Faribo Black Giant Hybrid (65 days)

5

Herbs

Herbs add a gourmet touch to food that not only improves the flavor but also appeals to our senses of sight and smell in a most tantalizing manner.

It is no culinary secret that soup stock, butter, eggs, milk, and cheese quickly absorb herb flavoring. To achieve maximum flavor, mix the herbs with one of these ingredients and let stand for a few hours before using. A bit of practice coupled with critical sampling will soon enable you to add the gourmet touch to almost any food.

Although there are more than 60 well-known and popular herbs used throughout the country, you can revolutionize both your garden and your culinary skills with only a few of them. The following are recommended for their ornamental and aesthetic values as well as culinary use: anise, borage, caraway, chives, dill, fennel, florence, parsley, peppermint, rosemary, sage, spearmint, sweet basil, sweet majoram, summer savory, and thyme.

Herbs do well in any ordinary well-drained soil; a good supply of six varieties can be grown on a border strip of garden that is only 20 feet long and four feet wide. Herbs require no more attention than other garden plants, and the results can be most rewarding from an ornamental as well as a practical point of view.

HOW TO GROW AND USE HERBS

Herb	Planting	Description	Uses	Harvest
Anise (*Pimpinella anisum*)	Full sun; well-drained loam. Soak seed 24 hr in tepid water. Thin as required.	Annual; 2 ft; graceful plant with small white flowers and straw-colored seed. Quite potent.	Green leaves in salads, soups, stews, and for garnish. Seeds in cakes and cookies. Oil in liqueurs, medicines, and perfumes.	Cut green leaves as needed. When seeds turn grayish, clip umbels and dry in cool, airy location. Store.
Borage (*Borago officinalis*)	Full sun; dry, well-drained soil. Easily transplanted.	Annual; 1½ ft, star-shaped blue flowers.	Excellent bee forage. Good for cut flowers. Leaves minced and used in teas and salads.	Cut young leaves anytime. Cut flowers anytime.
Caraway (*Carum carui*)	Full sun; dry, friable soil. Hardy, but slow in germination.	Biennial; 1½-2 ft, lacey, creamy, yellow flowers. Dark brown seeds with lighter-colored ridges.	Green leaves in stews, soups, salads. Seeds in cakes, bread, sauerkraut, and cheeses. Oil in liqueurs, medicines, and for perfumes.	Cut seed heads when no longer green and dry in cool, airy location. Store in glass jars.
Chives (*Allium schoenprasum*)	Spring or fall, indoors or outdoors Seed or divisions. Full sun.	Perennial with onion-like tops. Lavender flowers. Vigorous; grows in thick clumps.	Flavor salads, soups, omelets, cheeses, and appetizers.	Cut leaves as needed about 2 inches above bulblets.
Dill (*Anethum graveolens*)	Early spring in average garden soil after it is warm. Full sun. Thin or transplant to stand 1 ft apart in the row.	Annual; 2-3 ft. Threadlike foliage and greenish-yellow flowers. Young tender green shoots used for flavoring.	Leaves and shoots in fish sauces, potato salad, and cottage cheese. Dried dill weed condiment in soups, stews, and omelets. Seeds for pickling, vinegars, and condiment.	Cut when seeds are ripe; hang whole sprays up to dry. Store in glass jars.

HOW TO GROW AND USE HERBS *(continued)*

Herb	Planting	Description	Uses	Harvest
Florence Fennel or Finocchio (**Foeniculum dulee**)	Early spring in rich well-prepared soil. Thin to stand 10 inches apart in the row. Plants should be earthed up when half-grown and treated like celery.	Rapidly growing annual; 2½ ft with feathery foilage and enlarged leaf bases.	Both foliage and seed are used for flavoring food. Enlarged, blanched leaf bases are boiled or eaten raw like celery. Anise-like flowers.	Cut when blanched leaf bases are mature and when seeds are mature.
Parsley (**Petroselinum crispum**)	Soak seeds in tepid water 48 hr. Rich, moist soil, in full sun. Can thrive in partial shade.	Compact biennial grown as annual. 8-12 inches tall. Finely cut and curled leaves.	For garnish and flavor in meats, soups, salads, omelets. Parsley soup is delicious.	Cut fresh leaves and sprigs as needed. Cut and dry in fall and store in glass jars.
Peppermint (**Mentha piperita**)	Early spring by runners and stolons. Also propagated by slips and branches in moist sand.	Perennial, 2-3 ft. Vigorous in wet, favorable locations. Long narrow leaves. Flowers usually purple. Reddish undertone throughout plant.	Either fresh or dried leaves in teas, beverages, and jellies. Peppermint oil is used in medicines and to perfume many toiletries.	Cut fresh leaves as needed. For drying, cut stems when flowers start to bloom. Dry in shade and store in glass jars.
Rosemary (**Rosmarinus officinalis**)	Start seeds indoors and transplant in sunny, dry, well-drained soil in a sheltered location.	Perennial, 2-4 ft. Blue flowers. Leaves are ever-green, without stalks, and very fragrant.	Tender tips and buds used to flavor meats, sauces, soups, seafood, and poultry.	Cut fresh leaves anytime. For drying, gather as plants flower and dry in shade. Store in glass jars.
Sage (**Salvia officinalis**)	Seed or cuttings in good, well-drained garden soil in full sun.	Perennial, 1-2 ft. Light, woolly, wrinkled leaves. White, blue, or purple flowers.	Use dried in poultry stuffings and sausages. Flavors pork, veal, and cheeses. Sage is strong and should be used sparingly.	Cut sparingly first year. Tender tips and buds have most flavor. Strip leaves from stem and dry in shade. Store in glass jars.

Herb	Growing	Description	Uses	Harvesting and Storing
Spearmint (*Mentha spicata*)	Early spring by runners and stolons. Also propagated by slips and branches in moist sand.	Perennial, 2-3 ft. Vigorous in wet, favorable locations. Dark green, smooth, graceful plant with tiny, white flowers with purple markings.	Fresh leaves are minced to garnish and flavor peas and glazed carrots. Used in mint sauce and cold beverages. Use fresh and dried in teas and jellies.	Cut fresh leaves as needed. Cut stems when flowers start to bloom and dry in shade. Store in glass jars.
Sweet basil (*Ocimum basilicum*)	Full sun; well-drained garden soil. Easily grown in warm soil.	Compact annual 1-1½ ft tall. Pinch center bud out when seedling is 6 inches high to make more compact bush.	The flavor is flower-like and goes well with a wide variety of cooked foods. One of best of seasoning herbs.	Cut leaves as soon as plants are large enough to stand the operation. When flowers begin to open, cut leaves for drying and storage.
Sweet marjoram (*Origanum marjoram*)	Full sun in dry, well-drained garden soil. May be started indoors and transplanted when garden soil is warm.	Annual, 1-2 ft. Very fragrant and aromatic. Tiny, gray-green leaves covered with down.	Season sausages and poultry stuffings. Use mixed in salads or as garnish. Good in most cooked foods.	Cut fresh leaves as needed. When flowers start to appear, cut leaves and flowering tops, strip leaves, dry in shade and store in glass jars.
Summer savory (*Saturia hortensis*)	Sunny location in well-prepared, good garden soil. Also by division of rootstocks or cuttings.	Annual, 1-1½ ft. Long and narrow lance-shaped leaves. Pink to purplish small flowers.	Use fresh leaves in peas and snap beans or for garnish. Use dried leaves in sausages, meats, and poultry dressings.	Cut fresh leaves sparingly as needed. Gather plants when in full bloom, dry foilage thoroughly in shade, and store in glass jars.
Thyme (*Thymus vulgaris*)	Full sun in rather poor soil containing plenty of lime. Plants enjoy nestling against warm stones and do well in rock gardens, alongside stone walks, and on sunny banks.	Perennial, 6-12 in. tall. Grayish, tiny evergreen leaves. Small lilac to purplish flowers. This attractive plant improves the appearance of any garden or walkway.	Used to flavor wines, seafood, sauces, soups, stuffings and salads. Oil of thyme is used to perfume toiletries.	Cut fresh leaves as needed. For winter use, cut the stems before flowers appear and dry in an airy and shady place. Store in a glass jar.

6

Gardening Hints

1. All vegetable plants need good soil, enough water, enough sunlight, adequate spacing between plants, and proper temperature range for steady, vigorous growth.
2. For good sustained yield of top-quality vegetables over a long bearing season, the plants require a continuous supply of nutrients. Weeds must be kept to a minimum so that they do not steal the plant food and shade the plants.
3. If different varieties are planted during their proper season, the gardener can control or improve all of the plants' requirements, except the amount of sunlight they get.
4. If you dislike using an insecticide for bug control, you may want to "plant" some praying mantises and ladybugs in your garden. Both of these beneficial insects can be obtained from Burpee and Gurney. Also, encourage songbirds to stay near your garden by providing a bath and year-round feeding. Birds consume millions of insects.
5. Apply a complete, balanced fertilizer to the garden soil before sowing seeds or setting out plants. When plants are half-grown, make a second application in the form of top dressing.
6. The garden needs about an average of one inch of rainfall per week. When this does not occur, you must provide the water. In very dry wea-

ther, water the garden thoroughly to a depth of several inches about once a week.

7. Cultivate the soil very shallowly, one to two inches, as soon as the soil is workable after each good rainfall. This gardening practice destroys weeds, creates a dust mulch for retention of moisture, and keeps the soil receptive for the next rainfall.

8. Excessively heavy rainfall during the bearing season of vegetable crops tends to leach plant nutrients out of the soil. Replace these much-needed plant foods with a judicious application of top dressing, using a balanced fertilizer, compost, or well-rotted cow manure.

9. Plants yielding an abundance of fruits over a long bearing season benefit enormously from two to three well-spaced top dressings. Just remember to top dress sparingly, to keep fertilizer off foliage and roots, and to cultivate or rake it into the soil.

10. Do not make the mistake of trying to compare the nutrient requirements of a vegetable garden with those of field crops. Field crops, such as soybeans and corn, are "one-shot" affairs; that is, they bear only once, whereas many vegetable plants continue to bear and grow repeated yields of their fruits over a period of two or three months. Obviously, their nutrient requirements are much higher than those of field crops.

11. Mounding or hilling the soil with the hands around the stems of half-grown green beans has a very salubrious effect. It keeps the roots cooler, increases aeration of the soil, retains more moisture, helps control weeds, and keeps the plants from falling over. Young squash, tomato, pepper, eggplant, and cucumber plants and vines also benefit from this same treatment. Merely move the soil into place and leave it loose; do not pat or firm it down.

12. Newly transplanted seedlings cannot take the blistering heat of an extremely hot day nor the effects of a strong wind. You may have to shade and protect them with inverted baskets or cardboard boxes with holes cut in the sides for ventilation for two or three days.

13. Start a compost pile with green grass clippings, topsoil, and a sprinkling of a balanced fertilizer. Gradually add garden refuse, pea and bean vines, leaves, and more topsoil as these materials become available. Plan to keep a compost pile working for you all the time.

14. The real secret to growing fine lettuce plants is rapid growth and no crowding in the row. Rapid growth demands an abundance of plant nutrients and plenty of moisture. Fertilize, compost, and get the seedbed well prepared before sowing. Make adequate preparation, and the quality and quantity of harvest will be pleasing.

15. Garbage from the kitchen is rich in nitrogen and other plant nutrients.

Bury the garbage, spread out a bit, in a garden area for direct soil building and enrichment. It must be deep enough to avoid detection by animals. Add layers to the compost pile, covering with straw, grass clippings, leaves, or topsoil. Kitchen garbage is an excellent activator for the compost pile.

16. You are urged to give gardening a "one hundred percent" try for one full season. The outdoor exercise tones the muscles, relaxes the mind, and stimulates the appetite. Gardening affords an invigorating contrast to the often impersonal work some of us do at our regular jobs. A successful first season will make you fall in love with gardening.

17. *Succession of crops.* All garden space should be kept fully occupied throughout the growing season. In arranging the garden, all early maturing crops should be grouped so that as soon as one crop is harvested another takes its place. For example, early peas or beans can very properly be followed by late cabbage, celery, carrots, or beets; early sweet corn or potatoes can be followed by kale, spinach, or turnips.

18. *Intercropping.* It is not always necessary to wait until the early crop is entirely removed. A later crop may be planted between rows of potatoes. As a general rule, crops subject to attack by the same diseases and insects should not follow each other.

19. *Saving* the late tomatoes. Even up to the first frost there will be green tomatoes on the vines. Before the frosts come, pick all the tomatoes and wrap them individually in about three layers of newspapers. Store them, three or four layers deep, in open crates or boxes. The boxes may be kept in any warm area, and the tomatoes will ripen without aid of light in two to four weeks, depending on the temperature and the condition of the tomatoes when wrapped. A surplus of smaller green tomatoes could be used for relishes, pickling, etc.

20. *Hybrid seed and hybrid plants.* It is a well-established fact that hybrid vegetable plants are more disease-resistant and yield more uniform fruits over a longer season than comparable standard varieties. Consequently, the extra cost is entirely justifiable, and competent, experienced gardeners prefer the hybrids.

21. *Harvesting.* It is mandatory that you keep all cucumbers, squash, peppers, eggplant, peas, beans, etc. picked as they reach maturity. If fruits are left on plants and vines until the seeds inside them reach full maturity and ripen, the plants and vines will show a marked decrease in production. In some instances, they will stop bearing completely.

22. *Hills versus groups.* Most of us have grown up with the idea of hills of squash, hills of cucumbers, etc. Many gardeners actually draw soil up into a hill or mound to plant these vegetables. However, this is not good gardening practice, simply because a hill or mound of soil loses its moisture

content much faster than soil that is level with the surface of the earth. Accordingly, let us talk about groups of squash, groups of cucumbers, etc. Do not mound or draw up the soil into a hill; instead, prepare the soil for planting on the level surface.

23. Take full advantage of the expertise of your county extension and agricultural agents on all facets of vegetable gardening. These people are extremely knowledgeable and enjoy being of assistance.

24. Prevent or control most plant diseases by growing disease-resistant varieties, by keeping garden refuse cleaned up, by removing and burning "sick" plants, and by planting the same variety in a different location each year.

25. Send for seed catalogs in January to allow ample time for planning the early garden. If animal pests are likely to be a nuisance, send for literature about Havahart® traps. Obtain your strawberry plants from specialists who handle only the best.

26. Control harmful insects by using one of the excellent all-purpose sprays or dusts on the market. Examine your plants carefully, and either handpick the bugs or spray or dust at first signs of insect infestation.

27. *Feeding seedlings in a sterile medium.* Make a liquid fertilizer by dissolving one tablespoon of 10-10-10 in a gallon of water. Or use two tablespoons of 5-10-5 to a gallon of water. This fertilizer may be applied to the seedlings at five- to seven-day intervals.

28. When leaves of herbs are continually being cut or picked for fresh use, the plant is hard put to maintain its vigor. Top dressing with a complete fertilizer, or the use of a liquid fertilizer, at three- or four-week intervals will enable the plant to remain healthy and productive.

29. *Pollination of sweet corn.* Sweet corn pollination is best achieved by planting the corn in blocks. For example, four 25-foot rows are far superior to one 100-foot row. Sweet corn tends to cross-pollinate with field corn, so, if you have a choice, do not plant sweet corn adjacent to field corn.

30. Did you ever stop and think about the enormous amount of time and energy expended on lawns—which are primarily for decorative purposes? If you put this same amount of time and energy into the growing of snap beans, tomatoes, and squash, you would be positively astonished at the savings on your grocery bill.

31. Vegetable plants faithfully reflect the fertility of the soil in which they are grown. Soils that are deficient in organic matter and low in nutrients will not produce top-quality vegetables.

32. Keep a record of your gardening activities. Your specific knowledge about successful gardening will expand quite rapidly if you take the time to keep a brief record of your activities. Record varieties, planting dates,

time to first fruit, and length of bearing season. This may seem like a lot of extra work, but you can record four hours of gardening activity in about five minutes of writing. Good records enable you to plan a better, more productive garden for the coming year. In two short growing seasons you will become a successful, experienced gardener.

7

Strawberries

Strawberries are grown successfully in every state. They are easy to grow, and beginners are proud of their fine berries.*

BEARING

Standard varieties set in the spring of one year will bear their best crop in May or June of the next year. Everbearing varieties set in the spring produce berries in late summer and fall of the same year.

PLANTING

Early spring planting is of the greatest importance in growing strawberries. This means just as early in the spring as weather permits preparation of the land. If the plants are established while the soil is still cool and moist, a good stand results. If the plants are dormant and there is good irrigation, later setting is possible, but it is not as easy. Planting time is usually February,

---

*This chapter courtesy of W. F. Allen Company.

171

March, and early April in the Southern states; March and April in the middle
states; April and May in the Northern states.

Ozark Beauty Strawberry

PLANTING DISTANCES

In general, we recommend setting plants 18 to 20 inches apart in rows
four feet apart. This requires a little over 7000 plants per acre (see page 173).
Somewhat closer planting is satisfactory in small gardens where space is limited, or for the hill system (as with everbearers), or for late setting where a
good stand is uncertain.

For the small garden, order seven plants for each ten feet of row you
want to set, or plan on one plant for each five square feet. Thus, for a plot
ten by ten feet, you would need about 20 plants.

SOIL AND LOCATION

Any soil that makes good yields of garden or field crops will produce
strawberries in abundance, whether that soil is a light sandy loam or a heavy
clay. Here are some pointers.

PLANTS FOR VARIOUS PLANTING DISTANCE

Rows (distance apart)	In the row (inches)	Total plants per acre
3 ft	18	9680
3 ft	24	7260
3-1/2 ft	18	8297
3-1/2 ft	24	6223
4 ft	18	7260
4 ft	24	5445
3-2/3 ft	18	7128

1. In rolling country a sloping field gives better air drainage and less injurious frost.
2. Run the berry rows across a steeply sloping field rather than up and down to help prevent erosion.
3. Follow a hoed crop to make less weeds and grass for the strawberries to contend with.
4. Avoid sod land that may harbor grub worms that will cut or injure your plants. Treatment for grub worms makes the use of sod land much safer.
5. Change the place of the strawberry bed every few years. It will help to keep up the vigor and growth and reduce the danger of a buildup of disease and insect trouble.
6. Most important of all, select land that holds moisture well because (a) it is naturally springy, (b) it has a high water table, (c) lots of organic matter in the form of animal manures or green crops has been incorporated in the soil. Of course, if irrigation is available, you can give the plants water when necessary.

IRRIGATION

It would be most worthwhile to use irrigation for strawberries—for establishing the new bed, as well as at fruiting time. Irrigation is not mandatory, but if you have a frost during bloom, irrigation during the danger hours can save strawberry crops from frost and freeze damage with temperatures as low as 20°F.

LAND PREPARATION

In late winter or very early spring the land should be plowed or spaded to a depth of six to eight inches. Then it should be leveled off with a harrow or rake to form a smooth friable planting bed. Following are some hints that will help you to produce bigger, better crops of berries.

1. In late summer plow under a heavy growth of green crops such as peas, beans, clover, sowed corn, weeds, grass, etc. All of these rot quickly and are much more valuable for the strawberry crop if plowed under while still green.
2. An early fall sowing of rye or wheat will give a heavy sod that can be plowed under in late winter or very early spring. This will be easier to handle if disked up thoroughly before plowed.
3. Apply horse, cow, hog, or sheep manure at the rate of five to 20 tons per acre. This is the best of all preparations for a fine crop of berries. Results are almost equally good if one of these applications has been made for the previous crop. For small areas a good guide in the application of manure is to figure on one to two bushels for every 100 square feet.

PUTTING PLANTS IN GROUND

Any method of planting that leaves the roots reasonably straight down in the soil is good. The roots should be spread with the soil pressed tightly against them and the bud just at the surface. With plants that have very long roots, clip them off to about four or five inches; this will not hurt the plants and will make a good job of setting easier. No matter how long or how short the leaf stems, fruit stems, or roots may be at the time of setting, the bud must be just at the surface.

A good garden trowel is the best setting tool for work in small plots; in larger fields it is common practice to use a transplanter. With a transplanter it is very important that the setting depth of the plants be checked behind the planter.

CHEMICAL FERTILIZER

On very fertile soils no chemical fertilizer is needed. Have a soil test made and follow the recommendation of your local supplier or county agent.

LIME

If other crops, weeds, or grass have made a good growth on the land you have selected for strawberries, it does not need lime.

A pH range of 5.7 to 6 is best; up to 7 is satisfactory if the organic content of the soil is fairly high.

CARE OF PLANTS

Plants should be set as soon as you get them, if possible. Dip the roots in water and keep them protected when you take them to the garden or field for setting. A hot day is bad for setting strawberry plants. A hot windy day is terrible. A cool cloudy day is fine. If plants must be kept for a while, small lots can be kept in the family refrigerator. The very best way to hold plants is in cold storage between 29 and 32°F. Never, never put plants in a freezer where temperatures will go below 28°F.

CULTIVATING, HOEING, AND TRAINING

Shallow cultivating and hoeing (not to exceed two inches) kills weeds, conserves moisture, and enables new runners to take root.

Uncover the buds; failure to do this will give you a poor stand.

Most of the training of new runners is done at hoeing time. Train the first strong new runners out like spokes from a wheel and root them until a fruiting row 1-1/2 to 2-1/2 feet wide has been formed. Four to eight plants per square foot of fruiting bed is enough; whenever possible, later runners should be cut off.

MULCHES

Mulching is necessary for winter protection in all the Northern states and would be helpful in many fields as far South as Virginia and Kentucky. In addition to giving protection from cold, mulching helps to keep down weeds and grass, to conserve soil moisture, and to keep the fruit bright and clean.

The mulch should be applied in the fall after frost and light freeze (25 to 28°F) have occurred but before hard freezing (20°F or lower). It should be removed, at least partly, soon after growth starts in the spring.

Wheat, straw, and marsh grass are considered the best materials. Rye straw, pine needles, coarse strawy manure, buckwheat hulls, and various kinds of hay are satisfactory. In some sections, sawdust has been used with good results. Use whatever you have or can buy at a reasonable price.

TYPES OF PLANT

Early Varieties

Earlibelle–vigor and beauty
Plants: Small but great for producing runners. Productive. Adapted for Virginia south.
Berries: Medium to large. Bright red. Glossy and firm. Slightly tart.
Something Special: Earlibelle is outstanding for firmness, toughness, and flesh and skin color in freezing and canning.

Sunrise–the good grower
Plants: Very vigorous. Good producers of fine berries. Excellent resistance to disease. Grow well even in dry weather.
Berries: Conic. Medium to large. Firm, light, bright red and attractive.
Something Special: High flavor makes the Sunrise delicious for table use. A little light in color for best freezing. Great for shipping.

Midseason Varieties

Catskill–the leader
Plants: Widely adapted. Very productive. Make runners freely. Vigorous grower. Hardy. Resistant to verticillium wilt.
Berries: Very large. Long conic. Not too firm. Bright crimson skin, light red flesh. Mildly subacid.
Something Special: Good for desserts. Excellent for freezing. Loaded with vitamin C.

Surecrop–for sure crops
Plants: Widely adapted upper south to north. Large size. Vigorous producer. Free in runner production under most conditions. One of the very best for resistance to diseases of plant or foliage. Drought resistant.
Berries: Large. Round Conic. Irregular. Firm. Glossy. Medium red skin. Light red flesh. Tart.
Something Special: Fine for desserts. Excellent for freezing.

Late Varieties

Albritton–the one with class
Plants: Vigorous. Make runners freely. High yields in North Carolina and parts of Virginia.

Berries: Large. Uniform. Conic. Very firm. Glossy, bright red skin. Solid red flesh. Excellent flavor.

Something Special: Beautiful berries. Easy to sell. Excellent for shipping and freezing.

Jerseybelle—the "belle" of berries

Plants: Large. Good runner makers. Productive from southern New Jersey northward. Susceptible to leaf diseases, red stele, and verticillium wilt.

Berries: Large. Showy. Glossy. Medium red. Blunt conic. Tender skin. Prominent seeds.

Something Special: Size and beauty make Jerseybelle great for local markets and pick-your-own. Not too good for freezing.

Everbearing Varieties

Gem (Superfection)—old favorite

Plants: Hardy. Good producer. Drought susceptible.

Berries: Light red. Irregular. Tart. Medium firm.

Something Special: Attractive berries for table use or local market.

Ozark Beauty—good eating

Plants: Good runner production. Good yielder.

Berries: Large. Sweet. Good flavor. Firm.

Something Special: Pretty plants and good yields from June until first frost. Good freezer.

8

Fertilizers

This chapter explains how to calculate small measures of fertilizers from recommended applications by weight for large areas.

Books and bulletins on agriculture and gardening usually give recommendations for the use of fertilizers and lime in tons or pounds per acre, or in pounds per thousand or hundred square feet. The gardener often finds it difficult to convert these weights into the measures needed for a small plot or for a single row or a single plant. Tables 8-1 and 8-2 make the conversions for him, using the common household measurements of pints, cups, tablespoons, and teaspoons.

For example, if 300 pounds of superphosphate or mixed fertilizer are recommended per acre, you will find by turning to Table 8-1 that this means seven pounds per 1000 square feet or 11 ounces (1-1/2 cups) per 100 square feet. Then, turning to Table 8-2, you will find that two cups per 100 square feet means 1/2 cup for each 10-foot row if the rows are three feet apart, or six tablespoonsful for each plant if the plants are spaced 5 × 5 feet. A large number of such conversions are given for various kinds of fertilizer material and to fit various needs.

The rates to be selected for the various fertilizing materials depend on the soil and its previous treatments and the requirements of the plants. Certain materials—ground limestone, where needed, and superphosphate—are used in relatively large quantities; other materials, such as borax, are used sparingly. For example, small supplemental additions of ammonium nitrate can be beneficial to tomatoes, whereas large quantities would injure the plants.

The values tabulated are near enough for all practical purposes, though they are only approximate, since the weight of a given volume of a material will vary with its moisture content and texture. The standard pint, cup, table-spoon (tbs), and teaspoon (tsp) are used for liquid measure. Level measures are used.*

TABLE 8-1

WEIGHTS OF VARIOUS FERTILIZING MATERIALS PER ACRE, PER 1000 SQUARE FEET, PER 100 SQUARE FEET, AND THE APPROXIMATE EQUIVALENT-VOLUME MEASURES FOR 100 SQUARE FEET, GROUPED ACCORDING TO WEIGHT

Materials	*Acre*	*Weights specified per* 1000 sq ft	100 sq ft	*Volume Measure for 100 sq ft*
Weight about the same	Pounds	Pounds	Pounds	Pints
as that of water	1300	30	3	3
Examples: ammonium	870	20	2	2
nitrate, ammonium	435	10	1	1
sulfate, potassium				Cups
chloride, sodium	220	5	½	1
nitrate	110	2½	¼	½
				Pints
Weight about 1-3/10	5660	130	13	10
that of water	3485	80	8	6
Examples: ground	870	20	2	1½
limestone, ground			Ounces	
dolomitic limestone,	565	13	21	1
potassium sulfate				Cups
	280	6½	11	1
			Pounds	Pints
Weight about 9/10	1960	45	4½	5
that of water	1650	38	3¾	4
Examples: ammonium	1220	28	2¾	3

*For materials not included in the lists, carefully weigh a full pint and determine approximately the group to which it belongs.

TABLE 8-1 (continued)

WEIGHTS OF VARIOUS FERTILIZING MATERIALS PER ACRE, PER 1000 SQUARE FEET, PER 100 SQUARE FEET, AND THE APPROXIMATE EQUIVALENT-VOLUME MEASURES FOR 100 SQUARE FEET, GROUPED ACCORDING TO WEIGHT

Materials		Weights specified per		Volume Measure for 100 sq ft
	Acre	*1000 sq ft*	*100 sq ft*	
phosphates, superphos-phates; mixed	1000	23	2¼	2½
			Ounces	
fertilizers (5-10-5, 10-6-4	785	18	30	2
10-10-10, etc.)	610	14	21	1½
	390	9	15	1
				Cups
	300	7	11	1½
	200	4¾	7½	1
	100	2¼	3½	½
			Pounds	Pints
Weight about 8/10	1740	40	4	5
that of water	650	15	1½	2
Examples: aluminum			Ounces	Cups
sulfate, bonemeal,	175	4	6½	1
magnesium sulfate				Tbs
(Epsom salts), urea	44	1	1½	4
			Pounds	Pints
Weight about 7/10	1740	40	4	6
that of water	1525	35	3½	5
Examples: activated	650	15	1½	2
sewage sludge, granu-			Ounces	
lar borax, urea-form	300	7	11	1
				Cups
	150	3½	5½	1
			Pounds	Pints
Weight about 6/10	1300	30	3	5
that of water	545	12½	1¼	2
Examples: cottonseed			Ounces	
meal, fish scrap,	260	6	10	1
sulfur, tankage				Cups
	130	3	5	1
			Pounds	Pints
Weight about 5/10	1100	25	2½	5
that of water	435	10	1	2

TABLE 8-1 (continued)

WEIGHTS OF VARIOUS FERTILIZING MATERIALS PER ACRE, PER 1000 SQUARE FEET, PER 100 SQUARE FEET, AND THE APPROXIMATE EQUIVALENT-VOLUME MEASURES FOR 100 SQUARE FEET, GROUPED ACCORDING TO WEIGHT

Materials	*Acre*	*1000 sq ft*	*100 sq ft*	*Volume Measure for 100 sq ft*
Example: hydrated lime	220	5	Ounces 8	1
	110	2½	4	Cups 1
Manure (moist):	Tons		Pounds	Bushels
loose	13	600	60	2
packed	13	600	60	1
Dry straws or leaves packed tightly with hands	5	250	25	2

Courtesy of United States Department of Agriculture.

TABLE 8-2

FERTILIZERS, APPROXIMATE EQUIVALENT-VOLUME OF MATERIALS TO USE IN THE ROW AND PER PLANT AT VARIOUS RATES PER 100 SQUARE FEET

Rates per 100 square ft	*Rates per 10 feet rows spaced*			*Rates per plant spaced*		
	3 ft	*2 ft*	*1 ft*	*5 x 5 ft*	*2¼ x 2¼ ft*	*2 x 1½ ft*
Pints	Pints	Pints	Pints	Pints	Cups	Cups
10	3	2	1	2½	1	½
	Cups	Cups	Cups	Cups		
6	3½	2½	1¼	3	½	¼
5	3	2	1	2½	½	¼
					Tbs	Tbs
4	2½	1½	¾	2	6½	3
3	1¾	1¼	½	1½	5	2½

TABLE 8-2 (continued)

FERTILIZERS, APPROXIMATE EQUIVALENT-VOLUME OF MATERIALS TO USE IN THE ROW AND PER PLANT AT VARIOUS RATES PER 100 SQUARE FEET

Rates per 100 square ft	Rates per 10 feet rows spaced			Rates per plant spaced		
	3 ft	2 ft	1 ft	5 x 5 ft	2¼ x 2¼ ft	2 x 1½ ft
Pints	Cups	Cups	Cups	Cups	Tbs	Tbs
2½	1½	1	½	1¼	4	2
			Tbs			
2	1¼	¾	6½	1	3¼	1½
1½	¾	½	5	¾	2½	1
					Tbs	Tbs
1	½	6	3¼	½	1½	2½
Cups				Tbs		
1½	½	5	2½	6	1	1½
	Tbs				Tsp	
1	5	3¼	1½	4	2½	¾
½	2½	1½	¾	2	1¼	½
Tbs			Tsp	Tsp		
4	1¼	2½	1¼	1	½	¼
	Tsp					
1	1	½	⅓	+	⅙	1/12
Bushels	Bushels	Pecks	Quarts	Bushel	Quarts	Quarts
2	½	1½	6	½	3	1½
	Peck			Peck		
1	1	1	3	1	1½	¾

Courtesy of United States Department of Agriculture.

It will be useful to remember: (1) A pint of water weighs just a little more than a pound (actually, 1.046 pounds). (2) An acre is equivalent to 43,560 square feet (a plot about 209 feet square). (3) A pint is equivalent to two cups, or 32 tablespoons, or 96 teaspoons.

MIXING LIQUID FERTILIZERS

Dried blood (12 percent nitrogen): 4 teaspoons per gallon of water.
Steamed bone meal (11 percent phosphorus): 1 tablespoon per gallon of water.
Complete fertilizer (such as 10-10-10): 2 tablespoons per gallon of water.

Ground limestone: 2 tablespoons per gallon of water.

Muriate of potash (50 percent potash): 1/2 teaspoon per gallon of water.

Nitrate of soda (16 percent nitrogen): 1 tablespoon per gallon of water.

Cow manure (well-rotted): 1 dry quart to 2 gallons of water.

Hen manure (guano): 1 dry pound to 5 gallons of water.

Horse and cow manure must be stirred once or twice a day for a week before they are ready to use. Fertilizing with liquid manure or other liquid fertilizers is done in the same way as watering, except that none of it must be allowed to touch the foliage. Liquid fertilizers and manures are readily absorbed by the plants' root structures. Using liquid fertilizer is the quickest way to apply plant nutrients to the soil and thus to the plant itself.

9

Save Your Own
Garden Seed

There are many ways to travel along the road to independence and self-sufficiency. One of them could be the saving of your own garden seed. The advantages are obvious when you give it a bit of serious thought. First, prices are climbing steadily, and second, we have already experienced shortages of several varieties. Both these tendencies will worsen as inflation takes its toll and the numbers of gardeners increase rapidly because of economic necessity. Furthermore, the seeds you save from your own crops should be an excellent choice simply because they are adapted to your local soil and climatic conditions.

Most authorities on horticulture do not recommend the saving of seed from the home vegetable garden. They cite the facts that hybrids produce more uniform and larger yields than standard varieties. Commercial seed are produced and processed under more uniform and scientific conditions than those grown in the home garden, with a consequent higher percentage of germination. Their clinching argument is that some varieties have U.S. Variety Plant Protection, which prohibits unauthorized seed multiplication. We are thoroughly acquainted with several hundred varieties and the only one that we recall as being in this category is the Burpee Golden Zucchini.

Our contention is that our contemporary society depends on strict regimentation and narrowly defined specialists who purposely bombard the public with a lot of nonsense in order to further their own interests.

Seed collection should have special appeal for the organic gardener who wants seeds that have never been exposed to chemicals or pesticides.

Our ancestors a century back into history did not have the handicap of vested interests and pie-in-the-sky advertising. Consequently, they saved their own garden seeds from year to year and produced about 95 percent of their annual supply of food. The only time they bought seed was to get a start of a new species or variety.

You can be highly successful at saving your own seed if you will observe the following conditions:

1. Select the very best *standard* varieties of the seed you initially purchase to start your garden. Hybrids will either be infertile, or they will revert to the dominant strain of one of the parent stock. In either case, hybrids will not reproduce, true to form, from seed you save.

2. During the growing season, select the most vigorous plant exhibiting the best characteristics of its kind, for that particular variety, and mark it for future identification with a piece of cloth, a piece of string, or something similar. Your careful selection of the finest, most vigorous stock will eventually result in a superior strain or subvariety that is especially suited to your local climate and soil. When the seeds or fruits reach the desired stage of maturity or overripeness on your previously marked plants, harvest, process, and store for future use. What we have just pointed out is that you *must* start selecting seed before harvesting from those plants that have produced best. This method of seed selection is far superior to making a random selection from a mixture of seed harvested indiscriminately. You cannot expect seed to grow into plants that are superior to their parent plant. Consequently, it only makes good sense to select your seed from plants that have already demonstrated to at least some degree that they possess the desired traits in greater measure than the average plant, and are thus more likely to concentrate and pass on these desired traits in the offspring.

The time required for harvestable seed to develop varies from one crop to another. However, the significant factor is whether the plant needs one season or two for full development and seed production. Those that produce seed in one season—the annuals—include most of the favorite vegetables that are grown by home gardeners. These are comprised of the following: beans, cantaloupe, corn (pop and sweet), cucumber, eggplant, lettuce, mustard greens, peas, peanuts, peppers (hot and sweet), potatoes, pumpkin, radishes, spinach, squash (summer and winter), sunflower, tomatoes, and watermelon.

Beans and peas to be saved for seed, or for table use in their dried form, can be left on the plants until thoroughly dry and then harvested for shelling.

Legumes are easily shelled by filling a gunnysack one-quarter full and tramping (walking) on it to break open the pods. Of course, you can get the same results by tramping on a thin layer of beans or peas in a box or tub. Now you can pick out the larger pieces of pods by hand and pour a mixture of legumes and pods from one large pan to another in a moderate breeze (create your own breeze with a fan) to blow the debris away. Small quantities of both beans and peas are easily shelled by hand. Store the seed in clean containers in a dry place having a uniform temperature.

Corn (pop and sweet) should be left on the stalk until the ears are quite dry. When you pick the ears, strip back the husks and hang them in a dry area to become completely dehydrated. When the kernels have shrunk to minimum size and become thoroughly dry, shell them out, package and store for future use.

Cantaloupe, cucumber, pumpkin, squash, and watermelon are all vine crops having comparatively large seeds that are easily collected from the ripe fruit. Select the earliest-maturing fruit of each variety and leave it on the vine to become fully ripe. This actually means that you should be sure that it is overripe before you pick it for seed collection. All of them will change color after ripening, and you should not harvest fruits for seed until the change in color occurs. For example, cucumbers turn to a gorgeous, golden hue before they are ready to be picked for their seed. When the fruit is ready for seed collection, cut it in half and scrape the contents of the seed cavity into a glass, porcelain, or wooden container. Cover with water and let the mixture ferment for a day or two to separate the seeds from the mucillaginous membrane to which they are attached. When you think they have fermented enough, pour in more water and stir vigorously. The immature seed and pulp will float on top, with the good seed resting on the bottom of the container. Pour off the waste products and thoroughly wash the seeds with fresh water. You can obtain good results from seed collecting without fermenting the seeds from pumpkin, squash, and watermelon. Merely wash the seeds thoroughly and pick off any pulp adhering to the seed. Scatter thinly on a towel and dry thoroughly. Keep on dry paper for a week or longer in a dry place before packaging and storing in a dry area.

Do not pick the eggplant you have saved for seed collection until the first frost is expected. Let it remain on the plant until the seeds turn brown.

Let your peppers stay on the plant until thoroughly ripe—red or golden —and rather soft. The seeds of all fleshy crops are processed in the same manner as those of cantaloupe and cucumber.

Lettuce for seed collection is best done by choosing those plants that tend to bolt (go to seed) at the latest time. The lateness in bolting is a very desirable trait in lettuce. It may be necessary to stake and support the taller tops to keep them from falling over. If the seed heads appear reluctant to ripen, split them with a sharp knife. When the seeds have fully developed, shake them into a paper bag or other container. Spread out on paper in a dry, warm area to shed any residual moisture before packaging and storing.

Radishes are cross-pollinated by insects, and you will have better results by growing only one variety. Choose the earliest and largest plants for seed collection and stake the seed pod stems to prevent breakage. When seedpods are mature, cut the stems and hang the pods in a dry, warm place to lose any remaining moisture. When thoroughly dry, shell out the contents, package, and store.

Tomatoes for seed collection should be left on the plant until overripe. Two tomatoes will furnish enough seed for the average home garden. Quarter these tomatoes and squeeze the insides into a glass, porcelain, or wooden container and mash them thoroughly, but gently, so as not to injure the seed. Fill the container with water and let the mixture stand for two days. The pulp will float to the top and can be poured off with the liquid, leaving the seeds on the bottom. Wash the seeds thoroughly and spread out to dry on a towel or other absorbent, flat surface. When thoroughly dry, package and store in a dry place having a uniform temperature.

So far, we have been talking about the annuals, vegetables that produce their seeds for propagation during a single gardening season. Now it is time to think about the biennials, which do not mature and produce seeds until their second year or second gardening season. The biennials include beets, cabbage, carrots, onions, parsley, parsnips, rutabagas, and turnips.

The collection of beet seed is made during the second season. Harvest the roots from the first season and keep them in cool storage during the winter. In early spring transplant them back into the garden in rows with the crown level with the ground. Let the plants develop seed stalks and grow to maturity. Cut the seed stalks and hang in a dry, ventilated place to shed all their residual moisture. When thoroughly dry, shake out and remove the seeds for packaging and storing.

The same procedure for seed collection is used with all the biennials. However, you should cut the tops of beets, carrots, parsnips, rutabagas, and turnips about one-half inch above the crown and be careful not to injure it. Also, dig or harvest the roots carefully so that you will not bruise or injure the tap root.

All of the root crops can be stored in the ground if they are protected from freezing. You may want to experiment with the biennials that you cultivate for seed collection by simply cutting the tops and then mulching with a thick layer of spoiled hay. Remove the mulch in the spring at about the same time you would normally transplant roots or sow seeds for that variety.

There are some limitations on saving your own seeds of varieties that belong to the same species, are pollinated by insects, and will cross with one another. This classification fits the following members of the cabbage family: broccoli, brussels sprouts, cabbage, cauliflower, kale, and kohlrabi. Seed production in the home garden is feasible only when a single member of this family is grown.

Viability of seed varies with different species and does not appear to be the least bit related to size, as the uninitiated may think. We believe that a mathematical average of seeds used in the home garden would give them a useful life of four years. However, the viability would depend on species, variety, care used in seed collection, method of packaging, and temperature and humidity of the storage area. When you consider all the variables that can affect the useful life of seeds, you begin to appreciate the fact that fresh seeds are highly desirable. Consequently, date the seeds that you collect and try to use them the following year. On the other hand, do not hestitate to use seeds that you have kept for three years. Just remember that seed deteriorates with age, and the percentage of germination will continue to decrease with each passing year. Consequently, you must sow or plant more of them in order to get the desired stand.

10

Drying Food

ADVANTAGES

1. Reduction in bulk and weight. Five pounds of fresh fruit will yield
   about one pound of dried fruit. This loss of weight is due to the reduction of moisture content from about 80 percent in the fresh raw
   state to about 20 percent after being dried. You can easily verify this
   weight loss. Weigh the batch of fruit after it is prepared for drying,
   then weigh the same batch again after it has been dried. There is also
   a corresponding decrease in bulk.

   There may be a greater loss of weight and bulk in vegetables, because more moisture is removed; the remaining moisture content in
   the dried produce is close to 10 percent.
2. Ease of storage. You can store three or four times more dried food
   in a given area than is possible with either canned or frozen foods.
   The packaging is much less expensive, and dried food is not dependent on a constant flow of electricity and will not freeze and burst
   when for some unexpected reason it is exposed to freezing conditions.
3. Initial starting costs. You can start drying food (fruits and vegetables) without spending a single penny for equipment. The sun, am-
   bient temperature, or atmospheric heat and natural air are all free

gifts from a bountiful nature. Whatever else is needed for sun and air drying of produce can be found in any average home.

4. Various methods used. There are no set procedures for home drying of foods similar to the uniform methods employed in canning and freezing. The various methods include air drying, sun drying, string drying, oven drying, steam drying, and electrically heated dehydrators.

The numerous methods all have the common denominators of heat and air flow. These two elements are the requisites for all food drying.

5. Quality. Nothing is added, and the only thing removed is water. Some loss of vitamins A and C occurs, but with this exception, dried fruits and vegetables contain the same nutritive values found in fresh produce. Similar losses occur in cooking, canning, and freezing of food.

6. Satisfaction. Absolutely nothing compares with the feeling of self-sufficiency that comes from having a reserve supply of top-quality food that is free of additives. No artificial coloring, no flavor enhancers, and no long-term preserving agents—and no dependence on public utilities or freezing weather.

DISADVANTAGES

There are some disadvantages to food drying, and you should study them carefully to determine if they outweigh the advantages.

1. Some vegetables lose their green and yellow colors and turn to a neutral gray when sun-dried. The leafy greens become brown and in some instances rather unappetizing, although most of their nutritive values are retained.

2. The drying process is time-consuming. However, it costs nothing (or at most a few pennies when using a light bulb in a box) and is almost foolproof.

3. The appearance of your dried foods will not compare, in some instances, with those prepared commercially, and the flavor may not be the same. This difference in appearance and flavor is due to the differences in the techniques used. The food-producing industry sulfurs fruits and adds coloring, flavoring, and preserving agents to ensure that the products have a pleasing appearance and the ability to hold up under excessively long and sometimes adverse storage conditions.

SELECTION

Select blemish-free fruits and vegetables of the highest quality when they reach peak maturity. Drying will not improve the quality of the fruits and vegetables that you preserve in this manner. Consequently, it is readily apparent that you must start with firm, fresh, ripe, perfectly clean foods. Choose as carefully as you would for immediate use at the table. Handle them carefully to prevent any bruising or crushing.

Apples, berries, apricots, cherries, dates, figs, grapes, nectarines, peaches, pears, plums, prunes, and rhubarb are fruits that dry well.

Larger fruits like apples, nectarines, peaches, and pears should be cut into slices or wedges of a uniform size (not thicker than 1/4 inch) to expedite drying and to ensure that all are through drying at the same time. It is important to have uniformity in thickness of pieces for even, thorough drying of the entire batch. It is best to leave those vitamin- and mineral-rich peelings on the fruit for better nutrition.

Nature provides a waterproofing substance in the form of a wax-like coating on the skins of firm berries like blueberries, cranberries, gooseberries, and huckleberries. This same or similar coating is present on the skins of cherries, figs, grapes, plums, and prunes. All of the foregoing dry better, more easily and more quickly if this waterproofing substance is removed before preservation by drying is started.

Removal of the waterproofing substance is accomplished by dipping the fruit in briskly boiling water for 30 to 60 seconds, followed by a dunking in very cold water, and then draining thoroughly. Lay the fruit on absorbent toweling and cover with the same material to quickly remove all excess moisture. You may use a wire basket, a colander, or an 18-inch square of cheesecloth for this operation. The cheesecloth is more desirable, because it takes less heat from the boiling water and warms the cold water less.

This boiling water treatment not only removes the waterproofing substance but also causes "checking" or minute cracking of the tough outer skin, thereby allowing internal moisture to escape much faster.

Small fruits like cherries, dates, figs, grapes, plums, and strawberries are best dried whole. Sweet cherries and strawberries make delightfully different "natural candies" when dried with their stems left on. They are tastier, with their natural sugars concentrated, than any man-made confection. They are to be treasured for holiday or special occasion gifts. Dried fruits store well in tightly sealed glass jars that are kept in a cool, dark place. Naturally, they keep well in sealed plastic bags in the refrigerator. They keep indefinitely when frozen in rigid freezer containers.

The list of vegetables that dry well includes most everything that is grown in the home garden, namely: beans (all types and varieties), broccoli, cabbage, carrots, comfrey, corn (pop and sweet), cucumbers, celery leaves (stalks do not dry well), garlic, kale, mustard greens, okra, onions, parsley, parsnip, peas, peanuts, hot and sweet peppers, pumpkin, summer and winter squash, spinach, Swiss chard, and tomatoes.

TESTS FOR DRYNESS IN FRUITS

Fruits are dry enough to store well when no appreciable moisture can be squeezed from a piece of the fruit when cut apart in the middle. Another good indication of proper drying is the "leathery" dry and shriveled outside appearance with just a bit of detectable softness in the middle of the piece. Fruit that is stored without being sufficiently dry will mold and become inedible. Your sense of taste will also help you determine when fruit is dry enough, but not overdried. When just right, it is flavorful and sweet. When overdried it becomes hard and brittle and loses its flavor. Pay close attention to this phase of the preservation process, and you will quickly become quite expert.

It is easier to determine when vegetables are dry enough for packaging and storing. There can be no mistaking dried beans and peas, for they will rattle, shrivel, change color, and become hard when dry.

Sweet corn turns semi-transparent and becomes very hard when dry. It can be pulled, shucked, and desilked. There is no need to blanch; simply cut it off the cob and put it in a shallow tray, not more than one inch deep. Dry it in a 140°F oven for two or three hours. Remove and stir thoroughly and allow to cool for a few minutes, then replace in the oven and repeat the process until the corn is dry. Decrease the time in oven between drying and cooling periods as it becomes drier.

Cucumbers, sweet peppers, and summer squash are brittle to crisp. As a general rule, most vegetables are "brittle" or "tough-to-brittle" when dry enough to store well for long periods of time. A final word about "doneness." When foods are still hot or even warm from the sun or dryer, they will seem to be more pliable, moister, and softer than they actually are. Take a small sample and cool it—then examine and decide if it is done.

STORAGE

There are two major schools of thought as to when dried food is ready to package and store, and both are logical. Both are effective, and it may take several years of close observation before you decide which is better, if ever.

The first premise is that you cool the dried food and immediately package it in suitable bags, containers, or jars.

The second premise is that you should *condition* the dried fruits and vegetables before packaging them for storage. This method allows you to observe what is happening to the dried food for the first few days. Here is the way to proceed: Pour the cooled, dried food into large-mouthed, open containers, such as crocks or enamelware. Store these open containers in a warm, dry room for 10 to 15 days, stirring the contents daily and bringing the bottom layer up toward the top. Once you are sure that no mold is forming and that the contents are storing well, it is time to expose the dried produce to "high heat" to ensure that no insect eggs or harmful spoilage will develop. Do this by spreading the dried food about one-inch thick on cookie sheets or shallow trays. Process for about 10 minutes in a 170° oven. Cool thoroughly before packaging and storing. It may be advantageous for you to package enough for one meal in each package and label and date it with a felt or nylon marker.

The twin enemies of dried foods are insects and moisture. Sealed brown bags, glass jars and other containers are suitable as long as you can make them moisture- and insect-proof. All dried food containers should be stored in a dry, cool place. If glass jars are used, either cover with paper to exclude light or store in a dark place. Light has an adverse effect on the dried food. Make an occasional inspection for signs of moisture or insects. If either one is detected, open the container and reheat the dried food for about 10 minutes at 170°F. Cool and reseal in a fresh container.

Drying Food

After you see how easy it is to dry so many things right on the plant where they grew—and then experience the pleasure of drying green beans, apples, and other fruits and vegetables on pieces of string—you are almost sure to become interested in drying them at a more rapid rate than nature provides when they are at maximum size or all in one piece.

When starting out to dry foods for the first time, take an easy, relaxed approach and do a maximum amount of experimentation, coupled with close observation and note-taking. You can experiment and gain useful information about preserving food by drying at any time of the year, inside your home. Start by placing properly prepared fruits and vegetables on shallow trays or cookie sheets and then put them on or near the "hottest" areas in your home. These areas will include radiators, hot water heaters, fireplaces, and tops of refrigerators.

Alternatively, you could start your initiation by stringing some green beans and apple slices on pieces of twine and hanging them from a nail or rafter in any well-ventilated area. Check them daily and note changes in color and size. This will cost very little, and the experience will teach you quite a bit. If it is out of your garden season, buy a few green beans and apples in order that you may start learning by doing. Processing foods by drying is something that is as old as our recorded civilization but is little understood and practiced by the vast majorities of people throughout the industrial world of today.

Preserving food by drying is the oldest and simplest way known to mankind. However, it is little understood because it is not practiced by canning and freezing adherents. Also, the so-called convenience foods have further heightened dependence of people on local marketing whims. However, worldwide inflation, aggravated by explosive increases in population, coupled with ever-increasing shortages of food, may cause some of us to strive for self-sufficiency. If so, the first major step along the way could logically be a garden of our own and the natural preservation of all, or almost all of our food.

DRYING FRUITS AND VEGETABLES

Drying Green Snap Beans

The oldest and still the best method to use in the drying of green beans is that where the end product is known as "leather breeches." Use only select, tender green beans. Take a three- or four-foot length of strong thread or twine and tie a kitchen match stem (or similar-sized piece of wood) onto one end and put the other end through the eye of a long needle. A long needle is easier to work with. Now, push the needle through the center of the bean, pushing the beans together down against the other end of the thread, filling it from end to end but leaving enough room on the needle end to make a loop to put over a nail or enough to tie to a rafter. Hang the string of beans on a nail or rafter in a warm, airy space, but never in direct sunlight. The direct rays of the sun appear to rob the beans of some of their flavor. For the first two or three days there will not be much difference in their size and appearance. However, during the next four or five days the beans will start to dry up and change to a light brown color. During the next seven to ten days the beans will become noticeably lighter in color and considerably smaller, shrinking to less than one-half their original size. The beans are now completely dehydrated and may be stored in paper bags or boxes and kept in an area that is dry. Storage life is almost indefinite when they are kept in a dry area that is free of rodents and insects. The drying time may vary as much as two weeks, depending on the variables of the moisture content of the beans, the relative humidity, the average temperature, and ventilation of drying area.

When you get ready for a meal of "leather breeches," pull them off the string (unless you did this before storing) and drop your dried green beans into a pot of boiling water. Add one or two pieces of salt pork, bacon, or ham and cook slowly for two or three hours. Add just enough hot water to keep them covered while cooking and take care not to cook them too long. An occasional sampling will let you know when they are at their best—tender, but not mushy, not overcooked.

Apples, peaches, pumpkin, winter squash, and many other fruits and vegetables can be dried and preserved for future use by this identical, time-proven method. Slice the pieces to be strung and dried into sections or pieces about 1/4 inch thick. Handle carefully to keep them from being sliced through so as to fall off the string. You can readily restore dried foods to almost their original texture by soaking them in water for periods of two to eight hours. However, you must use only as much water as the food will absorb or use any excess to cook with. Dried fruits are "extra tasty" because of their concentrated sugar and make dandy snacks. To reconstitute, cover with water and soak for two or three hours until swollen and softened. Dried vegetables require three cups of water for each cup of dried produce. Allow to soak long enough for the liquid to be returned to the vegetable. You can now proceed with regular recipes. Do not waste the food values that accumulate in the water used to reconstitute dehydrated fruits and vegetables. A bit of experience and observation will soon teach you the time and water needed for revitalizing various fruits and vegetables.

HOW TO DRY BEANS

As you probably know, beans of all kinds are rich in protein and can be substituted for meat in many satisfying and healthful meals. All of them are easy to grow and can be left on the plant until dry enough to shell and store. Well, almost all of them; both limas and soybeans will sometimes split and drop their beans on the ground just about the time they are getting dry enough to harvest. You can eliminate this problem by picking these varieties at the very first indication of split pods and dropped beans. Shell them and spread them out on an old sheet or a clean floor to lose their last bit of moisture. When you think they are dry enough to store, put them in shallow trays and heat for about 10 to 15 minutes in an oven with a temperature of 170°– 180°F. This will eliminate any weevils or bugs and drive out any remaining moisture. As soon as they cool, store them in glass jars or coffee cans tightly closed to prevent entry of moisture. Moist beans will spoil and become unusable. You can "buy" extra protection from weevils and other bugs by placing a dried hot pepper in each container of dried beans. Red pepper is a very effective insect repellent.

If you should encounter a period of continual rainfall or damp weather while waiting for your beans to dry in the pods while still in the garden, pull up the entire   plant and hang it upside down in a sheltered, well-ventilated area. The beans will now dry instead of rotting in the pods, and your crop will be saved.

Many varieties are excellent when dried, and you should grow whatever you think will suit you best, keeping in mind that Pintos are both tasty and versatile and the Red Kidney is an old favorite. Of course, the October, or Cranberry and White Marrowfat, along with Pinto and Red Kidney, are the standard Bush Shell Beans. Then, again, you should not forget that the Kentucky Wonder, both pole and bush, are excellent when used as young green beans and are highly desirable as dry shell beans. The list is almost inexhaustible and the only real mistake you can make is not to grow and dry your own crop of beans.

DRYING HERBS

Herbs have been used throughout the centuries to enhance the best cuisines all over the world.

The most pleasurable way to improve your at-home dining is to experiment with herbs in all your cooking. For example, dried beans can have a delicate and different flavor with each method of preparation if you will experiment by adding very small amounts of the following, either singly or in various combinations: oregano, parsley, rosemary, sage, savory, sweet basil, and thyme—easy does it. Try small amounts singly at first, and then various combinations. If you will pursue this effort diligently, you cannot help but be pleased and surprised at the results.

Regardless of whether you grow your own herbs or gather them from the wild, it is very important that you dry and store them properly in order to preserve their flavor and oils. Gather the herbs in the late morning on a sunny day, using a sharp knife or scissors to cut the stems. Cut annuals back to the ground, leaving about half of the stalk of biennials and perennials. The blossoms of many impart a bitter taste; also, as buds and flowers are set, most of the plant's energy goes into this effort at the expense of the leaves. Harvesting is done in late summer and early fall.

Tie a comfortable handful tightly with strong twine. Hang the bunches of herbs upside down in a well ventilated dark attic or similar area. Herbs should be dried in darkness to retain more of their volatile oils and flavor.

In lieu of a dark place to dry them, place the tied bunches in brown paper bags to exclude light, tying the ends of the bags. Hang the bags from nails or rafters in any well ventilated place—garage, barn, or breezeway.

To dry leaves or herbs too small to be tied in bunches, place them in shallow boxes and stir them every other day to keep them from molding. Another good way is to spread them on newspapers or on an old sheet in a well ventilated, dark area.

Drying time will take from one to as much as two weeks. They are dry when you can crumble them into small pieces between your fingers. In some instances, it may take a bit longer to dry. They must be crumbly and completely dry before storing. During damp weather, or in areas with constant high humidity, it may be necessary to place your herbs on cookie sheets or shallow trays in a warm oven for five to 15 minutes to get them completely dry.

Now you can hold the stem in one hand and, starting from the base, strip all the leaves off with the other hand. Crumble the leaves very finely. Those stems can be used as you use pickling spices to impart flavor and aroma to broths, soups, and stews if they are stored in air-tight glass containers. Store herbs in tightly covered glass jars or bottles in a dark place. They deteriorate when exposed to light. If your storage area is not dark, cover the containers with brown paper, either taped or tied in place, to exclude all light. Do not experiment with other types of containers, because none are as satisfactory as glass.

SUN DRYING

To dry fruits and vegetables in the sunshine, you must protect the produce from insects. First, select an area in your yard that receives sunshine all day long. A picnic table, a folding, portable table, or a board supported by cinder blocks will provide a drying surface. Place the produce to be dried on cookie sheets, shallow trays, clean sheets, or brown wrapping paper. Spread the fruit or vegetable out in a single layer to facilitate air flow and better drying.

Use large pieces of fine material or netting placed over the produce to keep insects away. White-colored material absorbs less sunlight, allowing more to pass through to the produce. Make a raised border at the sides and ends of drying area with bricks or wood blocks to hold the cloth above the produce. Weight the netting down around the outside of these supports to prevent it from blowing away.

Each evening you must bring the produce indoors before dew begins to collect. You will appreciate using cookie sheets and shallow trays when you are moving the produce indoors in the evening and outside as soon as the dew is drying in the morning. Sun drying works best in the southwestern part of the United States in areas that have lots of sunshine accompanied by low humidity.

Solar ovens are used to good advantage in sunny sections of the country with high humidity.

AIR DRYING

This method of preservation may be used if you have a screened or glassed-in patio or porch. It works best in areas with low humidity. Of course, you may dry food in your attic or in any room of your home that is well ventilated.

Prepare the produce and place it in a single layer on clean paper or sheets. If your patio or porch is not screened, protect the produce with netting. When it begins to shrink and shrivel, turn it over to expose the other side to the air. This facilitates thorough drying. Air drying, due to lack of the sun's heat, requires more time than sun drying.

OVEN DRYING

This is a way to speed up the drying process, but it may result in the loss of more nutrients.

Place the produce on cookie sheets or in shallow trays in a single layer. Dry it in an oven heated to 180–200°F with the door partly open to permit some air flow and to induce drying instead of cooking. Complete drying will take from one to four hours.

STEAM DRYING

This is another rapid method of drying. It is similar to the double-boiler method of cooking and requires a special stove-top dryer having a lower section that is filled with water. Provision is made for filling and escape of excess steam. Hot steam heats the top of the dryer, where the produce is placed for drying. This double-boiler method of drying keeps the surface temperature in the range of 190–200°F.

STRING DRYING

This is the simplest method of all and is a variation of air, sun, and oven drying. One-quarter-inch slices of produce are strung on string and suspended from a nail or rafter in a warm, insect-free porch or attic, or above or adjacent to, a cook or heating stove.

ELECTRIC DEHYDRATORS

Electric dehydrators come in a large variety of sizes and prices. The larger models have large-capacity sliding trays, which enable you to dry much bigger amounts of produce at one time.

BULB-IN-BOX DRYER

You can fabricate a very inexpensive, small, indoor dryer in an hour or so.

The materials you will need are a cardboard box, eight to 12 inches deep, 10 to 12 inches wide and 14 to 20 inches long, and a portable trouble light. If you do not have a trouble light, fabricate a substitute from a suitable length of electric cord, a socket, and a plug cap. You will also need a cookie sheet or piece of sheet metal cut to fit the top of the box, enough aluminum foil to line the inside of the box, and a small amount of black paint.

Start this project by painting the bottom of the cookie sheet or the piece of sheet metal with the black paint to maximize heat absorption. Then line the inside of the box with aluminum foil, shiny side up. This foil effectively contains the heat from the light bulb and gives maximum heating effect. Cut a small hole in the end of the box, near the bottom, to pass the plug cap through. Place the light bulb setup in the center of the box and lead the plug and cord through the hole in the end of the box. Place the cookie sheet over the top of the box (black side down) and fill with a layer of sliced fruit or vegetables. Plug it in, and you are in business.

In 12 to 18 hours the produce will be dry and ready for storage for future use or for snacking at any time.

This little, inexpensive, indoor dryer can be put together for four to six dollars and will operate for pennies per day. Your only subsequent cost for operation is the electricity used by the light bulb.

The heat delivered to the cookie sheet or piece of sheet metal can be increased by one or all of the following adjustments:

1. Increase the wattage of the light bulb from 100 to 150 or more.
2. Decrease the "effective" size of the box by filling in the sides and ends with crumpled paper—between the aluminum foil and the box.
3. Decrease the distance between the bottom of the cookie sheet and the heat source by lowering it into the box—toward the light bulb. This means that you must provide a fairly level means of support for the cookie sheet to be set on. Cut six lengths of stiff wire from three coat hangers, or use similar stiff wire. Measure up from the floor (or down from the top) the level at which you want the cookie sheet to

be above the light bulb and scribe a straight line alongside of the box. Do this on both sides. Measure accurately and punch holes on a horizontal line so that cookie sheet will be nearly level. Start two inches from the end of the cookie sheet and mark four to six equidistant spots to insert wires for the supporting grill. Push a nail through the cardboard sides and insert the stiff wires. Experience will soon show you how to manage this little unit for peak efficiency.

The capacity can be increased by using longer boxes and adding extra lights—or simply by making additional units. Of course, it is a simple matter to "trap the heat" and increase drying temperature by covering the entire unit with a larger box. A good, desirable temperature for the surface of the cookie sheet is in the range of between 110 and 140°F. Lower temperatures are too slow, and much hotter temperatures will result in cooking versus drying. If you start with the light bulb within four or five inches of the bottom of the cookie sheet, you will not have much adjustment to make for desired heat level.

CABINET TYPE DRYER

If you have carpentry tools and the requisite skill, you can build a cabinet-type dryer equipped with a wall-type, thermostatically controlled, electric heater that is equipped with a small circulating fan. Something on the order of 800 to 1200 watts will be sufficient.

Basically, the design consists of a square cabinet with rough dimensions of two feet by four to five feet high. The top is equipped with a sliding lid to open as desired for controlling the flow of air and temperature to some extent. The heating unit is installed in the base. This does not have to be an electric wall-type heater equipped with a fan. You can use a heating plate or a cluster of heavy-duty light bulbs in porcelain sockets. Ventilation for adequate air flow can be provided by adjustable openings around the base. Further refinement can be made by directing the breeze from a small fan into an opening in the base.

A well-fitting, hinged door on the front is a necessity. Slides are provided at distances of three or four inches apart to support the drying trays, which are loaded into the cabinet through the door opening. The bottom set of slides should be eight to 12 inches above the base. There is a bit of controversy about what materials can best be used for the bottoms of the drying trays. It must be constructed so as to let a good flow of air through and around the produce being dried. Hardware cloth and aluminum screen are two possibilities. Fiberglass screen is considered highly desirable by some people. Whatever you use, be careful not to contaminate your food with cadmium and zinc, which may come off certain types of wire screening. Of course, you must be prudent and observe all applicable precautions when using electrical apparatus.

You will need a thermometer to measure temperatures in various levels of your dryer. Temperatures ranging from 100 to 140°F will dry fruits and vegetables in several hours without excessive loss of nutrients.

The drying process can be improved by a regular rotation of the trays. Remove the top tray. Move all trays upward one level. Now place the top tray in the bottom position. Repeat this procedure at regular one- or two-hour intervals.

SOLAR DRYER

You can build a solar dryer for small-scale outdoor drying when high humidity will not allow successful, natural air or sun drying. The angled glass top acts to collect and intensify the sun's heat. This heating effectively lowers the relative humidity inside the dryer so that the drying process is accelerated.

Neither dimensions nor materials need be kept to any set specifications. Consequently, you can put a solar dryer together in your spare time, using almost any material available.

The basic requirements for a solar dryer are:

1. A rectangular frame, similar to a cold frame, with rough dimensions of 2 × 6 feet. In the interests of efficiency it should be about three times as long as it is wide, to minimize shading by the ends. The back should be about twice as high as the front. Anything from 12 to 18 inches will be satisfactory for the height of the front.

2. A glass cover to concentrate the heat from the sun. The glass cover should be angled or sloped from back to front in order to intensify maximum heat from the sun. An angle of 25 degrees is about the correct slope for the central section of the United States running east and west. You may want to increase or decrease this angle a bit for best performance in your exact latitude. The cover can be made from two or three pieces of glass the thickness of ordinary window glass. Most building supply outlets carry this type of glass and cut it to desired sizes. Alternatively, you can use a big 3 × 6-foot storm sash; failing to find that, you can use any size window sashes that are available and build the frame to accommodate their size.

3. The outer shell and top cover of glass will trap the heat from the sun. However, to keep this heat from being dissipated rapidly, and

to greatly increase the dryer's effectiveness, you should insulate the inside. A further refinement, but one that is worthwhile, is to paint the interior black to maximize heat absorption and retention. Almost any kind of insulation will be effective. You can use multiple layers of cardboard, fiberglass, particle board, scrap plywood, sawdust, or sheetrock. Naturally, a solar dryer will work without insulation and without a black interior—these refinements merely make it much more efficient.

4. Since you are dealing with a box of hot air that is intended to be used for drying produce, it will be necessary to provide holes around the bottom of the front and end panels for entry of outside air. You can set up a natural convection current by drilling vent holes along the top section of the back. Cold air will enter through the bottom holes and, because of the heating effect on the inside of the dryer, will rise and exit through the vent holes at the top of the back section. This is exactly the desirable flow of air that you want to generate for the best drying effect. Holes should be about one-half inch or more in diameter. You will have to experiment with both number and location to get most desirable effect. Extra holes are easily plugged. You can use short pieces of garden hose to keep the holes open if you use fiberglass or sawdust insulation. Cover outside openings with screen or gauze to keep the bugs out.

5. Make your drying trays large enough to just fit comfortably inside the dryer. Loading and unloading of trays from dryer can be through a hinged top or a door on the back section.

6. The desired temperature of 120 to 150°F can be attained on sunny days in a well-constructed dryer. Regulation of air flow by closing and opening of air holes and/or by cracking the seal on the glass cover will vary inside temperature.

11

Fruits, Berries, Grapes, And Nuts

The following information is quoted verbatim from Stark Bro's Catalog. Stark Bro's are the oldest orchardists in America (est. 1816) and the largest in the world.

Home fruit gardens often bear delicious fruit in two years.

On a spot about the size of your living room you can have your own home fruit garden. You can harvest big, delicious apples for pies, sauces, jellies, salads or eating fresh. You can enjoy sweet, naturally tree-ripened peaches, or reach out and pick the fine flavored pears. Just imagine the joy you'll get from making fresh cherry pies and cobblers. Or, the thrill your children will feel when they pick fruit from the back yard.

Sounds like a dream! But, it can come true with Stark Bro's dwarf-size fruit trees with a pedigree. Our process enables us to control the size of the tree. In fact, the fruit from your dwarf trees often will be bigger than fruit from big, space-claiming standard trees. And, you get quicker crops with proper care. Your trees will probably bear the second or third year.

WHAT YOU SHOULD KNOW ABOUT POLLINATION

Most of the peach, nut prune, apricot and pie cherry trees listed in this catalog do not require cross pollination (pollen from another variety). All other fruit trees require another tree to provide proper pollination in order to bear abundant fruit. The chart below lists all varieties requiring pollinators. Many neighborhoods have enough fruit trees growing to insure pollination of your fruit trees, but if you are not absolutely sure of those available in your area, we recommend you follow the pollination chart below to insure proper pollination.

The following fruit trees are self-fertile (do not require another variety for cross pollination):

Golden Delicious, Red Rome Beauty, Stark Tropical Beauty and Jonathan apples. All peaches and nectarines, except Stark Hal-Berta Giant, Stark Honeydew Hale and J. H. Hale Peaches.

Duchess and Kieffer Pear.

All Pie Cherries.

All prunes, except Burbank Grand Prize, Blufre.

All Apricots.

Most nut trees. (Pecans are sometimes self-fertile, but to insure maximum crops plant another variety.)

These pollination requirements apply to all tree sizes (dwarf, semidwarf or standard) of a particular variety.

We recommend pollinators for the following fruit trees. For maximum crops, we suggest the fruit trees indicated in the right-hand column.

Type of Fruit Requiring Pollinator	Suggested Pollinator
All apples, EXCEPT Golden Delicious—Jonathan Red Rome Beauty Stark Tropical Beauty	Any other variety of apple tree except the Winesaps and Stark Scarlet Styamared. Most potent pollinators: Starkrimson, Starkspur EarliBlaze, and Starkspur Golden Delicious.
Peaches: Stark Hal-Berta Giant Stark Honeydew Hale J. H. Hale	Any other variety of peach tree. Most potent pollinators: Burbank July Elberta, Starking Delicious, and Stark Early Elberta.
All pears, EXCEPT: Duchess and Kieffer	Any other variety of pear tree, except Magness. (Bartlett and Seckel are not compatible.) Most potent pollinators: Starking Delicious and Moonglow.
All sweet cherries	Venus, Stark Gold or Van.

Type of Fruit Requiring Pollinator	Suggested Pollinator
All plums, EXCEPT: Giant Damson and Green Gage	Any other variety of plum tree. Most potent pollinator: Redheart.
Prunes: Burbank Grand Prize	Blufre or Stanley.

Here's why fall is the perfect planting time for 2/3 of the nation:

1. In the fall, trees stop new growth and are at an ideal stage to dig and transplant to their permanent place in your yard.
2. In the fall, the soil is nearly always in the best condition—warm, moist and mellow—for planting fruit trees.
3. Fall planted trees become firmly established over the winter and are ready to start vigorous growth the following spring. This often pays off as a full year's headstart over trees planted in the spring.

MINI-TREES

Stark Bro's Research Brings You the Miniature Fruit Tree

It's so revolutionary you don't need a big yard to grow your own fresh fruit.

For many years Stark Bro's has been looking for a smaller fruit tree especially for people with a limited space available. Some time ago, we learned about the pioneering efforts of Mr. Fred Anderson of California, who had been working with nectarines to develop a genetic or "natural" dwarf tree. When he told us he had been successful, we jumped at the chance to buy the rights to it. So we offer this fantastic new development to you.

Now you can harvest fresh, top quality, large peaches or nectarines on a tiny plot of ground or even on your patio or apartment balcony.

You can grow plenty of tree-ripened, naturally good peaches and nectarines on a spot no bigger than 4' X 5' in your yard or garden.

Just follow the planting instructions carefully both for yard and container planting.

Be sure your trees get plenty of sunlight, fertilizer and moisture. And you'll have peaches and nectarines for fresh eating, preserves, canning and cooking before you know it.

These amazing little trees are easily kept to smaller than six feet tall. And they'll grow in your lawn or garden anywhere a shrub will.

Ideal for yard or garden plantings where space is a problem.

Grow Stark Miniatures anywhere you'd plant a bush or a shrub. You'll get lovely spring-time blossoms, a beautiful, bushlike ornamental tree—and, best of all, you'll reap the delicious, extra benefits of your own fresh fruit.

These hardy, vigorous growing little trees will really stand out wherever you plant them. Their naturally compact growth and beautiful foliage rivals the most outstanding ornamentals. And the fresh fruit you'll harvest can actually make them pay for themselves.

We suggest a large, well-drained redwood box with a minimum depth and width of 18 to 20 inches. A medium coarse potting mixture of approximately 2 parts good garden soil, 1 part sand, and 1 part humus (such as peat moss) is ideal. Several applications of a well-balanced fertilizer such as Stark Tre-Pep are recommended during the growing season. Watering is essential—keep the soil moist, but not waterlogged. Prune the tree back 1/3 to 1/2 at planting time, and selectively prune new growth to allow plenty of sunshine into the branches. Place in a sunny spot (6 to 8 hours of sun or partial shade daily minimum). In the Central and Northern states when temperature drops below 20 degrees, move the containerized miniature trees into a sheltered area or unheated garage during the winter months to prevent freezing of the roots. Some winter chilling is essential to maintain winter dormancy and insure normal growth next season.

APPLES

The World's Best All-purpose Golden Apple

®Starkspur Golden Delicious—Stark Bro's paid $51,000 for the original tree.

Elon Gilbert originated this superb tree, and we paid him $51,000 for the original tree and full U.S. Patent Rights. You can't get this tree from anyone but Stark Bro's. And you can't go wrong with a Starkspur Golden Delicious.

Starkspur Golden Delicious is the perfect teammate for Starkrimson Delicious. Both are fast profit makers for home and commercial orchards. Both do well in limited space. Both have superb flavor, aristocratic shape. And both bear more apples quicker than any other trees around. They are perfect pollenizers for each other.

Starkspur Golden Delicious is truly the best all-purpose apple in the world. It's prized for eating fresh, cooking, baking, canning, jelly and apple butter. It keeps well after being sliced and it's ideal for salads. Also a favorite for baby food.

Starkspur Golden Delicious Apple (Semi-dwarf Apple Tree)

Its wonderful flavor is distinctive, the same that made the Stark Golden Delicious a world favorite. The Starkspur Golden Delicious has an aristocratic shape. It's longer and more typey than even the Stark Golden Delicious.

It's extra large, often measuring 4 inches or more.

Keeping ability is exceptional. The fruit stays solid, crisp and juicy in poly bags in your refrigerator throughout the winter.

Starkspur Golden Delicious is hardy in tree and bud. It will withstand lower temperatures and more severe conditions than standard-size trees. It has three sets of blooms, so if frost gets the first two, the third bloom can come through with a crop.

You get bigger crops faster. The numerous fruit spurs assure greater production on a regular and annual basis with less pruning and little or no propping. And you'll get crops the second or third year after planting.

It's the ideal tree size. Dwarf and semi-dwarf Starkspur Golden Delicious let you plant more trees in the same area. Pick most of the fruit without any ladder or a small stepladder. Pruning and spraying is easier, too.

Your apples ripen in early October in Zone 6. Trees do best in Zones 5 to 8.

SOME "BEAR FACTS" ABOUT APPLES

Scientific evidence proves that the minerals and vitamins in apples help digestion, nerves, skin, eyes, teeth, gums as well as the general healthy growth of the human body.

Tests at the University of Michigan show that apples can help reduce colds and other respiratory ailments.

And naturally tree-ripened apples from your own Stark Bro's trees have that fantastic flavor you'll thoroughly enjoy.

Apples are especially welcome in many homes because many varieties keep so well. In fact, by selecting certain varieties that keep especially well, others that ripen early, you can enjoy fresh apples all year 'round. In addition, apples are perhaps the most versatile of all fruits, delicious fresh, fine for freezing or canning, wonderful in pies, and great for applesauce and apple butter. And what child doesn't love a candy apple on a stick?

Your Stark Bro's trees will grow in most any yard or garden soil. If it's a heavy soil, you can give the tree a head start by mixing in up to 50 percent peat when you fill the planting hole.

Most apple varieties do well anywhere in Zones 5 to 8. If you live in Zones 3 and 4 you'll have to be a little more selective and grow varieties like McIntosh, Cortland, Wealthy, Spartan and Northern Spy.

In Zone 9, where winters are warm, you can now plant Stark Tropical Beauty Dwarf trees with the same success as apple growers in the colder regions.

Most apple trees need other apple varieties to bear heavy crops. There may be enough apple trees nearby for this cross pollination, but you should always plant two or more varieties if you have the space. Starkspur Golden Delicious is the perfect pollinator because it produces three successive sets of blooms.

Young trees should be shaped to provide a strong framework to carry heavy loads of fruit. Many experts recommend the modified-leader form, where a central main branch has symmetrically placed side branches all the way to the top. These side branches should form wide angles with the trunk; 10 o'clock, 2 o'clock are ideal. This spreading can be encouraged by using shaped laths or with stakes and strong twine.

Developed through years of research, the Stark dwarf apple tree makes growing your own fruit easier than ever before.

With normal pruning, this little tree will seldom grow more than 8 to 10 feet tall. At maturity, you can pick 4 to 6 bushels of delicious fresh fruit every summer without dangerous (or high) ladders.

Scientific engineering makes the difference. And Stark Bro's dwarfing process is so unique, it was once patented.

Just look at the four different parts that are hand grafted in every Stark dwarf apple tree.

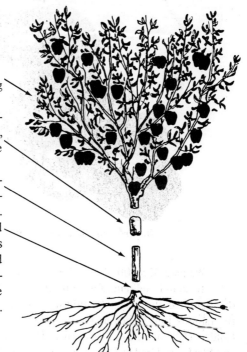

1. One-year-old well-branched top of superior record-bearing variety.
2. Unique dwarfing section controls size of tree naturally, yet allows top to produce full-size fruit.
3. Two-year-old hardy trunk section makes tree sturdy and resistant to winter damage.
4. Well-developed three-year-old vigorous hardy seedling roots selected for deep rooting and spreading characteristics. Insures good, solid anchorage for the life of the tree.

You'll harvest your first crop of delicious, vitamin rich, homegrown fruit usually within 2 to 3 years after planting. And with care, your dwarf tree will live and bear for many, many years.

You pay a little extra for Stark Bro's handmade dwarf tree with a pedigree. But you get the perfection of an ornamental fruit bearing tree that best meets the needs of the home grower.

We've improved the world's 2 most famous apples and now you can pick them from dwarf trees in your yard.

Starkrimson Delicious Apple (Suburbia Today)

We paid $76,000.00 to develop these trees.

It sounds unbelievable, but it's true. Stark Bro's paid $25,000.00 for the rights to the original semi-dwarf Starkrimson tree, new improvement in the famous Red Delicious family; and $51,000.00 for the original Starkspur Golden Delicious Semi-Dwarf tree. The pedigreed Starkrimson Red Delicious and Starkspur Golden Delicious you get are direct-in-line descendants of these two expensive mother trees.

Now you can grow and harvest these two tasty apples right in your own backyard. You get big, shiny Red Delicious or Golden Delicious Apples often in just 2 to 3 years. And Stark Bro's revolutionary dwarfing process controls the size of the tree without affecting the size of the fruit, to give you the size tree perfect for your needs.

And you can plant your trees on a spot no larger than your living room. Your family, neighbors and friends can watch this miracle of nature as the blossoms turn into tiny apples that grow into full-size fruit that's often 4 inches or more in diameter. These trees will bring years of enjoyment and eating pleasure. Stark Bro's Starkrimson Red Delicious and Starkspur Golden Delicious are truly horticultural marvels.

The Starkrimson Red Delicious, discovered in Hood River, Oregon, in 1956, was so important to the world of horticulture that a burglar-proof cage with a burglar alarm was built to protect the trees. These trees are invaluable because true-to-variety apples cannot be grown from seeds. They can only be produced with scions from the original tree.

Stark Red Rome (Law)

First Crop Pays for Your Trees

Stark Bro's Starkrimson Red Delicious and Starkspur Golden Delicious apples are the famous apples with 5-pointed crown. You pay as much as 15 cents apiece for them at stores and fruitstands.

But, you can get them fresh from your own backyard for even lower cost per bushel in just a few years. The first couple of bushels you pick will pay for your trees. And you'll harvest your first crop in the second or third year.

You'll save money on fresh fruit when your apple trees start producing. And you'll be adding beauty and value to your property.

Imagine picking Golden Delicious and Red Delicious apples from trees no taller than a lilac bush. Trees that take up only a few feet of space in shrub borders, at the corner of your house or as part of a hedge. Trees that often begin bearing fruit only 18 months to two years after planting.

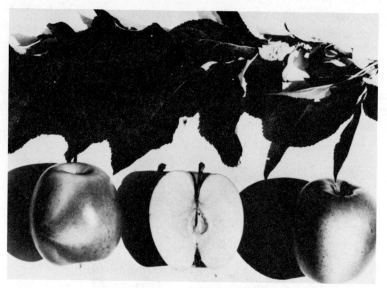

Blushing Golden Apple (Griffith Strain)

Harvest Your Apples for Fresh Eating, Cooking or Canning

When your trees start producing, you'll have plenty of delicious, fresh fruit for your family and friends to enjoy. And there are literally dozens of ways to serve your orchard-fresh apples. You can freeze them, can them, even store them in poly bags in your refrigerator. That is if you don't eat them all up!

Gala Apple

Starkspur Means More Fruit Per Limb, More Fruit Per Tree

Starkspur dwarf and semi-dwarf apple trees produce more fruit because each limb has more fruit-bearing spurs. The illustration below shows the difference between a spur-type and a regular limb.

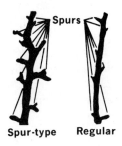

Spurs

Spur-type   Regular

The Starkspur apple tree is a natural or genetic semi-dwarf, but the root system is in no way restricted. It has the identical strong, sturdy roots of a standard-size tree. This means your Starkspur tree has the best anchorage of any semi-dwarf tree. Dwarf-size trees result from the 4-part grafting system explained on page 209.

Starkspur trees seldom need propping, because their stiff, strong framework supports huge quantities of fruit without assistance.

Starkspur Earliblaze Apple

Starkspur trees have less sucker growth and water sprouts. Instead of this wasteful vegetative growth, these trees develop productive spur growth.

Starkspur trees are hardier in tree and bud. Even when other trees have failed to produce, Starkspur trees most always bear large crops.

Greater Production. Starkspur trees can actually outproduce a standard tree. Count on twice as much fruit during the first ten years.

Less Spray. Starkspur trees are more compact, so it's faster and easier to get the job done. Smaller equipment is usually adequate, too.

Less Pruning. Starkspur trees require very little pruning after they are in good production.

Easy Picking. Starkspur trees grow more compactly, so you don't need tall ladders to harvest the fruit. It's a "Picker's Paradise."

PEACHES

"Bear Facts" About Peaches

Peaches will do well in any home yard or garden. (If planting in very tight clay, add 1/3 peat moss.) When planting peach trees, be sure to follow instructions regarding soil preparation and Tre-Pep fertilizer carefully, because vigorous growth is important to the health of the young peach tree.

Peaches grow best in Zones 5 to 8 (see Zone Map, page 215), but a few Stark Bro's varieties such as Starking Delicious, Burbank July Elberta, and Desertgold do well in the cooler parts of Zone 9 and the West Coast peach growing areas.

Peaches are at their delicious best when you pick them right off the tree, or about one day before they're eating ripe, and let them ripen in a cool place for 24 hours. Incidentally, the peach is the most popular canning fruit around, and there are dozens of excellent recipes available.

To get your peach trees to bear bigger fruit, it's important to thin fruit to 8 inches apart on early ripening varieties and 6 inches apart on later ripening varieties.

You can expect fresh peaches the second year after planting your Stark Bro's trees, with full production being reached in the fourth or fifth year.

Most peaches are self-pollinating, so you can plant a single tree with confidence. However, if you're planting J. H. Hale, Honeydew Hale or Hal-Berta Giant, you need to plant another variety to assure proper pollination.

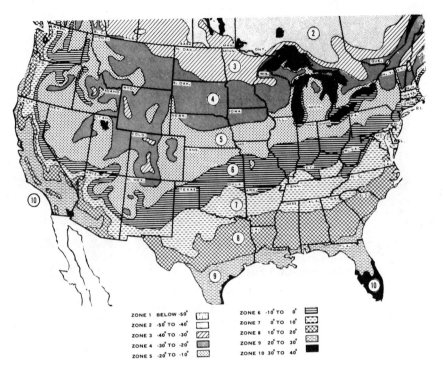

ZONE 1	BELOW -50°		ZONE 6	-10° TO 0°	
ZONE 2	-50° TO -40°		ZONE 7	0° TO 10°	
ZONE 3	-40° TO -30°		ZONE 8	10° TO 20°	
ZONE 4	-30° TO -20°		ZONE 9	20° TO 30°	
ZONE 5	-20° TO -10°		ZONE 10	30° TO 40°	

We suggest Burbank July Elberta for its wide popularity, magnificent flavor, hardiness, and all 'round usefulness.

Suggestion: If you live in a peach growing area where cold winter temperatures are a problem, or in the colder parts of Zone 5, we suggest you consider the Stark Bro's varieties developed for winter-cold resistance.

These include Reliance, Stark Sure-Crop, Stark FrostKing, and Sunapee. Reliance has fruited after winters of 25 below in New Hampshire. Sunapee and FrostKing have withstood New York winter temperatures of 20 below.

®*Starking Delicious*

Smith Strain. One of our earliest quality freestones. Sold only by Stark Bro's.

We paid $10,000 to bring you Starking Delicious, the highest quality very early peach we grow. Excellent flavor and hardiness are like those of its famous parent, the Burbank Elberta Peach, but Starking Delicious ripens a full three weeks earlier—in mid-July in Zone 6. The red, golden skinned fruit is large, often 3 inches or more. When fully ripe, it's perfectly freestone. It

Starking Delicious Peach

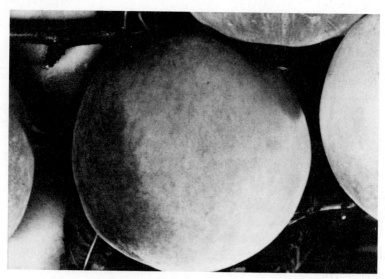

Halberta Giant

makes heavenly pies and desserts, and is a good canning and freezing variety. Does best in Zones 5 to 8, but also does well in the cooler parts of Zone 9 and in West Coast peach areas.

Suggestion: Starking Delicious is ideal for the backyard grower and the roadside market orchard.

Com-Pact Redhaven

Pratt Strain. A hardy, naturally dwarfed yellow freestone.

Redhaven Peach

Now you can grow delicious, full-sized Redhaven peaches on a naturally semi-dwarf tree that stays medium sized and most highly productive for the cubic space it occupies in your home fruit garden. Compact Redhaven's dense, lovely dark green foliage turns its setting into one of the most beautiful sites around your home. Hardier than Elberta, this little tree withstands cold winter weather and sudden drops in temperature. Its all over red peaches are the highest quality and ready for picking in Zone 6 by late July. Redhaven's unique flavor and good color make it a worldwide favorite. Does best in Zones 5 to 8.

Suggestion: ComPact Redhaven's semi-dwarf size gives the home gardener the perfect opportunity to grow this favorite peach of commercial orchardists.

Autumn Gold

Desertgold

Now you can grow peaches even where "warm" winters cause others to fail.

Desertgold is good news for every peach lover who lives where peaches usually can't be grown. Since it has a very low chilling requirement (350 to 400 hours below 45°), you can grow these luscious beauties even where it never frosts. Its delicious yellow flesh is freestone when fully ripe, and the golden fruits are lightly blushed with red. Trees bear heavy crops of medium-size fruits, ripening them very early in the season. Grows best in Zones 8 and 9.

Stark Early White Giant Peach

Sunbright Peach

Mrs. Stark's Old-fashioned Peach Preserves

2 Quarts Burbank July Elberta (About 10 peaches)
6 Cups Sugar
Yield: 7 half pints of delicious preserves

Peel and slice peaches. Mix with sugar. Let stand and combine for 12 to 18 hours. Then, place on stove and bring slowly to a boil, stirring frequently to prevent sticking. After about 40 minutes, the fruit will become clear and begin to thicken into syrup. Skim if needed, and pour boiling hot into sterilized canning jars. Put on caps, and you're done. It's one of the easiest, best-tasting recipes we've tried.

NECTARINES

Nectarines: Beautiful, Fuzzless Peaches, Queen Fruit of Today

You can grow these luxury-quality nectarines right in your own backyard. Just like those sold for fancy prices, if you're lucky enough to find them, the nectarines you pick will be sleek and fuzzless. So you can eat everything but the seed, skin and all. Juicy flesh is a rich, golden yellow—flavor is really "out of this world," distinctively different from peaches. A royal treat for eating fresh and in desserts, nectarines are also great for canning or freezing.

Stark Bro's nectarine trees are vigorous and productive, and as hardy or hardier than most peaches. No pollinator variety is needed. Standard size trees reach 16 to 18 feet at maturity. Nectarines are ornamental, too. Masses of bright pink blossoms perfume the air in early Spring. Plant some of these wonderful nectarine trees, and start enjoying "the queen fruit of today."

®Stark Red Gold

Magnificent flavored fruit is golden fleshed, smooth textured and juicy. This freestone nectarine is handsomely red, and it keeps very well under refrigeration. One of the most productive nectarines of all! Fruit ripens in mid-August in Zone 6. Grows best in Zones 5 to 8.

®Stark Sun Glo

A royal treat just released in dwarf size. Magnificent "fuzzless peach" provides the utmost in luxury taste. SunGlo is the largest, finest flavored of all the new Anderson series of Stark Nectarines (an exclusive strain of superior quality developed by a famous plant hybridizer and Stark Bro's). It has a mild, sweet, rich, distinctive flavor, completely free from the pit. Ripe fruits weigh up to a pound each. Dwarf trees grow only 8 to 10 feet tall.

Skin is an appetizing bright red. Flesh is exceptionally juicy and golden yellow in color. You eat everything but the seed—skin and all! Keeps its full flavor when frozen or canned.

Ripens in late July in Zone 6. Can be grown anywhere peaches are grown. Zones 5 to 8.

®*Burbank Flaming Gold*

Resembles Stark Early Flame. Luther Burbank called this his very finest Freestone Fuzzless Peach. Medium large size. Vivid red and gold skin. Most delicious flavor of all Nectarines. A favorite for eating fresh, freezing, canning. Ripe in mid-August in Zone 6. Does best in Zones 5 to 8.

Mericrest

Now you can enjoy exotic nectarines even where only the hardiest of peaches can possibly bear. In addition to being super hardy, new Mericrest is highly disease resistant. Medium sized with sleek, smooth skin, the golden fleshed freestone fruits have an especially tangy, aromatic flavor. Plentiful crops are ripe 'n' ready to enjoy in early August in Zone 6. Grows best in Zones 5 to 8.

®*Stark Early Flame—King Strain*

Extra early hybrid in Burbank Flaming Gold Nectarine . . . and has same fuzzless skin and refreshing flavor. Medium large fruit with golden flesh that is firm, juicy. Bright red on gold. Wonderful for eating fresh, canning, freezing. Ripe in latter part of July in Zone 6. Hardy wherever peaches grow. Does best in Zones 5 to 8.

APRICOTS

The apricot trees below will produce fruit without cross-pollination. Prune your apricot trees to a wedge shape. Spurs on branches produce fruit from about three years, and pruning makes the tree form new branches loaded with fruit bearing spurs. Wilson Delicious and Stark Earli-Orange are available in semi-dwarf and standard-size trees.

Wilson Delicious Apricot

Beautiful large fruit has thick, luscious orange yellow flesh with a rich distinctive flavor. The tree is very hardy, bears large crops even when others fail. Fine for eating fresh, canning, cooking, freezing, and drying. Also a good seller on local markets. Semi-dwarf tree is 12 to 15 feet tall at maturity. Ripens in early July in Zone 6. Does best in Zones 5 to 8.

®*Stark Earli-Orange Apricot—Roberts Strain*

The best early apricot—rich orange colored flesh, excellent flavor. Firm and juicy—a perfect freestone. The tree is a vigorous heavy bearer. This variety and the Wilson Delicious will thrive wherever peaches are grown. The Earli-Orange does triple duty—as an ornamental in the spring, as a fruit tree in early summer, and as a shade tree, too. Fine for eating fresh, cooking, canning, freezing, and local market. Semi-dwarf tree reaches 12 to 15 feet at maturity. Ripens in late June in Zone 6. Does best in Zones 5 to 8.

Hungarian Rose Apricot

Closely resembles the famous Wilson Delicious. Half of the deep orange skin is blushed with flashing red. Hungarian Rose is a richly flavored freestone with a special sweetness that makes it just right for eating, canning, drying, freezing, and marketing. Tree reaches a mature height of about 15–20 feet. Ripens in early July in Zone 6. Does best in Zones 6 to 8.

®*Stark Giant Tilton Apricot—Freiman Strain*

This spectacular mutation has multiplied all the qualities for which the standard Tilton apricot has long been famous. But the incredible size is what's most impressive. It's the largest apricot we've ever tested here at Stark Bro's. Giant Tilton is juicy and brimming with flavor. Each beautiful orange oval fruit is blushed with red on the "sunny" side. Giant tilton trees grow strongly, bearing abundant crops even in seasons when other varieties are sparse. Ripens in early July in Zone 6. Grows best in Zones 5 to 8.

Fresh Apricot Jam

8 cups apricots (pitted and chopped)
1 cup pineapple
10 cups granulated sugar
1/2 cup lemon juice

Mix fruits with sugar; refrigerate overnight. Bring to a rolling boil; boil for 8 minutes. Add lemon juice; boil for 2 minutes longer. Seal in sterilized jars. Yield: 8 pints.

PRUNES

Earliblue

Earliest ripening prune we have ever tested.

Matures in late July in Zone 6 almost two months ahead of Stanley and Blufre, and is easier to grow. Earliblue fruits are medium in size and an attractive purplish blue in color. The flesh is yellow, sweet, juicy and delicious, one of the highest quality prunes on the horticultural scene today.

The Earliblue trees are somewhat upright, very hardy, young bearing and attractive, well adapted to the home orchard. If you are going to plant one prune tree, Earliblue is the one to choose. They bloom late to escape spring frost and are self-pollinating. Does best in Zones 5 to 8.

®*Burbank Grand Prize*

Far Superior to Ordinary Prunes. Trees sold only by Stark Bro's.
Golden Yellow Flesh is Firm and Tender . . . Juicy and Sweet.
Very Large Fruit . . . Long-shaped . . . often measuring 3 inches.
Hardy Tree. Taste thrill for Eating Fresh.
Fine for canning, market. Ripe about mid-August in Zone 6.
Does best in Zones 5 to 8.

Blufre

Flavor even more delicious than Stanley prune.

A large blue prune with firm yellow flesh. Stanley-President Hybrid. Has a delightfully sweet flavor which is more delicious than that of the Stanley prune. Freestone.

Tree bears big crops—one of the most productive prune trees we have ever grown.

Extra hardy; bears young.

Fine for eating fresh; wonderful for canning, processing, drying, baby foods, etc.

Ripens in early September in Zone 6 (just ahead of Stanley prune).
Does best in Zones 5 to 7.

Stanley

Bears tremendous crops. Stark record-bearing strain.

This prune is similar to Blufre prune but it ripens a week later. This tree often starts to bear at 3 years. Bears big crops every year. Fruit is freestone.

Tree is extra hardy. A favorite prune with both home and commercial growers.

Sweet, pleasing flavor.

Rich yellow flesh is firm.

Ripens in Zone 6 early in September.

Does best in Zones 5 to 7.

PLUMS

Plant Stark Bro's plum trees for a fresh flavor treat in your backyard.

From Springtime, when they are completely covered with dazzling white flowers, until the plump, full colored fruit is harvested, Stark plum trees are a source of beauty and pleasure. Plums have a refreshing, tart sweetness and are excellent for eating out of hand. They make delicious preserves, jams and jellies. In addition, they are excellent as a stewed fruit and tops for pastries, pies and tarts.

To insure proper pollination plant 2 plum varieties. Redheart is our best pollenizer. Burbank Elephant Heart must have a Redheart planted nearby for proper pollination.

®Starking Delicious—Johnson Strain

Trees sold only by Stark Bro's.

Hardiest Japanese-type plum tree we have ever tested! Bore so heavily it had to be thinned after 17° below zero in the Stark-Burbank Test Orchard. Tree is amazingly resistant to disease also. Extra heavy bearer—usually loaded every year. And has long life, too. For even larger fruit, plums should be thinned to 4 inches apart early in the season.

Excitingly delicious flavor.

Extra large size.

Hard to beat for eating fresh, for desserts, jelly, and canning.

Ripe in Zone 6 about early August.

Does best in Zones 5 to 9.

Redheart

Large, new red fleshed midsummer plum—a cross between Wickson and Duarte. Bright red flesh, becoming somewhat deeper red at full maturity. Fine grained texture is firm-melting. Ripens to its full delicious flavor even when picked firm-ripe. Larger fruit will result from 4-inch spacing between plums early in season. Fine pollenizer, especially for Elephant Heart Plum.

Sweet, rich, delicious flavor.
Tree is hardy, heavy producer.
Fruit is crisp . . . keeps well and ships well.
Fine for eating fresh, preserves, jelly and canning.
Ripe early in August in Zone 6.
Does best in Zones 5 to 9.

Giant Damson

Largest and best of all the Damson plums! This tree is easy to grow, and it bears immensely big crops! Every home should have Stark Giant Damson Plums for their many, many uses. Fruit has rich, delicious flavor, and it's delightfully juicy—a real jam maker. It's a big profit-maker for commercial growers, too.

Medium-size fruit.
Keeps well.
Tree is hardy, vigorous.
Wonderful for making jams, jellies, and preserves.
Ripe in early September in Zone 6.
Does best in Zones 5 to 7.

PEARS

Some "Bear Facts" About Pears

Pears, one of the most delectable of fruits, are never better than when homegrown. Because you get what you almost never see in the stores: full juicy, fruity flesh. The long life and ease of cultivation of the pear tree makes it an excellent choice for any yard.

Pears will grow almost any place that apples will—and some places they won't. Generally, they do best in Zones 5, 6, 7 and 8, but several of our varieties will grow as far south as the Gulf States.

You'll find that pears are very adaptable, deep-rooted trees—diligent in finding their own nourishment—so don't over-fertilize. They do best in heavy loam, though they'll grow in many soils. (We've seen them flourish with proper care on sandy soils and clay!)

With a few exceptions, pears, as with most fruit trees, need to be near another variety to bear abundant crops of fruit. However, if you have room for only one pear tree, Duchess is ideal. It is self-pollinating and will produce big crops.

All pear trees should be harvested just as they begin to ripen (when color changes from green to light yellow-green), and allowed to finish ripening in a cool place—an air-conditioned room is ideal. This develops the full-flavor qualities of the pear better than if left to ripen on the tree.

If the fireblight disease is a problem in your area, we suggest that you plant only those highly resistant varieties such as Starking Delicious, Moonglow and Magness. Other resistant varieties are Tyson, Seckel and Duchess. Remember, too, that dwarf-size trees are more blight-resistant than Standards.

For a succession of beautiful fruit, just follow our suggestions and choose pears to give delicious eating all season long.

Starking Delicious Pear

®*Starking Delicious Pear—Cook Strain*

Blight resistant. Trees sold only by Stark Bro's.

Starking Delicious is our best pear for the home fruit grower. It's the most disease resistant pear we've ever tested. The tree is extremely healthy and hardy, and gives exceptional fruit-bearing performance year after year.

Extra large Starking Delicious pears have golden skin, smooth white flesh, and a sweet, rich flavor that makes them perfect for eating fresh, desserts or canning. In a refrigerator they'll keep until Christmas.

To get best quality from this pear you should leave it on the tree until it's a yellow-green color, then allow it to ripen at a temperature of 70-75°F for 5 to 10 days. This brings the fruit to its maximum flavor and quality.

Suggestion: Pick at the yellow-green stage, refrigerate until Christmas, then ripen at room temperature for delicious holiday eating.

Starking Delicious will ripen in early September in Zone 6 and grows best in Zones 5 to 8. It's truly the perfcct pear for the home fruit grower.

Note: When planting Starking Delicious, be sure to plant another pear variety for proper pollination.

Seckel Pear–Improved Stark Strain

Blight resistant. Also called "Sugar" or "Candy" Pear.

"If you've ever eaten one of these little pears, you'll stand around the tree and wait for the next one to ripen," says Harry Guengerich, Stark Bro's Research Director. They're that sweet and taste that much like candy. Seckel's golden yellow skin takes on a light red blush when that famous "sugar candy" taste is ready.

One of the finest pears ever developed, with a sweet spicy taste for eating out of hand. Absolutely great in fresh desserts. And Seckel is a pear your family can enjoy year 'round, because its flavor stays with it when canned.

Seckel is at its tasty best when harvested when the green turns to yellow-green, and ripened in a cool dark place.

Seckel will ripen about mid-September in Zone 6, and does well in Zones 5 to 8.

Suggestion: When planting a Seckel pear also plant another pear variety such as Tyson pear. Tyson is another "Sugar" pear that ripens in mid-August. Plant both varieties and you'll have sweet eating for two months.

Anjou Pear

Recommended for northern and central sections of the country.

Anjou pears are large yellow-green pears with clear, smooth skin and a sweet, mild, delicious flavor. It was developed for growing in northern and central sections of the country.

Anjou grows very well in the areas it was developed for, and is fine for eating fresh, canning and preserves.

Standard Tree fruit ripens in late September in Zone 6. Does best in Zones 5 to 7.

Suggestion: Pick Anjou when yellow-green. Let it ripen in a cool room.

Note. When planting Anjou be sure to plant another pear variety for proper pollination.

®*Starkrimson Pear—Kalle Strain*

Trees sold only by Stark Bro's. Grows best in northern and central areas. One of the most beautiful—and delicious—of all pears. Ripens to a solid, bright red all over with juicy, rich, sweet, melts-in-your-mouth flesh. You've probably seen these big red pears priced at a premium in your supermarket.

It's an excellent pear for eating fresh, and a good canning variety.

In Zone 6 it's ready for picking in mid-August, and does best in Zones 5 to 7.

Available only on Stark Bro's dwarf-size young bearing trees.

Suggestion: For best quality, pick the whole crop as soon as the first pear or two drop, or as the red brightens, then let ripen in a cool, dark place.

Note. When planting Starkrimson, be sure to plant another pear variety for proper pollination.

Comice Pear—Bear Creek Strain

Our best winter pear. Christmas Gift-pack favorite.

Comice is a magnificent premium pear developed in the heart of France, and known as the "Connoisseur's choice."

Comice pears are extremely large. This, together with the attractive appearance of the fruit, sets it apart from all others.

It's an excellent fresh eating pear with a flavor so delicious that it's a favorite in Christmas gift packs.

An excellent choice if you want a truly delicious prize-winning pear.

Ripens in late September in Zone 6, does best in Zones 5 to 7.

Suggestion: We especially recommend Comice for home fruit growers living in the West, although it will do well wherever pears are grown.

Note. When planting Comice, be sure to plant another pear variety for proper pollination.

CHERRIES

Some "Bear Facts" About Cherries

Here's a true luxury fruit! Always high priced, they're seldom top quality like those you grow in your own yard. Both sweet and pie cherries are very ornamental, with lovely spring blossoms, glossy green foliage and bright fruit clusters, followed by golden autumn colors.

Sweet cherry trees are larger and more upright than pie varieties. Some prefer to prune them for easier care and harvest. During dormancy, you cut back upright branches to more horizontal ones. This spreading shape can also be encouraged with young trees (using an l-shaped lath or twine and stakes), resulting in less pruning and longer bearing. All sweet cherries require a pollinator variety to bear well. Pie cherries grow in a compact, spreading shape. Hardier than the "sweets," they bloom late enough to escape spring frosts. For even smaller trees, try dwarf North Star, or the semi-dwarf varieties Starkspur Montmorency, Meteor or Suda. All pie cherries bear heavily without a pollinator.

Plant your cherries where water won't collect around the trunk during wet periods. In clay soils, peat should be added (up to 50 percent) to fill dirt when planting. Use Stark Tre-Pep regularly during the first 3 years, switching then to Stark Orchard Fertilizer as production begins.

To control leaf spot or brown rot, use Stark Home Orchard Spray. In areas where ripening time is often rainy or humid, Bing cherries are subject to cracking. To avoid this problem, try resistant types like Venus, Van or Stark Gold. Birds seldom bother Stark Gold, but others can be protected by hanging foil strips or using netting.

®Starkspur Montmorency—Carnefix Strain

Now the finest pie cherry in the world grows on a super-productive semi-dwarf tree. Sold only by Stark Bro's.

A great cherry for pies, canning, preserving, quick-freezing and eating right off the tree, too. After you try it, you'll see why many call it the world's best pie and canning cherry.

Although the "Monts" are so-called "pie or sour" cherries, Starkspur Montmorency is not really sour. When fully ripe, it's delicious—a favorite with children.

Extra large (biggest of the "pie or sour" cherries), brilliant red fruit and tender, yellow flesh. A strong grower, hardy, and resistant to disease. A sure and young bearer. Less susceptible to cracking caused by wet weather.

Blooms late in season—often the first year. Provides a striking ornamental effect for your yard or orchard. Ripens in Zone 6 in early June. Does best in Zones 4 to 7.

North Star Dwarf Cherry Tree

Hardiest of all cherries; smallest growing too. Extra delicious for pies and cobblers.

Montmorency Cherry

Originated by the Minnesota Fruit Experimental Farm, this marvelous genetic dwarf tree grows to only about 6 to 9 feet tall at maturity. Yet it bears cherries as big as, or bigger than, the fruit from large trees. Because it bears early, you get big crops sooner than you would from standard-size trees. Deep rich color, large, tart flavor. Very good for pies, cooking, freezing. Ripens about the middle of June in Zone 6. Does best in Zones 4 to 8.

BLACKBERRIES

A taste treat enjoyed for generations.

Everyone loves the rich flavor of blackberries—and the best ones ever are homegrown. Stark Bro's offers a hardy, delicious variety that's sure to please your whole family.

Darrow Blackberry

Easy to grow berries ripen early and continue to bear over a long period. High quality glossy black berries are firm and large—often measure 1 inch and 3/4-inch wide. Vigorous cane grows tall and erect, yields big crops every year. Rich, delicious flavor for eating fresh, canning or making jam. Grows best in Zones 5 to 8.

BLUEBERRIES

Plant two varieties for best results.

Grow blueberries for tempting pies, muffins or for eating fresh. If soil conditions in your area are less than ideal for growing blueberries, create your own soil by using compost or other organic material and aluminum sulphate. We recommend planting two varieties of blueberries for pollination to get results.

Earliblue Blueberry

Large, full-flavored berries ripen early in the season. Earliblue's exceptional taste lets you make the best pies, tarts and other desserts—even if you have no experience. Hardy bushes are so attractive you can plant them in your yard as ornamentals. We ship hardy 3-year-old bushes.

Coville Blueberry

Beautiful clusters of powdery blue berries grow on hardy bushes which reach a mature height of about 6 feet. Berries are large, with good quality and color. Coville ripens late—makes a perfect match for Earliblue to extend the ripening season. We ship healthy 3-year-old bushes with strong, well-developed root systems.

RASPBERRIES

Heritage Everbearing Red Raspberry

Newest, most outstanding everbearer is perfect for home gardens. Pick plenty of big berries in July, again in September till late fall. Enjoy the sweet flavorful berries fresh from the patch or freeze them. Sturdy upright canes need no support, usually bear first season after planting. Grows best in Zones 4 to 8.

Black Hawk Raspberry

Improved early ripening black raspberry—exceptional because of its ability to bear big crops in spite of hot, dry weather. Berries are uniformly large and juicy with a distinctive sweet flavor. Delicious fresh, in desserts— keep their flavor well when frozen. Best in Zones 5 to 8.

Latham Red Raspberry

Size, flavor and hardiness make it the most popular of all red raspberries. This new virus-free selection is unexcelled for desserts, freezing or canning. One of the best for eating fresh. Heavy-bearing and highly adaptable to many types of soil. Fruit is large and firm. Ripens mid-July. Grows best in Zones 3 to 8.

Southland Raspberry

Brand new ever-bearing red variety, developed in North Carolina especially for growing in upper- and mid-South. Yields continuously from early summer to freezing in areas where many other varieties fail completely. Vigorous, disease resistant, very hardy, productive. Hard-to-beat goodness all season for fresh eating and pies and other desserts. Grows best in Zones 5 to 8.

Bristol Raspberry

Best midseason black raspberry. Berries are very large and roundish. A delicious favorite for eating fresh, in desserts or frozen. Bristol berries are jet black, rich-flavored and juicy. Large vigorous upright plants that don't need staking. Does best in Zones 5 to 8.

GRAPES

Stark Bro's Grape Vines Grown in the Ozarks, Under Ideal Conditions for Finest Root Development

Growing your own grapes—it's easy. There's always room for a few grape vines . . . on fences, arbors, over unsightly buildings. Stark Grape Vines are grown in the Ozark Mountains, where we have found ideal conditions for the finest root development. They grow and bear at a very early age—often in two years or less. Make your own wine, grape juice, jelly, conserve. Have fresh grapes from early summer till winter. You can, when you plant varieties ripening in succession as listed below.

Golden Muscat

Midseason golden grape.
One of the finest grapes ever developed. Sweeter, larger, more luscious than many of the wonderful "Old Country" sweet grapes which make Europe famous for its vineyards. Very large, heavy fruit clusters.

Blue Boy Grape (Cook Strain)

Vigorous, hardy, and extremely productive.

Large, oval golden berry.

Juicy, tender flesh—aromatic, sweet, wine-like, refreshing, with wonderful muscat flavor.

Very good to best quality.

Fine for eating fresh, for jelly and juice.

Does best in Zones 5 to 8.

Steuben

New, late, midseason grape.

Steuben has a delicious, sweet flavor with a distinctive spicy tang. Its huge, long-tapered clusters are compact and usually heavily shouldered. Berries are medium size. Ripens midseason—2 to 3 days after Concord.

Vigorous, productive, hardy vines—bore full crop following 20° below zero.

Keeps well in storage.

Fine for eating fresh, jam, jelly, fair for wine making.

Does best in Zones 5 to 8.

Stark Blue Boy—Cook Strain

Vines sold only by Stark Bro's.

Improved Concord type grape. Ripens one week before Concord. If you like Concord grapes, you'll love our new Blue Boy. Flavor is smoother and more mellow than Concord and Hicks. Large, attractive bunches hang on the vine for 3 weeks or longer. Grows well in poor soils.

Large, flavorful grapes in tight clusters.

Vigorous, productive, winter hardy.

Early ripening.

Fine for eating fresh, jam, jelly and juice.

Excellent keeping quality.

Does best in Zones 5 to 8.

Catawba

Late-ripening grape.

For more than 100 years, the Catawba grape has been popular for table, champagne making, wine making. Berries are red, medium size; large clusters. One of best keepers of all grapes.

Firm, juicy berries, with sprightly, sweet, rich flavor.

Wonderful for eating fresh, jelly, best for wine making.

Does best in Zones 5 to 9.

Delaware

Medium-early-ripening.

Small, red grape with remarkable rich, delicate flavor. Unsurpassed quality. Medium size clusters. Adaptable to various soils.

Bears abundantly.

Keeps and ships well.

Favorite for eating fresh, jelly, excellent for wine making.

Does best in Zones 5 to 8.

Vinered

New, late-ripening grape.

An attractive new light red grape. Ripens just before Catawba to extend the picking season. Its pleasant flavor and tender skin make it an excellent grape for dessert use. Good for wine making. Vigorous, productive, hardy vine. Bears abundantly. Large to very large clusters, with medium compactness. Berry size is slightly larger than Catawba. Fine for eating fresh, for jelly, juice. Does best in Zones 5 to 7.

Himrod Seedless

Very early golden-yellow grape.

This hybrid Seedless Golden Grape is a delicious blend of the flavors of its parents—the Thompson Seedless and the Ontario Grapes. Ripens early.

Hardy vines.

Fruit keeps in good condition in storage until late December.

A fine table grape.

Does best in Zones 5 to 9.

Buffalo Grape

New, extra early blue-black grape.

The finest quality, very early ripening grape—it's the first Blue-Black Grape ready for delicious eating. Has the highest quality of all early-ripening black grapes. Flavor is best of early grapes. Clusters are medium to large, compact and well-filled with uniformly large berries.

Juicy flesh, very sweet and pleasing to taste.

Productive, hardy vines—have produced big, beautiful crops in spite of hot, dry weather.

Excellent for eating fresh, fair for wine making, jam, jelly, marmalade.

Fine for home and commercial plantings.

Does best in Zones 5 to 8.

NUTS

Some "Bear Facts" About Nuts

When you plant a nut tree in your yard, you get the best of both beauty and productivity. As a majestic hardwood shade tree, it offers a cool retreat from summer's heat. It will also pay you a rich reward of large, delicious nuts. You won't even have to pick them, just gather the fallen ripe nuts from the ground. These practical, dual purpose trees have also brought spectacular prices when mature trees are sold for furniture wood.

Nut trees are very easy to grow, and require little or no care once they're established. Most nut trees grow a long taproot, and they need special attention when transplanted. At Stark Bro's, we take extra care in digging, handling and shipping. To complete this special attention, you should dig a large, deep hole to accommodate this long root.

If your soil is heavy, mixing in up to 50 percent peat will help your nut trees get a faster start. Newly planted trees respond well to regular watering especially if you use Stark Tre-Pep. Mulching is also beneficial. Bearing trees will produce more if you apply Stark Orchard Fertilizer.

As the young nut tree develops, you should prune to keep it growing in a pyramid shape with a single main trunk. A young tree will benefit greatly from a Stark Tree Guard to protect the tender bark. Nut trees are usually not bothered by insects or diseases. If aphids should become so overwhelming as to seriously weaken the tree, you can use Stark Home Orchard Spray or other suitable insecticides.

Stark Bro's offers two types of nut trees: grafted and seedgrown. Certain improved varieties can be propagated only by grafting. This is very similar to apple grafting. Seedling trees grow on their own roots. This is the standard way to propagate many nut species.

®Starking Hardy Giant Pecan—James Strain

Sold only by Stark Bro's.

Extremely hardy—has survived winters of 20 degrees below zero and still produced. "One of the finest I have seen," says a horticulturist with the U.S. Department of Agriculture. The large nuts—often over 1-1/2 inches—ripen in early September in Zone 6. Paper thin shells are easy to crack. Kernels are golden yellow, plump and solid. Makes an excellent lawn and shade tree, with spreading glossy green leaves. Variety is self-fruitful. Bears young and heavy. Does best in Zones 6 to 9.

Starking Hardy Giant Pecan

Missouri Hardy Pecan Seedling

Here's the hardiest pecan tree Stark Bro's has ever tested. These seedgrown trees are an ideal selection for planting in cold Northern areas and other locations considered unfavorable to pecans. The nuts are medium large, rich and highly flavored. Vigorous trees bear young and regularly. Grows best in Zones 5 to 9.

®*Stark Kwik-Krop Walnut–Boellner Strain*

Sold only by Stark Bro's.

Extremely young bearing tree yields big crops of delicious walnuts usually within two years after planting. Kwik-Krop is a hardy hybrid of the American Black Walnut. Plump, rich flavored kernels can be removed in quarters or halves. Large, slightly pointed nuts have thin shells for easy cracking. Should be cured for 2 to 3 weeks. Ripens early in mid-September in Zone 6, grows best in Zones 5 to 9. Tree reaches a mature height of about 65 feet.

Carpathian Hardy English Walnut–Somers Strain

Seedgrown. Ideal multi-purpose tree for the home landscape, the Carpathian gives you bumper crops of plump English-type walnuts from a lushly foliaged shade tree. Grown from seed selected from outstanding parent trees that bear bountiful crops even after –30° winters. When tree reaches full height of about 30 feet, it should yield an average crop of 3 to 4 bushels of husked nuts. Grows best in Zones 5 to 9. For best crops, plant a pair or pollinate with any other walnut.

Butternut

A beautiful, wide spreading shade tree. Kernel is rich, spicy, very high in oil content and extremely fragrant. Excellent for making cookies or cake— one of the best nuts you'll find for eating fresh. Tree reaches a mature height of about 50 feet. Grows best in Zones 4 to 7.

Chinese Chestnut

Grow meaty, nutritious chestnuts just two years after planting. Everyone loves them fresh, baked or toasted. Grows rapidly into a well-shaped tree—just right for the backyard grower who wants a lovely shade tree and abundant nut producer. Should be planted in pairs for pollination. Tree reaches a mature height of about 40–50 feet. Best in Zones 4 to 8.

American Filbert (Hazelnut)

Great for backyard grower. Small size shrub reaches a height of just 5 to 7 feet. Provides medium size easy-to-crack nuts. Kernels are crisp and delicious, a favorite with nut lovers the world over. We recommend you plant two for cross-pollination and better crops. Does best in Zones 4 to 9.

12

Soil Testing[*]

Sudbury Soil Testing equipment has been designed primarily to enable the practical man who has not had special training in soil chemistry to determine the direction he should follow in his fertilizer program in order to produce maximum crop yields at minimum fertilizer costs.

The *Scientific American* says: "Each year gardeners and farmers spend millions of dollars for 'complete' fertilizers that contain a set ration of the three principal plant foods—nitrogen, phosphorus and potash. This gunshot application of plant foods may not have enough of one, or too much of another, chemical to supply the needs of the particular soil. A soil test will show what is present and what is lacking, and the grower may buy only those chemicals needed to make his soil highly productive. The possible economy is obvious."—Arthur Hawthorne Carhart.

From *Gardener's Chronicle*: "A complete fertilizer is a balanced fertilizer only when it supplies to the plant the elements nitrogen, phosphorus and potash which otherwise would not be present in sufficient quantities in the soil for normal healthy growth. Several systems of testing soils for the presence of available plant nutrients and toxic substances have been developed within the last few years. Much valuable information may be obtained by the use of these systems. Tests can be made by any person who can read and follow directions."—Dr. James Tyson, well-known agronomist.

---

*The information in this chapter is excerpted from the Sudbury soil-testing publication with the kind permission of The Sudbury Laboratory, Inc.

SOIL SHOULD BE ANALYZED

"Plants, like animals, require food in order to live, grow and reproduce themselves. Plant food consists of chemical compounds of ten elements, viz: carbon, hydrogen, oxygen, phosphorus, potassium, nitrogen, sulphur, calcium, iron and magnesium. Plants receive the first three from the air and water. The supply, practically speaking, is unlimited. They receive the remainder from the soil. But the supply of soil elements is not by any means unlimited, as the great bulk of the soil consists of useless material, and the amount of plant food elements in it is relatively small.

"This is not particularly true of nitrogen, phosphorus and potash. The supply of those elements in the soil is so small that the repeated yearly removal of small portions in the crops which are sold soon depletes the supply to a point below the requirements of maximum crop growth. Replenishment can be accomplished by adding the necessary chemicals to the soil. That is what fertilizers are. Crude chemicals to be applied to the soil for the purpose of replenishing the supply of one or more of the plant foods in that soil.

"It follows that the value of fertilizer is in proportion to the amount of plant food which it contains. It is evident also that in order to produce the desired results on any given piece of soil, a fertilizer must carry the element of plant food which is not being furnished to the crop in adequate amounts by that soil.

"If, for example, a soil is failing to supply as much nitrogen as the crop needs it should be treated with a nitrogenous fertilizer. In such a case a phosphoric or potassic fertilizer might be entirely useless." (The foregoing is an excerpt from *Massachusetts College Extension Bulletin No. 74*, by A. E. Beaumont.)

GENERAL INFORMATION

Before making any tests, see that the test tubes and corks are absolutely clean. The accuracy of these tests depends on clean equipment.

Select the soil to be tested about two inches under the surface and be careful not to touch it with the hands, or put it into any container that might contaminate it. Probably the best way is to dig out a soil sample with a spoon and put it in a clean drinking glass. Cigarette ashes will sometimes change the test, so it is better not to smoke while working with the soil test equipment. It is also well always to keep the test tube corked until the test is complete, for some of the liquids are sensitive to reactions from the air.

Never pour any soil testing solution back into the bottles once it has been taken out. If too much solution is poured into the test tube, it is a mistake to pour any of the excess material back into the bottle, as this practice will lead to contamination of the solutions.

If your soil testing solutions are not contaminated, and are kept tightly corked, there is no reason why their effectiveness should deteriorate with time. The colors in your color charts will not fade unless exposed to the direct rays of the sun for long periods. We have made a sincere attempt to produce a soil testing kit that will be a permanent piece of farm and garden equipment.

Sudbury Soil Testing Equipment is *not* designed to test fertilizers, and you will not get correct results if nitrogen, phosphorus, or potash have been added to the soil within 30 days from the time the test is made. Nor will it be possible for you to check the accuracy of your test by putting nitrate of soda, acid phosphate, or potash in the soil testing solution.

Keep in mind that soil chemistry is not an exact science, and that the plants themselves still hold many secrets. However, procedures and recommendations made herein are based upon information that we believe to be reliable.

TESTING pH (ACIDITY OR ALKALINITY)

We suggest that you begin testing for acidity (lime). This is the simplest and, according to many, the most important test. It is called the lime test because most soils are acid, and lime is the ordinary agent to correct this condition. The test really assists in determining the amount of lime or ammonium sulphate required to properly adjust the soil so that it will produce the best results with the particular plant you intend to grow.

Soil is referred to as being sweet or sour—acid or alkaline. Sweet or alkaline soil means that it tests on the pH scale above 7, while sour or acid soil means that it tests on the pH scale below 7.

To determine the acidity or alkalinity of the soil sample, fill the test tube that has a red cork (always use the same test tube and the same cork for the acidity test) one-quarter full of fine dry soil. Avoid touching soil samples with your hands. Then pour into the partially filled test tube the acidity or lime testing solution, until the test tube is half full. Shake the mixture thoroughly (be sure that the test tube is closed with the cork, not your finger). Now allow the soil to settle. Some soils settle rapidly, while others may take several hours. It is well to allow the solution to set overnight, if possible. The transparent liquid above the soil can then be compared with the colors on our lime color chart. There is an advantage in comparing these colors in daylight.

It is entirely possible that the test will not produce an exact comparable color, but a shade in between two colors shown on the chart, in which case it will be necessary to estimate the pH of your test.

If the soil condition as it exists does not meet with your plant requirements, it can easily be changed. Lime is the accepted material used for sweetening soil (raising the pH). Five pounds of finely ground limestone will raise the pH of 100 square feet of soil 3/4 of a pH point. This is approximately equal to one ton of lime per acre. Many months will elapse before the full effect of the lime is apparent.

Never spread lime directly on manure or commercial fertilizer.

Although lime is not a fertilizer, it does promote bacterial growth. It makes available more natural plant foods already found in the soil. On some of our sour soil lime not only sweetens it and promotes bacterial action but it also makes phosphorus more available, which otherwise plants could not use. Agricultural authorities are putting more emphasis each year on the importance of lime, and we advise you to be sure to check the pH of your soil and the pH preference of the plants you intend to grow in order to avoid disappointment.

If sulphur or aluminum sulphate is used to lower the pH of the soil, 1-1/2 pounds of either material is considered sufficient to lower the pH reading 3/4 of a point when applied to 100 square feet—or 600 pounds per acre.

Certain plants, such as azaleas, gardenias, rhododendrons, laurel, and so on, must have a sour soil condition if they are to do their best. Other plants prefer sweet soil in order to thrive.

On our lime color chart "A" equals 7-1/2 of the pH scale, which means that soil testing "A" is slightly sweet. "B" equals 6-3/4 on the pH scale and indicates the soil is very slightly acid. "C" equals 6 pH; "D" equals 5-1/4 pH; "E" equals 4-1/2 pH.

TESTS FOR PLANT FOOD DEFICIENCY

Commercial fertilizer formulas are always stated in percentage of nitrogen, phosphorus, and potash, and in that order. In other words, if the formula on a bag of fertilizer is marked 10-2-12, it means that it contains 10 percent nitrogen, 2 percent phosphorus, and 12 percent potash.

Because nitrogen is represented by the first figure in the formula on the fertilizer bag, let us test for this material next.

Fill one test tube (one having a white cork) one-quarter full of solution No. 2; then add solution No. 3 until it is half full. Be sure to use a test tube with a white cork for all nitrogen tests.

Now, take the other test tube that has a white cork and fill it one-quarter full of dry soil. Pour the contents of the first tube containing the two solutions into the one containing the soil. Close the test tube with a white cork and shake until the solutions are well mixed.

LIST of pH PREFERENCE FOR VEGETABLES, FRUIT TREES AND FIELD CROPS ACCORDING TO OUR CHART

Crop	pH	Crop	pH	Crop	pH	Crop	pH
Alfalfa	A	Corn	B	Lima beans	B	Rape	B
Apple	C	Cotton, upland	C	Millet	B	Raspberries	B
Artichoke (Jerusalem)	A	Cowpeas	C	Milo, dwarf yellow	C	Red clover	B
Asparagus	A	Cowpea, common	B	Mushroom	B	Rhubarb	B
Barley	A	Crabapple	B	Muskmelon	B	Rutabaga	B
Beans	C	Cranberries	E	Oats	B	Rye	C
Beet (sugar)	A	Cucumber	B	Okra	B	Salsify	B
Beet (table)	A	Currants	C	Onions	C	Shallot	C
Blackberries	C	Eggplant	B	Orange (sweet)	B	Sorghum	C
Blueberries	E	Endive	B	Parsley	B	Soybeans	B
Blue Grass	A	Garlic	B	Parsnips	B	Spinach	C
Broccoli	B	Gooseberry	C	Peaches	C	Squash	C
Brussels sprouts	B	Grapefruit	B	Pears	B	Strawberries	C
Buckwheat	C	Grapes	D	Peas	D	Swiss chard	B
Cabbage	A	Horseradish	B	Peanuts	B	Tobacco (according to species)	A to D
Canteloupe	B	Kale	B	Peppers	B	Tomatoes	C
Carrots	A	Kohlrabi	B	Pineapple	B	Turnip	C
Cauliflower	A	Kentucky coffee	B	Plums, American	B	Vetch	C
Celery	A	Leek	B	Potatoes	B	Watercress	B
Cherry (sweet)	B	Lemon	A	Potatoes (sweet)	A	Watermelon	B
Chicory	B	Lentil	C	Pumpkin	C	Wheat	A
Chives	B	Lespedeza	C	Quince	C		
Clover	A	Lettuce	A	Radish	A		

pH PREFERENCE OF FLOWERS According to Our Chart

Plant	pH	Plant	pH	Plant	pH	Plant	pH
Acacia	A	Cyclamen	C	Heliotrope	C	Peony	B
African daisy	B	Cypress	C	Hemlock	C	Petunia	A
African violet	B	Daffodil	B	Hibiscus, Chinese	B	Phlox	C
Ageratum, blue	B	Dahlia	B	Hickory	B	Pine	D
Almond	B	Daisy	B	Holly	B	Pitcher plant	E
Alyssum	B	Delphinium	C	Hollyhock	C	Pogonia, rose	E
Amaryllis	C	Deutzia	A	Honeysuckle bush	A	Pointsettia	A
Anemone	B	Didiscus	B	Hyacinth	B	Poppy	C
Arbor Vitae	A	Dogwood	B	Hydrangea, blue	B	Primrose	B
Aster	B	Easter lily	C	Hydrangea, pink	C	Primula	B
Azaleas	E	Euphorbia	C	Indianpipe	C	Pyrethrum	E
Bachelor's button	B	Feverfew	B	Iris	B	Red hot poker	B
Barberry	A	Ferns	D	Iris, Japanese	D	Rhododendron	B
Bayberry	D	Fir	D	Ivy, Boston	D	Rose	E
Begonia	C	Forget-me-not	A	Ivy, English	A	St. Paulia	B
Bleeding heart	B	Foxglove	B	Jack-in-pulpit	B	Salpiglosis	B
Birch, American white	D	Fuschia	B	Jacob's ladder	B	Scabiosa	B
Bouvardia	C	Gardenia	C	Laurel	C	Snapdragon	B

ph PREFERENCE OF FLOWERS According to Our Chart (continued)

Flower	pH	Flower	pH	Flower	pH	Flower	pH
Boxwood	B	Genista	B	Ladyslipper	A	Snowdrop	E
Burning bush	C	Geranium	C	Ladyslipper, showy	A	Spirea	B
Butterfly bush	B	Gerbera	B	Larkspur	A	Spruce, Colorado	B
Calendula	A	Gladiolus	A	Lilac	B	Star of Bethlehem	B
Calla lily	E	Godetia	E	Lily	B	Stocks	B
Candytuft	B	Goldenrod	B	Lupine	B	Sunflower	B
Canna	B	Grass, Bermuda	B	Magnolia, sweet bay	B	Swainsonia	A
Carnation	B	Grass, colonial bent	B	Marigold	B	Sweet peas	A
Centaurea	B	Grass, creeping bent	B	Mignonette	B	Sweet William	A
Cineraria	A	Grass, Italian rye	A	Mock orange	B	Trailing arbutus	E
Chrysanthemum	B	Grass, panic	B	Morning glory	E	Tuberose	B
Clarkia	B	Grass, perennial rye	B	Myrtle	B	Tulips, common	B
Clematis	A	Grass, rough blue	A	Mysotia	B	Verbena	B
Columbine	B	Grass, squirrel tail	B	Narcissus	A	Violet	B
Coral bells	B	Grass, Sudan	B	Nasturtium	C	Violet, dog's tooth	C
Coreopsis, trefoil	D	Grass, wood reed	D	Orchid	A	Water lily	C
Cosmos	B	Gypsophila	B	Osage, orange	D	Wisteria	B
Coxcomb	B	Hawthorne	B	Palm, cocos	B	Woodbine	B
Crocus	B	Heather	B	Pansy	D	Yucca	B
						Zinnia	B

Allow the mixture of soil and soil testing solution time to separate. In sandy soils, this separation will take place in minutes, while in some clay soil, it may take hours for the soil to separate from the solution. In any case, compare the color of the clear liquid with the color chart as soon as it is possible, because we have found that allowing the solution to contact the soil for an extended period may neutralize the chemicals and cause the color to fade.

"A" on the color chart indicates the minimum of nitrogen required, while "B," "C," "D," and "E" indicate deficiency. Even with an "A" reading we recommend that your fertilizer should contain two percent nitrogen, while "B" requires three percent, "C" four percent, "D" six percent, and "E" eight percent.

The required amount of nitrogen may be applied in a standard mixed fertilizer, or it may be applied separately, or the fertilizer mixture may be made at home. Commercial dried blood contains from nine to fourteen percent nitrogen. Tankage contains six to ten percent nitrogen, plus four to twelve percent phosphorus. Nitrate of soda contains 15 percent nitrogen and raises the pH of the soil. Ammonium sulphate contains 20 percent nitrogen and lowers the pH of the soil. There are many other forms of nitrogen, but the above are the most common.

Leafy vegetables are apt to be heavy consumers of nitrogen, and they should be supplied with this plant food in order to produce tender juicy leaves. Lawns are also heavy feeders of this essential plant food. Too much nitrogen will often produce a rank growth at the expense of flowers and fruits. Extremely dark green brittle foliage accompanied by weak stems is a pretty good indication of too much nitrogen.

Many people have a tendency to overfeed with nitrogen, because in most forms it is quickly available and shows results almost at once. However, remember in feeding plants, as well as animals and humans, it is necessary to have a balanced ration.

The next figure on the fertilizer bag represents the percentage of phosphorus that the formula contains.

Fill one test tube having a blue cork one-eighth full of solution No. 4; then add solution No. 5 until it is half full. Be sure to use a test tube with a blue cork for all phosphorus tests.

Now, take the other test tube that has a blue cork and fill it one-quarter full of fine soil. Pour the contents of the first tube containing the two solutions into the one containing the soil. Close the tube with a blue cork and shake until the soil and solutions are well mixed.

Allow this mixture to stand until the soil settles; the clear liquid should then be stirred for 30 seconds with the tin rod that you will find in this kit. Compare with those on color phosphorus chart. If no color develops after stirring with the tin rod, add a few more drops of Solution No. 4 and stir again with the tin rod.

On the phosphorus chart "A" again represents the minimum amount required, while "B," "C," "D," and "E" indicate a deficiency. Even with an "A" reading we recommend that the fertilizer should contain two percent phosphorus, "B," four percent; "C," eight percent; "D," 12 percent; and "E," 16 percent.

In some types of soil a greenish color will be obtained instead of blue. The tests should be judged on the depth of color in this case.

It is believed that phosphorus promotes a rapid development and stimulates flower and seed production. Many soils are low in phosphorus because barnyard manures, which are notoriously short on this material, have been used as fertilizer.

The most common form of applying phosphorus is in the form of acid phosphate, which contains 16 percent phosphorus. Super-phosphate contains 20 percent phosphorus, and bonemeal contains 23 percent.

The last figure in the formula on the fertilizer bag denotes the percentage of potash that it contains.

Fill one test tube having a yellow cork one-quarter full of solution No. 6, then add solution No. 7 until it is half full. Be sure to use a test tube with a yellow cork for all potash tests.

Now take the other test tube that has a yellow cork and fill it one-quarter full of dry soil. Pour the contents of the first tube containing the two solutions into the one containing the soil. Close the test tube with a yellow cork and shake until the solutions are well mixed.

Allow this mixture to stand until the soil settles and a clear liquid can be compared with the color chart.

As before, "A" on the color chart indicates the minimum of potash required, while "B," "C," "D," and "E" represent deficiency. With an "A" reading the fertilizer should contain two percent potash, "B," four percent; "C," eight percent; "D," 12 percent; and "E," 16 percent.

Potash seems to be essential in promoting root growth. In the vegetable kingdom, potatoes, asparagus, beets, carrots, radishes, and rhubarb all seem to respond to extra potash feeding. And all tuberous flowers should be fed generous portions of this material. Unleached wood-ashes contain three to seven percent potash, while muriate of potash and sulphate of potash as well as potassium nitrate are all 46 percent pure potash.

After you have developed the percentage of each of the three principal plant food elements that your particular soil requires, apply this complete formula at the rate of five pounds per 100 square feet, which is approximately one ton per acre.

We are aware of the fact that the fertilizer recommendations developed by using a Sudbury Soil Testing Kit may sometimes result in an amount of fertilizer far in excess of the amount locally used on farms. Sometimes the amount indicated cannot be justified by the money value of one crop. Nevertheless, the kit will indicate the direction that you should travel in applying needed plant food to your particular soil. In any case, regardless of the economics of the growing operation, plant nutrient shortages, we believe, are quite accurately indicated by this equipment. After putting hundreds of thousands of Sudbury Soil Testing Kits in the hands of all kinds of people in all parts of the world, working with all kinds of crops, we are convinced that if the fertilizer recommendations that are developed by a careful soil test are followed, amazing crops will be produced.

This Sudbury Soil Testing Kit supplies information on the principal elements needed by plant life to produce abundant crops—nitrogen, phosphorus, and potash—and on the degree of alkalinity or acidity. While most commercial fertilizer manufacturers include sufficient additional "trace elements" in many of their formulas, sometimes special soil conditions require unusual analyses to detect these deficiencies. For normal use, we believe that such tests tend to complicate more than help, but when testing for any of the minor trace elements is required, write for particulars and prices for this special equipment.

From time to time, purchasers of Sudbury Soil Testing Kits ask for a table like the pH preference table as it would apply to plant nutrients. We believe that such a table is not necessary, because if the fertilizer recommendations developed by using Sudbury Soil Testing Kits are followed, amazing crops will result. These recommendations are based on nutrient requirements for average crops. We know that the nutrient requirements vary from crop to crop, but the recommendations that we use have proved successful for many years under every imaginable condition.

WHAT TO DO AFTER YOU TEST YOUR SOIL

Many times you will find that the formula for the fertilizer the soil needs to produce maximum crop yields is not locally available. You can take a good standard formula fertilizer that may be available and adjust it to meet your soil requirements.

Every bag of fertilizer has the formula printed on the container, even though it is sold under a trade name, such as "Agrico," "Vigoro," etc. Suppose you find that the formula is 4-12-4, which means it contains four percent nigrogen, 12 percent phosphorus, and four percent potash. If you want to increase the amounts of nitrogen, phosphorus, or potash, here's what you add and how much:

APPROXIMATE AMOUNTS OF FERTILIZER TO APPLY

| *Per 100 sq ft—5 lb* | *Per acre—2000 lb* |

NITROGEN

For each 2% you wish to increase nitrogen content, add 0.62 lb of nitrate of soda (15% nitrogen content) to the 5 lb of commercial fertilizer or 0.21 lb of Sudbury Unit X "Tailor-Made" Fertilizer.

NITROGEN

For each 2% you wish to increase nitrogen content, add 250 lb of nitrate of soda (15% nitrogen content) to the 2000 lb of commercial fertilizer or 84 lb of Sudbury Unit X "Tailor-Made" Fertilizer.

PHOSPHORUS

For each 2% you wish to increase the phosphorus content, add 0.55 lb of Super-phosphate (18% phosphorus content) to the 5 lb of commercial fertilizer or 0.22 lb of Sudbury Unit Y "Tailor-Made" Fertilizer.

PHOSPHORUS

For each 2% you wish to increase the phosphorus content, add 222 lb of Super-phosphate (18% phosphorus content) to the 2000 lb of commercial fertilizer or 89 lb of Sudbury Unit Y "Tailor-Made" Fertilizer.

POTASH

For each 2% you wish to increase the po potash content, add 0.2 lb of muriate of potash (50% potash content) to the 5 lb of commercial fertilizer or 0.23 lb of Sudbury Unit Z "Tailor-Made" Fertilizer.

POTASH

For each 2% you wish to increase the potash content add 80 lb of muriate of potash (50% potash content) to the 2000 lb of commercial fertilizer or 89 lb of Sudbury Unit Z "Tailor-Made" Fertilizer.

Add this complete fertilizer at the rate of 5 lb per 100 sq ft, or 2000 lb per acre.

Your Sudbury Soil Test Kit shows the nutrient deficiencies of your soils and you can then decide whether to apply sufficient quantities to replace them all at once, or to apply in installments over a longer period. Some economists say that one should not expect to spend more than 10 percent of the value of the crop for fertilizer, and the expenditure of $40 to $50 per acre might not seem justified for many crops. On the other hand, up to triple or quadruple yield often can be expected by proper fertilization of depleted soils and may justify almost fantastic expenditures for fertilizer.

Appendix A

Planning, Planting, Pruning and Proper Care.

PLAN BEFORE YOU PLANT

Possibly you've already given a great deal of thought as to where you're planting your new tree. Or maybe you don't really have much choice with a very limited space. But your tree will reward you with better crops if it's planted in the place it likes best. And you can avoid many future problems by considering every aspect of the planting spot.

If your tree had its choice, it would ask for a sunny place with well-drained, fertile soil. But it will be quite satisfied with just half a day's worth of sunlight. Drainage is nearly always good enough to keep your trees "happy." If your soil is heavy clay, some peat added to the soil at planting time helps a lot.

If you aren't lucky enough to have super-rich soil, don't be discouraged. Most fruit trees are very adaptable, getting along amazingly well even when the soil is none too good. In fact, many productive commercial orchards are on land where hardly any other crop could succeed.

If you'd like your tree to become a landscaping asset, choose the planting place with this in mind. Imagine it as a full-grown tree, and check everything out: Wires overhead? Sidewalk underneath? Does it obstruct something I want to see? Can I keep an eye on it from the house? Will other trees be in the way . . . allowing for their additional growth in the meantime?

Even a year or two after planting, your tree will be *very* difficult to transplant. So it really pays to take the time to plant it in just the right place.

This Appendix is excerpted from Paul Stark, Jr's "Guide to Successful Planting and Growing" with the kind permission of Stark Bro's Nurseries & Orchards Company, Louisia, Mo.

LEAVE SPACE FOR FUTURE PLANTINGS

Once you've experienced the joys of
growing your own fruit, you'll soon be
wanting to plant more trees. Take my word
for it; someday you'll thank me. Chances
are, you'll want to plant other varieties to
extend your fresh fruit enjoyment over the
entire season. So if you'll just space your
first trees to "leave room for a few more
down at the end," these reserved planting
places will be there when you're ready.

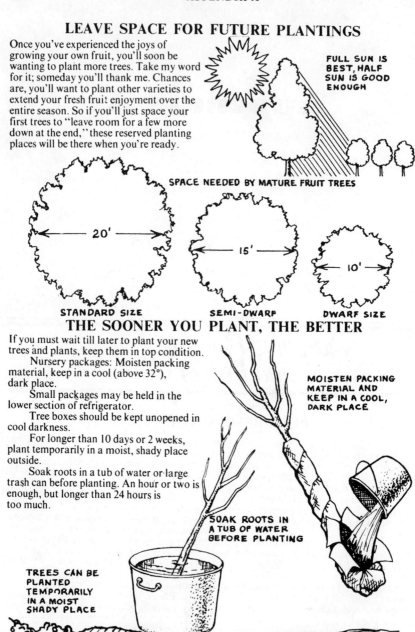

FULL SUN IS
BEST, HALF
SUN IS GOOD
ENOUGH

SPACE NEEDED BY MATURE FRUIT TREES

20'

15'

10'

STANDARD SIZE   SEMI-DWARF   DWARF SIZE

THE SOONER YOU PLANT, THE BETTER

If you must wait till later to plant your new
trees and plants, keep them in top condition.
  Nursery packages: Moisten packing
material, keep in a cool (above 32°),
dark place.
  Small packages may be held in the
lower section of refrigerator.
  Tree boxes should be kept unopened in
cool darkness.
  For longer than 10 days or 2 weeks,
plant temporarily in a moist, shady place
outside.
  Soak roots in a tub of water or large
trash can before planting. An hour or two is
enough, but longer than 24 hours is
too much.

MOISTEN PACKING
MATERIAL AND
KEEP IN A COOL,
DARK PLACE

SOAK ROOTS IN
A TUB OF WATER
BEFORE PLANTING

TREES CAN BE
PLANTED
TEMPORARILY
IN A MOIST
SHADY PLACE

GIVE YOUR NEW TREE A $10.00 HOLE

Old time gardeners say you need a ten dollar hole for a five dollar tree. Even though prices have changed, the principle has not. Roots grow faster when they're spread out than when they're cramped into a small hole. And they grow especially better in soil that's been loosened, if you add some peat -- up to ⅓ -- to the mixture.

Better leave the tree soaking in a bucket of water while you dig, to keep its roots from drying. If you keep the topsoil in a separate pile, you can put it in the bottom of the hole where it'll do the most good. Air pockets can be avoided by working the fine soil carefully around the roots, then tamping down the planting completely to firm the soil. If you leave it slightly underfilled, it'll be easier to do a good job of watering.

Now, water your new tree. Deep, thorough soaking is best, preferably with a solution of Stark Tre-Pep. This starter fertilizer helps trees and plants grow quickly and vigorously. Give Stark Tre-Pep a try; you're sure to be mighty pleased with the results! After watering, be sure to finish filling up hole to ground level.

I wish there were some way we could send out one of these ten dollar holes with every tree sold by Stark Bro's. But of course, we can't. So it's up to you to get out there and dig for it.

There's one more thing I wouldn't want you to forget: Remove the wired name tag. As the tree grows, this small piece of wire can choke off the circulation, damaging or killing the tree. If you'd like to keep the tag on your tree, tie it on loosely with soft twine.

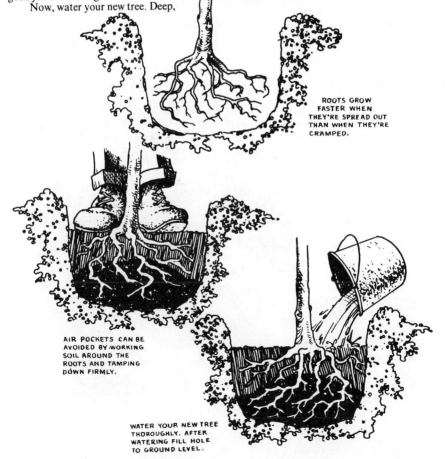

ROOTS GROW FASTER WHEN THEY'RE SPREAD OUT THAN WHEN THEY'RE CRAMPED.

AIR POCKETS CAN BE AVOIDED BY WORKING SOIL AROUND THE ROOTS AND TAMPING DOWN FIRMLY.

WATER YOUR NEW TREE THOROUGHLY. AFTER WATERING FILL HOLE TO GROUND LEVEL.

GRAFTED TREES NEED SPECIAL PLANTING ATTENTION

All Stark Bro's fruit trees are grafted or budded, the only methods for growing true-to-name planting stock. You can see where the fruiting variety on top is joined to the root variety on the bottom by a change in bark or by a slight offset angle. For certain dwarf fruit trees, it's very important to keep this graft above the ground. Otherwise, roots could develop from above the graft. Then your tree could grow to full size by bypassing its dwarfing parts.

Four-part dwarf apple trees should be planted about 1 inch deeper than the soil line from the nursery row. Their grafted dwarfing interstem is high enough so there's no chance of the top rooting. But for dwarf pears, peaches, nectarines and semi-dwarf apricots and plums, the bud-graft line should remain at or above the ground. Standard size fruit trees will be better off with a slightly deeper planting, too.

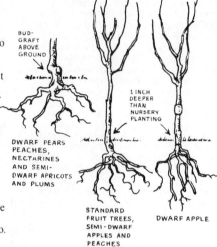

BUD-GRAFT ABOVE GROUND

1 INCH DEEPER THAN NURSERY PLANTING

DWARF PEARS PEACHES, NECTARINES AND SEMI-DWARF APRICOTS AND PLUMS

STANDARD FRUIT TREES, SEMI-DWARF APPLES AND PEACHES

DWARF APPLE

DECORATE YOUR PATIO WITH TUBBED MINIATURE FRUIT TREES

Here's an exciting way to grow delicious fruit on a tiny tree. Select one of the miniature varieties listed in your Stark Bro's catalog. Plant it in a redwood planter box about 20 inches tall. I like to use a growing mixture of ½ good garden soil, ¼ coarse sand and ¼ peat.

Water regularly, much like you'd care for other potted plants. Keep the soil moist, but avoid getting it waterlogged. Monthly feedings till July 1 with Stark Tre-Pep should keep it happy and healthy.

Your patio fruit trees should get at least 6 to 8 hours of good sunlight daily during the growing season. During the winter, after it drops below 20°, move your tubbed tree to a sheltered area or unheated garage. But don't bring it indoors, because it needs to be cold during winter dormancy to bloom and grow normally next spring.

PRUNE YOUR NEW TREE

To get a new fruit tree off to the right start, nothing is more important than pruning at planting time. Yet all too often, this initial pruning is overlooked by the home grower. Many beginners seem to balk at the basic idea. But if the bareroot tree is left unpruned, it may not grow well. And it will take longer to bear the plentiful crops it should.

I think I know why. You might fear it hurts the tree. Or you might think it's wasteful to give your tree a substantial setback in size. You might even mistakenly feel this pruning will delay the first crop of fruit.

Here's why you should prune, there are three basic reasons: survival, stimulation and shaping. First, a tree needs pruning to grow. In digging and handling, any bareroot tree has been disturbed. It has lost some tiny feeder roots, the ones needed to absorb moisture and nutrients. But the top is still full size. This imbalance can cause the tree to put out weak, retarded growth.

In addition, cutting the tree back stimulates stronger, more vigorous growth from the remaining buds. Usually after a single growing season, the tree you prune will be bigger than a matching unpruned tree.

Most important, your fruit tree needs to be shaped. The husky young trees you get from Stark Bro's have far too many branches. Left unpruned, your tree would become a crowded thicket nearly impossible to correct in later years.

To become a strong, heavy-bearing tree, your tree should have just a few well-placed branches. I suggest you select three to five of the strongest branches about 4 - 6 inches apart, arranged somewhat evenly around the trunk. Cut off all the rest of the branches and prune back by ⅓ the ones that remain. Leave the top central branch a little longer than the side branches.

Young cherry trees are often unbranched. So just trim back the top to about 36 inches. After the new side branches have grown 3 to 5 inches, cut the trunk back about six inches more. This leaves only the lower wide-angled branches.

It's not really difficult, just grit your teeth and do it. Even though you may be cutting off more than seems right, it's far better to overprune at planting time than to underprune.

I can assure you that this pruning will result in a sturdier, healthier tree. You'll be getting the right start toward a strong framework, and you'll be rewarded with bigger, better crops of fruit.

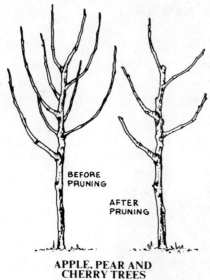

**APPLE, PEAR AND
CHERRY TREES**

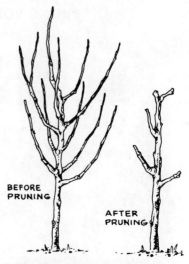

**PEACH, NECTARINE, PLUM
AND APRICOT TREES**

Miniature fruit trees need only light pruning, removing crowded branches and any less than 5" above ground. Trim back all that remain by just a few inches.

Paul's Pointers

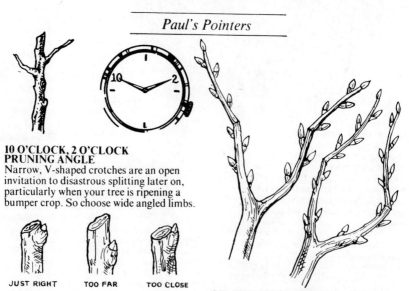

10 O'CLOCK, 2 O'CLOCK PRUNING ANGLE
Narrow, V-shaped crotches are an open invitation to disastrous splitting later on, particularly when your tree is ripening a bumper crop. So choose wide angled limbs.

JUST RIGHT   TOO FAR   TOO CLOSE

PRUNING TO A BUD
Make sharp, clean cuts close enough so there won't be a clumsy stub left that's hard to heal over. But stay far enough above the bud so it won't die back. Slant your cuts as shown, and the new growth will develop beautifully.

SELECT BUDS AIMED IN THE RIGHT DIRECTION
Every branch has buds pointing in various directions. Since the bud farthest out on the branch usually becomes the strongest new branch, make your cut above one that's aimed outward. This helps your tree grow into a spreading shape.

HELP YOUR NEW TREE TO THRIVE

You've already taken care of the most important things: your tree has been carefully planted and properly pruned. But during the first few seasons, there are several extra things that you should do. And it makes all the difference between a tree that's just growing and a tree that's really thriving.

STAKING SHADE TREES

Sometimes, staking for the first few seasons can help a new tree get started. That's because the wind can whip the top around so hard it actually pulls them out of the desired straight upright position.

For the most part, you should only need to stake taller shade trees, especially those with lots of branches. Properly pruned fruit trees hardly ever require staking.

TENDER TRUNKS NEED PROTECTION

Rabbits chew. The sun scalds. And lawn mowers scrape. In each case, the result is the same: a badly damaged tree. But it's so easy to protect this tender bark on young trees. You can wrap the trunk with heavy paper, burlap or special tree wrap, but these must be renewed every so often. They also tend to look untidy. I'm convinced Stark Tree Guards are the best way to protect young trees. These heavy-duty plastic spirals are easy to use and last for years. I recommend you check them once a year to make sure they haven't become too tight, and to remove any grass that's grown inside. Every tree I've seen protected with a Stark Tree Guard has been spared the bark damage that so often harms young trees.

SOAK WATERING DURING DRY SPELLS

If Summer brings about an inch of rainfall every ten days or so, consider yourself blessed and put away the hose. But if it gets really dry, your new tree will respond well to a good, thorough soaking. I think the best way to do this is to let your garden hose trickle slowly. This gives the water a chance to soak in instead of running off. Give your tree enough water to soak the ground all around the roots.

Even if you're in the midst of a brown-lawn drought, don't water too often. Once every 10 days or 2 weeks is plenty.

If there's anything worse than dry, thirsty roots, it's waterlogged, drowning roots.

Unless you're in an area where irrigation is usually needed for normal plant growth, you probably won't need to water after the first growing season.

CULTIVATE AND MULCH

I always like to keep the surface of the soil loosely worked-up during the Spring months. And my trees seem to like it, too. Then when Summer arrives, I cover this cultivated soil with a thick blanket of mulch. It does wonders to keep the ground cool and moist, and it also prevents weeds from crowding. Use peat, chopped leaves, straw, compost, grass clippings or well-rotted manure, they're all good. 4 to 6 inches deep is about right, but keep the mulch a few inches away from the trunk. Then, in late Fall or early Winter, remove this mulch. If you put it away in some out-of-the-way place, you can use the same mulching material again the following season.

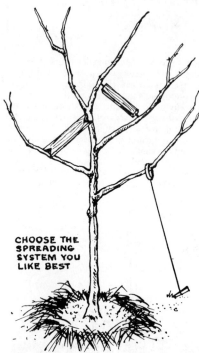

CHOOSE THE SPREADING SYSTEM YOU LIKE BEST

The sooner branches are spread, the better. But one year old branches are usually too small. And after they're four years old, branches usually get too set in their ways. So between two and four years old, a branch is ripe for spreading. Usually after being held down for one growing season, a branch will keep its new position, and spreaders can be removed and used to spread higher up branches.

Once your tree is spread, every branch will get better sunlight. And it'll be in good shape to hold up heavy bumper crops of fruit in the years to come. You should get fruit sooner, too, because the nearly horizontal branch puts more of its strength into growing fruit buds, less into excessive leafy growth.

FOR FASTER GROWTH, FERTILIZE

Help your new tree grow more vigorously with regular feedings of Stark Tre-Pep or Stark Orchard Fertilizer. You'll be amazed with the results! Make your last feeding of the season before July 1st to allow the new growth to mature before frost.

BRANCH SPREADING

Your tree doesn't always know what's best for it. Given its own way, many a fruit tree will develop only upward growing branches with narrow V-shaped crotches. Certain varieties are notorious for this! It usually delays the tree's first bearing for several years. And then the structural weakness of this "natural shape" allows the fruit-heavy branches to split off.

Not only that, but when all the branches grow upward, they crowd each other for light and air circulation. And this problem only gets worse as the years go by.

So here's how to help your tree develop a sturdy uncrowded structure that will bear earlier. It's called branch spreading. You just pull down the tree's side branches to the ideal 10 o'clock, 2 o'clock position and make them stay there. To hold them in this position, wedge in a tree spreader you've made, cut to the right length. These are easily made from wood slats, notched at the ends, or from wood cleats with nails at each end (nail heads cut off).

Another way to spread branches is to bend them down to nearly horizontal, tieing them in that position with soft twine to a stake driven into the ground. Just make sure the twine doesn't become "choking tight".

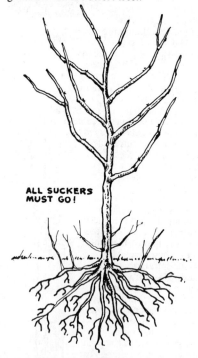

ALL SUCKERS MUST GO!

REMOVE SUCKERS

Any branch growing near the ground should be cut off. They only sap the tree's strength. And if they're growing from the roots, they aren't the fruiting variety you want.

TREE DEVELOPMENT

"The best time to prune is when the knife is sharp", old time gardeners say. That's not exactly true, because fruit trees develop better if they're pruned at just the right time in just the right way.

Years of experience have taught me that fruit trees are naturally inclined to take certain shapes. Following their natural forms, you can prune them into strong, better bearing trees. If you keep up with your pruning and shaping each year, you'll be making mostly small, easy-to-heal cuts. That's far better than letting things get out of hand and doing a lot of heavy pruning.

Keep these main objectives in mind before you make a single cut. You want to help the tree form a strong framework. Any crossing or interfering branches should be removed. Any weak or narrow-angled branches must go. You want to keep your

tree from becoming too thick and crowded and to keep its height reasonable. All these objectives promote improved bearing, which is surely your overall aim.

Try to follow the shaping of these model trees in the drawings, yet allow your tree to express some of its own individuality. You're bound to be mighty pleased with the results.

OFF SEASON PRUNING

Sometimes, pruning should be done even when the season isn't the best. If a branch is broken by the wind or by a heavy load of fruit, emergency treatment is called for. Prune back the ragged edges, making a smooth cut that leaves no stubby stump. Fast-growing "watersprouts" can just as well be removed as soon as you see them, rather than waiting till later.

APPLE, PEAR, CHERRY AND BLUE PLUMS

These trees are best grown with one central trunk with outward growing side branches arranged evenly around the trunk. Each side branch should be about 4 to 8" above the last. Late Winter/early Spring pruning is best. Except for cherries, some spreading will probably be needed, (see page 11). At 5 to 6 years of age, cut this central trunk back to about 6 to 7' from the ground. Prune it back to a strong, outward growing side branch. Avoid trimming off the stubby side branches, called spurs. That's where your next crop will be growing.

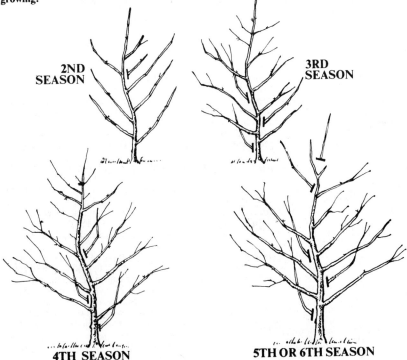

2ND SEASON

3RD SEASON

4TH SEASON

5TH OR 6TH SEASON

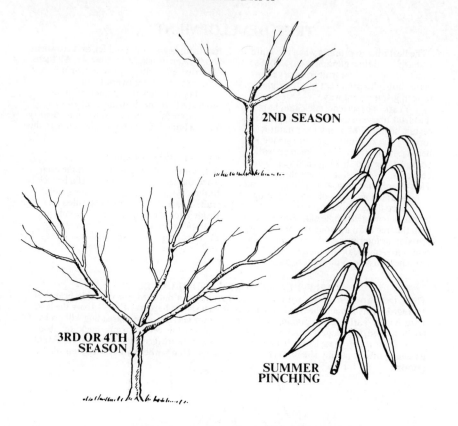

2ND SEASON

3RD OR 4TH
SEASON

SUMMER
PINCHING

PEACH, NECTARINE, APRICOT AND RED PLUM

These vigorous trees like to spread, so select 3 nearly-horizontal branches to form its framework. If you looked down at the tree, it should be shaped much like a pinwheel. The center should be kept fairly open to let in plenty of sunlight. Fruit develops on twigs of last season's growth. To encourage huskier twigs, I recommend Summer pinching for peaches and nectarines. It keeps their size down, too. In early June, hand pinch or prune 2 inches off the end of each soft, leafy shoot. Repeat in late July if side shoots grow strongly. The resulting bushy limb growth should be thinned out by about half in early Spring.

IF YOUR FRUIT TREE REFUSES TO BEAR

Fruit trees are supposed to be fruitful, aren't they? So when they don't bear, there must be a reason. Often you can do something to help bring them into bearing.

First, how old is your tree? Most dwarf fruit trees will bear their first crop the 2nd or 3rd season after planting. But for various reasons, certain trees may not be ready for bearing till a year, even two years later. Standard size trees take longer: apples and pears, from 3 to 5 years; peaches and nectarines, about 2 or 3 years; cherries, apricots and plums, from 3 to 5 years.

Has your tree bloomed? If a tree is growing in partial shade or rich soil or if it has been heavily fertilized, it often develops excessive branch growth at the expense of fruit production. Less fertilizer stimulation or limb spreading (see page 11), should bring it into bearing. Severe pruning may also be the problem.

Was it subject to cold damage? If the past winter was unusually cold, or if there was a freak cold spell in the early Fall or late Spring, this could have damaged the blooms. Fortunately, this is unlikely to happen again the following season.

BEARING PROBLEMS (CONT.)

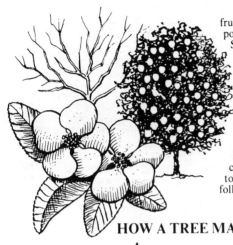

Is a pollinator variety present? Some fruit varieties cannot set fruit by their own pollen (consult the charts on pages 20-23). Should this be the problem, you should plant a pollinator tree to get abundant crops from both. Any spraying done while your tree is in bloom is likely to harm the bees. No bees, no pollination, no fruit.

Did it bear too heavily last season? Some varieties get into the habit of biennual bearing -- big crop one year, very little the next. Proper thinning (see page 24) usually corrects this problem, allowing the tree to save some of its strength for the following year.

HOW A TREE MAKES FRUIT

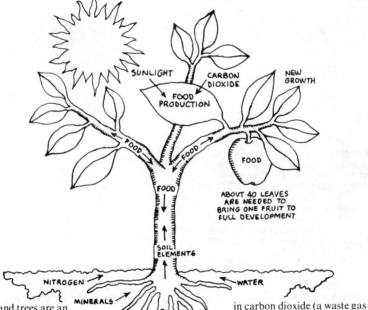

Plants and trees are an important part of the complicated balance of all life on earth. Just like all other living things, they require a balanced diet. But unlike animals, plants can take their nourishment directly from the soil and the air . . . with some help from the sun.

Their tiny, hairlike roots take in water with dissolved nitrogen and minerals. Using small pores in their leaves, plants breathe in carbon dioxide (a waste gas from animals). With the energy of sunlight and a process called photosynthesis, they produce basic food elements. This food is used for the plant's continued growth and for its reproductive efforts.

Remember, what we see as fruit, the tree has intended as a seed pod. This pod is attractive to animals to bribe them into carrying the seeds to new planting locations.

A LITTLE KNOWN FACT
THAT MAKES ALL THE DIFFERENCE

Most every time a fruit tree won't bear, you
can trace it back to a lack of balance in the
tree's life system. Here's how it works: the
roots take water, nitrogen and other soil
elements. And the leaves take in air and
sunlight to produce food. When the tree has
more food than it needs for itself, it uses the
surplus to make fruit.

Normally, there is a healthy balance
between the leaves and the roots . . . they
work well together. But sometimes, outside
influences can upset this balance. By taking
corrective measures, the balance can be
restored, and both you and your tree will be
better off.

How can you tell if your tree gets out
of balance? If a tree has plenty of soil
elements but is low on food reserves, the
leaves will be dark green, slender twigs
grow very long (over 15" annual growth for
a mature apple tree). This is the normal
state for a young tree, but when it causes
nonbearing in an older tree, try some of
these corrective measures:

1. Withhold fertilizer, discontinue
   cultivation
2. Protect leaves from insects and
   diseases
3. Prune lightly, mostly thinning out to
   let the remaining branches get more
   light
4. Bend limbs down (see page 11) so
   center of tree gets more light

If a tree has plenty of food reserves, but
lacks sufficient soil elements, the leaves will
be light green, slender twigs will be
short (less than 10" annual growth for a
mature fruit tree). This tree is weak, and
even though it often bears a lot of under-
sized fruit, it lacks the healthy growth
needed for continued production. Try these
corrective measures:

1. Apply fertilizer with high nitrogen
   content, Stark Orchard Fertilizer.
   recommended
2. Water well if the soil is dry
3. Prune in early Spring, shortening
   new growth by ⅓
4. Spray regularly to keep leaves
   healthy

If you can help your tree maintain this
healthy balance, it can produce big crops of
fruit year after year. So if you can help tip
the scale in the right direction, it's well
worth your time and trouble.

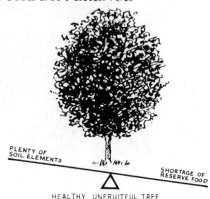

PLENTY OF
SOIL ELEMENTS   SHORTAGE OF
                                 RESERVE FOOD

HEALTHY UNFRUITFUL TREE

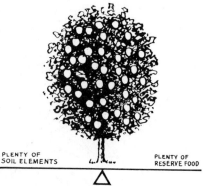

PLENTY OF   PLENTY OF
SOIL ELEMENTS   RESERVE FOOD

VIGOROUS FRUITFUL MATURE TREE

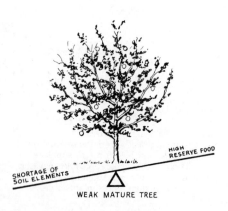

                                 HIGH
                                 RESERVE FOOD
SHORTAGE OF
SOIL ELEMENTS

WEAK MATURE TREE

VARIETY FACTS

What a wonderful selection of fruits are available to the backyard grower! With a full range of ripening times, flavors and qualities for every use, you can pick the variety that's just right for your family.

These charts make it easy to select pollination partners. Just match up the pollination needs of a variety in the first column with the pollen type in the third column. Many varieties need no pollinator, so the first column indicates "SP" for "self-pollinating."

For each variety, I've listed the expected ripening time for here in northern Missouri. As you'd guess, further South they'll ripen somewhat earlier. And further North, ripening will be later. Weather conditions also affect ripening. In addition, I've indicated the most enjoyable ways to use each variety. Perhaps this will help you select other varieties to round out your fruit tree plantings.

APPLES

Pollen Needs	Variety	Pollen Type	Ripens	Winter Keeping	Fresh Eating	Cooking	Canning	Freezing	Young Bearing
A or B	®Stark Earliest	B	Late June		--	--			--
A or B	Lodi, Early Golden	B	Early July		--	--	--		--
A or B	®Starkspur Lodi	B	Early July		--	--	--		
A or B	Early McIntosh	B	Early Aug.		--	--			
A or B	Summer Champion®	B	Early Aug.		--.	--			
A or B	®Starkspur EarliBlaze	B	Mid-Aug.		--	--	--		--
SP	Wealthy Double Red	B	Mid-Aug.		--	--			--
A or B	®Stark Gala	B	Late Aug.		--	--			--
A or B	Prima	B	Late Aug.		--	--	--		--
A or B	®Stark McIntosh Double Red	B	Late Aug.	--	--	--			--
A or B	Ozark Gold	B	Early Sept.		--	--			--
A or B	®Starkspur McIntosh	B	Early Sept.	--	--	--			--
A or B	®Stark RedGold	B	Early Sept.		--				
A or B	Priscilla	B	Mid-Sept.		--	--	--		
SP	®Stark Jon-A-Red	A	Mid-Sept.	--	--	--	--		--
SP	Grimes Golden Double Life®	B	Mid-Sept.	--	--	--			--
A or B	Cortland	B	Late Sept.	--	--	--	--		--
A or B	Spartan	B	Late Sept.	--	--	--			
A or B	®Starking Delicious	A	Late Sept.	--	--				--
A or B	®Starking Full Red Delicious	A	Late Sept.	--	--				--
A or B	®Stark Red Bouquet Delicious	A	Late Sept.	--	--				--
A or B	®Starkrimson Delicious	A	Late Sept.	--	--				--
A or B	®Starkspur Red Delicious	A	Late Sept.	--	--				--
A or B	®Stark Jumbo	A	Early Oct.	--	--	--	--		--
A or B	IdaRed	B	Early Oct.	--	--	--	--	--	
A or B	®Stark Jonalicious	B	Early Oct.	--	--	--	--		
SP	®Stark Golden Delicious	A	Early Oct.	--	--	--	--	--	--
SP	®Starkspur Golden Delicious	A	Early Oct.	--	--	--	--	--	--

Pollen Needs	Variety	Pollen Type	Ripens	Winter Keeping	Fresh Eating	Cooking	Canning	Freezing	Young Bearing
SP	®Starkspur Red Rome Beauty	B	Mid-Oct.	--	--	--	--		--
SP	®Stark Red Rome Beauty	B	Mid-Oct.	--	--	--	--		--
A or B	®Stark Splendor	B	Mid-Oct.	--	--	--	--		--
A or B	®Stark Blushing Golden	A	Mid-Oct.	--	--	--	--	--	--
A or B	®Stark Red Winesap	C	Mid-Oct.	--	--	--	--		
A or B	Turley Winesap	C	Mid-Oct.	--	--	--	--		
A or B	®Starkspur Winesap	C	Mid-Oct.	--	--	--	--		--
A or B	®Stark Scarlet Staymared	C	Late-Oct.	--	--	--	--		
A or B	®Stark Red York	B	Late-Oct.	--	--	--	--	--	
A or B	Northern Spy. Double Red	B	Late Oct.	--	--	--	--		
A or B	®Starkspur Arkansas Black	B	Late Oct.	--	--	--			--
SP	®Stark Tropical Beauty	A	Late Oct.		--	--			

PEACHES AND NECTARINES

Pollen Needs	Variety	Pollen Type	Ripens	Winter Keeping	Fresh Eating	Cooking	Canning	Freezing	Young Bearing
SP	®Stark Early White Giant	D	Early July		--	--			--
SP	Desertgold	D	Early July		--				--
SP	®Stark EarliGlo	D	Mid-July		--	--			--
SP	®Starking Delicious	D	Mid-July		--	--			--
SP	Candor	D	Mid-July		--	--	--	--	--
SP	®Stark Sure-Crop	D	Mid-July		--	--	--		--
SP	Com-Pact Redháven	D	Late July		--	--	--	--	--
SP	Redhaven	D	Late July		--	--		--	--
SP	®Stark EarlyFlame Nect.	D	Late July		--	--	--		--
SP	Reliance	D	Early Aug.		--	--			--
SP	®Stark SunGlo Nect.	D	Early Aug.		--	--	--	--	--
SP	®Stark SunBright	D	Early Aug.		--	--	--	--	--
SP	®Burbank July Elberta	D	Early Aug.		--	--	--	--	--
SP	®Stark Sunburst Nect.	D	Early Aug.		--	--	--	--	--
SP	®Stark Starlet	D	Early Aug.		--	--	--	--	--
SP	®Stark Delicious Nect.	D	Early Aug.		--				--
SP	Glohaven	D	Early Aug.		--	--	--'	--	--
SP	Sunapee	D	Early Aug.		--·		--		--
SP	Loring	D	Early Aug.		--	--	--	--	--
SP	Babygold 5	D	Early Aug.			--	--		--
SP	Mericrest	D	Early Aug.		--	--	--	--	--
SP	Cresthaven	D	Mid-Aug.		--	--	--	--	--

PEACHES AND NECTARINES

Pollen Needs	Variety	Pollen Type	Ripens	Winter Keeping	Fresh Eating	Cooking	Canning	Freezing	Young Bearing
SP	Madison		Mid-Aug.		--	--	--		--
SP	⊛Burbank Flaming Gold Nect.	D	Mid-Aug.		--				--
SP	⊛Stark Early Elberta	D	Mid-Aug.		--	--	--	--	--
SP	⊛Stark FrostKing	D	Mid-Aug.		--	--	--	--	--
SP	⊛Stark RedGold Nect.	D	Mid-Aug.		--	--	--	--	--
SP	Belle of Georgia	D	Late Aug.		--	--	--		--
SP	⊛Stark Elberta Queen	D	Late Aug.		--		--	--	--
D	J. H. Hale	--	Late Aug.		--	--	--	--	--
D	⊛Stark Honeydew Hale	--	Late Aug.		--	--	--	--	--
SP	Redskin	D	Late Aug.		--	--	--	--	--
D	⊛Stark Hal-Berta Giant	--	Late Aug.		--	--	--	--	--
SP	Monroe	D	Early Sept.		--		--	--	
SP	⊛Stark Autumn Gold	D	Early Sept.		--	--	--	--	--

PLUMS-APRICOTS

Pollen Needs	Variety	Pollen Type	Ripens	Winter Keeping	Fresh Eating	Cooking	Canning	Freezing	Young Bearing
SP	⊠Stark Earli-Orange Apricot		Late June		--	--	--	--	--
SP	⊠Stark Giant Tilton Apricot		Early July		--	--	--	--	
SP	Wilson Delicious Apricot		Early July		--	--	--	--	--
SP	Hungarian Rose Apricot		Mid-July		--	--	--		
J	Santa Rosa Plum	J	Mid-July		--		--		--
J	⊠Stark Giant Cherry Plum	J	Mid-July				--		--
SP	Earliblue Prune	I	Late July		--	--	--		
K	Underwood Plum	K	Late July		--	--	--		
J	Redheart Plum	J	Early Aug.		--				
J	⊛Starking Delicious Plum	J	Early Aug.		--		--		--
K	Ember Plum	K	Early Aug.		--	--	--		
J	Ozark Premier Plum	J	Mid-Aug.		--		--		--
J	⊛Burbank Red Ace	J	Mid-Aug.		--				--
I	⊛Burbank Grand Prize Prune	I	Mid-Aug.		--		--	--	--
SP	Green Gage Plum	I	Mid-Aug.		--	--	--		
SP	Blufre Prune	I	Early Sept.		--	--	--		--
J	⊛Burbank Elephant Heart	J	Early Sept.		--				--
SP	Damson	I	Early Sept.			--			
SP	Stanley Prune	I	Early Sept.		--		--		

CHERRIES

Pollen Needs	Variety	Pollen Type	Ripens	Winter Keeping	Fresh Eating	Cooking	Canning	Freezing	Young Bearing
SP	Early Richmond	F	Mid-June		--	--	--	--	--
H	Vista	G	Mid-June		--	--	--	--	--
H	Emperor Francis	G	Mid-June		--	--	--	--	--
SP	North Star	F	Mid-June			--	--	--	--
G or H	Van	H	Mid-June		--	--	--	--	--
H	Napoleon (Royal Ann)	G	Mid-June		--	--	--	~	--
G or H	Venus	G	Mid-June		--	--	--	--	--
H	Bing	G	Mid-June		--	--	--	--	--
G or H	Hedelfingen	H	Mid-June		--	--	--	--	--
H	ⁿStark Lambert	G	Mid-June		--	--	--	--	--
G or H	Schmidt's Biggareau	H	Mid-June		--	--	--	--	
SP	ⁿStark Montmorency	F	Late June		--	--	--	--	--
SP	ⁿStarkspur Montmorency	F	Late June		--	--	--	--	--
G or H	ⁿStark Gold	H	Late June		--	--	--	--	--
SP	Meteor	F	Early July		--	--	--	--	--
SP	Suda Hardy	F	Early July			--	--	--	--

PEARS

Pollen Needs	Variety	Pollen Type	Ripens	Winter Keeping	Fresh Eating	Cooking	Canning	Freezing	Young Bearing
L-M-N	Tyson	M	Early Aug		--	--	--		--
L-M-N	ⁿStarkrimson	M	Mid-Aug.		--	--	--		
L-M-N	Fame	M	Mid-Aug.		--				
L-M-N	Moonglow	M	Mid-Aug.		--	--	--		--
L or M	Bartlett	N	Late Aug.		--	--	--		--
L-M-N	ⁿStarking Delicious	M	Early Sept		--	--	--		
L-M-N	Magness	--	Mid-Sept.		--				
L-M-N	ⁿStark Grand Champion	M	Mid-Sept.	--	--	--	--		
L or M	Seckel	N	Mid-Sept.	--	--	--			--
SP	Duchess	L	Late Sept	--	--	--	--		--
L-M-N	Buerre Bosc	M	Late Sept	--	--				--
L-M-N	Anjou	M	Late Sept	--	--				
L-M-N	Comice	M	Early Oct	--	--	--	--		--
SP	Kieffer	M	Mid-Oct.	--	--				--

IT'S FUN TO HARVEST DELICIOUS TREE-RIPENED FRUIT

Now you're ready to enjoy your delicious home grown fruit. They'll be best it you wait till just the right time to pick them. Lots of folks have never eaten tasty, tree-ripened fruit. This is a special delicacy, an additional benefit to you when you grow your own fruit.

Apples tell you they're ripe by losing the last traces of their green background color and by developing their full bright color. Most important they become less tangy-tart and sweeter in taste. You'll also notice the seeds turn from white to brown. When you're picking, just lift it upward quickly. If it's ready, it will come loose without damage to the tree.

Pears are different. You have to pick them before they ripen while they're still hard and yellow-green. Wait till they start to turn yellow, perhaps a few will drop off the tree. They should then part from the branch easily. Handle with care, and place in a cool room to ripen. Check frequently, it may take a few days, a week, or even longer.

Pick your peaches at the last minute, when they're ripe 'n' ready to enjoy. A gentle twist will loosen all fruits that are ready. Store at room temperature for a day, to bring out the finest flavor.

One sure sign that red cherries are getting ripe is when the birds start visiting your tree for breakfast. But when it's lunch and dinner, too, you'll probably want to keep these freeloaders away. About the only good way to do this is to cover your tree with lightweight netting. Stark Bro's Garden Net keeps your fruit safe from attack. It's easy to use and lasts for years. I suggest you give it a try.

Cool storage of apples for winter enjoyment.
Tasty, fresh fruit is a special treat during the bleak winter months. Fortunately, many varieties of apples keep their fine eating qualities for a long time with proper storage. Check the chart on page 20-21 to see which varieties store best.

If you're planning to store your apples, pick them a bit early, just as they start to ripen. Handle them carefully to avoid bruises that could develop into spoilage. The ideal storage spot is humid and cool, from 32° to 40°. If you place them in perforated plastic freezer bags and keep them in your refrigerator, this should work well. Any cool area in your house, the basement or an unheated porch perhaps, might also be O.K. for a while.

You can also extend the enjoyment of many pears in much the same way. After you've picked the unripe fruit, place it in cool storage immediately. Bring them out to ripen at room temperature when you're ready to use them.

I think it's best to inspect stored fruit every week or so to check for any spoilage. That way, you can remove any that are developing soft spots or brown areas. This keeps the spoilage from "spreading" to nearby fruit. Remember, "One bad apple spoils the whole barrelfull."

THIN YOUR FRUIT FOR BEST SIZE, AND BIGGER TOTAL CROPS.

Thin tiny fruits within 3 weeks after bloom so your tree can produce large fruits you'll be proud of. Apples and pears should be about 8 inches apart; peaches and nectarines, 8 inches apart for early types, 5 inches for late ripeners; and apricots and large plums, 4 inches apart. Of course, damaged or misshapen fruit should be the first to go.

There's more to growing enjoyment than fresh fruit.

YOU'LL BE NUTTY ABOUT NUTS.

I'll never understand why everyone doesn't plant at least one or two nut trees in his yard. Just think, it's probably the greatest combination ever: a magnificent hardwood shade tree plus a yearly crop of big, meaty nuts.

In fact, there's only one bad thing I'd have to say about nut trees: they can be so stubborn in getting started. Once they're growing, they're about as carefree as a tree can be. So the extra attention you give nut trees at planting time is well worth it when you consider how trouble-free they'll be in all the years ahead.

Many nut trees have just one main root, almost like a giant skinny carrot. Since this long taproot mustn't be trimmed or bent, you'll want to dig a very deep hole, about the $20 size.

If your soil's on the heavy side, mixing in up to ⅓ peat helps a lot. As you're filling in the hole, stop to tamp it down every few inches. This eliminates air pockets. When the hole is nearly full, pour in a bucket of water treated with Stark Tre-Pep.

After it has soaked in, give it another bucketful.

Now comes the "hard" part. Muster the courage to give your new tree a drastic pruning, cutting off at least ⅓ to ½ of the top. This forces it to grow a strong sprout that will become the main

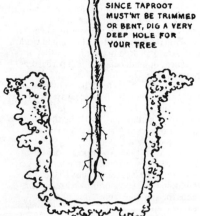

SINCE TAPROOT MUST'NT BE TRIMMED OR BENT, DIG A VERY DEEP HOLE FOR YOUR TREE

trunk. If you didn't prune, it would probably grow many smaller sprouts. And since this is way too low for side branches to start, you'd have to trim off all but one. Take my word for it, this severe pruning at planting time gets your new tree off to the best possible start.

Your nut tree will respond well to a couple more soakings with Stark Tre-Pep before July 1. Mulching helps keep the soil cool and moist. Since the trunk is especially vulnerable to sunscald and rodent damage, I highly recommend using a Stark Tree Guard.

As your young tree grows, you should prune to keep it growing in a pyramid shape with a single main trunk. Bearing trees will produce bigger crops if you apply Stark Orchard Fertilizer.

BERRY BUSHES, SO EASY TO GROW

Just about the only way to get really delicious raspberries and blackberries is to have your own "berry patch". They like lots of sun and moisture, so try to find a planting spot where they'll get plenty of both.

As you plant your new berry bushes, avoid getting them too deep. The crown should be right at the soil level with the roots just under the surface. Water well with a Stark. Tre-Pep solution and prune back the stems to about 2 inches. Additional fertilizing in late Spring and early Summer results in more vigorous new growth. Spring cultivation and Summer mulching is very beneficial.

Berry bushes bear only on one-year old stems. So as soon as the canes have produced fruit, prune them back to the ground to make room for the strong new canes. In addition, some pruning should be done every Spring to keep the plants from becoming tangled and to improve their ability to bear. You may want to stake or trellis-train your berry plants to keep them more compact and upright.

HERE'S A TIME SAVING TIP ON HOW TO SIMPLIFY PRUNING. Plant one of the new everbearing red raspberries listed in Stark Bro's catalog. Then prune all the canes to the ground every Spring. Then you'll get a single large crop of berries in the Fall from the new canes that grew during the Summer.

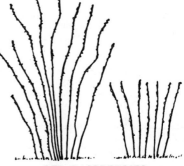

PLANT 3 TO 5 FEET APART

2"

LEAVE ABOUT 6 FEET BETWEEN ROWS

RED RASPBERRIES -- Prune in the Spring, cutting young canes back to 4-5 feet. Remove entirely all weaker canes, leaving only 8 or 9 stronger ones.

BLACK RASPBERRIES -- When new shoots are 3 feet tall, snip off the tips. This results in vigorous side branches, which are pruned back to about 10 inches in the Spring.

BLACKBERRIES -- In the Spring, prune each main cane back to 3 or 4 feet. Then cut back side branches to leave 5 or 6 buds on each.

"Leaving 3 to 4 strong canes per foot of row promotes better bearing."

RED RASPBERRIES

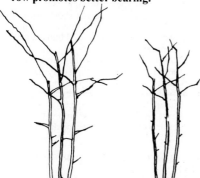

BLACKBERRIES

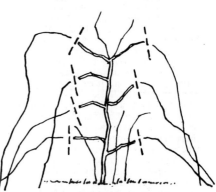

BLACK RASPBERRIES

BLUEBERRIES

If your soil is on the acid side, or if you're willing to make it acid, you've already met the major requirement of successful blueberry growing.

Pick a sunny, well drained place to plant them, preferably where the soil has lots of organic matter. Consider planting them as a beautiful, productive hedge. Follow the planting instructions on page 6, spacing them 4-6 feet apart. Don't plant too deep, and finish the job with a Stark Tre-Pep solution soaking.

Trim your new plants moderately, pruning back by about one half. To keep your blueberries happy and fruitful, cultivate in the Spring, mulch heavily during the Summer, and keep their soil acid. Aluminum sulphate treatments may be needed to maintain this necessary acidity.

Let your plants save their strength the

first year by removing the flowers. For best crops, plant another variety for proper pollination. Blueberries ripen over several weeks, so plan to pick more than once. If birds become a bother, protect your crop with Stark Garden Net.

GRAPES ARE GREAT FOR HOMEOWNERS

There's something about a bountiful harvest of delicious grapes that really makes a man feel like a king! Yet this richly rewarding experience is well within the reach of most everybody.

Select a sunny spot for your new grape vines and follow the planting instructions on page 31. If you're willing to work plenty of organic matter into the soil, your vines will grow better. Compost, chopped leaves, peat moss, or rotted manure are all good. Complete with a thorough soaking with Tre-Pep solution, and get ready for great results.

Prune your new vine heavily, leaving only 2 or 3 buds on its strongest stem. As it grows, you'll be keeping only the most vigorous sprout to form the main stem. Shallow cultivation during the early growing months and Summer mulching can do wonders for your grape vines.

To start out the second year, begin training the vine on a permanent support. Make sure this trellis support is strong enough, because it will soon be holding up lots of heavy bunches of grapes. Select the best side canes to form the "double T" shape. This training is followed in most vineyards because it's the most productive.

Your crop of grapes will be produced on new growth from one-year old stems. So it pays to keep old wood to a bare minimum. In late Winter from the third

year on, your grape vine should be pruned severely. On each of the four "arms", select a good pencil-size stem as the fruiting cane, trimming it back to keep about 8 to 10 buds. Near the base of each of these fruiting canes, also leave a stubby stem with 2 buds to form next year's fruiting canes. All other canes are pruned away. You keep doing this each year to maintain your vine in the very best bearing condition. I know this pruning sounds mighty drastic, but take my word for it, it really works!

Muscadine grapes are more productive with a different type of training. This "single T" shape has a row of short, upward growing branches. In late Winter, the canes are cut back to leave only 3 or 4 buds above the horizontal main stem.

To get the best quality fruit, you may need the protection of regular spraying. Black rot causes reddish-brown spots on leaves first, then on the fruit which shrivels and dries up. Berry moth appears as worms feeding on the fruit. Control both with Stark Home Orchard Spray and destroy fallen leaves and fruit.

IT'S FUN TO MAKE YOUR OWN WINE

An extra opportunity open to everyone who grows their own grapes is the creation of special homemade wines. To get the "vintage quality" you'll really be proud of, you should start with special French hybrid varieties of grapes. Several of the best types of wine grapes are offered by Stark Bro's.

Some of these varieties are also fine for fresh eating, giving you a very versatile crop. It's almost like having your cake and eating it, too!

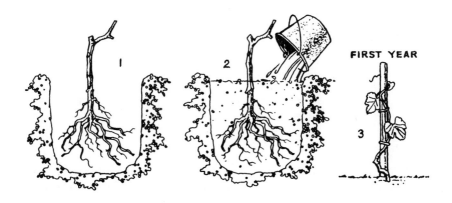

1. Dig hole big enough to give the roots plenty of "elbow room". Plant slightly deeper than it grew at the nursery.
2. Fill hole about ¾ full, soak well with a solution of Stark Tre-Pep. Finish filling the hole.
3. Prune back to 2 or 3 buds, later leaving only the strongest new cane. Train to stake during first Summer, pinching back all side shoots to two leaves each.

PRUNING EXAMPLES

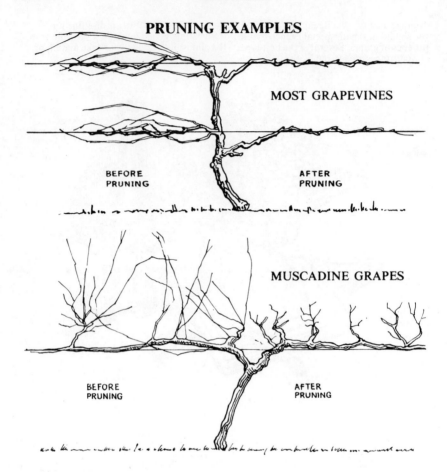

MOST GRAPEVINES

BEFORE
PRUNING

AFTER
PRUNING

MUSCADINE GRAPES

BEFORE
PRUNING

AFTER
PRUNING

Appendix B

Home CANNING of Fruits and Vegetables

Organisms that cause food spoilage—molds, yeasts, and bacteria—are always present in the air, water, and soil. Enzymes that may cause undesirable changes in flavor, color, and texture are present in raw fruits and vegetables.

When you can fruits and vegetables you heat them hot enough and long enough to destroy spoilage organisms. This heating (or processing) also stops the action of enzymes. Processing is done in either a boiling-water-bath canner or a steam-pressure canner. The kind of canner that should be used depends on the kind of food being canned.

Right Canner for Each Food

For fruits, tomatoes, and pickled vegetables, use a boiling-water-bath canner. You can process these acid foods safely in boiling water.

For all common vegetables except tomatoes, use a steam-pressure canner. To process these low-acid foods safely in a reasonable length of time takes a temperature higher than that of boiling water.

A pressure saucepan equipped with an accurate indicator or gage for controlling pressure at 10 pounds (240° F.) may be used as a steam-pressure canner for vegetables in pint jars or No. 2 tin cans. If you use a pressure saucepan, add 20 minutes to the processing times given in this publication for each vegetable.

Getting Your Equipment Ready

Steam-Pressure Canner

For safe operation of your canner, clean petcock and safety-valve openings by drawing a string or narrow strip of cloth through them. Do this at beginning of canning season and often during the season.

Check pressure gage.—An accurate pressure gage is necessary to get the processing temperatures needed to make food keep.

A weighted gage needs to be thoroughly clean.

A dial gage, old or new, should be checked before the canning season, and also during the season if you use the canner often. Ask your county home demonstration agent, dealer, or manufacturer about checking it.

This Appendix is excerpted from Home and Garden Bulletin No. 8 with the kind permission of the U.S. Department of Agriculture.

271

If your gage is off 5 pounds or more, you'd better get a new one. But if the gage is not more than 4 pounds off, you can correct for it as shown below. As a reminder, tie on the canner a tag stating the reading to use to get the correct pressure.

The food is to be processed at 10 pounds steam pressure; so—

If the gage reads high—	If the gage reads low—
1 pound high—process at 11 pounds.	1 pound low—process at 9 pounds.
2 pounds high—process at 12 pounds.	2 pounds low—process at 8 pounds.
3 pounds high—process at 13 pounds.	3 pounds low—process at 7 pounds.
4 pounds high—process at 14 pounds.	4 pounds low—process at 6 pounds.

Have canner thoroughly clean.—Wash canner kettle well if you have not used it for some time. Don't put cover in water—wipe it with a soapy cloth, then with a damp, clean cloth. Dry well.

Water-Bath Canner

Water-bath canners are available on the market. Any big metal container may be used as a boiling-water-bath canner if it is deep enough so that the water is well over tops of jars and has space to boil freely. Allow 2 to 4 inches above jar tops for brisk boiling (see sketch). The canner must have a tight-fitting cover and a wire or wooden rack. If the rack has dividers, jars will not touch each other or fall against the sides of the canner during processing.

If a steam-pressure canner is deep enough, you can use it for a water bath. Cover, but do not fasten. Leave pet-cock wide open, so that steam escapes and pressure does not build up inside the canner.

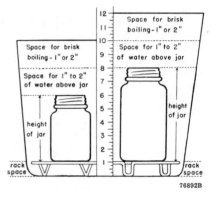

76892B

Glass Jars

Be sure all jars and closures are perfect. Discard any with cracks, chips, dents, or rust; defects prevent airtight seals.

Select the size of closure—widemouth or regular—that fits your jars.

Wash glass jars in hot, soapy water and rinse well. Wash and rinse all lids and bands. Metal lids with sealing compound may need boiling or holding in boiling water for a few minutes—follow the manufacturer's directions.

If you use rubber rings, have clean, new rings of the right size for the jars. Don't test by stretching. Wash rings in hot, soapy water. Rinse well.

Tin Cans

Select desired type and size.—Three types of tin cans are used in home canning—plain tin, C-enamel (corn enamel), and R-enamel (sanitary or stand-ard enamel). For most products plain tin cans are satisfactory. Enameled cans are recommended for certain fruits and vegetables to prevent discoloration of food, but they are not necessary for a wholesome product.

The types of cans and the foods for which they are recommended are:

Type of can	Recommended for—
C-enamel....................	Corn, hominy.
R-enamel....................	Beets, red berries, red or black cherries, plums, pumpkin, rhubarb, winter squash.
Plain	All other fruits and vegetables for which canning directions are given in this bulletin.

In this bulletin, directions are given for canning most fruits and vegetables in No. 2 and No. 2½ tin cans. A No. 2 can holds about 2½ cups, and a No. 2½ can about 3½ cups.

Use only cans in good condition.—See that cans, lids, and gaskets are perfect. Discard badly bent, dented, or rusted cans, and lids with damaged gaskets. Keep lids in paper packing until ready to use. The paper protects the lids from dirt and moisture.

Wash cans.—Just before use, wash cans in clean water; drain upside down. Do not wash lids; washing may damage the gaskets. If lids are dusty or dirty, rinse with clean water or wipe with a damp cloth just before you put them on the cans.

Check the sealer.—Make sure the sealer you use is properly adjusted. To test, put a little water into a can, seal it, then submerge can in boiling water for a few seconds. If air bubbles rise from around the can, the seam is not tight. Adjust sealer, following manufacturer's directions.

76627B

A can sealer is needed if tin cans are used.

General Canning Procedure

Selecting Fruits and Vegetables for Canning

Choose fresh, firm fruits and young, tender vegetables. Can them before they lose their freshness. If you must hold them, keep them in a cool, airy place. If you buy fruits and vegetables to can, try to get them from a nearby garden or orchard.

For best quality in the canned product, use only perfect fruits and vegetables. Sort them for size and ripeness; they cook more evenly that way.

Washing

Wash all fruits and vegetables thoroughly, whether or not they are to be pared. Dirt contains some of the bacteria hardest to kill. Wash small lots at a time, under running water or through several changes of water. Lift the food out of the water each time so dirt that has been washed off won't go back on the food. Rinse pan thoroughly between washings. Don't let fruits or vegetables soak; they may lose flavor and food value. Handle them gently to avoid bruising.

Filling Containers

Raw pack or hot pack.—Fruits and vegetables may be packed raw into glass jars or tin cans or preheated and packed hot. In this publication directions for both raw and hot packs are given for most of the foods.

Most raw fruits and vegetables should be packed tightly into the container because they shrink during processing; a few—like corn, lima beans, and peas— should be packed loosely because they expand.

Hot food should be packed fairly loosely. It should be at or near boiling temperature when it is packed.

There should be enough sirup, water, or juice to fill in around the solid food in the container and to cover the food. Food at the top of the container tends to darken if not covered with liquid. It takes from ½ to 1½ cups of liquid for a quart glass jar or a No. 2½ tin can.

Head space.—With only a few exceptions, some space should be left between the packed food and the closure. The amount of space to allow at the top of the jar or can is given in the detailed directions for canning each food.

Closing Glass Jars

Closures for glass jars are of two main types:

Metal screwband and flat metal lid with sealing compound. To use this type, wipe jar rim clean after produce is packed. Put lid on, with sealing compound next to glass. Screw metal band down tight by hand. When band is tight, this lid has enough give to let air escape during processing. Do not tighten screw band further after taking jar from canner.

Screw bands that are in good condition may be reused. You may remove bands as soon as jars are cool. Metal lids with sealing compound may be used only once.

Porcelain-lined zinc cap with shoulder rubber ring. Fit wet rubber ring down on jar shoulder, but don't stretch unnecessarily. Fill jar; wipe rubber ring and jar rim clean. Then screw cap down firmly and turn it back ¼ inch. As soon as you take jar from canner, screw cap down tight, to complete seal.

Porcelain-lined zinc caps may be reused as long as they are in good condition. Rubber rings should not be reused.

75944B

Exhausting and Sealing Tin Cans

Tin cans are sealed before processing. The temperature of the food in the cans must be 170° F. or higher when the cans are sealed. Food is heated to this temperature to drive out air so that there will be a good vacuum in the can after processing and cooling. Removal of air also helps prevent discoloring of canned food and change in flavor.

Food packed raw must be heated in the cans (exhausted) before the cans are sealed. Food packed hot may be sealed without further heating if you are sure the temperature of the food has not dropped below 170° F. To make sure, test with a thermometer, placing the bulb at the center of the can. If the thermometer registers lower than 170°, or if you do not make this test, exhaust the cans.

To exhaust, place open, filled cans on a rack in a kettle in which there is enough boiling water to come to about 2 inches below the tops of the cans. Cover the kettle. Bring water back to boiling. Boil until a thermometer inserted at the center of the can registers 170° F.—or for the length of time given in the directions for the fruit or vegetable you are canning.

Remove cans from the water one at a time, and add boiling packing liquid or water if necessary to bring head space back to the level specified for each product. Place clean lid on filled can. Seal at once.

Processing

Process fruits, tomatoes, and pickled vegetables in a boiling-water-bath canner according to the directions on page 10. Process vegetables in a steam-pressure canner according to the directions on page 16.

Cooling Canned Food

Glass jars.—As you take jars from the canner, complete seals at once if necessary. If liquid boiled out in processing, do not open jar to add more. Seal the jar just as it is.

Cool jars top side up. Give each jar enough room to let air get at all sides. Never set a hot jar on a cold surface; instead set the jars on a rack or on a folded cloth. Keep hot jars away from drafts, but don't slow cooling by covering them.

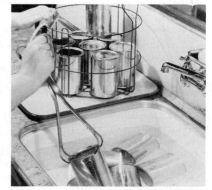

BN21476

76619B

Cool jars top side up on a rack, leaving space between jars so air can circulate.

Cool tin cans in cold water; change water frequently to cool cans quickly.

Tin cans.—Put tin cans in cold, clean water to cool them; change water as needed to cool cans quickly. Take cans out of the water while they are still warm so they will dry in the air. If you stack cans, stagger them so that air can get around them.

Day-After-Canning Jobs

Test the seal on glass jars with porcelain-lined caps by turning each jar partly over in your hands.   To test a jar that has a flat metal lid, press center of lid; if lid is down and will not move, jar is sealed.   Or tap the center of the lid with a spoon.   A clear, ringing sound means a good seal.   A dull note does not always mean a poor seal; store jars without leaks and check for spoilage before use.

If you find a leaky jar, use unspoiled food right away.   Or can it again; empty the jar, and pack and process food as if it were fresh.   Before using jar or lid again check for defects.

When jars are thoroughly cool, take off the screw bands carefully.   If a band sticks, covering for a moment with a hot, damp cloth may help loosen it.

Before storing canned food, wipe containers clean.   Label to show contents, date, and lot number—if you canned more than one lot in a day.

BN21468

Wash bands; store them in a dry place.   **Label jars after they have been cooled.**

Storing Canned Food

Properly canned food stored in a cool, dry place will retain good eating quality for a year.   Canned food stored in a warm place near hot pipes, a range, or a furnace, or in direct sunlight may lose some of its eating quality in a few weeks or months, depending on the temperature.

Dampness may corrode cans or metal lids and cause leakage so the food will spoil.

Freezing does not cause food spoilage unless the seal is damaged or the jar is broken.   However, frozen canned food may be less palatable than properly stored canned food.   In an unheated storage place it is well to protect canned food by wrapping the jars in paper or covering them with a blanket.

On Guard Against Spoilage

Don't use canned food that shows any sign of spoilage.   Look closely at each container before opening it.   Bulging can ends, jar lids, or rings, or a leak— these may mean the seal has broken and the food has spoiled.   When you open a container look for other signs—spurting liquid, an off odor, or mold.

It's possible for canned vegetables to contain the poison causing botulism— a serious food poisoning—without showing signs of spoilage.   To avoid any risk of botulism, it is essential that the pressure canner be in perfect order and that every canning recommendation be followed exactly.   Unless you're absolutely sure of your gage and canning methods, boil home-canned vegetables before tasting.   Heating usually makes any odor of spoilage more evident.

Bring vegetables to a rolling boil; then cover and boil for at least 10 minutes. Boil spinach and corn 20 minutes.   If the food looks spoiled, foams, or has an off odor during heating, destroy it.

Burn spoiled vegetables, or dispose of the food so that it will not be eaten by humans or animals.

How To Can Fruits, Tomatoes, Pickled Vegetables

Fruits, tomatoes, and pickled vegetables are canned according to the general directions on pages 5 to 8, the detailed directions for each food on pages 11 to 16, and the special directions given below that apply only to acid foods.

Points on Packing

Raw pack.—Put cold, raw fruits into container and cover with boiling-hot sirup, juice, or water. Press tomatoes down in the containers so they are covered with their own juice; add no liquid.

Hot pack.—Heat fruits in sirup, in water or steam, or in extracted juice before packing. Juicy fruits and tomatoes may be preheated without added liquid and packed in the juice that cooks out.

BN21474

To hot pack fruit, pack heated fruit loosely into jars.

BN21469

Cover fruit with boiling liquid before closing jar and processing in boiling-water bath.

Sweetening Fruit

Sugar helps canned fruit hold its shape, color, and flavor. Directions for canning most fruits call for sweetening to be added in the form of sugar sirup. For very juicy fruit packed hot, use sugar without added liquid.

To make sugar sirup.—Mix sugar with water or with juice extracted from some of the fruit. Use a thin, medium, or heavy sirup to suit the sweetness of the fruit and your taste. To make sirup, combine—

4 cups of water or juice.....	2 cups sugar.....	For 5 cups THIN sirup.
	3 cups sugar.....	For 5½ cups MEDIUM sirup.
	4¾ cups sugar...	For 6½ cups HEAVY sirup.

Heat sugar and water or juice together until sugar is dissolved. Skim if necessary.

To extract juice.—Crush thoroughly ripe, sound juicy fruit. Heat to simmering (185° to 210° F.) over low heat. Strain through jelly bag or other cloth.

To add sugar direct to fruit.—For juicy fruit to be packed hot, add about ½ cup sugar to each quart of raw, prepared fruit. Heat to simmering (185° to 210° F.) over low heat. Pack fruit in the juice that cooks out.

To add sweetening other than sugar.—You can use light corn sirup or mild-flavored honey to replace as much as half the sugar called for in canning fruit. Do not use brown sugar, or molasses, sorghum, or other strong-flavored sirups; their flavor overpowers the fruit flavor and they may darken the fruit.

Canning Unsweetened Fruit

You may can fruit without sweetening—in its own juice, in extracted juice, or in water. Sugar is not needed to prevent spoilage; processing is the same for unsweetened fruit as for sweetened.

Processing in Boiling-Water Bath

Directions.—Put filled glass jars or tin cans into canner containing hot or boiling water. For raw pack in glass jars have water in canner hot but not boiling; for all other packs have water boiling.

Add boiling water if needed to bring water an inch or two over tops of containers; don't pour boiling water directly on glass jars. Put cover on canner.

After jars are covered with boiling water, place lid on water-bath canner and bring water quickly back to boiling.

When water in canner comes to a rolling boil, start to count processing time. Boil gently and steadily for time recommended for the food you are canning. Add boiling water during processing if needed to keep containers covered.

Remove containers from the canner immediately when processing time is up.

Processing times.—Follow times carefully. The times given apply only when a specific food is prepared according to detailed directions.

If you live at an altitude of 1,000 feet or more, you have to add to these processing times in canning directions, as follows:

Altitude	Increase in processing time if the time called for is—	
	20 minutes or less	More than 20 minutes
1,000 feet	1 minute	2 minutes.
2,000 feet	2 minutes	4 minutes.
3,000 feet	3 minutes	6 minutes.
4,000 feet	4 minutes	8 minutes.
5,000 feet	5 minutes	10 minutes.
6,000 feet	6 minutes	12 minutes.
7,000 feet	7 minutes	14 minutes.
8,000 feet	8 minutes	16 minutes.
9,000 feet	9 minutes	18 minutes.
10,000 feet	10 minutes	20 minutes.

To Figure Yield of Canned Fruit From Fresh

The number of quarts of canned food you can get from a given quantity of fresh fruit depends upon the quality, variety, maturity, and size of the fruit, whether it is whole, in halves, or in slices, and whether it is packed raw or hot.

Generally, the following amounts of fresh fruit or tomatoes (as purchased or picked) make 1 quart of canned food:

Pounds

Apples	2½ to 3
Berries, except strawberries	1½ to 3 (1 to 2 quart boxes)
Cherries (canned unpitted)	2 to 2½
Peaches	2 to 3
Pears	2 to 3
Plums	1½ to 2½
Tomatoes	2½ to 3½

In 1 pound there are about 3 medium apples and pears; 4 medium peaches or tomatoes; 8 medium plums.

Directions for Fruits, Tomatoes, Pickled Vegetables

Apples

Pare and core apples; cut in pieces. To keep fruit from darkening, drop pieces into water containing 2 tablespoons each of salt and vinegar per gallon. Drain, then boil 5 minutes in thin sirup or water.

In glass jars.—Pack hot fruit to ½ inch of top. Cover with hot sirup or water, leaving ½-inch space at top of jar. Adjust jar lids. Process in boiling-water bath (212° F.)—

Pint jars	15 minutes
Quart jars	20 minutes

As soon as you remove jars from canner, complete seals if necessary.

In tin cans.—Pack hot fruit to ¼ inch of top. Fill to top with hot sirup or water. Exhaust to 170° F. (about 10 minutes) and seal cans. Process in boiling-water bath (212° F.)—

No. 2 cans	10 minutes
No. 2½ cans	10 minutes

Applesauce

Make applesauce, sweetened or unsweetened. Heat to simmering (185°–210° F.) ; stir to keep it from sticking.

In glass jars.—Pack hot applesauce to ¼ inch of top. Adjust lids. Process in boiling-water bath (212° F.)—

Pint jars_____	10 minutes
Quart jars_____	10 minutes

As soon as you remove jars from canner, complete seals if necessary.

In tin cans.—Pack hot applesauce to top. Exhaust to 170° F. (about 10 minutes) and seal cans. Process in boiling-water bath (212° F.)—

No. 2 cans_____	10 minutes
No. 2½ cans_____	10 minutes

Apricots

Follow method for peaches. Peeling may be omitted.

Beets, Pickled

Cut off beet tops, leaving 1 inch of stem. Also leave root. Wash beets, cover with boiling water, and cook until tender. Remove skins and slice beets. For pickling sirup, use 2 cups vinegar (or 1½ cups vinegar and ½ cup water) to 2 cups sugar. Heat to boiling.

Pack beets in glass jars to ½ inch of top. Add ½ teaspoon salt to pints, 1 teaspoon to quarts. Cover with boiling sirup, leaving ½-inch space at top of jar. Adjust jar lids. Process in boiling-water bath (212° F.)—

Pint jars_____	30 minutes
Quart jars_____	30 minutes

As soon as you remove jars from canner, complete seals if necessary.

Berries, Except Strawberries

● **Raw Pack.**—Wash berries; drain.

In glass jars.—Fill jars to ½ inch of top. For a full pack, shake berries down while filling jars. Cover with boiling sirup, leaving ½-inch space at top. Adjust lids. Process in boiling-water bath (212° F.)—

Pint jars_____	10 minutes
Quart jars_____	15 minutes

As soon as you remove jars from canner, complete seals if necessary.

In tin cans.—Fill cans to ¼ inch of top. For a full pack, shake berries down while filling cans. Fill to top with boiling sirup. Exhaust to 170° F. (10 minutes) ; seal cans. Process in boiling-water bath (212° F.)—

No. 2 cans_____	15 minutes
No. 2½ cans_____	20 minutes

● **Hot Pack.**—(For firm berries)— Wash berries and drain well. Add ½ cup sugar to each quart fruit. Cover pan and bring to boil; shake pan to keep berries from sticking.

In glass jars.—Pack hot berries to ½ inch of top. Adjust jar lids. Process in boiling-water bath (212° F.)—

Pint jars_____	10 minutes
Quart jars_____	15 minutes

As soon as you remove jars from canner, complete seals if necessary.

In tin cans.—Pack hot berries to top. Exhaust to 170° F. (about 10 minutes) and seal cans. Process in boiling-water bath (212° F.)—

No. 2 cans_____	15 minutes
No. 2½ cans_____	20 minutes

Cherries

● **Raw Pack.**—Wash cherries; remove pits, if desired.

In glass jars.—Fill jars to ½ inch of top. For a full pack, shake cherries down while filling jars. Cover with boiling sirup, leaving ½-inch space at top. Adjust lids. Process in boiling-water bath (212° F.)—

Pint jars_____	20 minutes
Quart jars_____	25 minutes

As soon as you remove jars from canner, complete seals if necessary.

In tin cans.—Fill cans to ¼ inch of top. For a full pack, shake cherries down while filling cans. Fill to top with boiling sirup. Exhaust to 170° F. (about 10 minutes) and seal cans. Process in boiling-water bath (212° F.) —

No. 2 cans_____ 20 minutes
No. 2½ cans_____ 25 minutes

● **Hot Pack.**—Wash cherries; remove pits, if desired. Add ½ cup sugar to each quart of fruit. Add a little water to unpitted cherries to keep them from sticking while heating. Cover pan and bring to a boil.
In glass jars.—Pack hot to ½ inch of top. Adjust jar lids. Process in boiling-water bath (212° F.) —

Pint jars_____ 10 minutes
Quart jars_____ 15 minutes

As soon as you remove jars from canner, complete seals if necessary.
In tin cans.—Pack hot to top of cans. Exhaust to 170° F. (about 10 minutes) and seal cans. Process in boiling-water bath (212° F.) —

No. 2 cans_____ 15 minutes
No. 2½ cans_____ 20 minutes

Fruit Juices

Wash; remove pits, if desired, and crush fruit. Heat to simmering (185°–210° F.). Strain through cloth bag. Add sugar, if desired—about 1 cup to 1 gallon juice. Reheat to simmering.
In glass jars.—Fill jars to ½ inch of top with hot juice. Adjust lids. Process in boiling-water bath (212° F.) —

Pint jars_____ 5 minutes
Quart jars_____ 5 minutes

As soon as you remove jars from canner, complete seals if necessary.
In tin cans.—Fill cans to top with hot juice. Seal at once. Process in boiling-water bath (212° F.) —

No. 2 cans_____ 5 minutes
No. 2½ cans_____ 5 minutes

Fruit Purees

Use sound, ripe fruit. Wash; remove pits, if desired. Cut large fruit in pieces. Simmer until soft; add a little water if needed to keep fruit from sticking. Put through a strainer or food mill. Add sugar to taste. Heat again to simmering (185°–210° F.).
In glass jars.—Pack hot to ½ inch of top. Adjust lids. Process in boiling-water bath (212° F.) —

Pint jars_____ 10 minutes
Quart jars_____ 10 minutes

As soon as you remove jars from canner, complete seals if necessary.
In tin cans.—Pack hot to top. Exhaust to 170° F. (about 10 minutes), and seal cans. Process in boiling-water bath (212° F.) —

No. 2 cans_____ 10 minutes
No. 2½ cans_____ 10 minutes

Peaches

Wash peaches and remove skins. Dipping the fruit in boiling water, then quickly in cold water makes peeling easier. Cut peaches in halves; remove pits. Slice if desired. To prevent fruit from darkening during preparation, drop it into water containing 2 tablespoons each of salt and vinegar per gallon. Drain just before heating or packing raw.

BN21470

Peaches can be peeled easily if they are dipped in boiling water, then in cold water.

● **Raw Pack.**—Prepare peaches as directed above.

(*Continued on next page*)

In glass jars.—Pack raw fruit to
½ inch of top. Cover with boiling
sirup, leaving ½-inch space at top of
jar. Adjust jar lids. Process in boiling-water bath (212° F.)—

Pint jars_____ 25 minutes
Quart jars_____ 30 minutes

As soon as you remove jars from canner, complete seals if necessary.

In tin cans.—Pack raw fruit to ¼
inch of top. Fill to top with boiling
sirup. Exhaust to 170° F. (about 10
minutes) and seal cans. Process in
boiling-water bath (212° F.)—

No. 2 cans_____ 30 minutes
No. 2 ½ cans_____ 35 minutes

● **Hot Pack.**—Prepare peaches as directed above. Heat peaches through in
hot sirup. If fruit is very juicy you
may heat it with sugar, adding no
liquid.

In glass jars.—Pack hot fruit to ½
inch of top. Cover with boiling liquid,
leaving ½-inch space at top of jar.
Adjust jar lids. Process in boiling-
water bath (212° F.)—

Pint jars_____ 20 minutes
Quart jars_____ 25 minutes

As soon as you remove jars from
canner, complete seals if necessary.

In tin cans.—Pack hot fruit to ¼
inch of top. Fill to top with boiling
liquid. Exhaust to 170° F. (about 10
minutes) and seal cans. Process in
boiling-water bath (212° F.)—

No. 2 cans_____ 25 minutes
No. 2½ cans_____ 30 minutes

Pears

Wash pears. Peel, cut in halves, and
core. Continue as with peaches, either
raw pack or hot pack.

Plums

Wash plums. To can whole, prick
skins. Freestone varieties may be
halved and pitted.

● **Raw Pack.**—Prepare plums as directed above.

In glass jars.—Pack raw fruit to
½ inch of top. Cover with boiling
sirup, leaving ½-inch space at top of
jar. Adjust jar lids. Process in boiling-water bath (212° F.)—

Pint jars_____ 20 minutes
Quart jars_____ 25 minutes

As soon as you remove jars from canner, complete seals if necessary.

In tin cans.—Pack raw fruit to ¼
inch of top. Fill to top with boiling
sirup. Exhaust to 170° F. (about 10
minutes) and seal cans. Process in
boiling-water bath (212° F.)—

No. 2 cans_____ 15 minutes
No. 2½ cans_____ 20 minutes

● **Hot Pack.**—Prepare plums as directed above. Heat to boiling in sirup
or juice. If fruit is very juicy you may
heat it with sugar, adding no liquid.

In glass jars.—Pack hot fruit to ½
inch of top. Cover with boiling liquid,
leaving ½-inch space at top of jar. Adjust jar lids. Process in boiling-water
bath (212° F.)—

Pint jars_____ 20 minutes
Quart jars_____ 25 minutes

As soon as you remove jars from canner, complete seals if necessary.

In tin cans.—Pack hot fruit to ¼
inch of top. Fill to top with boiling
liquid. Exhaust to 170° F. (about 10
minutes) and seal cans. Process in
boiling-water bath (212° F.)—

No. 2 cans_____ 15 minutes
No. 2½ cans_____ 20 minutes

Rhubarb

Wash rhubarb and cut into ½-inch
pieces. Add ½ cup sugar to each quart
rhubarb and let stand to draw out juice.
Bring to boiling.

In glass jars.—Pack hot to ½ inch
of top. Adjust lids. Process in boiling-water bath (212° F.)—

Pint jars_____ 10 minutes
Quart jars_____ 10 minutes

As soon as you remove jars from
canner, complete seals if necessary.

In tin cans.—Pack hot to top of
cans. Exhaust to 170° F. (about 10

minutes) and seal cans. Process in boiling-water bath (212° F.) —

No. 2 cans_____ 10 minutes
No. 2½ cans_____ 10 minutes

Tomatoes

Use only firm, ripe tomatoes. To loosen skins, dip into boiling water for about ½ minute; then dip quickly into cold water. Cut out stem ends and peel tomatoes.

76787B

To peel tomatoes, dip them in boiling water, then quickly in cold water to loosen skins.

76792B

To raw pack tomatoes, put peeled tomatoes in jars and press down to fill spaces.

● **Raw Pack.**—Leave tomatoes whole or cut in halves or quarters.

In glass jars.—Pack tomatoes to ½ inch of top, pressing gently to fill spaces. Add no water. Add ½ teaspoon salt to pints; 1 teaspoon to quarts. Adjust lids. Process in boiling-water bath (212° F.) —

Pint jars_____ 35 minutes
Quart jars_____ 45 minutes

As soon as you remove jars from canner, complete seals if necessary.

In tin cans.—Pack tomatoes to top of cans, pressing gently to fill spaces. Add no water. Add ½ teaspoon salt to No. 2 cans; 1 teaspoon to No. 2½ cans. Exhaust to 170° F., (about 15 minutes) and seal cans. Process in boiling-water bath (212° F.) —

No. 2 cans_____ 45 minutes
No. 2½ cans_____ 55 minutes

● **Hot Pack.**—Quarter peeled tomatoes. Bring to boil; stir to keep tomatoes from sticking.

In glass jars.—Pack boiling-hot tomatoes to ½ inch of top. Add ½ teaspoon salt to pints; 1 teaspoon to quarts. Adjust jar lids. Process in boiling-water bath (212° F.) —

Pint jars_____ 10 minutes
Quart jars_____ 10 minutes

As soon as you remove jars from canner, complete seals if necessary.

In tin cans.—Pack boiling-hot tomatoes to ¼ inch of top. Add no water. Add ½ teaspoon salt to No. 2 cans; 1 teaspoon to No. 2½ cans. Exhaust to 170° F. (about 10 minutes) and seal cans. Process in boiling-water bath (212° F.) —

No. 2 cans_____ 10 minutes
No. 2½ cans_____ 10 minutes

Tomato Juice

Use ripe, juicy tomatoes. Wash, remove stem ends, cut into pieces. Simmer until softened, stirring often. Put through strainer. Add 1 teaspoon salt to each quart juice. Reheat at once just to boiling.

In glass jars.—Fill jars with boiling-hot juice to ½ inch of top. Adjust

(*Continued on next page*)

jar lids. Process in boiling-water bath
(212° F.) —

    Pint jars_____ 10 minutes
    Quart jars_____ 10 minutes

As soon as you remove jars from
canner, complete seals if necessary.

In tin cans.—Fill cans to top with
boiling-hot juice. Seal cans at once.
Process in boiling-water bath (212°
F.) —

    No. 2 cans_____ 15 minutes
    No. 2½ cans_____ 15 minutes

How To Can Vegetables

Can vegetables according to general directions on pages 5 to 8, the detailed
directions for each vegetable on pages 18 to 28, and special directions below that
apply only to vegetables.

Points on Packing

Raw pack.—Pack cold raw vegetables (except corn, lima beans, and peas)
tightly into container and cover with boiling water.

Hot pack.—Preheat vegetables in water or steam. Cover with cooking liquid
or boiling water. Cooking liquid is recommended for packing most vegetables
because it may contain minerals and vitamins dissolved out of the food. Boiling
water is recommended when cooking liquid is dark, gritty, or strong-flavored, and
when there isn't enough cooking liquid.

Processing in a Pressure Canner

Use a steam-pressure canner for processing all vegetables except tomatoes and
pickled vegetables. A pressure saucepan may be used for pint jars and No. 2
cans (see p. 3).

Directions.—Follow the manufacturer's directions for the canner you are
using. Here are a few pointers on the use of any steam-pressure canner:

● Put 2 or 3 inches of boiling water in the bottom of the canner; the amount
of water to use depends on the size and shape of the canner.

● Set filled glass jars or tin cans on rack in canner so that steam can flow
around each container. If two layers of cans or jars are put in, stagger the
second layer. Use a rack between layers of glass jars.

● Fasten canner cover securely so that no steam can escape except through
vent (petcock or weighted-gage opening).

● Watch until steam pours steadily from vent. Let it escape for 10 minutes
or more to drive all air from the canner. Then close petcock or put on weighted
gage.

● Let pressure rise to 10 pounds (240° F.). The moment this pressure is
reached start counting processing time. Keep pressure constant by regulating
heat under the canner. Do not lower pressure by opening petcock. Keep drafts
from blowing on canner.

● When processing time is up, remove canner from heat immediately.

With glass jars, let canner stand until pressure is zero. Never try to rush
the cooling by pouring cold water over the canner. When pressure registers zero,
wait a minute or two, then slowly open petcock or take off weighted gage.
Unfasten cover and tilt the far side up so steam escapes away from you. Take
jars from canner.

To process vegetables, bring pressure in canner up to 10 pounds, then start to count processing time.

With tin cans, release steam in canner as soon as canner is removed from heat by opening petcock or taking off weighted gage. Then take off canner cover and remove cans.

Processing times.—Follow processing times carefully. The times given apply only when a specific food is prepared according to detailed directions.

If you live at an altitude of less than 2,000 feet above sea level, process vegetables at 10 pounds pressure for the times given.

At altitudes above sea level, it takes more than 10 pounds pressure to reach 240° F. If you live at an altitude of 2,000 feet, process vegetables at 11 pounds pressure. At 4,000 feet, use 12 pounds pressure; at 6,000 feet, 13 pounds pressure; at 8,000 feet, 14 pounds pressure; at 10,000 feet, 15 pounds pressure.

A weighted gage may need to be corrected for altitude by the manufacturer.

To Figure Yield of Canned Vegetables From Fresh

The number of quarts of canned food you can get from a given amount of fresh vegetables depends on quality, condition, maturity, and variety of the vegetable, size of pieces, and on the way the vegetable is packed—raw or hot pack.

Generally, the following amounts of fresh vegetables (as purchased or picked) make 1 quart of canned food:

	Pounds		*Pounds*
Asparagus	2½ to 4½	Okra	1½
Beans, lima, in pods	3 to 5	Peas, green, in pods	3 to 6
Beans, snap	1½ to 2½	Pumpkin or winter squash	1½ to 3
Beets, without tops	2 to 3½	Spinach and other greens	2 to 6
Carrots, without tops	2 to 3	Squash, summer	2 to 4
Corn, sweet, in husks	3 to 6	Sweetpotatoes	2 to 3

Directions for Vegetables

Asparagus

● **Raw Pack.**—Wash asparagus; trim off scales and tough ends and wash again. Cut into 1-inch pieces.

In glass jars.—Pack asparagus as tightly as possible without crushing to ½ inch of top. Add ½ teaspoon salt to pints; 1 teaspoon to quarts. Cover with boiling water, leaving ½-inch space at top of jar. Adjust jar lids. Process in pressure canner at 10 pounds pressure (240° F.)—

Pint jars	25 minutes
Quart jars	30 minutes

As soon as you remove jars from canner, complete seals if necessary.

In tin cans.—Pack asparagus as tightly as possible without crushing to ¼ inch of top. Add ½ teaspoon salt to No. 2 cans; 1 teaspoon to No. 2½ cans. Fill to top with boiling water. Exhaust to 170° F. (about 10 minutes) and seal cans. Process in pressure canner at 10 pounds pressure (240° F.)—

No. 2 cans	20 minutes
No. 2½ cans	20 minutes

● **Hot Pack.**—Wash asparagus; trim off scales and tough ends and wash again. Cut in 1-inch pieces; cover with boiling water. Boil 2 or 3 minutes.

In glass jars.—Pack hot asparagus loosely to ½ inch of top. Add ½ teaspoon salt to pints; 1 teaspoon to quarts. Cover with boiling-hot cooking liquid, or if liquid contains grit use boiling water. Leave ½-inch space at top of jar. Adjust jar lids. Process in pressure canner at 10 pounds pressure (240° F.)—

Pint jars	25 minutes
Quart jars	30 minutes

As soon as you remove jars from canner, complete seals if necessary.

In tin cans.—Pack hot asparagus loosely to ¼ inch of top. Add ½ teaspoon salt to No. 2 cans; 1 teaspoon to No. 2½ cans. Fill to top with boiling-hot cooking liquid, or if liquid contains grit use boiling water. Exhaust to 170° F. (about 10 minutes) and seal cans. Process in pressure canner at 10 pounds pressure (240° F.)—

No. 2 cans	20 minutes
No. 2½ cans	20 minutes

Beans, Dry, With Tomato or Molasses Sauce

Sort and wash dry beans (kidney, navy, or yellow eye). Cover with boiling water; boil 2 minutes, remove from heat and let soak 1 hour. Heat to boiling, drain, and save liquid for making sauce.

In glass jars.—Fill jars three-fourths full with hot beans. Add a small piece of salt pork, ham, or bacon. Fill to 1 inch of top with hot sauce (see recipes below). Adjust jar lids. Process in pressure canner at 10 pounds pressure (240° F.)—

Pint jars	65 minutes
Quart jars	75 minutes

As soon as you remove jars from canner, complete seals if necessary.

In tin cans.—Fill cans three-fourths full with hot beans. Add a small piece of salt pork, ham, or bacon. Fill to ¼ inch of top with hot sauce (see recipes below). Exhaust to 170° F. (about 20 minutes) and seal cans. Process in pressure canner at 10 pounds pressure (240° F.)—

No. 2 cans	65 minutes
No. 2½ cans	75 minutes

Tomato sauce.—Mix 1 quart tomato juice, 3 tablespoons sugar, 2 teaspoons salt, 1 tablespoon chopped onion, and ¼ teaspoon mixture of ground cloves, allspice, mace, and cayenne. Heat to boiling.

Or mix 1 cup tomato catsup with 3 cups of water or soaking liquid from beans and heat to boiling.

Molasses sauce.—Mix 1 quart water or soaking liquid from beans, 3 tablespoons dark molasses, 1 tablespoon vinegar, 2 teaspoons salt, and ¾ teaspoon powdered dry mustard. Heat to boiling.

Beans, Dry, Baked

Soak and boil beans according to directions for beans with sauce.

Place small pieces of salt pork, ham, or bacon in earthenware crock or a pan.

Add beans. Add enough molasses sauce to cover beans. Cover crock and bake 4 to 5 hours at 350° F. (moderate oven). Add water as needed—about every hour.

In glass jars.—Pack hot beans to 1 inch of top. Adjust jar lids. Process in pressure canner at 10 pounds pressure (240° F.)—

Pint jars_____ 80 minutes
Quart jars_____ 100 minutes

As soon as you remove jars from canner, complete seals if necessary.

In tin cans.—Pack hot beans to ¼ inch of top. Exhaust to 170° F. (about 15 minutes) and seal cans. Process in pressure canner at 10 pounds pressure (240° F.)—

No. 2 cans_____ 95 minutes
No. 2½ cans_____ 115 minutes

Beans, Fresh Lima

Can only young, tender beans.

● **Raw Pack.**—Shell and wash beans.

In glass jars.—Pack raw beans into clean jars. For small-type beans, fill to 1 inch of top of jar for pints and 1½ inches for quarts; for large beans, fill to ¾ inch of top for pints and 1¼ inches for quarts. Beans should not be pressed or shaken down. Add ½ teaspoon salt to pints; 1 teaspoon to quarts. Fill jar to ½ inch of top with boiling water. Adjust jar lids. Process in pressure canner at 10 pounds pressure (240° F.)—

Pint jars_____ 40 minutes
Quart jars_____ 50 minutes

As soon as you remove jars from canner, complete seals if necessary.

In tin cans.—Pack raw beans to ¾ inch of top; do not shake or press beans down. Add ½ teaspoon salt to No. 2 cans; 1 teaspoon to No. 2½ cans. Fill cans to top with boiling water. Exhaust to 170° F. (about 10 minutes) and seal cans. Process in pressure canner at 10 pounds pressure (240° F.)—

No. 2 cans_____ 40 minutes
No. 2½ cans_____ 40 minutes

● **Hot Pack.**—Shell the beans, cover with boiling water, and bring to boil.

In glass jars.—Pack hot beans loosely to 1 inch of top. Add ½ teaspoon salt to pints; 1 teaspoon to quarts. Cover with boiling water, leaving 1-inch space at top of jar. Adjust jar lids. Process in pressure canner at 10 pounds pressure (240° F.)—

Pint jars_____ 40 minutes
Quart jars_____ 50 minutes

As soon as you remove jars from canner, complete seals if necessary.

In tin cans.—Pack hot beans loosely to ½ inch of top. Add ½ teaspoon salt to No. 2 cans; 1 teaspoon to No. 2½ cans. Fill to top with boiling water. Exhaust to 170° F. (about 10 minutes) and seal cans. Process in pressure canner at 10 pounds pressure (240° F.)—

No. 2 cans_____ 40 minutes
No. 2½ cans_____ 40 minutes

Beans, Snap

● **Raw Pack.**—Wash beans. Trim ends; cut into 1-inch pieces.

In glass jars.—Pack raw beans tightly to ½ inch of top. Add ½ teaspoon salt to pints; 1 teaspoon to quarts. Cover with boiling water, leaving ½-inch space at top of jar. Adjust jar lids. Process in pressure canner at 10 pounds pressure (240° F.)—

Pint jars_____ 20 minutes
Quart jars_____ 25 minutes

As soon as you remove jars from canner, complete seals if necessary.

In tin cans.—Pack raw beans tightly to ¼ inch of top. Add ½ tea-

(*Continued on next page*)

spoon salt to No. 2 cans; 1 teaspoon to No. 2½ cans. Fill to top with boiling water. Exhaust to 170° F. (about 10 minutes) and seal cans. Process in pressure canner at 10 pounds pressure (240° F.)—

    No. 2 cans_____ 25 minutes
    No. 2½ cans_____ 30 minutes

● **Hot Pack.**—Wash beans. Trim ends; cut into 1-inch pieces. Cover with boiling water; boil 5 minutes.

In glass jars.—Pack hot beans loosely to ½ inch of top. Add ½ teaspoon salt to pints; 1 teaspoon to quarts. Cover with boiling-hot cook-

BN21475

To hot pack snap beans, cover cut beans with boiling water and boil 5 minutes.

BN21471

Then pack hot beans loosely in jar and cover with hot cooking liquid before processing in a pressure canner.

ing liquid, leaving ½-inch space at top of jar. Adjust jar lids. Process in pressure canner at 10 pounds pressure (240° F.)—

    Pint jars_____ 20 minutes
    Quart jars_____ 25 minutes

As soon as you remove jars from canner, complete seals if necessary.

In tin cans.—Pack hot beans loosely to ¼ inch of top. Add ½ teaspoon salt to No. 2 cans; 1 teaspoon to No. 2½ cans. Fill to top with boiling-hot cooking liquid. Exhaust to 170° F. (about 10 minutes) and seal cans. Process in pressure canner at 10 pounds pressure (240° F.)—

    No. 2 cans_____ 25 minutes
    No. 2½ cans_____ 30 minutes

Beets

Sort beets for size. Cut off tops, leaving an inch of stem. Also leave root. Wash beets. Cover with boiling water and boil until skins slip easily— 15 to 25 minutes, depending on size. Skin and trim. Leave baby beets whole. Cut medium or large beets in ½-inch cubes or slices; halve or quarter very large slices.

In glass jars.—Pack hot beets to ½ inch of top. Add ½ teaspoon salt to pints; 1 teaspoon to quarts. Cover with boiling water, leaving ½-inch space at top of jar. Adjust jar lids. Process in pressure canner at 10 pounds pressure (240° F.)—

    Pint jars_____ 30 minutes
    Quart jars_____ 35 minutes

As soon as you remove jars from canner, complete seals if necessary.

In tin cans.—Pack hot beets to ¼ inch of top. Add ½ teaspoon salt to No. 2 cans; 1 teaspoon to No. 2½ cans. Fill to top with boiling water. Exhaust to 170° F. (about 10 minutes) and seal cans. Process in pressure canner at 10 pounds pressure (240° F.)—

    No. 2 cans_____ 30 minutes
    No. 2½ cans_____ 30 minutes

Beets, Pickled

See page 12.

Carrots

● **Raw Pack.**—Wash and scrape carrots. Slice or dice.

In glass jars.—Pack raw carrots tightly into clean jars, to 1 inch of top of jar. Add ½ teaspoon salt to pints; 1 teaspoon to quarts. Fill jar to ½ inch of top with boiling water. Adjust jar lids. Process in pressure canner at 10 pounds pressure (240° F.)—

Pint jars_____ 25 minutes
Quart jars_____ 30 minutes

As soon as you remove jars from canner, complete seals if necessary.

In tin cans.—Pack raw carrots tightly into cans to ½ inch of top. Add ½ teaspoon salt to No. 2 cans; 1 teaspoon to No. 2½ cans. Fill cans to top with boiling water. Exhaust to 170° F. (about 10 minutes) and seal cans. Process in pressure canner at 10 pounds pressure (240° F.)—

No. 2 cans_____ 25 minutes
No. 2½ cans_____ 30 minutes

● **Hot Pack.**—Wash and scrape carrots. Slice or dice. Cover with boiling water and bring to boil.

In glass jars.—Pack hot carrots to ½ inch of top. Add ½ teaspoon salt to pints; 1 teaspoon to quarts. Cover with boiling-hot cooking liquid, leaving ½-inch space at top of jar. Adjust jar lids. Process in pressure canner at 10 pounds pressure (240° F.)—

Pint jars_____ 25 minutes
Quart jars_____ 30 minutes

As soon as you remove jars from canner, complete seals if necessary.

In tin cans.—Pack hot carrots to ¼ inch of top. Add ½ teaspoon salt to No. 2 cans; 1 teaspoon to No. 2½ cans. Fill with boiling-hot cooking liquid. Exhaust to 170° F. (about 10 minutes) and seal cans. Process in pressure canner at 10 pounds pressure (240° F.)—

No. 2 cans_____ 20 minutes
No. 2½ cans_____ 25 minutes

Corn, Cream-Style

● **Raw Pack.**—Husk corn and remove silk. Wash. Cut corn from cob at about center of kernel and scrape cobs.

In glass jars.—Use pint jars only. Pack corn to 1½ inches of top; do not shake or press down. Add ½ teaspoon salt to each jar. Fill to ½ inch of top with boiling water. Adjust jar lids. Process in pressure canner at 10 pounds pressure (240° F.)—

Pint jars_____ 95 minutes

As soon as you remove jars from canner, complete seals if necessary.

In tin cans.—Use No. 2 cans only. Pack corn to ½ inch of top; do not shake or press down. Add ½ teaspoon salt to each can. Fill cans to top with boiling water. Exhaust to 170° F. (about 25 minutes) and seal cans. Process in pressure canner at 10 pounds pressure (240° F.)—

No. 2 cans_____ 105 minutes

● **Hot Pack.**—Husk corn and remove silk. Wash. Cut corn from cob at about center of kernel and scrape cob. To each quart of corn add 1 pint boiling water. Heat to boiling.

In glass jars.—Use pint jars only. Pack hot corn to 1 inch of top. Add ½ teaspoon salt to each jar. Adjust jar lids. Process in pressure canner at 10 pounds pressure (240° F.)—

Pint jars_____ 85 minutes

As soon as you remove jars from canner, complete seals if necessary.

In tin cans.—Use No. 2 cans only. Pack hot corn to top. Add ½ teaspoon salt to each can. Exhaust to 170° F. (about 10 minutes) and seal cans. Process in pressure canner at 10 pounds pressure (240° F.)—

No. 2 cans_____ 105 minutes

Corn, Whole-Kernel

● **Raw Pack.**—Husk corn and remove silk. Wash. Cut from cob at about two-thirds the depth of kernel.

In glass jars.—Pack corn to 1 inch of top; do not shake or press down.

(*Continued on next page*)

76621B

A nail driven at an angle through the cutting board (see arrow) holds the cob steady and makes it easy to cut corn from the cob.

Add ½ teaspoon salt to pints; 1 teaspoon to quarts. Fill to ½ inch of top with boiling water. Adjust jar lids. Process in pressure canner at 10 pounds pressure (240° F.) —

Pint jars_____ 55 minutes
Quart jars_____ 85 minutes

As soon as you remove jars from canner, complete seals if necessary.

In tin cans.—Pack corn to ½ inch of top; do not shake or press down. Add ½ teaspoon salt to No. 2 cans; 1 teaspoon to No. 2½ cans. Fill to top with boiling water. Exhaust to 170° F. (about 10 minutes) and seal cans. Process in pressure canner at 10 pounds pressure (240° F.) —

No. 2 cans_____ 60 minutes
No. 2½ cans_____ 60 minutes

● **Hot Pack.**—Husk corn and remove silk. Wash. Cut from cob at about two-thirds the depth of kernel. To each quart of corn add 1 pint boiling water. Heat to boiling.

In glass jars.—Pack hot corn to 1 inch of top and cover with boiling-hot cooking liquid, leaving 1-inch space at top of jar. Or fill to 1 inch of top with mixture of corn and liquid. Add ½ teaspoon salt to pints; 1 teaspoon to quarts. Adjust jar lids. Process in pressure canner at 10 pounds pressure (240° F.) —

Pint jars_____ 55 minutes
Quart jars_____ 85 minutes

As soon as you remove jars from canner, complete seals if necessary.

76624B

To hot pack corn, put heated corn loosely in C-enamel cans; fill cans with boiling liquid.

In tin cans.—Pack hot corn to ½ inch of top and fill to top with boiling-hot cooking liquid. Or fill to top with mixture of corn and liquid. Add ½ teaspoon salt to No. 2 cans; 1 teaspoon to No. 2½ cans. Exhaust to 170° F. (about 10 minutes) and seal cans. Process in pressure canner at 10 pounds pressure (240° F.)—

No. 2 cans_____ 60 minutes
No. 2½ cans_____ 60 minutes

Hominy

Place 2 quarts of dry field corn in an enameled pan; add 8 quarts of water and 2 ounces of lye. Boil vigorously ½ hour, then allow to stand for 20 minutes. Rinse off the lye with several hot water rinses. Follow with cold water rinses to cool for handling.

Work hominy with the hands until dark tips of kernels are removed (about 5 minutes). Separate the tips from the corn by floating them off in water or by placing the corn in a coarse sieve and washing thoroughly. Add sufficient water to cover hominy about 1 inch, and boil 5 minutes; change water. Repeat 4 times. Then cook until kernels are soft (½ to ¾ hour) and drain. This will make about 6 quarts of hominy.

In glass jars.—Pack hot hominy to ½ inch of top. Add ½ teaspoon salt to pints; 1 teaspoon to quarts. Cover with boiling water, leaving ½-inch space at top of jar. Adjust jar lids. Process in pressure canner at 10 pounds pressure (240° F.)—

Pint jars_____ 60 minutes
Quart jars_____ 70 minutes

As soon as you remove jars from canner, complete seals if necessary.

In tin cans.—Pack hot hominy to ¼ inch of top. Add ½ teaspoon salt to No. 2 cans; 1 teaspoon to No. 2½ cans. Fill to top with boiling water. Exhaust to 170° F. (about 10 minutes) and seal cans. Process in pressure canner at 10 pounds pressure (240° F.)—

No. 2 cans_____ 60 minutes
No. 2½ cans_____ 70 minutes

Mushrooms

Trim stems and discolored parts of mushrooms. Soak mushrooms in cold water for 10 minutes to remove adhering soil. Wash in clean water. Leave small mushrooms whole; cut larger ones in halves or quarters. Steam 4 minutes or heat gently for 15 minutes without added liquid in a covered saucepan.

In glass jars.—Pack hot mushrooms to ½ inch of top. Add ¼ teaspoon salt to half pints; ½ teaspoon to pints. For better color, add crystalline ascorbic acid—$\frac{1}{16}$ teaspoon to half-pints; ⅛ teaspoon to pints. Add boiling-hot cooking liquid or boiling water to cover mushrooms, leaving ½-inch space at top of jar. Adjust jar lids. Process in pressure canner at 10 pounds pressure (240° F.)—

Half-pint jars_____ 30 minutes
Pint jars_____ 30 minutes

As soon as you remove jars from canner, complete seals if necessary.

In tin cans.—Pack hot mushrooms to ¼ inch of top of cans. Add ½ teaspoon salt to No. 2 cans. For better color, add ⅛ teaspoon of crystalline ascorbic acid to No. 2 cans. Then fill to top with boiling-hot cooking liquid or boiling water. Exhaust to 170° F. (about 10 minutes) and seal cans. Process in pressure canner at 10 pounds pressure (240° F.)—

No. 2 cans_____ 30 minutes

Okra

Can only tender pods. Wash; trim. Cook for 1 minute in boiling water. Cut into 1-inch lengths or leave pods whole.

In glass jars.—Pack hot okra to ½ inch of top. Add ½ teaspoon salt to pints; 1 teaspoon to quarts. Cover with boiling water, leaving ½-inch space at top of jar. Adjust jar lids. Process in pressure canner at 10 pounds pressure (240° F.)—

Pint jars_____	25 minutes
Quart jars_____	40 minutes

As soon as you remove jars from canner, complete seals if necessary.

In tin cans.—Pack hot okra to ¼ inch of top. Add ½ teaspoon salt to No. 2 cans; 1 teaspoon to No. 2½ cans. Fill to top with boiling water. Exhaust to 170° F. (about 10 minutes) and seal cans. Process in pressure canner at 10 pounds pressure (240° F.)—

No. 2 cans_____	25 minutes
No. 2½ cans_____	35 minutes

Peas, Fresh Blackeye (Cowpeas, Blackeye Beans)

● **Raw Pack.**—Shell and wash blackeye peas.

In glass jars.—Pack raw blackeye peas to 1½ inches of top of pint jars and 2 inches of top of quart jars; do not shake or press peas down. Add ½ teaspoon salt to pints; 1 teaspoon to quarts. Cover with boiling water, leaving ½-inch space at top of jars. Adjust jar lids. Process in pressure canner at 10 pounds pressure (240° F.)—

Pint jars_____	35 minutes
Quart jars_____	40 minutes

As soon as you remove jars from canner, complete seals if necessary.

In tin cans.—Pack raw blackeye peas to ¾ inch of top; do not shake or press down. Add ½ teaspoon salt to No. 2 cans; 1 teaspoon to No. 2½ cans. Cover with boiling water, leaving ¼-inch space at top of cans. Exhaust to 170° F. (about 10 minutes)

and seal cans. Process in pressure canner at 10 pounds pressure (240° F.)—

No. 2 cans_____	35 minutes
No. 2½ cans_____	40 minutes

● **Hot Pack.**—Shell and wash blackeye peas, cover with boiling water, and bring to a rolling boil. Drain.

In glass jars.—Pack hot blackeye peas to 1¼ inches of top of pint jars and 1½ inches of top of quart jars; do not shake or press peas down. Add ½ teaspoon salt to pints; 1 teaspoon to quarts. Cover with boiling water, leaving ½-inch space at top of jar. Adjust jar lids. Process in pressure canner at 10 pounds pressure (240° F.)—

Pint jars_____	35 minutes
Quart jars_____	40 minutes

As soon as you remove jars from canner, complete seals if necessary.

In tin cans.—Pack hot blackeye peas to ½ inch of top; do not shake or press peas down. Add ½ teaspoon salt to No. 2 cans; 1 teaspoon to No. 2½ cans. Cover with boiling water, leaving ¼-inch space at top of cans. Exhaust to 170° F. (about 10 minutes) and seal cans. Process in pressure canner at 10 pounds pressure (240° F.)—

No. 2 cans_____	30 minutes
No. 2½ cans_____	35 minutes

Peas, Fresh Green

● **Raw Pack.**—Shell and wash peas.

In glass jars.—Pack peas to 1 inch of top; do not shake or press down. Add ½ teaspoon salt to pints; 1 teaspoon to quarts. Cover with boiling water, leaving 1½ inches of space at top of jar. Adjust jar lids. Process in pressure canner at 10 pounds pressure (240° F.)—

Pint jars_____	40 minutes
Quart jars_____	40 minutes

As soon as you remove jars from canner, complete seals if necessary.

In tin cans.—Pack peas to ¼ inch of top; do not shake or press down. Add ½ teaspoon salt to No. 2 cans; 1 teaspoon to No. 2½ cans. Fill to top with boiling water. Exhaust to 170° F. (about 10 minutes) and seal cans. Process at 10 pounds pressure (240° F.)—

    No. 2 cans_____ 30 minutes
    No. 2½ cans_____ 35 minutes

● **Hot Pack.**—Shell and wash peas. Cover with boiling water. Bring to boil.

In glass jars.—Pack hot peas loosely to 1 inch of top. Add ½ teaspoon salt to pints; 1 teaspoon to quarts. Cover with boiling water, leaving 1-inch space at top of jar. Adjust jar lids. Process in pressure canner at 10 pounds pressure (240° F.)—

    Pint jars_____ 40 minutes
    Quart jars_____ 40 minutes

As soon as you remove jars from canner, complete seals if necessary.

In tin cans.—Pack hot peas loosely to ¼ inch of top. Add ½ teaspoon salt to No. 2 cans; 1 teaspoon to No. 2½ cans. Fill to top with boiling water. Exhaust to 170° F. (about 10 minutes) and seal cans. Process at 10 pounds pressure (240° F.)—

    No. 2 cans_____ 30 minutes
    No. 2½ cans_____ 35 minutes

Potatoes, Cubed

Wash, pare, and cut potatoes into ½-inch cubes. Dip cubes in brine (1 teaspoon salt to 1 quart water) to prevent darkening. Drain. Cook for 2 minutes in boiling water, drain.

In glass jars.—Pack hot potatoes to ½ inch of top. Add ½ teaspoon salt to pints; 1 teaspoon to quarts. Cover with boiling water, leaving ½-inch space at top of jar. Adjust jar lids. Process in pressure canner at 10 pounds pressure (240° F.)—

    Pint jars_____ 35 minutes
    Quart jars_____ 40 minutes

As soon as you remove jars from canner, complete seals if necessary.

In tin cans.—Pack hot potatoes to ¼ inch of top. Add ½ teaspoon salt to No. 2 cans; 1 teaspoon to No. 2½ cans. Fill to top with boiling water. Exhaust to 170° F. (about 10 minutes) and seal cans. Process in pressure canner at 10 pounds pressure (240° F.)—

    No. 2 cans_____ 35 minutes
    No. 2½ cans_____ 40 minutes

Potatoes, Whole

Use potatoes 1 to 2½ inches in diameter. Wash, pare, and cook in boiling water for 10 minutes. Drain.

In glass jars.—Pack hot potatoes to ½ inch of top. Add ½ teaspoon salt to pints; 1 teaspoon to quarts. Cover with boiling water, leaving ½-inch space at top of jar. Adjust jar lids. Process in pressure canner at 10 pounds pressure (240° F.)—

    Pint jars_____ 30 minutes
    Quart jars_____ 40 minutes

As soon as you remove jars from canner, complete seals if necessary.

In tin cans.—Pack hot potatoes to ¼ inch of top. Add ½ teaspoon salt to No. 2 cans; 1 teaspoon to No. 2½ cans. Fill to top with boiling water. Exhaust to 170° F. (about 10 minutes) and seal cans. Process in pressure canner at 10 pounds pressure (240° F.)—

    No. 2 cans_____ 35 minutes
    No. 2½ cans_____ 40 minutes

Pumpkin, Cubed

Wash pumpkin, remove seeds, and pare. Cut into 1-inch cubes. Add just enough water to cover; bring to boil.

In glass jars.—Pack hot cubes to ½ inch of top. Add ½ teaspoon salt to pints; 1 teaspoon to quarts. Cover with hot cooking liquid, leaving ½-inch space at top of jar. Adjust jar lids. Process in pressure canner at 10 pounds pressure (240° F.)—

    Pint jars_____ 55 minutes
    Quart jars_____ 90 minutes

(*Continued on next page*)

As soon as you remove jars from canner, complete seals if necessary.

In tin cans.—Pack hot cubes to ¼ inch of top. Add ½ teaspoon salt to No. 2 cans; 1 teaspoon to No. 2½ cans. Fill to top with hot cooking liquid. Exhaust to 170° F. (about 10 minutes) and seal cans. Process in pressure canner at 10 pounds pressure (240° F.)—

No. 2 cans_____ 50 minutes
No. 2½ cans_____ 75 minutes

Pumpkin, Strained

Wash pumpkin, remove seeds, and pare. Cut into 1-inch cubes. Steam until tender, about 25 minutes. Put through food mill or strainer. Simmer until heated through; stir to keep pumpkin from sticking to pan.

In glass jars.—Pack hot to ½ inch of top. Add no liquid or salt. Adjust jar lids. Process at 10 pounds pressure (240° F.)—

Pint jars_____ 65 minutes
Quart jars_____ 80 minutes

As soon as you remove jars from canner, complete seals if necessary.

In tin cans.—Pack hot to ⅛ inch of top. Add no liquid or salt. Exhaust to 170° F. (about 10 minutes) and seal cans. Process in pressure canner at 10 pounds pressure (240° F.)—

No. 2 cans_____ 75 minutes
No. 2½ cans_____ 90 minutes

Spinach (and Other Greens)

Can only freshly picked, tender spinach. Pick over and wash thoroughly. Cut out tough stems and midribs. Place about 2½ pounds of spinach in a cheesecloth bag and steam about 10 minutes or until well wilted.

In glass jars.—Pack hot spinach loosely to ½ inch of top. Add ¼ teaspoon salt to pints; ½ teaspoon to quarts. Cover with boiling water, leaving ½-inch space at top of jar. Adjust jar lids. Process in pressure canner at 10 pounds pressure (240° F.)—

Pint jars_____ 70 minutes
Quart jars_____ 90 minutes

As soon as you remove jars from canner, complete seals if necessary.

In tin cans.—Pack hot spinach loosely to ¼ inch of top. Add ¼ teaspoon salt to No. 2 cans; ½ teaspoon to No. 2½ cans. Fill to top with boiling water. Exhaust to 170° F. (about 10 minutes) and seal cans. Process in pressure canner at 10 pounds pressure (240° F.)—

No. 2 cans_____ 65 minutes
No. 2½ cans_____ 75 minutes

78351B

To raw pack squash, pack uniform pieces of squash tightly into jars.

78352B

Cover squash with boiling water just before closing jars and putting in pressure canner.

Squash, Summer

● **Raw Pack.**—Wash but do not pare squash. Trim ends. Cut squash into ½-inch slices; halve or quarter to make pieces of uniform size.

In glass jars.—Pack raw squash tightly into clean jars to 1 inch of top of jar. Add ½ teaspoon salt to pints; 1 teaspoon to quarts. Fill jar to ½

BN21467

When processing time is up, let pressure in canner drop to zero. Slowly open petcock or take off weighted gage. Unfasten cover, tilting far side up so steam escapes away from you.

inch of top with boiling water. Adjust jar lids. Process in pressure canner at 10 pounds pressure (240° F.) —

    Pint jars_____ 25 minutes
    Quart jars_____ 30 minutes

As soon as you remove jars from canner, complete seals if necessary.

In tin cans.—Pack raw squash tightly into cans to ½ inch of top. Add ½ teaspoon salt to No. 2 cans; 1 teaspoon to No. 2½ cans. Fill cans to top with boiling water. Exhaust to 170° F. (about 10 minutes) and seal cans. Process in pressure canner at 10 pounds pressure (240° F.) —

    No. 2 cans_____ 20 minutes
    No. 2½ cans_____ 20 minutes

● **Hot Pack.**—Wash squash and trim ends; do not pare. Cut squash into ½-inch slices; halve or quarter to make pieces of uniform size. Add just enough water to cover. Bring to boil.

In glass jars.—Pack hot squash loosely to ½ inch of top. Add ½ teaspoon salt to pints; 1 teaspoon to quarts. Cover with boiling-hot cooking liquid, leaving ½-inch space at top of jar. Adjust jar lids. Process in pressure canner at 10 pounds pressure (240° F.) —

    Pint jars_____ 30 minutes
    Quart jars_____ 40 minutes

As soon as you remove jars from canner, complete seals if necessary.

(*Continued on next page*)

In tin cans.—Pack hot squash loosely to ¼ inch of top. Add ½ teaspoon salt to No. 2 cans; 1 teaspoon to No. 2½ cans. Fill to top with boiling-hot cooking liquid. Exhaust to 170° F. (about 10 minutes) and seal cans. Process in pressure canner at 10 pounds pressure (240° F.) —

No. 2 cans_____ 20 minutes
No. 2½ cans_____ 20 minutes

Squash, Winter

Follow method for pumpkin.

Sweetpotatoes, Dry Pack

Wash sweetpotatoes. Sort for size. Boil or steam until partially soft (20 to 30 minutes). Skin. Cut in pieces if large.

In glass jars.—Pack hot sweetpotatoes tightly to 1 inch of top, pressing gently to fill spaces. Add no salt or liquid. Adjust jar lids. Process in pressure canner at 10 pounds pressure (240° F.) —

Pint jars_____ 65 minutes
Quart jars_____ 95 minutes

As soon as you remove jars from canner, complete seals if necessary.

In tin cans.—Pack hot sweetpotatatoes tightly to top of can, pressing

gently to fill spaces. Add no salt or liquid. Exhaust to 170° F. (about 10 minutes) and seal cans. Process in pressure canner at 10 pounds pressure (240° F.) —

No. 2 cans_____ 80 minutes
No. 2½ cans_____ 95 minutes

Sweetpotatoes, Wet Pack

Wash sweetpotatoes. Sort for size. Boil or steam just until skins slip easily. Skin and cut in pieces.

In glass jars.—Pack hot sweetpotatoes to 1 inch of top. Add ½ teaspoon salt to pints; 1 teaspoon to quarts. Cover with boiling water or medium sirup, leaving 1-inch space at top of jar. Adjust jar lids. Process in pressure canner at 10 pounds pressure (240° F.) —

Pint jars_____ 55 minutes
Quart jars_____ 90 minutes

As soon as you remove jars from canner, complete seals if necessary.

In tin cans.—Pack hot sweetpotatoes to ¼ inch of top. Add ½ teaspoon salt to No. 2 cans; 1 teaspoon to No. 2½ cans. Fill to top with boiling water or medium sirup. Exhaust to 170° F. (about 10 minutes) and seal cans. Process in pressure canner at 10 pounds pressure (240° F.) —

No. 2 cans_____ 70 minutes
No. 2½ cans_____ 90 minutes

Questions and Answers

Q. *Is it safe to process foods in the oven?*

A. No, oven canning is dangerous. Jars may explode. The temperature of the food in jars during oven processing does not get high enough to insure destruction of spoilage bacteria in vegetables.

Q. *Why is open-kettle canning not recommended for fruits and vegetables?*

A. In open-kettle canning, food is cooked in an ordinary kettle, then packed into hot jars and sealed without processing. For vegetables, the temperatures obtained in open-kettle canning are not high enough to destroy all the spoilage organisms that may be in the food. Spoilage bacteria may get in when the food is transferred from kettle to jar.

Q. *May a pressure canner be used for processing fruits and tomatoes?*

A. Yes. If it is deep enough it may be used as a water-bath canner (p. 4). Or you may use a pressure canner to process fruits and tomatoes at 0 to 1 pound pressure without having the containers of food completely covered with water. Put water in the canner to the shoulders of the jars; fasten cover. When live steam pours steadily from the open vent, start counting time. Leave vent open and process for the same times given for the boiling-water bath.

Q. *Must glass jars and lids be sterilized by boiling before canning?*

A. No, not when boiling-water bath or pressure-canner method is used. The containers as well as the food are sterilized during processing. But be sure jars and lids are clean.

Q. *Why is liquid sometimes lost from glass jars during processing?*

A. Loss of liquid may be due to packing jars too full, fluctuating pressure in a pressure canner, or lowering pressure too suddenly.

Q. *Should liquid lost during processing be replaced?*

A. No, never open a jar and refill with liquid—this would let in bacteria and you would need to process again. Loss of liquid does not cause food to spoil, though the food above the liquid may darken.

Q. *Is it safe to use home canned food if liquid is cloudy?*

A. Cloudy liquid may be a sign of spoilage. But it may be caused by the minerals in hard water, or by starch from overripe vegetables. If liquid is cloudy, boil the food. Do not taste or use any food that foams during heating or has an off odor.

Q. *Why does canned fruit sometimes float in jars?*

A. Fruit may float because pack is too loose or sirup too heavy; or because some air remains in tissues of the fruit after heating and processing.

Q. *Is it safe to can foods without salt?*

A. Yes. Salt is used for flavor only and is not necessary for safe processing.

Q. *What makes canned foods change color?*

A. Darkening of foods at the tops of jars may be caused by oxidation due to air in the jars or by too little heating or processing to destroy enzymes. Overprocessing may cause discoloration of foods throughout the containers.

    Pink and blue colors sometimes seen in canned pears, apples, and peaches are caused by chemical changes in the coloring matter of the fruit.

    Iron and copper from cooking utensils or from water in some localities may cause brown, black, and gray colors in some foods.

    When canned corn turns brown, the discoloring may be due to the variety of corn, to stage of ripeness, to overprocessing, or to copper or iron pans.

    Packing liquid may dissolve coloring materials from the foods. The use of plain tin cans will cause some foods to lose color (p. 4).

Q. *Is it safe to eat discolored canned foods?*

A. The color changes noted above do not mean the food is unsafe to eat. However, spoilage may also cause color changes. Any canned food that has an unusual color should be examined carefully before use (p. 8).

Q. *Does ascorbic acid help keep fruits and vegetables from darkening?*

A. Yes. The addition of ¼ teaspoon of crystalline ascorbic acid (vitamin C) to a quart of fruit or vegetable before it is processed retards oxidation, which is one cause of darkening of canned foods. One teaspoon of crystalline ascorbic acid weighs about 3 grams (or 3,000 milligrams).

Q. *Is it all right to use preservatives in home canning?*

A. No. Some canning powders or other chemical preservatives may be harmful.

Q. *Why do the undersides of metal lids sometimes discolor?*

A. Natural compounds in some foods corrode the metal and make a brown or black deposit on the underside of the lid. This deposit is harmless.

Q. *When canned or frozen fruits are bought in large containers, is it possible to can them in smaller containers?*

A. Any canned or frozen fruit may be heated through, packed, and processed the same length of time as recommended for hot packs. This canned food may be of lower quality than if fruit had been canned when fresh.

Q. *Is it safe to leave food in tin cans after opening?*

A. Yes. Food in tin cans needs only to be covered and refrigerated.

Q. *Is the processing time the same no matter what kind of range is used?*

A. Processing times and temperatures in this bulletin are for canning in a pressure canner or boiling-water bath with any type of range.

Q. *Can fruits and vegetables be canned without heating if aspirin is used?*

A. No. Aspirin cannot be relied on to prevent spoilage or to give satisfactory products. Adequate heat treatment is the only safe procedure.

Index

Acidity, soil 2, 240
Altitude canning problems 279, 285
Alfalfa 16
Alkalinity, soil 2, 240
Ancestors 41
Anise (*Pimpinella anisum*) 163
Annual, herbs 163-65
Aphids 69
Apples 203-14, 279
   drying techniques 42
   dwarf trees, 209-14
   mini-trees 205
   pollination 203-04
Applesauce 279-80
Apricots 220-22, 280
   Stark Earli-Orange 221
   Stark Giant Tilton 221
Ascorbic acid 291, 298
Asparagus 126-29, 286

Beans 44-52
   bush shell varieties 51
   drying methods 195, 286-87
   Dwarf horticultural 50
   Garbanzo 51
   green-shell 50
   leather breeches 42
   lima 48, 287
   Long Pod Fava (English broad bean) 50
   pickled 42
   pole 48
   Scarlet runner 52
   snap 46, 287
   soy 51-52
   Yard Long 52
Beets 53-54, 288
   pickled 280
Berries 280

The numbers in **boldface** refer to pages in the text
The numbers in lightface refer to pages in the Appendices

Berry
    bushes 267-68
Blackberries 230
Blackrot 40
Blanching 46, 73, 135
Blight 40
Blossom-end rot 112
Blueberries 230
Borage (*Borago officinalis*) 163
Botulism (food poisoning) 276
Broccoli 55-56
Brussels Sprouts 129-30
Buckwheat crops for soil
        improvement 16-17
Butternut 237

Cabbage 57-58
Canning
    leaks, testing for, 276
    liquids 284, 297
    open-kettle 296
    oven method 296
    pressure method 271, 284, 297
    with tin cans 272-75, 283, 285,
    298
    water-bath method 272, 278-79
Cantaloupe 130-31
Captan 41
Caraway (*Carum carui*) 163
Carbaryl 38
Caro-Red, "special" tomato 117
Carrots 58, 289
Castings, earthworm 14
Cauliflower 131-33
Celeriac 133
Celery 133-36
Celtuce 136-37
Chard 59-60
Chemical fertilizers 3-6
Cherries 228-29, 280
Chinese cabbage 138-39
Chinese chestnut 237
Chives (*Allium schoenprasum*) 80,
        81, 163

Choicest garden produce 45
Clayey soil 11, 14, 16
Clover 15
Cold-hardy plants 26
Collards 139-40
Comfrey 140-43
Compost 12, 167-68
Cooking liquid 284, 297
Corn 104-06, 289-90
Corn sirup for canning 277
Cover crops 16-17
Cowpeas 61
Crop rotation 169
Cucumbers 61-64
Cultivation 35, 167
Cutworm, protection against 119

Damping-off 40, 115
Dates for planting 22-25
Deciduous plant nutrients 10
Decomposition 10, 15
Determinate tomatoes 112
Dill (*Anethum graveolens*) 143, 163
Discoloration of canned foods 298
Doublerich "special" tomato 117
Downy mildew 63
Dry beans 51, 286-87
Drying foods 189-202
    fruits and vegetables 191-92
    methods 193-202
    pro's and con's 189-90
    storage 192-93
Dusting insecticides 39

Earliest planting dates 22-25
Eat-All Sweet Potato Squash 104
Economic aspects of gardening 1-2
Eggplant 65-67
Endive 144-45
English broad bean 50

English walnut 236
Escarole. *See* Endive

Fallacy, soil aeration, moles 18
Fava beans 50
Fencing, garden 18
Fennel, Florence (*Foeniculum dulee*)
    164
Fertilizers
    balanced 3-5
    kitchen garbage 167-68
    mixed liquid 68, 182-83
    with compost and manure 13
    weight-volume rates for various
        applications 179-82
    usage 5-6, 178-79
Filbert, American (Hazelnut) 237
Flea Beetles 114
Food coloring 17
Forcing 137
Frozen foods 298
Fruit canning 273-74, 277-78, 297
    of juices 281
    of purees 281
    yields 279
Fruit trees
    remedies if non-bearing 258-60
    varieties 261-64
    first-season care 255
    care and pruning 256-58
Fungicides 40
Furrow depths 46, 95
Fusarium wilt 112

Garbage for compost heaps 167-68
Gardening hints 41, 166-70
Garden seed, home grown 184-88
Garlic 81
Glass jars for canning 272-75, 277,
    284, 297
Grapes 232-35, 269-70

Green-manuring crops 15
Greens 294
Greens, mustard 149-50
Guaranteed analysis, fertilizers 5
Gumbo. *See* Okra
Gurney's White Beauty (low acid
    tomato) 117

Hardening off 116
Hardpan 15-16
Harvesting 54, 62-63, 69, 71, 93,
    161, 168, 265
Hazelnuts 237
Heat-loving plants 26
Herbs 162-65
    drying 196-97
Hominy 291
Honey in fruit canning 278
Hornworms 114
Horseradish 145-46
Host plants 18
How-to plant 251-52
Humus 10-11, 16-17
Hybrids 41, 113, 168, 185

Improving soil
    with grass 11
    with leaves 9
Indeterminate tomatoes 112
Indoor seeding 114
Insects, beneficial 40
Insecticides 38-40
Iron chelate 4
Iron for chlorophyl formation 4
Intercropping 76, 97, 168

Jerusalem artichoke 147-49
Juices:
    fruit 281
    tomato 283-84

Kale 67-70
Kohlrabi 70-71

Late-planting 27-31, 250
Leaching nutrients from soil 167
Leaf mold 10
Leaf spot 40
Legumes 15-16
Legume inoculation 41
Lettuce 72-75
Lima beans 48-50, 287
Lime 14-15
    hydrated 14
    quantities needed 15
    when and how to apply 15
    uses 14
Limestone 17
Liquid loss in canning 297

Malabar spinach 99
Maneb 41
Manuring, green
        See Green manuring
Maps, frost 36-37
Mice, control of 19
Millet 16
Minigardens 1-2
Mole damage 18-19
Mosaic 63
Mulches
    advantages 6
    grass clippings 8
    hay 6
    leaves 7
    manure 9
    organic 8
    pine needles 8
    plastic 6
Mulching paper 8
Muriate of potash 4
Mushrooms 291

Muskmelon See Cantaloupe
Mustard greens 149-50

Nectarines 219-20
    Stark Red Gold 219
    Stark Sun Glo 220
New Zealand spinach 99-100
Nitrogen
    abundant sources 4, 15-16, 245
    green manuring for 15
    utilization by plants 3-4, 245
Nitrogen-fixing bacteria 41, 52
Nutrients for plants 5, 10, 167
Nut trees 266
Nuts 235-37

Okra 75-77, 292
Onion family
    onion 77-80
    chives 80-81
    garlic 81
    leek 82-83
    shallot 83
Open-kettle canning 296
Open-pollination 104
Organic gardening 17-18
Organic matter
    materials 12-13, 15-17
    sources 9, 11, 15-16
Oven canning 296

Packing Methods:
    fruits 273, 277
    hot pack 273, 277, 284
    raw pack 273, 277, 284
    vegetables 273, 284
Parsley (*Petroselinum crispum*)
        83-84, 164
Parsnips 85-86

Peaches 214-18 , 281-82
 Starking Delicious 215-16
 Com-Pact Redhaven 216-17
Peanuts 151-52
Pears 224-28, 282
 Starking Delicious 226
 Starkrimson 227
Peas 87-90
 blackeye 292
 green 292-93
Pecans 235-36
 Missouri Hardy 236
 Starking Hardy Giant 235-36
Penetration, soil, green manure crop
  roots 15-16
Peppers 91-94
Peppermint (*Mentha piperita*) 164
Perennial herbs 163-65
Pest control 38-40
pH factor of soil 2-3, 240-41
Phosphoric acid
 sources 4, 246
 utilization by plants 4, 246
Physical barrier against moles 19
Pickles beets 288
Planning gardens 1-2, 20, 166-70,
  249
Planting dates 22-25
Planting late 250
Plums 223-24, 282
 Giant Damson 224
 Starking Delicious 223-24
Popcorn 152-54
Potash
 sources 4, 246
 utilization by plants 4, 246
Potatoes 94-96, 293
Potherbs. *See* Chard, Greens,
  Mustard greens, Spinach,
  Tampala
Preservatives, food 17, 298
Pressure canning 271; *see also*
  Steam pressure canning
Propagation of plants 141, 145-46,
  164-65

Prunes 222-23
 Blufre 222-23
 Earliblue 222
Pruning methods 253-54, 257-58
Pumpkin 155-56, 293-94
Purees of fruit, canned 281

Quantity of seeds 32-34

Radishes 21, 96-98
Raspberries 231
Recanning fruits 298
Recording your gardening activities
  169-70
Rhubarb 282-83
Rodent damage 19
Romaine or Cos lettuce 73
Rosemary (*Rosmarinus officinalis*)
  164
Rows, planting in 21, 104
Rubber canning rings 272, 274
Rutabaga 156-57
Rye 16

Sage (*Salvia officinalis*) 164
Salsify 157-58
Sealer test of tin cans 273
Seed collecting 184-88
Seed quantities per 100-ft row
  32-34
Seeding indoors 114
Seeding outdoors 114
Seedlings, feeding in a sterile medium
  169
Seedlings, watering 115-16
Sirups for canning and preserving
  277-78
Snap beans 46, 287
Soil testing 2-3, 238-48
 fertilizer indications 247-48
 pH preference, vegetables, field

Soil testing (*continued*)
 crops, fruit trees 242
 pH preference, flowers 243-44
 plant food deficiency 241,
  245-46
Sour soil 4, 240
Soybeans 16, 51-52
Spearmint (*Mentha spicata*) 165
Spinach 98-100, 294
Spoilage problems 276, 298
Spraying insecticides 38-40
Squash 294-95
 summer 100-03
 winter 100-04
Started plants 56, 66, 93, 105,
  114-15
Starter solutions 66, 109
Steam pressure canning 284
 for fruit 297
 safeguards 271, 297
Stolons 164-65
Stone mulch 118
Strawberries 171-77, 267
Subsoil channeling 15-16
Succession planting 2, 21, 168
Sudan grass 16
Sugar peas, edible-podded 143-44
Sugar Sirup for fruit canning 277
Sugarless canning 278
Summer savory (*Saturia hortensis*)
  165
Sunflower 158-59
Sweet basil (*Ocimum basilicum*)
  165
Sweet corn 104-06
Sweet marjoram (*Origanum
  majoram*) 165
Sweet Potatoes 106-09, 296
Sweet soil 4, 240

Tampala 99
Testing:
 glass jars 274

soil fertility 2-3, 238-48
tin cans 276
Thinning plants 35, 59, 99, 160
Thiram 41
Thyme (*Thymus vulgaris*) 165
Tin cans
 processing 273-75, 285
 types 272-73
Tobacco mosaic 116
Tomato juice 283-84
Tomatoes 109-23, 283
Top dressing 9, 120, 166, 169
Transplanting 109-10, 116, 134-35,
  167
Trellis 18, 48, 62, 99
Trickle irrigation 118-19
Turnips 124-25

Vegetables:
 canning methods 273-74, 284-85
 yield when canned 285
Vermiculite 115
Verticillium wilt 112
Vetch 15

Walnuts 236
Water-bath canning 272, 278-79
Watering methods 35, 38, 118-19,
  166
Watermelon 159-61
Weeding for controlled growth 11,
  35
What to grow 20
When to plant 21
Witloof chicory 137-38

Zineb 41
Zucchini 21, 102-03